THE BEGINNER'S DIGITAL PHOTOGRAPHY GUIDE

LONDON, NEW YORK, MUNICH,
MELBOURNE, DELHI

Senior Editor Nicky Munro
Project Art Editor Joanne Clark
Editor Hannah Bowen
Designer Simon Murrell

Jacket Designer Natasha Rees
Jacket Editor Manisha Majithia
Jacket Design Development Manager Sophia MTT

Producer, Pre-production Rebekah Parsons-King
Production Controller Mandy Inness

Managing Editor Stephanie Farrow
Senior Managing Art Editor Lee Griffiths

Written by Chris Gatcum

First published in Great Britain in 2013 by
Dorling Kindersley Limited
80 Strand, London WC2R 0RL
Penguin Group (UK)

2 4 6 8 10 9 7 5 3 1
010-186986-May/2013

A CIP catalogue record for this book
is available from the British Library.
ISBN 978-0-2411-8378-6

Printed and bound by Hung Hing

Discover more at
www.dk.com

CONTENTS

INTRODUCTION

The aim of this book is simple: to provide you with a solid foundation in digital photography. It cuts through the jargon and complicated technicalities that can make the subject unnecessarily intimidating, and shows you how to get the most out of your camera. It's not surprising that so many photographers feel daunted by all the buttons, dials, and menus found on modern digital cameras – and it's all too easy to switch to Auto and leave everything to the camera. But once you learn how satisfying it is to make the creative decisions yourself, and see how taking control can make such a huge difference to your pictures, you'll never look back. And it's really not as difficult as it might appear. Of course, it does take a little commitment, and you won't be able to master every technique without some practice, but the results are more than worth the effort. Your camera is an amazing piece of technology that's capable of transforming your pictures from average snapshots to something altogether more impressive. This book will completely demystify the world of digital photography for you, and will set you on the path to becoming not just a good photographer, but a great one.

ABOUT **THIS BOOK**

Each chapter of the book is full of practical "hands-on" tutorials that will help you get the best from your camera. Canon and Nikon dSLRs are used throughout, but even if your camera make or model is different, you'll find that most dSLRs (and many CSCs) have very similar functions and controls.

CAMERA SETTINGS KEY

The following icons are used throughout the book to show you precisely what settings were used for each of the final images.

SHOOTING MODES

P Program mode

Aperture Priority mode

Shutter Priority mode

Manual mode

METERING MODES

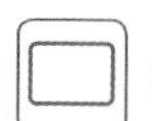
Multi-area

Centre-weighted

Spot

Partial

EXPOSURE

Aperture setting

Shutter speed

ISO setting

WHITE BALANCE

Auto

Daylight

Cloudy

Shade

Tungsten

Fluorescent

Flash

Custom

WHAT'S ON THE PAGES?

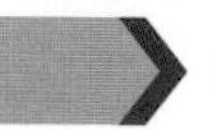

INTRODUCING |

At the start of every chapter you'll find "Introducing" pages that give you an overview of the particular subject covered. You won't be overloaded with technical information, but will learn all you need to gain the confidence and know-how to get started.

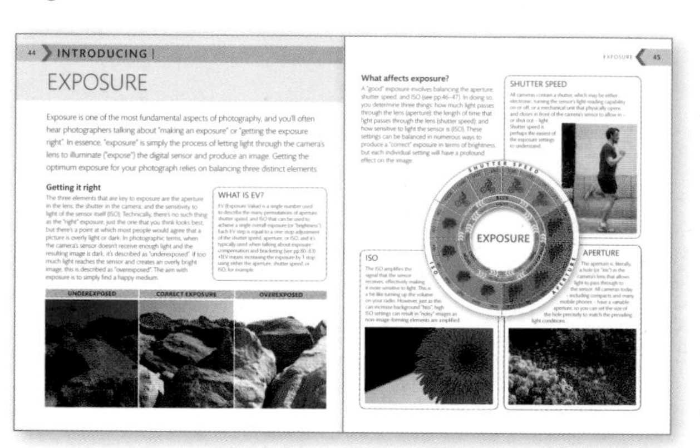

THINGS YOU'LL SEE

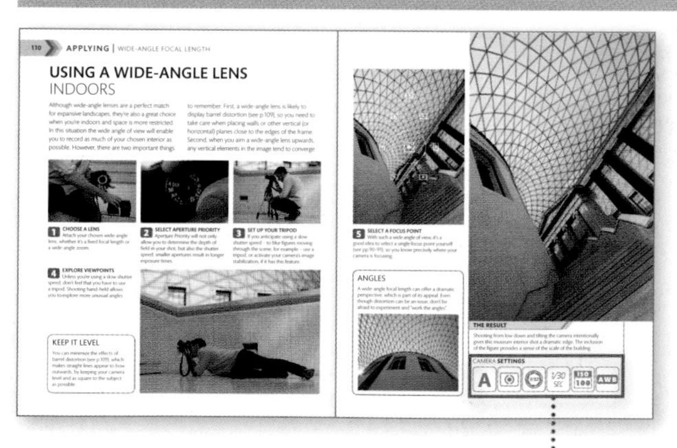

Camera settings Wherever you're shown how to apply a technique, you'll also see the final result, along with the settings used to get there (see also Key, left).

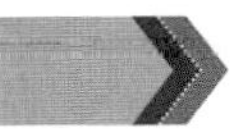

EXPLAINING |

If you see "Explaining" at the top of a page, you'll get a specific look at one aspect of photography. It could be an explanation of focal length, or the theory behind the colour of light (and why you might need to know about it). The concepts are presented clearly and simply throughout.

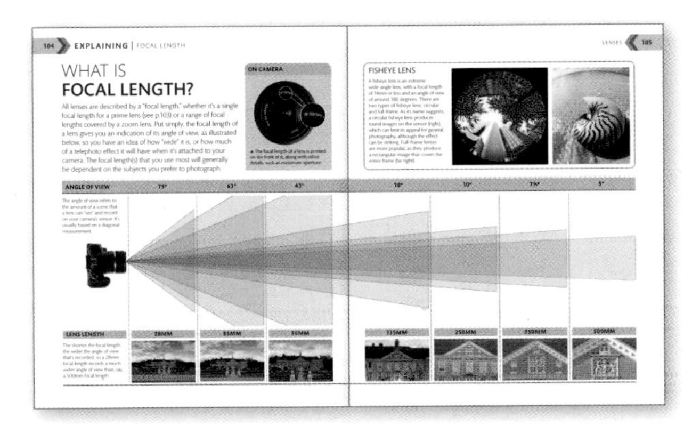

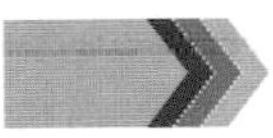

APPLYING |

The "Applying" pages provide you with illustrated tutorials on how to put all the theory into practice. The step-by-step instructions are so simple and straightforward that you really can't go wrong. You'll also find suggestions on how to apply the techniques to different subjects and situations.

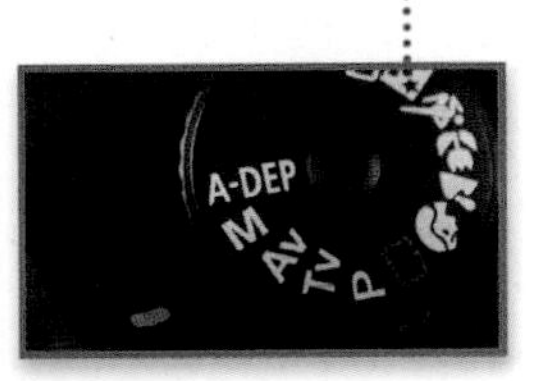

Close-up camera details The tutorials show you which buttons and dials you should be looking for on your camera. Most dSLRs (and many CSCs) have similar options, often in exactly the same place.

Boxes Handy tip boxes provide inspirational advice to expand your knowledge of the subject in question.

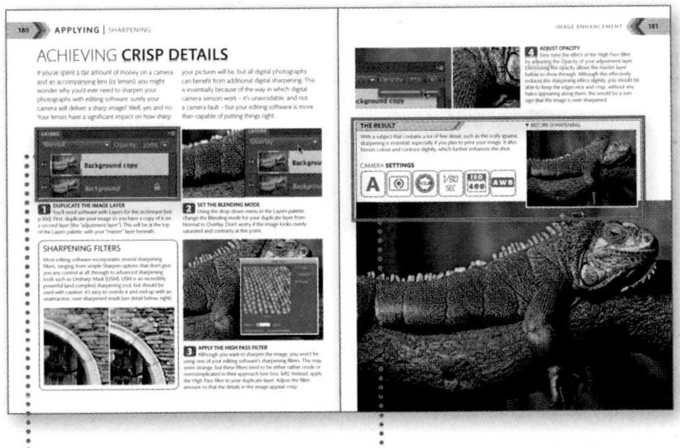

Screenshots Image editing can turn a good shot into a great one. Adobe's Photoshop Elements has been used throughout, but most editing software has a comparable range of features.

The result A brief overview of the final image explains how it was created and which techniques were used.

EQUIPMENT

EQUIPMENT

Your choice of camera is likely to come down to two things: the type of photography you want to do, and your budget. The camera isn't necessarily the end of your purchases, however. There are a lot of accessories available that aim to enhance your photography in some way, but lenses, tripods, and flashes are designed to expand your camera's capabilities and are often considered "must-have" items.

The essentials

Whether you want a camera that's light, foolproof, and requires minimal input, or one that allows you to take full creative control, this chapter will help you choose the ideal camera for you. The panel below gives a brief overview of the options available, and lists the pros and cons of each camera type. If you're serious about photography, then a camera with interchangeable lenses is definitely the most versatile option.

CAMERAPHONE

Has a fixed lens and minimal control over exposures, but with the advantage that you'll have it to hand at all times.

FUNCTIONALITY

- Fixed lens
- Few manual controls
- Easy to share images, either via email or text message, or by uploading to social networking sites
- Small, discreet, and pocketable

BASIC COMPACT

A modest zoom range and primarily automatic controls makes this an ideal point-and-shoot camera.

FUNCTIONALITY

- Zoom lens covering wide to telephoto focal lengths
- Automatic/semi-automatic shooting modes
- JPEG only
- Small and pocketable

ADVANCED COMPACT

Provides manual control, and in some cases Raw file capture, with the convenience of a portable size.

FUNCTIONALITY

- Zoom lens covering wide to telephoto focal lengths
- Automatic and manual shooting modes
- Range of creative controls
- Raw and JPEG capture
- Small and pocketable

EXTRAS

If you choose to invest in a dSLR or CSC, then there's a wide range of lenses, flash units, and other accessories that can help you take your photography to another level. And regardless of which type of camera you choose, a camera case and memory card are essential extras. This chapter will show you what's available so you can decide what you need.

PRIMARY CONSIDERATIONS:

- Lenses to expand your range of focal lengths
- An external flash for low-light shots and fill-flash
- A tripod
- A comfortable and accessible camera case or bag
- Spare battery and memory card(s)

BRIDGE/SUPERZOOM

Combines dSLR styling and features (including manual control) with a wide-ranging zoom lens.

FUNCTIONALITY

- All-encompassing zoom lens covering wide to super-telephoto focal lengths
- Non-interchangeable lens
- Small, compact-camera sized sensor
- Automatic and manual shooting modes
- Full range of creative controls
- dSLR-style handling

CSC

A full range of automatic, manual, and creative controls, plus interchangeable lenses, all in a small camera body.

FUNCTIONALITY

- Interchangeable lenses
- High quality dSLR-sized sensor
- Fully automatic to fully manual control
- Full range of creative controls
- Raw and JPEG capture
- Electronic viewfinder
- Compact and dSLR-style camera bodies available

DSLR

A tried-and-tested design and the favoured camera of countless enthusiast and professional photographers.

FUNCTIONALITY

- Wide range of lenses and accessories
- Full-frame and sub-full-frame sensor sizes available
- Full manual control over all aspects of your photography
- Raw and JPEG image capture
- Optical through-the-lens viewfinder
- Ergonomic design

ANATOMY OF A DSLR

Single lens reflex (SLR) cameras have been the camera of choice for professional and enthusiast photographers since the 1970s, but the actual SLR design dates back to the late 1940s. The reason for their popularity (and name) is down to the viewing system, which uses a pentaprism (a five-sided glass prism) to rotate the image coming through the lens so it can be viewed through an eye-level viewfinder. This "through-the-lens" (or TTL) viewing system means that the photographer gets an accurate view of what the camera is seeing, and what it will be recording, making it easy to frame a shot. Although initially designed for use with film, most SLRs are now digital, hence "digital SLR", or dSLR.

FRONT VIEW

The front of a dSLR is the "business end" of the camera. The camera's lens dominates, and aside from the lens release button, which allows you to remove and replace the lens, there are few additional controls on either entry-level cameras, such as this Nikon, or professional-specification (pro-spec) models, such as the Canon shown opposite.

OTHER MANUFACTURERS

No matter which manufacturer's cameras you look at, most dSLRs share a very similar design. The size of the camera body may vary slightly, and the controls that are available will be slightly different (and possibly in different locations), but the vast majority of cameras will have a mode dial on the top, an LCD screen dominating the back, a viewfinder "hump" above that, and, of course, an interchangeable lens on the front.

FRONT VIEW KEY

1 Shutter-release button

2 Autofocus (AF) assist lamp

3 Hotshoe (for mounting a flash)

4 Mode dial

5 Lens (see p.32 for anatomy)

6 Lens release button

7 Pop-up flash

8 Microphone

9 On/Off switch

10 Hand grip

SCREEN OPTIONS

If your dSLR camera has the ability to shoot video, then it will also offer Live View, which allows you to view and frame your shots using the rear LCD screen instead of the viewfinder. This can be a very useful feature, especially if your camera has a screen that folds out and can be rotated, as it will help you shoot from less conventional angles. In turn, this can help you create more dramatic images.

BACK VIEW

If the front of a dSLR camera is relatively sparsely populated, the back is almost certain to be bristling with buttons, switches, and control wheels. Although this may seem daunting at first, all manufacturers carefully consider which controls to put on the outside of the camera (and where), for instant access, and which to keep hidden in the menu system.

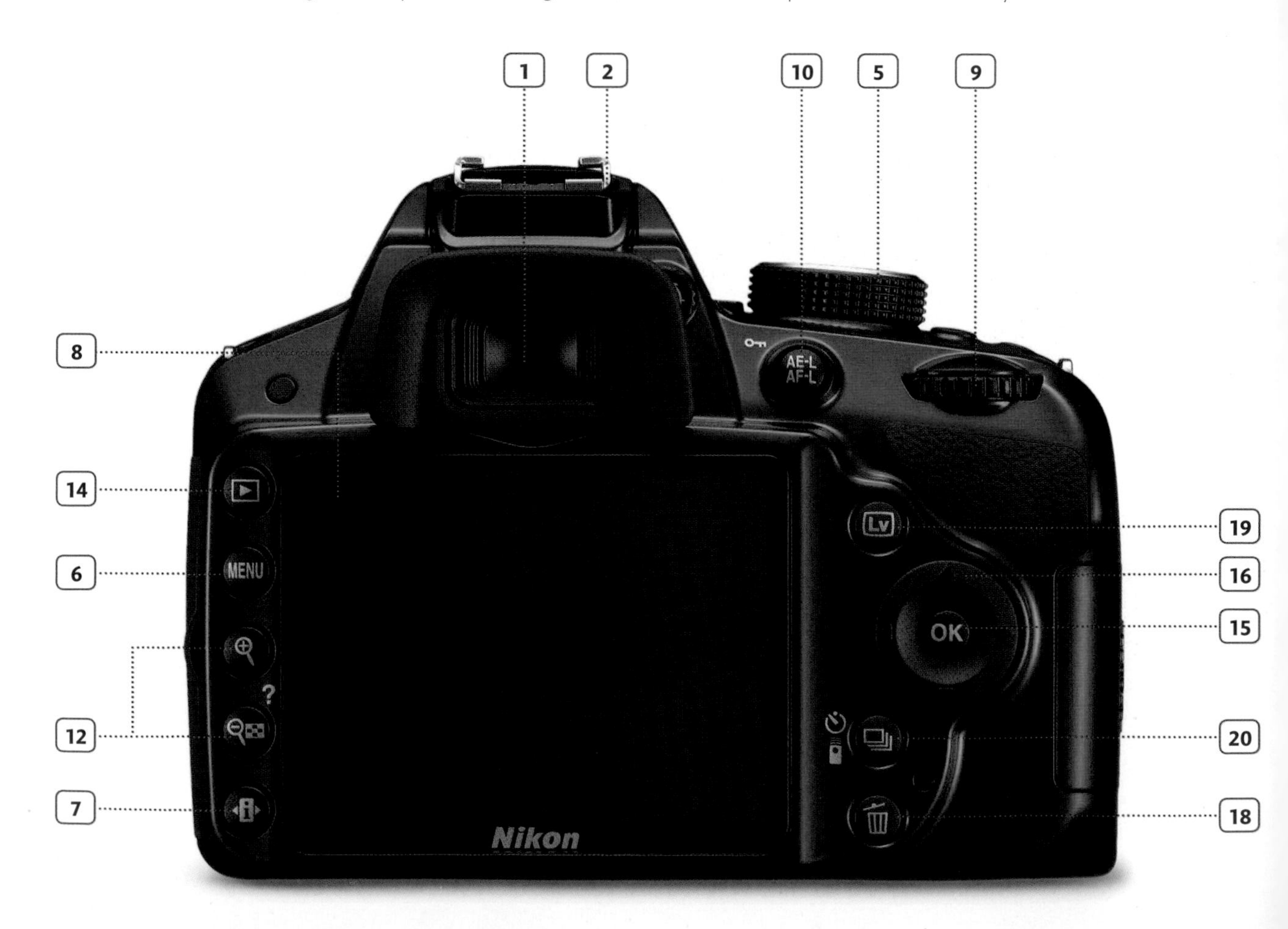

BACK VIEW KEY

1 Viewfinder
2 Hotshoe (for mounting a flash)
3 Movie mode/record button
4 Autofocus (AF) activation button
5 Mode dial
6 Menu button
7 Info button
8 LCD screen
9 Control wheel
10 Exposure/focus-lock button
11 AF point selection button
12 Playback zoom button
13 Quick Control button
14 Playback button
15 Set/OK button
16 Four-way control button
17 Lock
18 Delete button
19 Live View button
20 Drive mode selection button

On the entry-level Nikon (opposite), the buttons on the back are split logically between those that relate to functions requiring the LCD screen, and those that will be used primarily during shooting. The playback and menu buttons, plus playback zoom controls are on the left, for example, while the exposure and focus lock, Drive mode, and Live View buttons are on the right.

TOP VIEW KEY

1 Lens (see p.32 for anatomy)
2 Lens release button
3 ISO button
4 Shutter-release button
5 Control wheel
6 Mode dial
7 On/Off switch
8 Viewfinder
9 Hotshoe (for mounting a flash)
10 Autofocus (AF) mode button
11 LCD screen
12 Drive mode selection button
13 Metering pattern selection button
14 LCD illumination button
15 Movie mode/record button
16 Pop-up flash
17 Info button
18 Exposure compensation button

TOP VIEW

When you look at the top of a pro-spec camera next to an entry-level model, key differences tend to become more apparent. Pro-spec cameras don't usually have a pop-up flash, for example, and they use top-mounted LCD displays to relay the camera settings; this is useful if the camera is mounted on a tripod. The exposure mode dial tends to be significantly different too: entry-level cameras will usually have a selection of Scene Modes to choose from, in addition to the pro-spec options.

SIDE VIEW KEY

1 Lens (see p.32 for anatomy)
2 Pop-up flash
3 Hotshoe (for mounting a flash)
4 Viewfinder
5 Flash activation/mode button
6 Function button
7 Lens release
8 Connection port cover
9 Mode dial
10 Shutter-release button
11 Memory card compartment
12 Control wheel

CONNECTIVITY

With the rise of HD video modes, an increasing number of dSLR cameras now feature a mini HDMI socket, so you can connect your camera to a television and play movies (and images) directly from the memory card. Alternatively, you can download your images to a computer using the USB connection.

SIDE VIEW

Compared to the back and top, the sides of a dSLR are relatively spartan. There are no buttons or dials, as it would be easy to knock them by accident, so the camera designers use the sides to provide access points to the camera. These are typically arranged with the memory card compartment on the right (hand grip) side of the camera body, and the various connection ports and accessory sockets on the left, often behind a rubberized flap.

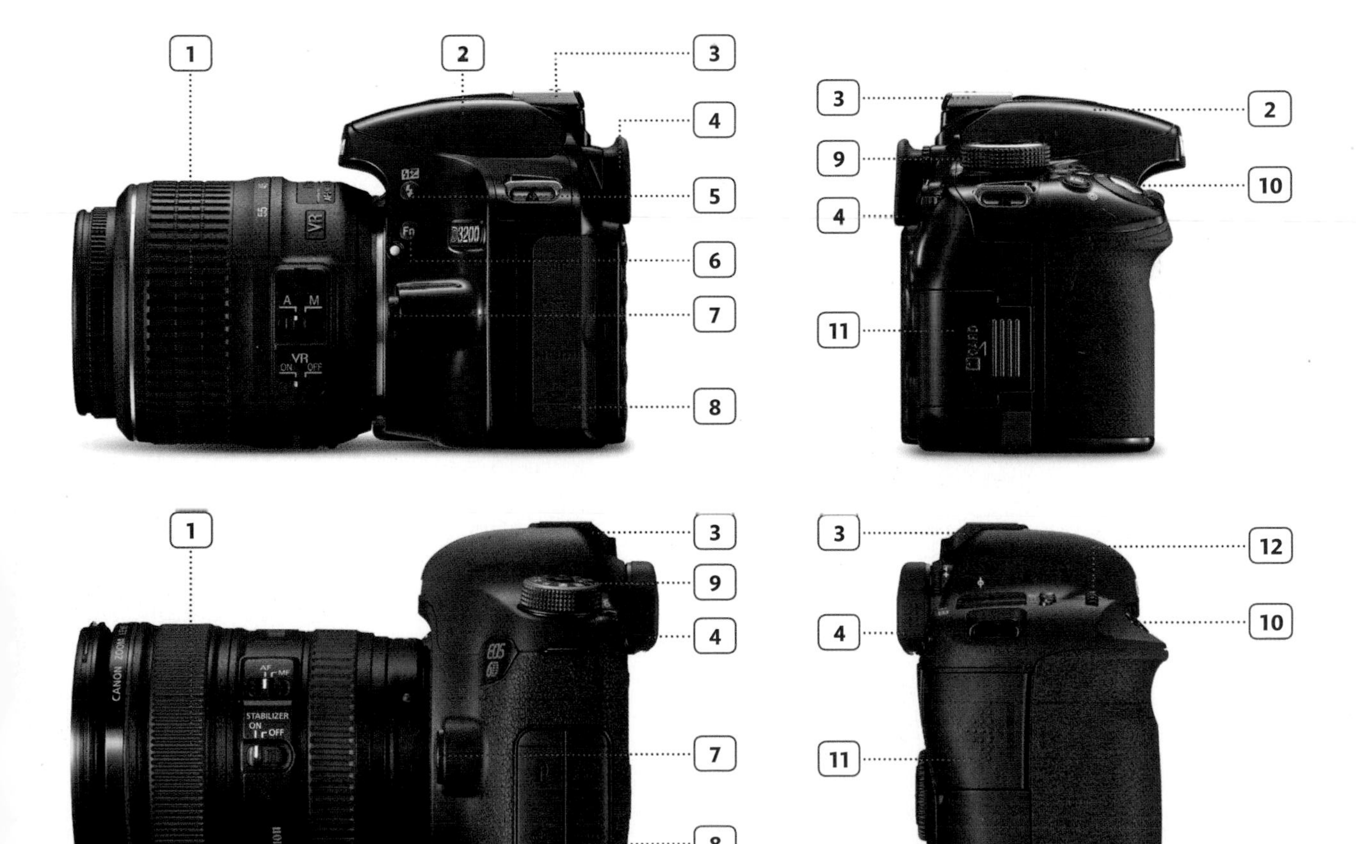

THROUGH THE **VIEWFINDER**

On dSLRs, as well as most bridge cameras and some CSCs, the viewfinder is your "window on the world". It's where you look at the scene you want to photograph and frame your shots. It's also where you view information about the camera settings. Aperture, shutter speed, and ISO will all be displayed, and you'll also be able to see which focus points are being used. Most cameras show additional information here too. The illustrations below use Canon and Nikon dSLRs as representative examples, so you may find they differ from your own camera. Either way, you should look at these two pages in conjunction with your camera manual.

VIEWFINDERS

Through a typical viewfinder, the image area will be relatively clear: apart from the Autofocus points (see p.89), which are usually overlaid, there will be few other elements to distract you from framing your shot. Instead, all the shooting information you might need will appear beneath the image, so you can quickly check your settings before you shoot.

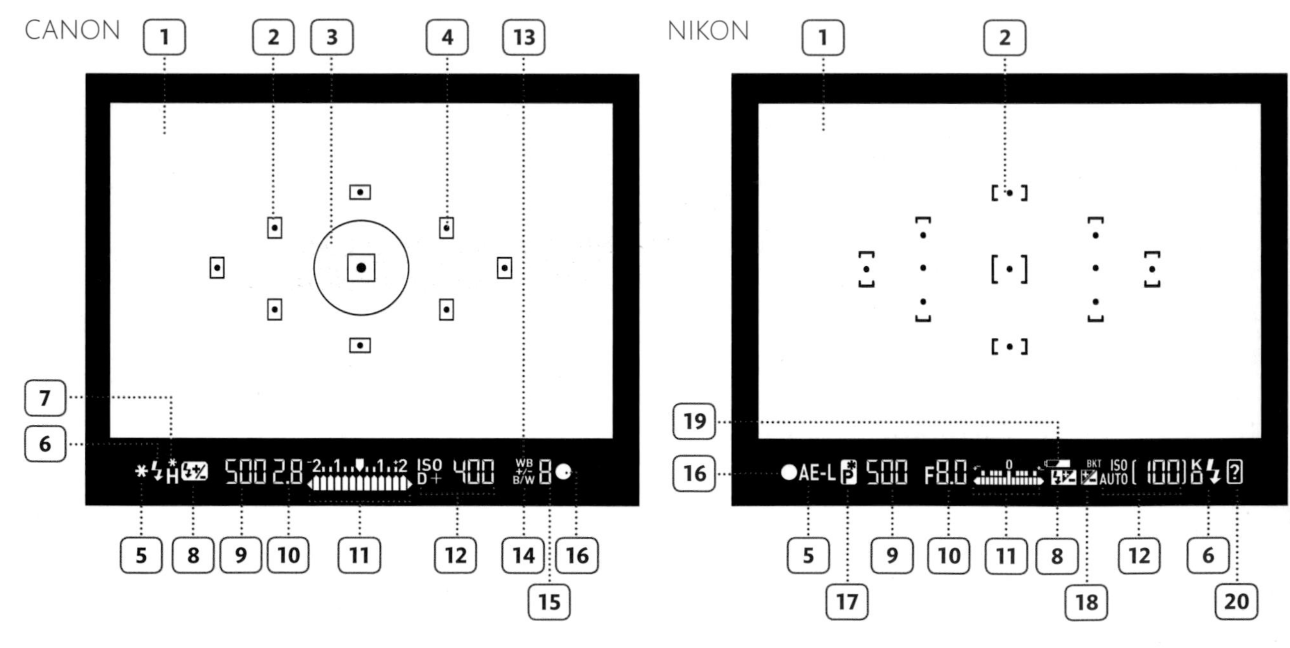

VIEWFINDER KEY

1 Focus screen
2 Autofocus (AF) point
3 Spot meter area
4 AF point activation indicator
5 Exposure lock active
6 Flash ready indicator
7 Flash mode
8 Flash compensation
9 Shutter speed
10 Aperture
11 Exposure level indicator
12 ISO settings
13 White Balance adjustment
14 Black-and-white mode
15 Maximum burst
16 Focus confirmation
17 Program shift (see pp.52–53)
18 Exposure compensation
19 Battery level
20 Warning indicator

ON THE **LCD SCREEN**

In the past, a camera's rear LCD screen was used for little more than reviewing images and accessing and viewing the various menu options. Today's screens are far more sophisticated, not only in terms of their specification (large sizes and high resolutions are now standard), but also in terms of the information they relay.

Some cameras even allow you to make the rear LCD screen "Live" so you can see a variety of settings, but also control them and make changes via the LCD screen. Again, Canon and Nikon cameras are shown as examples below, so refer to your own camera's LCD screen to get to know where things are.

LCD SCREENS

The amount of data that's displayed on the rear LCD screen varies between camera make and model. Certain camera models allow you to set the level of information depending on your needs, ranging from simple displays that show the essentials (exposure, white balance, and so on), through to displays packed with information.

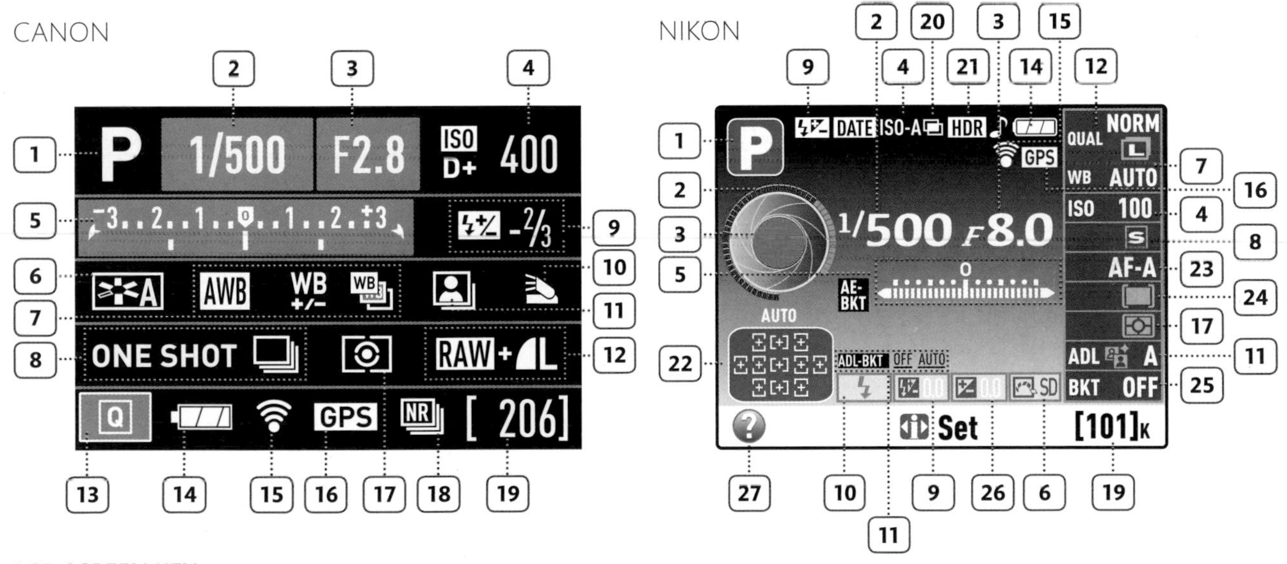

LCD SCREEN KEY

1 Exposure mode
2 Shutter speed
3 Aperture
4 ISO setting
5 Exposure level indicator
6 Picture style (see pp.48–49)
7 White Balance setting
8 Drive mode
9 Flash compensation
10 Flash active/flash mode
11 Auto Lighting Optimizer/ Active D-Lighting setting
12 Image quality
13 Quick Control
14 Battery level
15 Eye-Fi transmission status
16 GPS connection
17 Metering pattern
18 Multi-shot noise reduction
19 Shots remaining
20 Multiple exposure indicator
21 HDR indicator
22 Autofocus (AF) point indicator
23 Focus mode
24 AF area mode
25 Exposure bracketing indicator
26 Exposure compensation
27 Help icon

OTHER **CAMERA TYPES**

Compact system cameras, or CSCs, are the most recent development in camera technology and, at the time of writing, the fastest-growing in terms of popularity and sales. The reason for this is easy to understand: a CSC is typically far smaller and lighter than a dSLR, yet it features interchangeable lenses and a sensor size commonly associated with dSLR cameras. However, it's not the only alternative, and for some photographers a high-end compact or a bridge camera (see pp.26–27) is a perfect all-in-one solution.

COMPACT SYSTEM CAMERA (CSC)

There are generally two styles of CSC currently on the market: those that are similar to compact cameras (top), and those that take their styling lead from dSLRs, complete with mode dials and eye-level viewfinders (below). Which type is best for you depends on your style of photography: compact designs tend to favour go-anywhere spontanaeity.

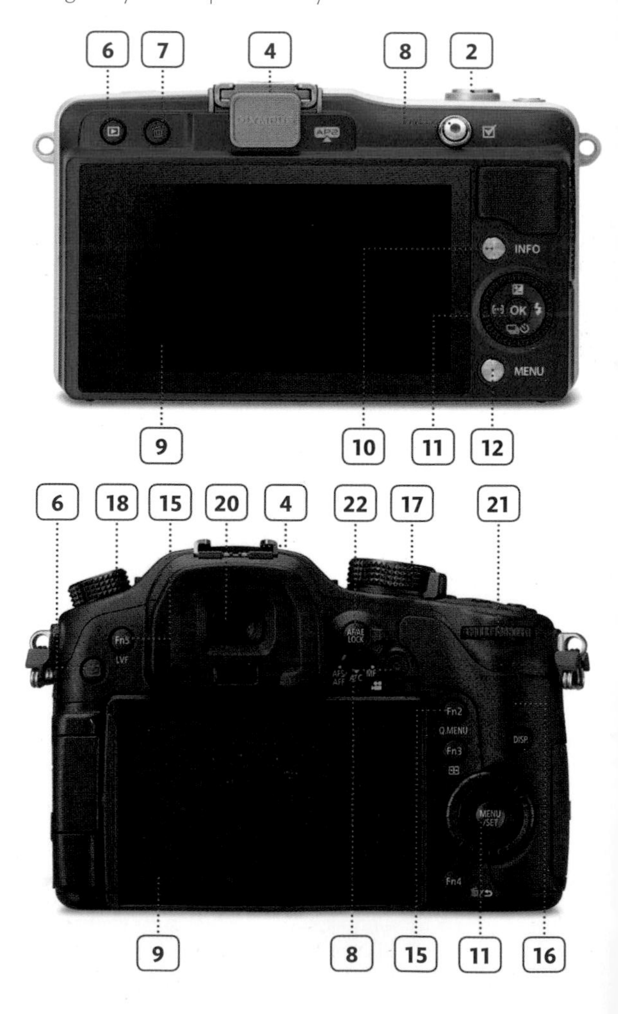

VIEWFINDER DIFFERENCES

One of the key differences between a CSC and dSLR camera is the viewfinder: a CSC uses an electronic viewfinder (EVF) rather than an optical viewfinder. Some CSCs have an EVF built in (in a dSLR style), while others have EVFs as an optional extra that slides into the accessory shoe. Some do away with an eye-level viewfinder altogether and simply use the LCD screen for framing.

COMPACT SYSTEM CAMERA KEY

1 Finger grip
2 Shutter-release button
3 Lens
4 Accessory shoe/hotshoe
5 Lens release button
6 Playback button
7 Delete button
8 Movie mode/record button
9 LCD screen
10 Info button
11 Control pad and camera function buttons
12 Menu button
13 Microphone
14 On/Off switch
15 Fn (Function) button
16 Speaker
17 Mode dial
18 Drive mode selector
19 Flash PC sync socket
20 Electronic viewfinder (EVF)
21 Control wheel
22 Focus lock (AF-L)/Focus mode selector
23 Image stabilization switch
24 White balance, ISO, and exposure compensation buttons

BRIDGE/SUPERZOOM

"Bridge", or "superzoom", cameras tend to have a pseudo-dSLR-style body shape and control layout, coupled with a fixed lens. The lens is usually an all-encompassing zoom covering a range of focal lengths, from wide-angle to super telephoto. This makes them incredibly versatile, but the small sensor inside is often the same size as those found in compact cameras.

HIGH-END COMPACT

A high-end compact camera will typically allow you to shoot Raw and JPEG images, just like a dSLR camera or CSC, and it will also offer similar levels of control, including Aperture Priority, Shutter Priority, and Manual shooting modes. The zoom lens is fixed, but it tends to put image quality ahead of the focal length range, allowing stunning images to be made.

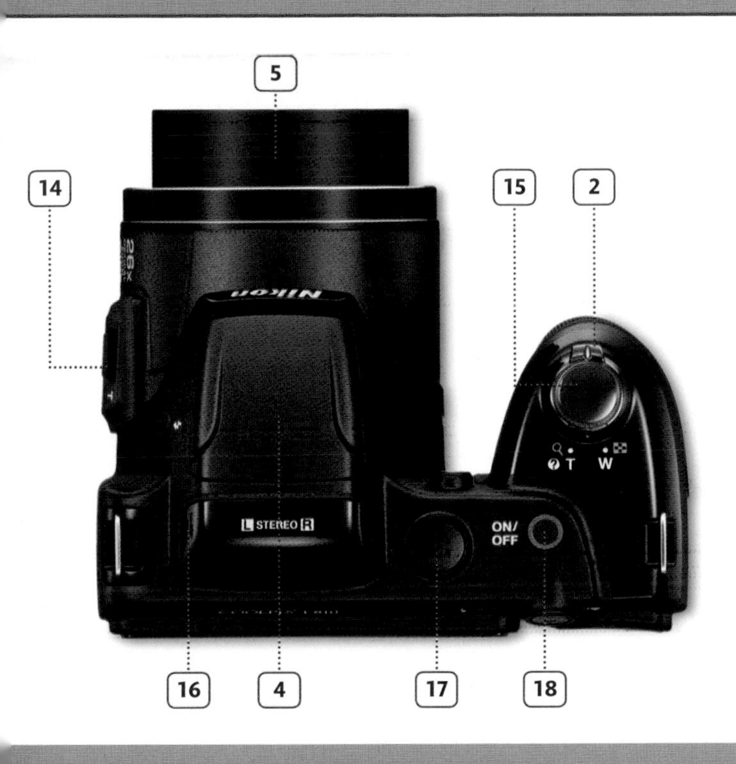

BRIDGE/SUPERZOOM AND HIGH-END COMPACT KEY

1. Finger grip
2. Zoom control
3. Autofocus (AF) illuminator
4. Pop-up flash
5. Lens
6. LCD screen
7. Flash ready indicator
8. Movie mode/record button
9. Scene mode selection
10. Control pad and camera function buttons
11. Menu button
12. Delete button
13. Playback button
14. Side-mounted zoom control
15. Shutter-release button
16. Microphone
17. Speaker
18. On/Off switch
19. Control wheel
20. Mode dial
21. Viewfinder
22. Hotshoe
23. Shortcut/Direct print button
24. AF point selection button
25. Metering pattern selection button
26. Exposure/focus lock button
27. Exposure compensation dial

HOLDING YOUR CAMERA

Imagine this scenario: you've spent hundreds (perhaps even thousands) of pounds on equipment; you've made sure that you've got everything just right in terms of exposure setting, white balance, focus, and framing; and you've triggered the shutter at the precise once-in-a-lifetime moment you want to record; and after all that, your image is blurred. It's extremely disappointing and frustrating, but camera shake – movement of the camera at the point of capture – is the number one culprit behind blurred images. However, you don't necessarily need any specialist equipment to remedy the problem: in most cases, you just need to ensure that you're holding your camera correctly.

CAMERA GRIP

To keep your camera as steady as possible (without using a tripod), hold it in your right hand, with your index finger close to the shutter-release button and your fingers around the camera's grip. Your left hand should support the lens, while also allowing you to control the zoom and focus rings. Keep your elbows tucked into your sides for added stability. The images on the far right show some of the most common mistakes.

REMEMBER...

- Hold your camera and lens with both hands
- Keep your elbows tucked in
- Press the shutter-release button gently
- Take your shot as you finish exhaling (on your "out breath")

✓ CORRECT GRIP

✓ CORRECT GRIP

✓ CORRECT GRIP

VARIATIONS

The standard camera grip (see below) works well in most situations, which is why it's seen as the "correct" way to hold your camera. Sometimes, however, alternative or modified grips, as shown here, may be preferable. These may be particularly useful when you're using a longer, or heavier, lens.

▲ CROSS-BRACING

▲ LONG LENS SUPPORT

✗ HOLDING THE CAMERA WITH ONLY ONE HAND

✗ STICKING YOUR ELBOWS OUT, REDUCING STABILITY

✗ LEAVING THE LENS UNSUPPORTED

✗ GRIPPING THE LENS TOO LOOSELY

VERTICAL SHOOTING

The same rules for holding your camera apply when you switch from shooting in the horizontal ("landscape") format to vertical ("portrait") format: keep your elbows tucked in; use your right hand to hold the camera, so you can trigger the shutter and use the control wheel to change settings; and support the lens from below.

STAYING STEADY

As well as making sure that you're holding your camera correctly (see pp. 28–29), it's equally important to adopt the most appropriate stance for your shooting position. In all instances the same basic grip is used for control and stability of the camera, but your stance will have a significant impact on your stability. The following are some of the most common shooting positions, showing the best stance, with the inset images showing the most common mistakes.

STANDING

It's likely that most of the time you'll be shooting from an upright standing position. While this may be the most comfortable, natural position, you still need to ensure that you're standing firm.

REMEMBER...

- Stand with your feet approximately shoulder-width apart
- Stand square-on to your subject, rather than twisting your body sideways

✗ TENSE, UNSTEADY STANCE

✓ CORRECT STANCE

CROUCHING

Shooting from a crouching position will enable you to explore different angles, allowing you to include more of the foreground in a shot, for example. However, unless you balance yourself properly, you'll find it hard to stay steady.

REMEMBER...

- Distribute your weight evenly and avoid leaning forwards
- Rest your elbows on your knees

✗ ELBOW UNSUPPORTED

✓ CORRECT STANCE

SITTING

You probably won't take photographs from a seated position all that often, but when you do, use your legs, knees, and feet to create a solid grounding.

REMEMBER...

- Keep your feet apart to create a stable base
- Rest your elbows on your knees to brace yourself

✗ BOTH ELBOWS UNSUPPORTED

✓ CORRECT POSITION

✗ FEET NOT FIRMLY PLANTED

LAYING DOWN

Shooting from a prone position allows you to capture an intriguing "worm's eye" view of the world. But while you're trying to find the right position it's easy to forget to hold your camera properly.

REMEMBER...

- Support yourself on your elbows comfortably
- Use your right hand to hold and operate the camera...
- ...and your left hand to support and control the lens

✗ AWKWARD GRIP

✓ CORRECT POSITION

ADDITIONAL **EQUIPMENT**

A dSLR camera or CSC is an interchangeable lens camera, so it perhaps goes without saying that you have the ability to change lenses – you may even have bought the camera with more than one lens to start with. Lenses will be covered in much greater detail later in the book, but this isn't the only purchase you're likely to make in your pursuit of great photographs. As well as your camera and lenses, there's a whole host of additional accessories that will help improve your pictures, ranging from a tripod to hold your camera steady, through to flashes and filters to expand your creative repertoire.

LENSES

Although most lenses have certain things in common (a focus ring and bayonet mount, for example), they don't all share exactly the same features. A zoom lock, for example, is generally found only on heavy, wide-ranging zooms, and is designed to stop the zoom from extending by itself because of the weight of the glass used in its construction. Some lenses also feature image stabilization technology, to help prevent camera shake (see p.107).

LENS ANATOMY

It's easy to assume that one lens is very much like another, but nothing could be further from the truth. Physical differences, such as the size of the focus and zoom rings, can make a huge difference to the handling of a lens, as can the range of focal lengths it covers (see pp.104–105).

LENS ANATOMY KEY

1. Filter thread
2. Front lens element
3. Manual focus ring
4. Focus distance scale
5. Zoom ring
6. Focal length setting
7. Focus mode (Auto/Manual)
8. Zoom lock
9. Lens mount
10. Electronic contacts

LENS TERMINOLOGY

There's quite a lot of jargon used in photography, and this is particularly true when you start to talk about lenses. If you're intending to buy a new lens, you'll encounter a world of acronyms and abbreviations that can be truly bewildering. The table to the right shows a few of the most commonly used terms that you're likely to come across, along with the different "codes" used by lens manufacturers to describe them.

TERM	DESCRIPTION
Aspherical (AS/ASP/ASPH)	Most lenses are curved in a "c" shape, but the surface of an aspherical lens doesn't conform to the shape of a sphere, so light is able to pass through it more evenly.
Image stabilization (IS/VR/OS/VC/PowerOIS)	A system that uses sensors to detect camera movement. A "floating" lens element inside the lens moves to counteract this movement.
Low dispersion glass (ED/UD/APO/LD/SD/HLD)	A type of glass used in the construction of a lens to reduce the appearance of coloured edges (known as "chromatic aberrations") in images.
Silent focus (USM/SWM/SWD/SDM/HSM/SSM/USD)	Some of the more advanced Autofocus systems in a lens use a "silent" motor that minimizes any noise associated with focusing the lens.

ATTACHING A LENS

1 ALIGN MARKS
There will be alignment marks on both the lens and the lens mount (either on the mount itself, or to the side) to ensure that you fit your lens correctly. Align the two marks...

2 SLIDE IN STRAIGHT
...and slide the lens into the lens mount. The lens should fit smoothly into the camera body, but if it doesn't, don't force it – remove the lens and realign.

3 TWIST AND LOCK
Once the lens is slid into the camera body, turn it to lock it in place. The direction in which you turn it will depend on your camera model, so check the manual.

LENS REMOVAL

To remove a lens, you reverse the process used to fit it. Press the lens release button (usually located next to the lens mount on the camera body) and turn the lens in the opposite direction to the way in which you attached it. Once the lens is detached, fit another lens or a cap to prevent dust getting into the sensor.

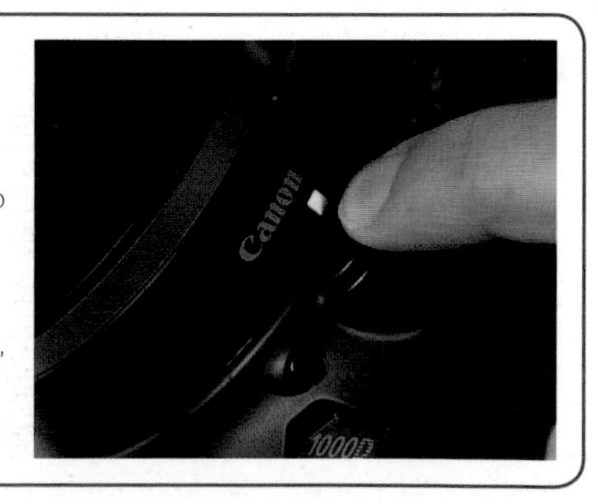

CAMERA SUPPORT

Image stabilization (sensor- or lens-based) does a great job of helping you to avoid blurred shots caused by camera shake, but these systems have their limits. They certainly won't help if you want to make very long exposures lasting half a second or longer. However, a solid tripod will hold your camera for as long as necessary, and providing it's set up correctly, will guarantee shake-free results. It also enables you to frame your shots very precisely, which is why every serious photographer should own one.

TRIPOD ANATOMY

Aside from their three-legged design, all tripods vary slightly. One of the main differences is in their construction: while most tripods are made of aluminium, some of the more costly models are made of lightweight carbon fibre, which is a bonus if you intend to carry one for long periods of time.

TRIPOD IN ACTION

There's no getting away from the fact that a tripod makes it much slower to take a shot than using your camera hand-held. However, this also gives you time to assess your scene and your camera settings, and really think about how you're going to get the best shot possible.

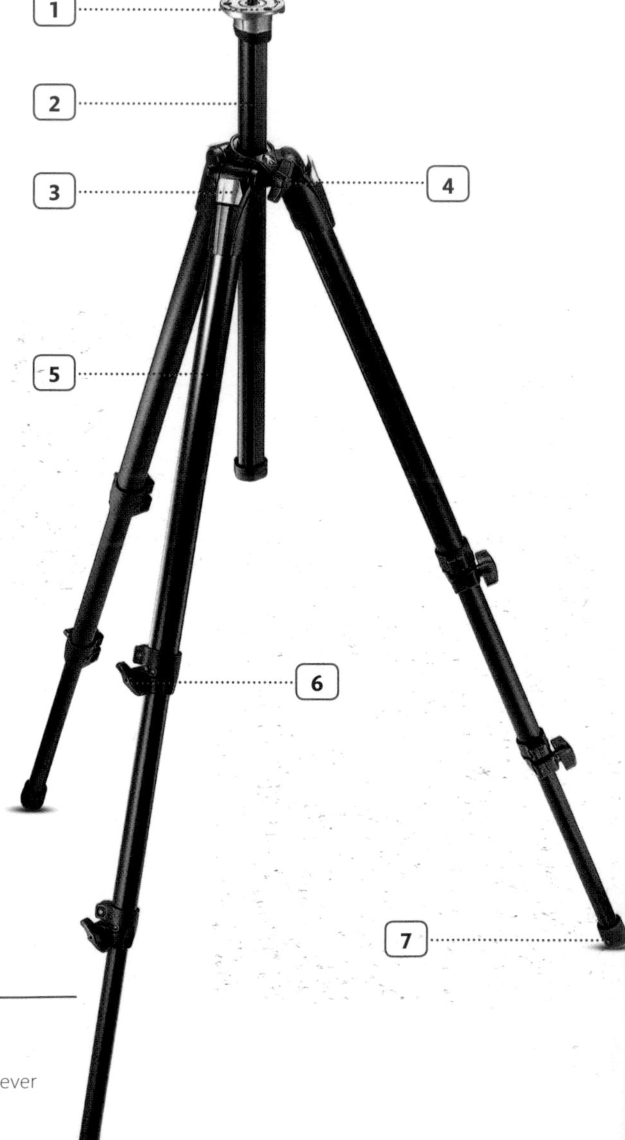

TRIPOD ANATOMY KEY

1. Tripod head mounting plate
2. Centre column
3. Leg angle lock/release
4. Centre column lock
5. Tripod leg
6. Leg extension locking lever
7. Foot

TRIPOD HEADS ANATOMY

A pan-and-tilt tripod head (right) enables you to move your camera in any one of three directions: tilt backwards and forwards; tilt side to side; and pan (rotate). Each of these movements is controlled independently, usually using large locking handles, so you have very precise control over the positioning of your camera. The downside is that it's big and bulky compared to a ball-and-socket head (below), and it takes longer to set up. A ball-and-socket head has just one lock: release it and you're free to turn, tilt, and twist your camera as you choose. This makes it much quicker to use than a pan-and-tilt head, but it doesn't offer the same level of accuracy.

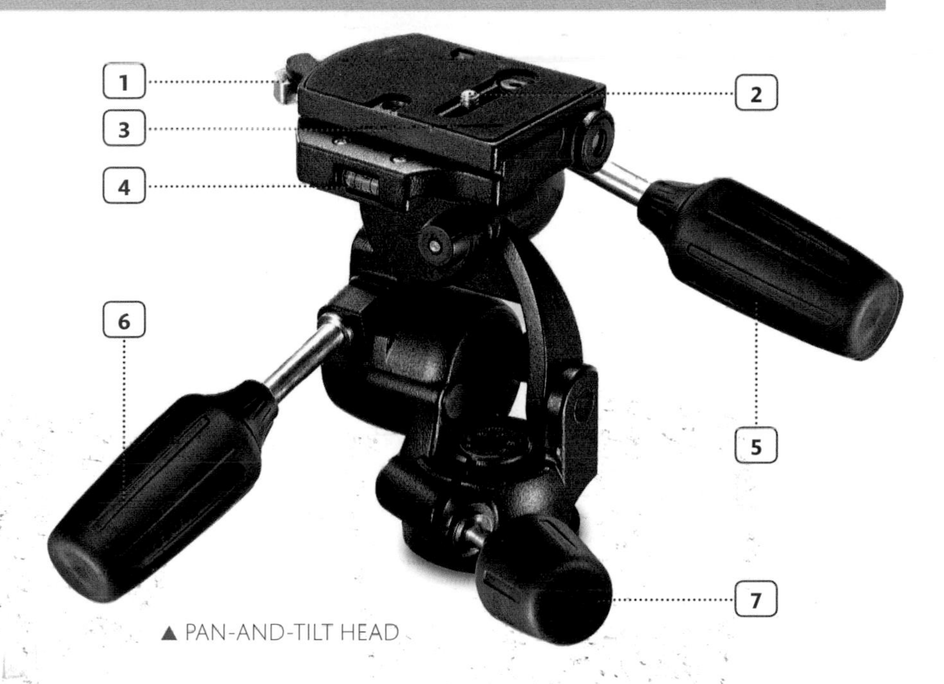

▲ PAN-AND-TILT HEAD

1 2 3 9 8 10

▲ BALL-AND-SOCKET HEAD

TRIPOD HEADS ANATOMY KEY

1. Quick-release lever
2. Mount thread (typically ¼in)
3. Camera/quick-release plate
4. Spirit level
5. Sideways tilt locking lever
6. Forward/back tilt locking lever
7. Panning locking lever
8. Ball and socket
9. Ball lock/release
10. Ball friction control

QUICK-RELEASE PLATES

Attaching and removing your camera from the tripod head is made much easier if the head has a "quick-release" system. This comprises a plate that's screwed into your camera's tripod socket, which simply clips on to the tripod head. A lever can be used to release the camera in an instant.

LIGHTING

All dSLR cameras and most CSCs have a hotshoe on top, which allows you to attach a flash. If your camera has a built-in pop-up flash, you might wonder why you'd want to attach a hotshoe flash, but in fact it opens up a lot of creative options: it's more powerful, has greater versatility, and, most importantly, can also be used away from the camera. Flash will be explored in greater detail in chapter 6 (see pp.150–63), but here you'll find a quick tour of the options that you're likely to encounter.

FLASH ANATOMY

When choosing a flash, a model that's fully dedicated to your camera is highly recommended, as it will automate the exposure process. A tilting head is also useful, as it will enable you to use "bounce flash" (see pp.156–57), while more powerful flash units will generally provide the greatest versatility when it comes to lighting a single figure or a group of people.

FLASH ANATOMY KEY

1. Slide out wide-angle diffuser
2. Flash tube/diffuser
3. Flash body
4. Autofocus illuminator
5. Foot
6. LCD panel
7. Mode selection button
8. Test button
9. Flash ready light
10. Locking wheel
11. Tilt angle indicator
12. Custom function settings
13. Zoom control
14. Power switch
15. Control panel navigation pad
16. Slave mode activation switch

OTHER FLASH TYPES

A hotshoe-mounted flash is ideal for shooting subjects situated some distance from the camera, but it's not so useful for close-ups, as the light will often pass straight over the top of the subject. Dedicated macro flash units get round this issue by positioning the flash much closer to the lens: a ring flash circles the lens entirely, while a twin flash uses two flash lights, which are controlled independently, to illuminate your subject.

▲ MACRO RING FLASH SET-UP

▲ TWIN FLASH SET-UP

OTHER LIGHTING ACCESSORIES

If you start to use flash on a regular basis you may wish to explore the wide range of different effects or "looks" that you can achieve with the help of additional flash accessories. Reflectors and diffusers, for example – both hand-held and flash mounted – can be used to soften the light and fill in shadows (see pp.130–33).

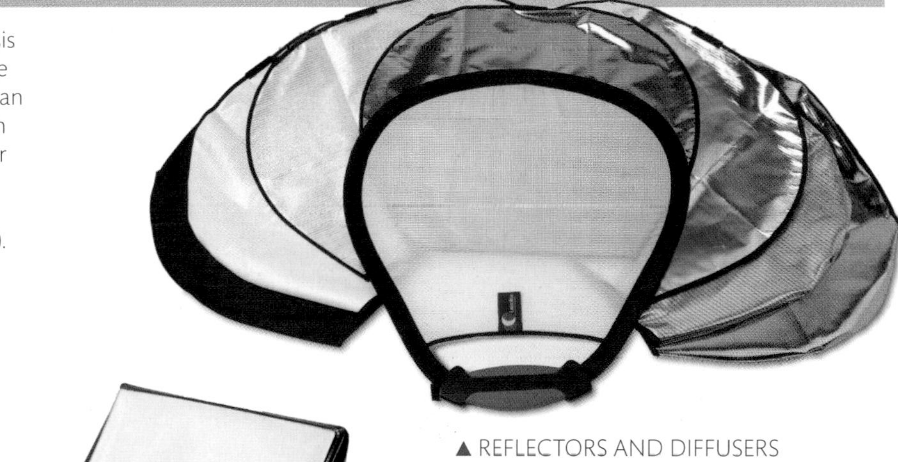

▲ REFLECTORS AND DIFFUSERS

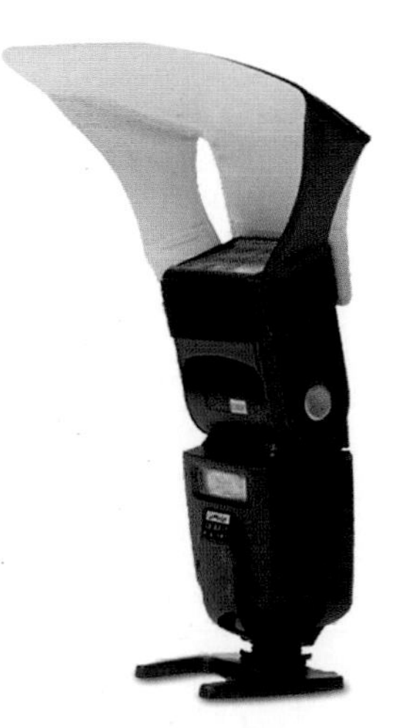

▲ FLASH REFLECTOR

▲ FLASH SOFTBOX DIFFUSER

▲ ON-CAMERA FLASH DIFFUSER

OTHER ACCESSORIES

The camera, along with lens, flash, and tripod, forms the backbone of most "general purpose" photography kits. However, beyond those four key items are other accessories that may well help in one way or another when you're out and about taking pictures. These range from bags or cases in which to store and carry your kit, to memory cards (most dSLRs and CSCs don't come with a memory card to begin with), and spare batteries.

BAGS AND CASES

Soft or hard, over-the-shoulder or backpack style – camera bags and cases come in a wide range of shapes, sizes, and materials, so there's sure to be one that suits your needs.

▲ TOP-LOADING CASE

▲ SHOULDER BAG

▲ RUCKSACK

▲ HARD CASE

LENS FILTERS

Although digital editing can replicate the effects of some of the traditional lens filters, there are at least two filters that are still invaluable, and whose effects can't be easily replicated. Neutral density (ND) filters block out light and allow you to extend exposure times (see pp.62–63), while polarizing filters intensify skies and cut through reflections.

▲ WITH ND FILTER

▲ WITHOUT ND FILTER

▲ NEUTRAL DENSITY FILTER

▲ POLARIZING FILTER

▲ WITH POLARIZER

▲ WITHOUT POLARIZER

MEMORY CARDS

There are several types of memory card currently in use, but your camera will only take one of them, so be sure to buy the right one. The capacity of all memory cards is measured in "gigabytes" (GB): if you intend to shoot video as well as still photographs, then a high-capacity card (16GB+) is recommended.

▲ COMPACT FLASH

▲ SD CARD

▲ SONY MEMORY STICK

1 OPEN MEMORY CARD SLOT Turn your camera off, then find the memory card slot (it's usually on the side of the camera) and slide it open.

2 CHECK THE DIRECTION The card will fit only one way, so check it's the right way round before sliding it into the camera.

3 INSERT THE CARD Press the memory card all the way into the slot (it will "click" into place), then close the slot.

BATTERIES

Today's camera batteries are long-lasting and reliable. However, like any batteries, they will eventually run out and need recharging. Batteries don't last for ever either, so at some point you'll need a replacement. To ensure that you're never caught out, it's a good idea to buy an additional battery to begin with.

▲ NIKON BATTERY

▲ CANON BATTERY

1 OPEN BATTERY COMPARTMENT Find the battery compartment, which is usually situated on the bottom of the camera. Press it to unlock it...

2 INSERT BATTERY ...and slide in the battery. As with memory cards, the battery will only fit one way and should never be forced.

3 LOCK BATTERY Push the battery all the way in until it clicks into place. Close and lock the compartment.

JPEG OR RAW?

With digital photography there are a couple of fundamental decisions that need to be made before you take a picture. The first question is what file format will you use? All dSLRs and CSCs (as well as some bridge and compact camera models) offer a choice of two formats – JPEG and Raw – which require slightly different approaches. As a general guide, Raw files require more work (sometimes a lot more) after they've been downloaded to your computer, but they're also capable of delivering slightly better quality images.

SHOOTING JPEGS

When your camera records a JPEG file, it processes the images so that all of the settings you've made are "burned" into the file. This means that the colour, contrast, sharpening, and everything else you can tweak or change on your camera is applied to the image before the information is saved to your memory card. However, a JPEG file is compressed using a "lossy" system, which means that information can be permanently lost when it's saved: you need to take care to avoid this.

Your camera will offer a number of JPEG quality options, typically ranging from Basic to Fine (see below). The higher the JPEG quality, the higher the quality of your images.

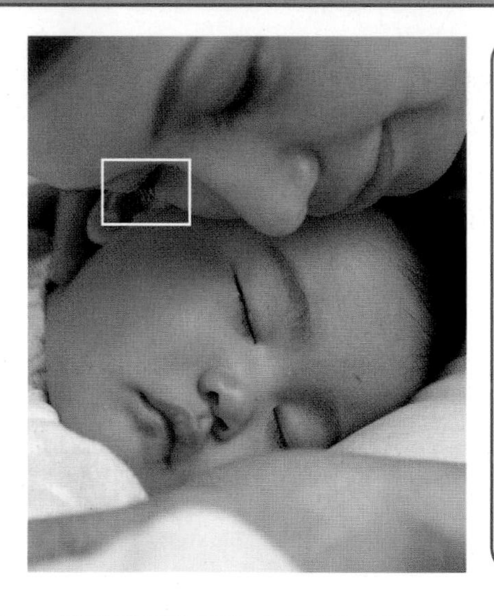

RAW FORMAT

The appeal of shooting Raw is simple: unlike a JPEG file, the camera doesn't process your image. Instead, you do this on your computer using Raw conversion or your image-editing software. This means you can change the appearance of a shot quite radically, without affecting the image quality. For example, you're free to change the white balance, contrast, and saturation, or even make changes to the exposure. These adjustments are only set when you resave the Raw file.

BASIC

▲ A Basic JPEG quality setting means a high level of compression is applied to reduce the file size as much as possible. This will also reduce the image quality, so this setting is best avoided.

NORMAL

▲ If your image will only ever be viewed on screen, then a Normal JPEG quality setting may suffice. However, it's much better to use a Fine setting and reduce the file size on your computer.

FINE

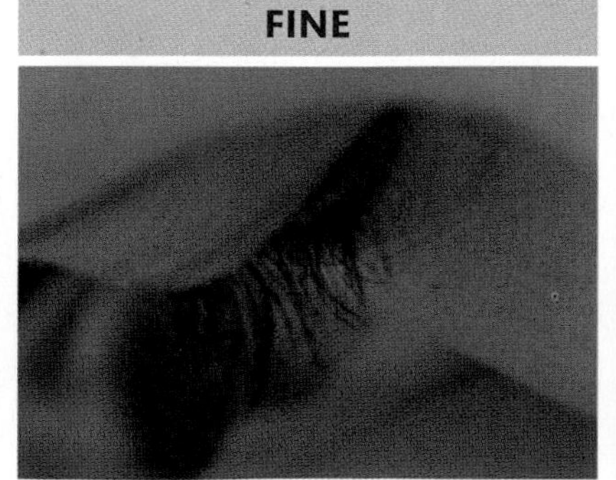

▲ A Fine JPEG setting applies the least amount of compression to your images, so you get the highest quality result. This is the best option for all your digital photographs.

SETTING IMAGE QUALITY

The image quality option is usually found within the camera's shooting menu, although it will only be available when you set your camera to record JPEGs: when it's set to Raw the image is either not compressed, or high-quality "lossless" compression is used. As a very simple rule, set the JPEG image quality to its highest setting and don't touch it again. You can reduce the quality/file size later if you need to, but it's impossible to recover detail lost by high compression levels.

1 CALL UP THE MENU Press the Menu button on the back of your camera and locate the correct shooting menu (you may need to consult your manual).

2 OPEN IMAGE QUALITY Navigate to Image Quality (or similar) using the control pad on the back of your camera and press OK/SET to display the quality options.

3 SET IMAGE QUALITY Select the quality setting you want to use and press OK/SET. Use the Menu button to close the camera menu and return to shooting mode.

IMAGE SIZE

As well as quality options, your camera is also likely to allow you to change the image size – measured in pixels or megapixels (MP). Unless you have very good reason to use a small size setting, it's best to shoot at the maximum image size available: you can always reduce the size of your images on your computer later if you want or need to, but enlarging "small" shots is certain to degrade the picture quality.

✗ Poor quality
✓ Fair quality
✓✓ Good quality
✓✓✓ Very good quality
✓✓✓✓ Excellent quality
✓✓✓✓✓ Press quality

RESOLUTION (PIXELS)	IMAGE SIZE	ON SCREEN	PRINT SIZE (INCHES)				
			4x6	5x7	8x10	16x20	20x30
640x480	0.3 MP	✓✓	✓	✗	✗	✗	✗
1280x980	1 MP	✓✓✓✓	✓✓✓✓	✓✓✓	✓✓	✗	✗
1600x1200	2 MP	✓✓✓✓	✓✓✓✓✓	✓✓✓✓✓	✓✓✓	✓	✗
2240x1680	4 MP	✓✓✓✓	✓✓✓✓✓	✓✓✓✓✓	✓✓✓✓✓	✓✓	✓
3032x2008	6 MP	✓✓✓✓	✓✓✓✓✓	✓✓✓✓✓	✓✓✓✓✓	✓✓✓✓	✓✓✓
3264x2448	8 MP	✓✓✓✓	✓✓✓✓✓	✓✓✓✓✓	✓✓✓✓✓	✓✓✓✓✓	✓✓✓✓
4000x3000+	12 MP+	✓✓✓✓	✓✓✓✓✓	✓✓✓✓✓	✓✓✓✓✓	✓✓✓✓✓	✓✓✓✓✓

2 EXPOSURE

EXPOSURE

Exposure is one of the most fundamental aspects of photography, and you'll often hear photographers talking about "making an exposure" or "getting the exposure right". In essence, "exposure" is simply the process of letting light through the camera's lens to illuminate ("expose") the digital sensor and produce an image. Getting the optimum exposure for your photograph relies on balancing three distinct elements.

Getting it right

The three elements that are key to exposure are the aperture in the lens; the shutter in the camera; and the sensitivity to light of the sensor itself (ISO). Technically, there's no such thing as the "right" exposure, just the one that you think looks best, but there's a point at which most people would agree that a picture is overly light or dark. In photographic terms, when the camera's sensor doesn't receive enough light and the resulting image is dark, it's described as "underexposed". If too much light reaches the sensor and creates an overly bright image, this is described as "overexposed". The aim with exposure is to simply find a happy medium.

WHAT IS EV?

EV (Exposure Value) is a single number used to describe the many permutations of aperture, shutter speed, and ISO that can be used to achieve a single overall exposure (or "brightness"). Each EV step is equal to a one-stop adjustment of the shutter speed, aperture, or ISO, and it's typically used when talking about exposure compensation and bracketing (see pp.80–83): +1EV means increasing the exposure by 1 stop using either the aperture, shutter speed, or ISO, for example.

UNDEREXPOSED | CORRECT EXPOSURE | OVEREXPOSED

What affects exposure?

A "good" exposure involves balancing the aperture, shutter speed, and ISO (see pp.46–47). In doing so, you determine three things: how much light passes through the lens (aperture); the length of time that light passes through the lens (shutter speed); and how sensitive to light the sensor is (ISO). These settings can be balanced in numerous ways to produce a "correct" exposure in terms of brightness, but each individual setting will have a profound effect on the image.

SHUTTER SPEED
1/500 1/250 1/125 1/60 1/30 1/15 1/8 1/4
BLUR
LIGHT
LESS LESS MORE MORE

APERTURE
f/32 f/22 f/16 f/11 f/8 f/5.6 f/4 f/2.8
DEPTH OF FIELD
LIGHT
MORE LESS MORE LESS

ISO
100 200 400 800 1600 3200 6400 12800
NOISE
LIGHT
LESS LESS MORE MORE

EXPOSURE

SHUTTER SPEED

All cameras contain a shutter, which may be either electronic, turning the sensor's light-reading capability on or off, or a mechanical unit that physically opens and closes in front of the camera's sensor to allow in – or shut out – light. Shutter speed is perhaps the easiest of the exposure settings to understand.

ISO

The ISO amplifies the signal that the sensor receives, effectively making it more sensitive to light. This is a bit like turning up the volume on your radio. However, just as this can increase background "hiss", high ISO settings can result in "noisy" images as non-image-forming elements are amplified.

APERTURE

The aperture is, literally, a hole (or "iris") in the camera's lens that allows light to pass through to the sensor. All cameras today – including compacts and many mobile phones – have a variable aperture, so you can set the size of the hole precisely to match the prevailing light conditions.

Shutter speed and movement

The shutter speed in your camera determines how long your sensor is exposed to light, which explains why it's also referred to as the "exposure time". The effect it will have on your image depends on whether there's any movement in the scene: slow shutter speeds will result in moving subjects appearing blurred (see pp.68–71), while fast shutter speeds can effectively "freeze" movement (see pp.64–67). If there is no movement at all in your subject (a building or a still life, for example), then all shutter speeds will produce an equally static result.

PRESSING THE SHUTTER

The shutter inside most cameras uses a pair of blades known as "curtains". The first curtain opens to start the exposure, then the second follows to end it. The length of time it takes for this to happen is the shutter speed, or exposure time, and determines the amount of movement blur that'll appear in your image.

CLOSED

1ST CURTAIN TRAVELLING

FULLY OPEN

2ND CURTAIN TRAVELLING

CLOSED

Aperture and depth of field

As it's not intuitive, aperture is the most difficult of the three exposure settings to grasp. It'll be explained in more detail later in the chapter (see pp.54–55), but the key thing to note is that the aperture affects what is known as "depth of field". Put simply, this is the amount of the scene that will appear sharp in your image: the greater the depth of field, the more elements will appear to be "in focus". This is an incredibly effective creative tool as it can be used blur parts of an image to isolate a subject or direct attention, or to make everything equally sharp.

CHANGING THE APERTURE SIZE

When you increase the size of the aperture, or "open up" the lens, you allow more light to reach the sensor. This reduces depth of field, so less of the scene appears in focus, but it allows a faster shutter speed and/or a lower ISO to be used.

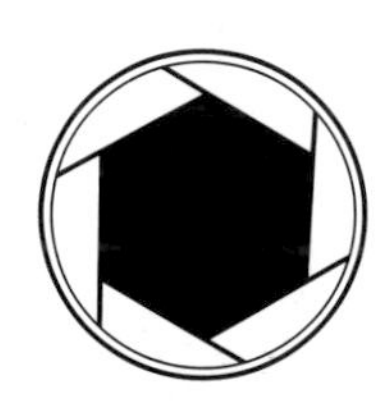
f/2.8

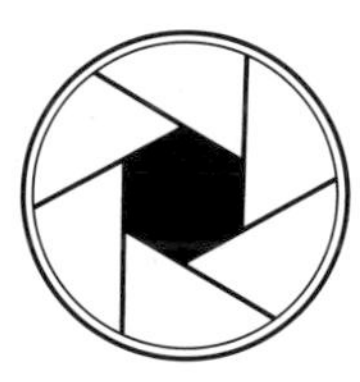
f/5.6

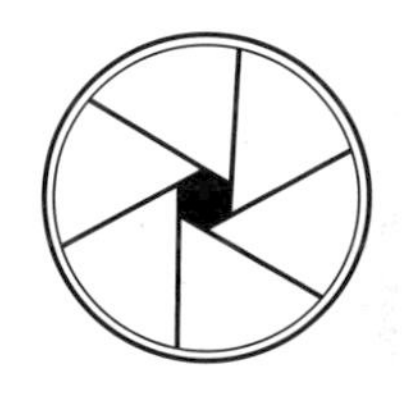
f/16

ISO and noise

At its most basic, the ISO setting controls how sensitive your sensor is to light: low ISO settings indicate low sensitivity, while high ISO settings equate to high sensitivity. On most cameras the ISO range starts at 100 (although some start at 200), and increases to ISO 3200, or higher (see right). However, as the sensitivity increases, so too does the "noise" in the image. This is effectively "interference", which is seen in an image as either coloured speckles (known as "chroma" noise) or an underlying granular texture (known as "luminosity" noise).

ISO SETTINGS

Noise Reduction (NR), whether in-camera or as a tool in your editing software, can help reduce the appearance of noise in your images. However, when you use NR you risk losing detail or reducing sharpness. As a general rule, it's always best to use the lowest ISO setting that you can.

1/100 SEC
1/30 SEC
1/15 SEC
1 SEC

f/5.6
f/16

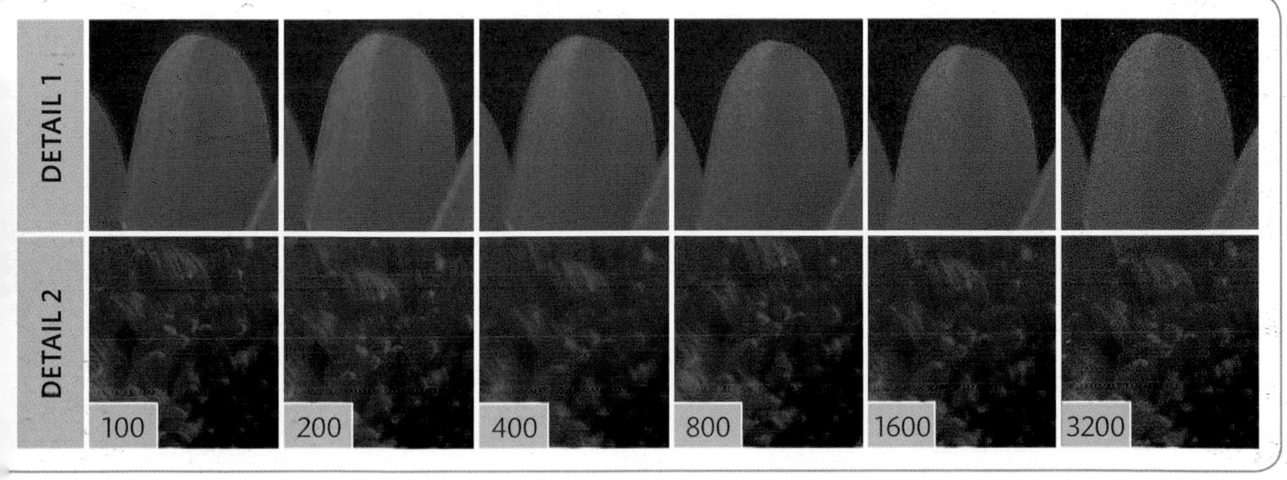
DETAIL 1
DETAIL 2
100
200
400
800
1600
3200

WHAT ARE **SCENE MODES?**

Your camera's Scene modes are designed to get you up and running with your camera in double-quick time, without you having to worry about technicalities such as exposure, white balance, and flash. As long as you know what it is that you're photographing, then the camera will do the rest, setting aperture and shutter speed, along with other parameters such as colour, contrast, and even the level of in-camera sharpening. All you need to do is frame the shot and press the shutter release.

OTHER SCENE MODES

The modes outlined in the table below are the quintet typically found on a dSLR or CSC mode dial, but they're not the only ones available. If you check your camera manual you may find that your particular model offers some or all of the following modes: Night portrait, Night landscape, Party/Indoor, Beach/Snow, Dusk/Dawn, Autumn foliage, Pet portrait, Candlelight, Food, Hi key, Low key, Fireworks, and Document.

COMPACT CAMERA CHEATS

If you think your compact camera doesn't offer control over aperture and shutter speed, think again. The various Scene modes available on most compacts do give you a modicum of control over your camera. If you want a wide aperture, for example, try using Portrait mode (regardless of what it is you're photographing), or if you want a fast shutter speed, try Sports mode. You may not have control over all aspects of your shot, but it's better than having none at all.

WHAT IT DOES	KEY SETTINGS
In Portrait mode your camera will set a wide aperture to throw potentially distracting background elements out of focus, although most cameras tend not to select the very widest lens setting. The colour and contrast are both set to produce natural-looking skin tones (through neutral colour and low-medium contrast), and in low-light situations the built-in flash will fire automatically.	■ Wide aperture (see pp.54–55; pp.58–59) ■ Automatic flash ■ Neutral (not overly saturated) colour
When you switch to Landscape mode, your camera assumes that you want as much of the scene as possible to be recorded sharply, so it will set a small aperture for a large depth of field (see pp.56–57). Colours are intensified slightly to add vibrance to your outdoor shots – especially greens (for trees and foliage) and blues (for sky and sea) – and the flash will be switched off, regardless of the ambient light levels.	■ Small aperture (see pp.54–57) ■ Vibrant colour ■ Flash off
With most cameras the difference between Child mode and Portrait mode is very small, but it is significant. Child mode uses the same wide aperture approach as Portrait mode (to blur backgrounds), but aims to use a slightly faster shutter speed to keep up with active youngsters. The colour is typically set to be a little more vibrant for brighter, fun-packed shots.	■ Wide aperture (see pp.54–55; pp.58–59) ■ Fast shutter speed (see pp.62–63) ■ Vibrant colour
Sports mode is all about freezing action, so your camera will select a fast shutter speed for split-second exposure times (usually accompanied by a wide aperture setting). If it needs to increase the ISO to achieve this, it will do so, even if that increases the level of noise in the image. Sports mode also sets the focus to Continuous mode so it can follow fast-moving subjects around the frame.	■ Fast shutter speed (see pp.62–67) ■ Continuous Autofocus (see pp.96–97) ■ Flash off
In Close-up mode, your camera will set a small aperture in an attempt to overcome the issues with focusing that are particular to this type of work. It will also keep the colours neutral, as it assumes a "natural" subject. However, unless you're using a dedicated macro lens, it can't help you to focus any closer. Flash is usually set to Auto as default in Close-up mode, but you can switch it off if you prefer.	■ Small aperture (see pp.54–55; pp.60–61) ■ Neutral colours ■ Automatic flash

WHAT ARE **AUTO** AND **ADVANCED MODES?**

If your camera has Scene modes then it will undoubtedly have an Auto mode, and it's highly likely that you will have Program (P), Aperture Priority (A or Av), Shutter Priority (S or Tv), and Manual (M) modes available too. It's these four more advanced settings that will enable you to take control of your camera – and your photography.

MOVIE MODE

The option to shoot High Definition (HD) movies on a dSLR or CSC is a relatively recent development, but one that's now taken for granted. Using your camera to record video footage allows you to get even more out of it, and the quality is so high that dSLRs and CSCs are being used to film professional music videos, advertisements, and even some low-budget movies.

ALTERNATIVE MODES

Not all cameras have the same modes, or indeed the same way of showing them on the mode dial. Canon uses Tv for Time Value (Shutter Priority) and Av for Aperture Value (Aperture Priority), for example. Some of their models also have A-DEP (Automatic Depth) mode, which uses the active autofocus points to set an aperture that will keep everything sharp. In a similar vein, some Pentax cameras feature an Sv (Sensitivity Value) mode, or "ISO Priority".

WHAT IT DOES	KEY SETTINGS
As the name suggests, Auto mode leaves all decision-making to the camera, so regardless of the subject you simply have to frame the shot and press the shutter-release. You don't have to worry about exposure, white balance, or any other technicalities, and, unlike Scene modes (see pp.48–49), you don't even need to tell the camera what your subject is: you just point and shoot.	■ Camera sets aperture, shutter speed, and ISO ■ Camera sets white balance ■ Flash is automatic ■ You have little control over other functions
When you switch to Program mode (see pp.52–53), you start to take a certain amount of control away from your camera and begin to have more input into how your photographs turn out. Although the camera sets the aperture and shutter speed automatically, this pairing can usually be adjusted, and you will also have control over the ISO, white balance, and certain other options, depending on your camera model.	■ Camera sets aperture and shutter speed ■ You set ISO ■ You can shift aperture/shutter pairing ■ You have control over all other functions
In Shutter Priority mode (see pp.62–73), you choose your preferred shutter speed and the camera selects the aperture setting that will provide you with the best overall exposure. Shutter Priority is best suited to subjects that need a specific shutter speed – to freeze fast-moving sports or wildlife subjects, for example, or to extend the exposure time and introduce motion blur.	■ You set shutter speed ■ Camera sets aperture ■ You have control over all other functions
Aperture Priority mode (see pp.54–61) is the longest-standing "semi-automatic" shooting mode, with only Manual mode having been around for longer. Aperture Priority works in much the same way as Shutter Priority, although you choose the aperture setting and the camera selects a shutter speed that it calculates will give the "correct" exposure. You have full control over all other camera functions.	■ You set aperture ■ Camera sets shutter speed ■ You have control over all other functions
In Manual mode (see pp.74–75) you only have yourself to blame if things go wrong. The camera will guide you towards the exposure that its programming deems most suitable, but ultimately it's down to you whether or not you choose to go with the camera's suggestion: you have full control over the aperture, shutter speed, ISO, and all other settings, and the camera won't override anything.	■ You set shutter speed ■ You set aperture ■ You have control over all other functions

TAKING **CREATIVE CONTROL**

While your camera's Auto and Scene modes will enable you to "point and shoot" and get a decent enough image most of the time, the fact that they leave the majority of decisions up to the camera does limit your creativity. However, you don't need to jump right in and start taking full manual control of your camera – far from it, in fact. To begin with, all you need to do is switch to Program mode, and take advantage of the added level of control it gives you. With this simple adjustment you'll start to make the most of your camera's tools, helping you to fully realize your photographic potential.

1 SELECT PROGRAM
The first step is the most significant: switch your camera's mode dial to Program.

2 PLAN YOUR SHOT
Where and what you photograph will have an impact on the settings you choose, so decide first what it is you're hoping to achieve with your picture.

3 SET ISO AND WHITE BALANCE
Call up the menu and set your camera's White Balance and ISO (this is not always possible in Auto or Scene modes). There are various White Balance modes to choose from (see pp.126–29), but for an interior shot like this, Incandescent/Tungsten is a good starting point.

4 CHECK EXPOSURE
In the viewfinder, your camera will indicate its recommended shutter speed and aperture combination (the "exposure pairing"), but, unlike Auto and Scene modes, Program gives you options.

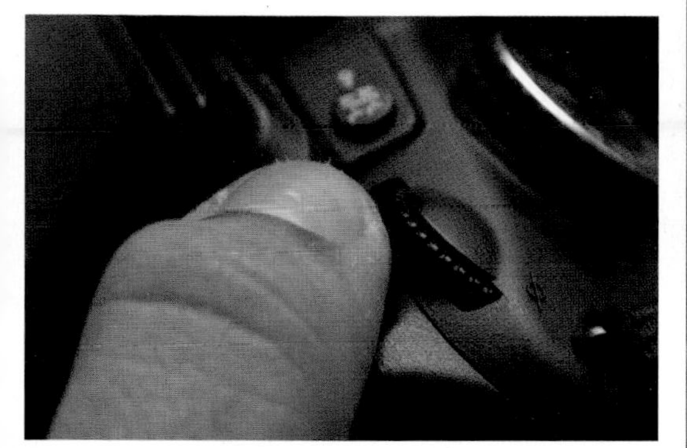

5 ADJUST EXPOSURE

Changing the exposure pairing is usually done with the camera's main control wheel. Note that the exposure shifts in a way that maintains the same overall brightness, so it won't make your picture any lighter or darker.

APERTURE

SHUTTER SPEED

6 SHIFT FOR APERTURE OR SHUTTER SPEED

The key difference between Auto/Scene and Program is the ability to "shift" the paired exposure setting. This will allow you to use a wider aperture to blur a background, for example, or set a slower shutter speed to blur any subject movement.

THE RESULT

It took several test shots to get this result, using Program mode and shifting the exposure to increase the shutter speed until the spinning top was blurred without becoming unrecognizable.

CAMERA **SETTINGS**

WHY USE **APERTURE PRIORITY MODE?**

When you switch your camera to Aperture Priority you're telling it that you're going to decide on the aperture that's used to take your photograph: the camera will then set the shutter speed automatically, so you achieve the correct exposure overall. More than this, when you choose the aperture, you're deciding what depth of field you want in your shot, which is one of the most important creative decisions you can make when taking a photograph.

IN-CAMERA

▲ You'll find Aperture Priority mode on your camera's mode dial, indicated by an A, or Av.

	IRIS	F/STOP	FOREGROUND FOCUS
WIDE APERTURE Setting a wide aperture opens up the iris to allow more light through the lens. However, it also reduces the depth of field so that only the point you focus on appears sharp: almost everything behind and in front of this point will be blurred. This is great when you want to conceal a distracting background.		f/2.8 f/4	f/2.8
MEDIUM APERTURE A medium aperture setting offers the best compromise between the amount of light passing through the lens and the depth of field. In addition, the lens usually delivers its best performance in terms of image sharpness at medium aperture settings.		f/5.6 f/8	f/8
SMALL APERTURE Setting a small aperture (sometimes referred to as "stopping down") restricts the amount of light passing through the lens. It also increases the depth of field, so much more of the scene appears in focus: if you use a very small aperture setting it's possible to get everything looking sharp.		f/11 f/16	f/16

LIGHT: MORE → LESS

DEPTH OF FIELD: LESS → MORE

What effects can I achieve?

The main reason for controlling the aperture is because it allows you to determine depth of field. This is the amount of the scene in front of and behind the actual focus point that appears sharp in your final image. Using a small aperture increases the depth of field, so more of your scene appears sharp, but it often results in longer shutter speeds (or higher ISO settings), which may mean that you'll need to use a tripod. Wider aperture settings reduce the depth of field and help ensure fast shutter speeds, but you need to bear in mind that choosing where to focus becomes even more important than usual.

DEPTH OF FIELD PREVIEW

When you look through your viewfinder, the lens will be set at its widest aperture so you see a bright image, but this won't show you the depth of field. Some (but not all) cameras feature a depth of field preview button, which is usually located beside the lens mount. The images below show the shot without preview (left) and with preview (right).

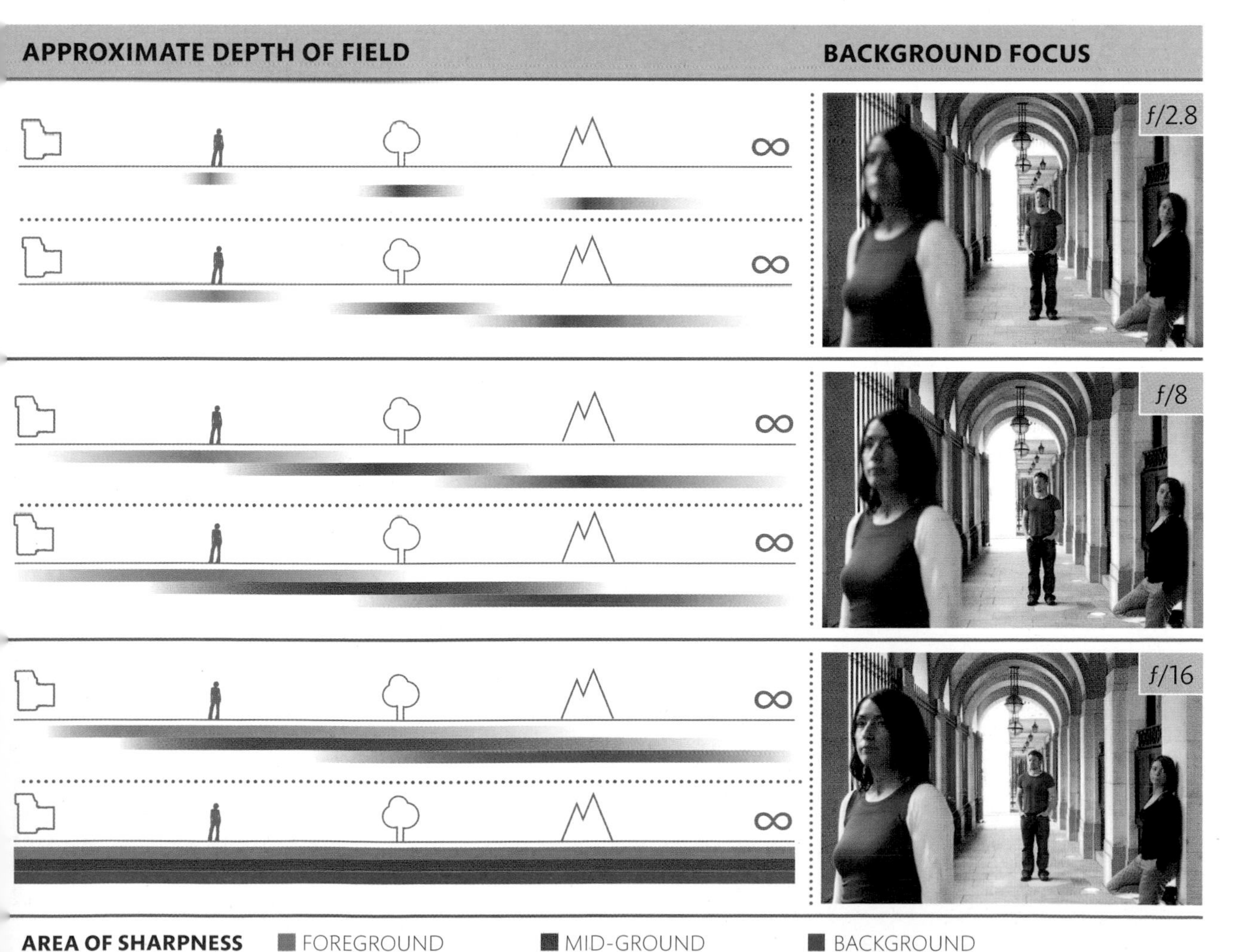

KEEPING EVERYTHING **IN FOCUS**

When you're presented with a stunning view, it's only natural to want everything in your photograph to be as sharp as it appears to the naked eye. The aperture in your lens is the primary means of controlling what is and isn't "in focus" (see pp.54–55) or, to use the correct terminology, determining the depth of field. For this type of shot – where you want the entire view to be as sharp as possible – you'll need to set a small aperture. It's also a good idea to start with the lowest ISO setting on your camera (see pp.44–47), as this will keep noise to a minimum and help maximize detail.

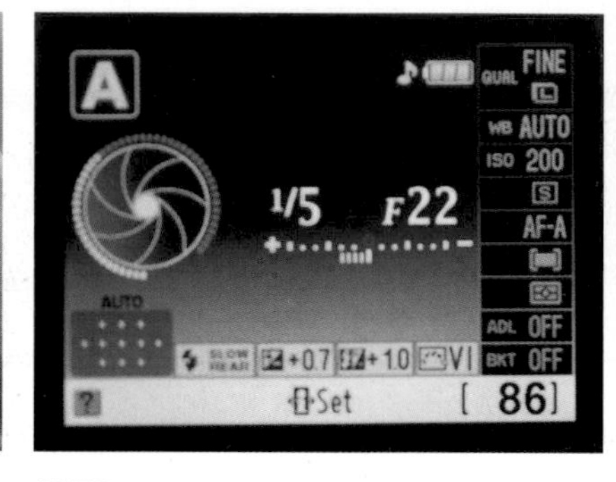

1 SELECT APERTURE PRIORITY
Aperture Priority should be your go-to mode whenever you want to control the depth of field, which is precisely what's required here.

2 SET APERTURE
With distant subjects, where everything in the shot is relatively far away, use the control wheel to set a medium-to-small aperture of f/8–f/16.

3 CHECK SHUTTER SPEED
A small aperture will lengthen the shutter speed, so be sure to check the camera's recommended exposure setting if you plan to shoot hand-held.

4 REVIEW THE IMAGE
Take a test shot at your chosen aperture and review the image. Use your camera's playback zoom controls to zoom in and check the depth of field. You should be able to scroll around the image, so look at both the closest and furthest areas of your shot.

HAZE

Whenever you're photographing distant subjects haze can be an issue, reducing contrast and clarity in your images. Fitting a UV or Skylight filter will help.

ALSO WORKS FOR...

Setting a small aperture so that you get a large depth of field is great for any situation where you want to show everything that's going on, rather than concentrating attention on a single person, area, or object. You can think of it as a general "establishing shot" that will give anyone looking at it a good idea of what it was you saw when you triggered the shutter.

THE RESULT

An aperture of f/13 guaranteed that the boats at the bottom of the frame and the distant buildings would appear equally sharp. The resulting 1/50 sec shutter speed was fast enough to avoid movement blur.

CAMERA **SETTINGS**

USING A **SHALLOW DEPTH OF FIELD** FOR **PORTRAITS**

Using a wide aperture is a classic portrait technique that's guaranteed to give your image maximum impact. The reason it works so well is because it can be used to focus the viewer's attention onto your subject (and away from any distractions). The technique can work particularly well with a telephoto focal length lens, not only because this provides you with a comfortable working distance (see pp.112–13), but also because by zooming in you'll reduce the depth of field further still.

1 POSITION YOUR SUBJECT
For a close-up portrait shot, position your subject away from the background and zoom in to fill the frame. This is usually more practical than reducing depth of field by trying to get very close to your subject.

2 SELECT APERTURE PRIORITY
For full control over the depth of field, set the exposure mode to Aperture Priority and let the camera choose the shutter speed.

3 SET A WIDE APERTURE
Dial in a wide aperture setting (small f-number). Note that prime lenses (see p.103) tend to have wider maximum apertures than zoom lenses.

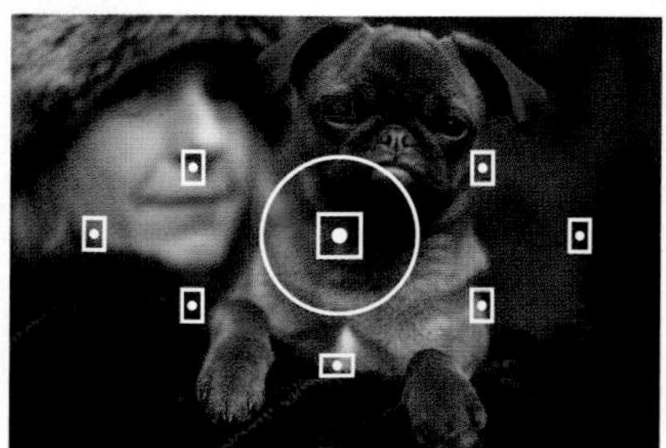

4 SELECT A FOCUS POINT
When you're using a wide aperture setting, focusing is critical because of the shallow depth of field. The best method is to pick the autofocus point yourself (see pp.90–91).

THE RESULT

Zooming in and setting a wide aperture has reduced the depth of field, with the nearest and furthest elements thrown out of focus. The light catching the puppy's eye draws further attention to her face.

CAMERA **SETTINGS**

ALSO WORKS FOR...

A shallow depth of field is great for unconventional portraits, in which the face isn't necessarily the sole focus of the image. In fact, it's a truly versatile creative technique that can be used whenever you want to make a specific part of a scene the centre of attention, regardless of your subject.

ISOLATING A SUBJECT FROM THE BACKGROUND

When you photograph subjects that are close to the camera the depth of field decreases at all aperture settings, so even if you're using a small aperture of f/16 or f/22 it's possible for the depth of field to cover little more than an inch or two with close-up subjects (or even less with extreme close-ups).

However, setting a wide aperture is still useful, as it determines how much (or how little) of the subject appears sharp in your final photograph. Here, using a wide aperture of f/2.8 ensures that the subject really stands out against a potentially distracting background.

1 CHOOSE YOUR LENS
For close-up photographs you can use a dedicated macro lens, but you may find that you can get close to your subject with a long focal length setting on a zoom lens, as here.

2 SET UP YOUR TRIPOD
It's a good idea to use a tripod, as it will enable you not only to hold the camera steady, but also focus precisely on your subject.

3 SELECT APERTURE PRIORITY
Switch your camera to Aperture Priority and select a wide aperture setting (f/2.8–f/4 is good). This will throw the background out of focus.

4 CHOOSE AN AUTOFOCUS POINT
Manually select the Autofocus (AF) point sitting over your subject, or over the part of the subject you want to appear sharp. This may be the central AF point (as here) or an off-centre point (see pp.94–95).

5 TRIGGER WITH SELF-TIMER
To reduce the risk of jogging the camera or changing the point of focus accidentally, trigger your camera's shutter with a remote release. If you don't have one, you can use the self-timer function instead.

6 EXPERIMENT WITH APERTURE

You don't always have to shoot with the lens "wide open" (at its widest aperture setting) to blur a background. In this shot the background is thrown out of focus even when a small aperture setting of f/22 is used, so the choice of aperture is more about the degree of background blur that you want – and, as you can see, that can make a big difference to the final result.

THE RESULT

A wide aperture setting of f/2.8 has transformed the leaves in the background into a creamy green blur, which allows the vivid red flower to take centre stage.

CAMERA **SETTINGS**

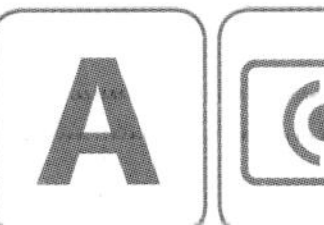

WHY USE **SHUTTER PRIORITY MODE?**

The shutter speed you use can have a profound effect on the resulting image – action may be captured in pin-sharp detail, blurred to convey a sense of motion, or even reduced to an abstract smear of colours. The precise effect you choose is going to be a technical and/or creative decision, but the mode of choice is Shutter Priority: you select the shutter speed and the camera will set a suitable aperture. The table below gives a very rough guide to some of the dramatic effects you can create.

IN-CAMERA

▲ You'll find Shutter Priority mode on your camera's mode dial, indicated by an S, or Tv.

SUBJECT	SUGGESTED SPEED	RESULT
SPORTS Sports photography is usually associated with high-impact, freeze-frame images of sports men and women captured at the peak moment of action, but blur can also be used to convey a sense of speed and movement.	**TO FREEZE** MINIMUM 1/500 SEC	
NIGHT LIGHTS If you want to achieve a fast shutter speed at night you'll usually have to use a wide aperture setting and a high ISO, which can lead to noisy images (see pp.46-47). This is why night shots tend to be taken with slower shutter speeds, which capture moving lights as a blurred trail.	**TO FREEZE** MINIMUM 1/500 SEC	
WILDLIFE As with sports photography, wildlife shots are usually crisp and clear, highlighting textures and markings, or focusing attention on the way in which the animals move. Extending the exposure time, however, is a great way of creating more abstract images of the natural world.	**TO FREEZE** MINIMUM 1/2000 SEC	
WATER Whether you depict moving water as "frozen", using a short shutter speed, or as a silky blur with a long exposure depends entirely on the mood you're trying to create. Images of pin-sharp droplets or crashing waves tend to be more dramatic, while misty water has a more atmospheric, ethereal feel.	**TO FREEZE** MINIMUM 1/1000 SEC	

ULTRA-LONG EXPOSURES

In Shutter Priority mode there's usually a shutter-speed limit of 30 seconds. You can extend this, however, by switching to Manual mode (see pp.74–75) and selecting Bulb (B) mode, if available, by scrolling the control wheel to the end of the shutter speeds. In B mode the shutter will be held open for as long as you hold the shutter-release button (or remote release), allowing you to make an exposure lasting minutes, or even hours. Recording star trails like these requires very long exposure times: ideally upwards of an hour. B mode is the only option here, and a tripod and remote release is essential.

SUGGESTED SPEED	RESULT	TIPS
TO BLUR 1/60 SEC +		■ Very rapid movement will blur at shorter shutter speeds than more moderate movement. ■ Panning (see pp.72–73) allows you to use slow shutter speeds while still retaining some sharpness in your subject.
TO BLUR 1/2 SEC +		■ Very slow shutter speeds (5 seconds +) can be used to make vehicles "disappear", leaving only their light trails. ■ A tripod is essential to avoid camera shake. ■ You should NEVER use flash to photograph moving traffic.
TO BLUR 1/125 SEC +		■ Telephoto lenses exaggerate movement, so use faster shutter speeds with long lenses. ■ When you're shooting hand-held, activate image stabilization, if available, to reduce camera shake.
TO BLUR 1/8 SEC +		■ 1/8 sec is usually slow enough to blur fast-moving water, but 1/2 sec or longer may be needed for a slower flow. ■ Use a neutral density filter so you can extend the exposure time and create a misty, milky effect (see pp.70–71).

FREEZING **MOVEMENT**

As you've already seen, the shutter speed you choose will have a profound effect on the way in which movement is recorded in your image, making Shutter Priority the go-to mode for moving subjects. This is especially true of fast-moving subjects, as the smallest difference in exposure time (and we're talking about thousandths of a second) can make the difference between a sharply recorded subject and one that's slightly blurred. However, it's not only extremely high-speed subjects that you need to think about: the branches of trees blowing in the wind, flowing water, or even people walking in the street are all examples of more modest movement that could appear blurred unless care is taken.

1 FRAME YOUR SUBJECT
No matter what you're photographing, always walk around your subject to determine the best viewpoint. For a shot like this, you'd need to pay careful attention to the background to ensure that the water droplets stand out.

2 SELECT SHUTTER PRIORITY
Set your camera to Shutter Priority so that you have full control over the shutter speed: the camera will select the aperture.

3 ADJUST SHUTTER SPEED
Select the shutter speed by turning the main control wheel on your camera. To freeze movement, aim for a shutter speed of at least 1/500 sec.

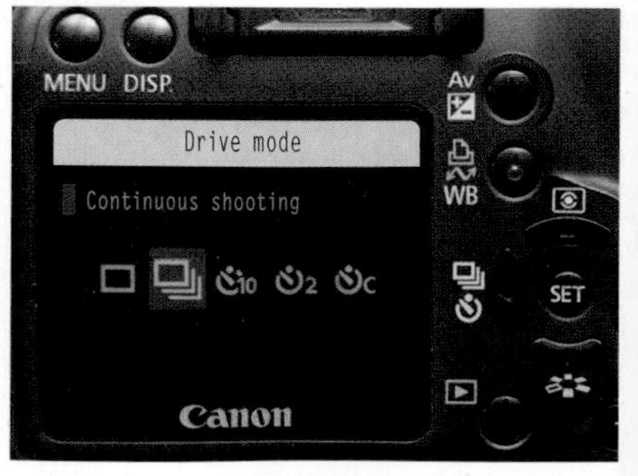

4 ACTIVATE CONTINUOUS DRIVE
Activating your camera's Continuous Drive mode allows you to make a number of exposures in rapid succession, so you can pick the best later.

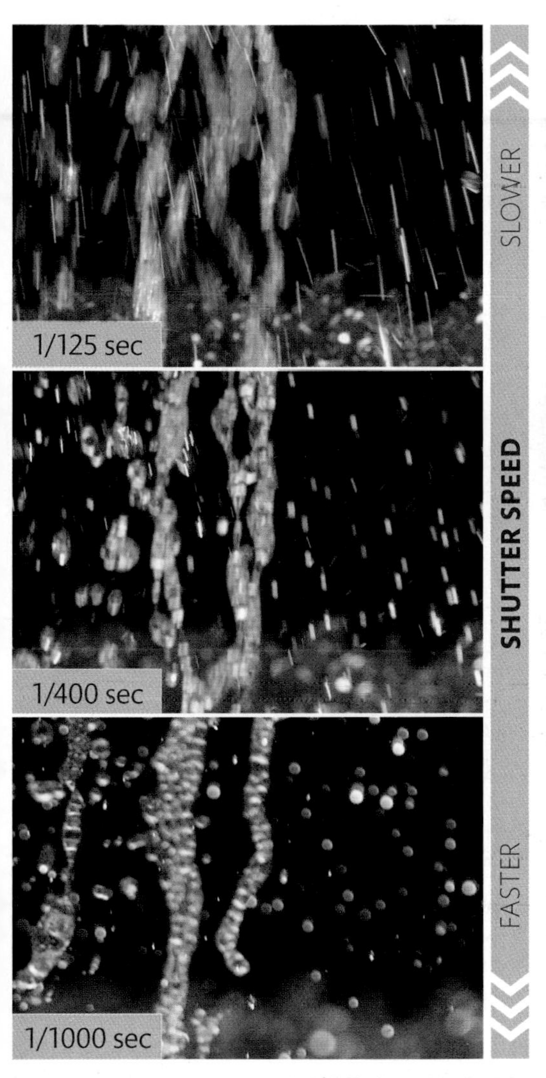

5 EXPERIMENT WITH SHUTTER SPEEDS
It's worth taking several shots using a variety of shutter speeds, so that you have a choice of exposures: sometimes a small amount of motion blur may be preferred to absolute sharpness.

SPEED OF MOVEMENT

The shutter speed you need to set to freeze your subject depends entirely on the speed at which it is moving: the faster the subject, the faster the shutter speed required to stop it in its tracks. If in doubt, use the fastest shutter speed possible and hope that it's quick enough.

THE RESULT

Ensuring that every tiny droplet was as sharp as possible meant using a fast shutter speed of 1/1600 sec. To achieve this we increased the ISO to 400.

CAMERA **SETTINGS**

FREEZING **EXTREME MOVEMENT**

When you aim your camera at something that's moving very quickly, you need split-second exposure times if you want to avoid motion blur. Shutter Priority is the obvious mode for this, but it's not as easy as just setting the fastest shutter speed available. You must also pay close attention to the aperture setting and ISO, because you need to make sure that enough light reaches the sensor in this briefest of moments. In turn, this may have an impact on depth of field, so accurate focusing is also critical: in extreme situations you may need to prefocus (see pp.98–99).

1 CHOOSE YOUR LENS
To get close to the action you'll need a long focal length lens, so fit a prime telephoto lens or a long-reaching zoom that extends to at least 200mm.

2 SET SHUTTER SPEED
Switch your camera to Shutter Priority mode and dial in a short shutter speed. How short will depend on the speed of your subject, but for this shot 1/4000 sec was needed.

3 INCREASE ISO
Unless it's really bright, you will probably have to increase the ISO so your camera can set an aperture. Treat ISO 1600 as the upper limit, however, to avoid excessive noise.

4 PREFOCUS
Because your camera's Autofocus (AF) system may not react quickly enough to a high-speed subject, it's a good idea to prefocus (see pp.98–99). Manual focus can be useful here, or you can use an off-centre AF point (see pp.94–95).

5 RELEASE THE SHUTTER
To stand the best chance of capturing the image you want, you should fire the shutter a split-second before your subject hits the zone of focus. This will compensate for the brief delay between pressing the button and the exposure being made.

ALSO WORKS FOR...

Ultra-short shutter speeds are useful for freezing subjects that you might not normally consider "high-speed", but that require surprisingly brief exposure times if you want to record all of their detail sharply. The beating wings of a bird can quickly become a blur, for example, and the time it takes for a tennis player to hit their serve or a golfer to play their stroke can be equally fleeting.

THE RESULT

Timing is everything with this type of shot. Practice is the only way of knowing what shutter speeds work best for you, and when precisely you need to trigger the shutter.

CAMERA **SETTINGS**

CREATING **MODERATE MOVEMENT BLUR**

While fast shutter speeds can be used to "freeze" a moving subject (see pp.64–67), the opposite is also true – slower shutter speeds can be employed intentionally to allow something to appear blurred in your picture. Again, Shutter Priority is the ideal mode for this, because it allows you to decide on the precise shutter speed you want to use (giving you full control over the level of blur), while the camera sets an aperture to match. This typically means that you'll be shooting with medium to small aperture settings (to restrict the amount of light passing through the lens). A low ISO setting is also a good starting point.

1 SET UP YOUR TRIPOD
A tripod is essential for avoiding camera shake when you're using a slow shutter speed. Make sure it's set up somewhere stable and the legs are locked.

2 FRAME YOUR SHOT
With your camera on a tripod you can frame your shot precisely, choosing to crop it so that the entire subject is seen or, as here, to zoom in for a slightly more abstract result.

3 SELECT SHUTTER PRIORITY
Turn your camera's mode dial to Shutter Priority so you can adjust the shutter speed.

4 ADJUST THE SHUTTER SPEED
On most cameras you set the shutter speed using a control wheel next to the shutter-release button.

5 CHECK THE EXPOSURE
Your camera will try to select a suitable aperture, but this isn't always possible. Review your image to make sure it's not overexposed.

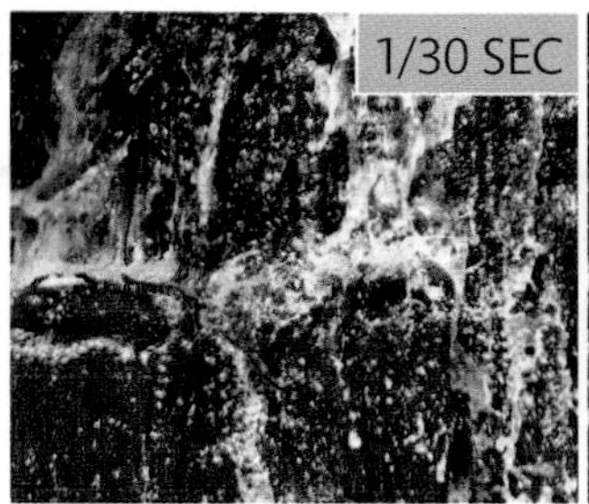

FASTER **SHUTTER SPEED** SLOWER

6 EXPERIMENT WITH SHUTTER SPEEDS

There are varying degrees of "slow" shutter speed, and each one will affect the way in which your subject is recorded. There's no reason why you shouldn't take several shots using different shutter speeds, increasing the amount of movement blur as you go, so you have a number of options to choose from.

THE RESULT

Careful selection of the shutter speed has allowed the water cascading over these rocks to appear blurred, while the camera has set an aperture that provides a good overall exposure.

CAMERA **SETTINGS**

CREATING **EXTREME MOVEMENT BLUR**

When you start using super-slow shutter speeds, the world can look very different. Ordinary streets take on a futuristic appearance thanks to trails of light left by otherwise invisible traffic; people walking will simply disappear; and water can be transformed to mist as exposure times are measured in seconds, rather than fractions of a second. A neutral density (ND) filter (see p.38) is essential for this technique if you're shooting in daylight, and may also prove beneficial in extending the exposure in low-light conditions. Don't forget that the stronger the filter, the longer your shutter speeds can be.

1 USE A TRIPOD
It goes without saying that you'll need to make sure your camera is locked down on a solid tripod so it can't move during your super-long exposure.

2 FIT A NEUTRAL DENSITY FILTER
An ND filter reduces the amount of light that comes through the lens, which enables you to extend exposure times. As it's "neutral", the colour in your image is unaffected by the filter.

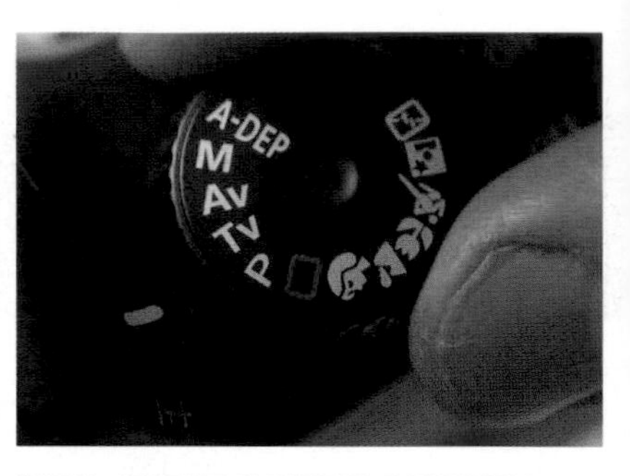

3 SELECT SHUTTER PRIORITY
Set your camera to Shutter Priority and dial in a slow shutter speed: most dSLRs and CSCs will allow you to set an exposure time of up to 30 seconds.

4 CHOOSE AN AUTOFOCUS POINT
In low-light situations it's a good idea to select the central Autofocus point (see pp.88–91), then lock focus and recompose your shot (see pp.92–93). Alternatively, you could focus manually.

5 TRIGGER WITH SELF-TIMER
Rather than press the shutter-release button yourself (which risks knocking the camera and causing camera shake), use your camera's self-timer or a remote release, if you have one.

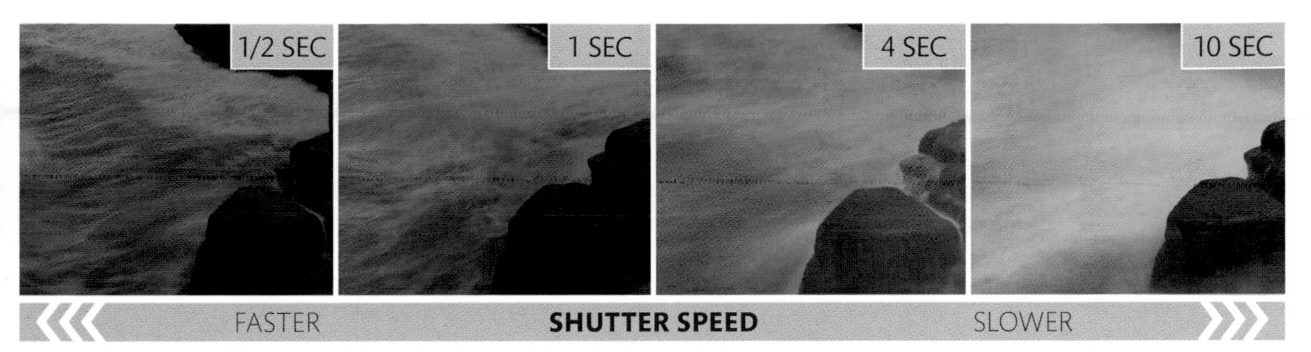

6 CONTROL THE BLUR

The level of blur in your image depends on two things: how quickly (or slowly) the subject is moving and the shutter speed you use. You probably won't have much control over the subject's speed, but you can still vary the way in which the movement is recorded. With water, the longer the exposure, the more "silky" it will appear.

THE RESULT

Using an ND filter on the lens allowed us to increase the exposure time to 20 seconds, even though there was still light in the sky when this shot was taken. As a result, the sea looks more like mist than water.

CAMERA **SETTINGS**

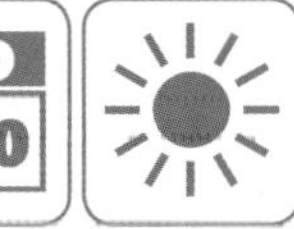

PANNING FOR **SHARPNESS AND BLUR**

Freezing and blurring movement are both ways in which you can control the appearance of motion in an image, but what if you want a sharp subject and a sense of motion too? The good news is that this is easily achievable. The solution is to "pan" with your subject, which basically means following them with your camera while you make your exposure. Although it's unlikely that the subject will be as tack-sharp as it would be if you used a motion-freezing shutter speed, it won't be blurred beyond recognition either; what blur there is will serve to enhance the idea that it's moving.

1 SELECT SHUTTER PRIORITY Turn the mode dial to Shutter Priority and choose your shutter speed: something in the region of 1/60 sec is a good starting point.

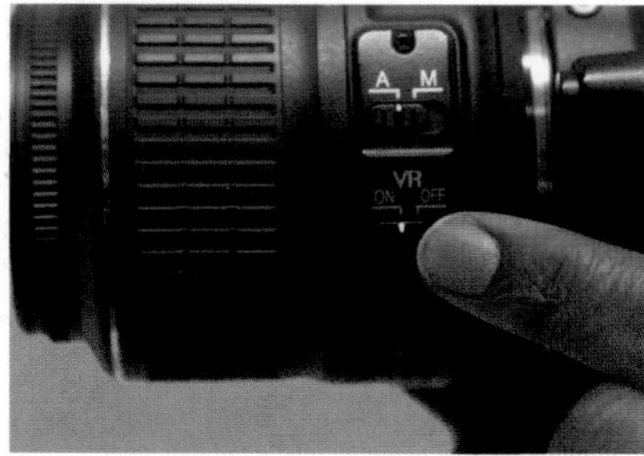

2 ACTIVATE IMAGE STABILIZATION (IS) For hand-held panning shots, switch your IS on. Some lenses offer an IS option specifically for panning, so activate this useful feature if you have it.

3 SELECT CONTINUOUS AUTOFOCUS Unless your subject is moving really fast, Continuous Autofocus (AF) mode is the best option as it will keep adjusting focus to keep your subject as sharp as possible.

4 TRACK YOUR SUBJECT Look through the camera's viewfinder and follow your subject as it approaches you.

5 PAN THE CAMERA Just before your subject reaches the point where you want to take your shot, gently press the shutter-release button. Continue to track your subject with your camera as you do so, turning at the waist so that you pan smoothly.

HIGH-SPEED PANNING

When you're photographing very fast-moving subjects, your AF system may not lock on accurately in time to capture the moment. In this situation, focus manually at a predetermined point and wait for your subject to arrive: don't forget to pan quickly as you take your shot though.

THE RESULT

Panning has created a more dynamic result than a "frozen" shot would have done: the blurred pedestrians and city backdrop contrast strongly with the sharper cyclist.

CAMERA **SETTINGS**

TAKING FULL **MANUAL CONTROL**

For some people, switching the camera to Manual mode is aspirational, as if it's somehow the sign of a great photographer. The truth is, Manual won't enable you shoot any better than you can in Aperture Priority or Shutter Priority modes. What it does do, however, is allow you to set the aperture and shutter speed yourself (as well as the ISO), and no matter where you point the camera it won't change the settings. In challenging lighting conditions this can be a good reason to take manual control of your camera, especially if you use it with a grey card too.

1 SET TO MANUAL
Whenever you want to set the aperture, shutter speed, and ISO yourself there's only one mode to choose, and that's Manual.

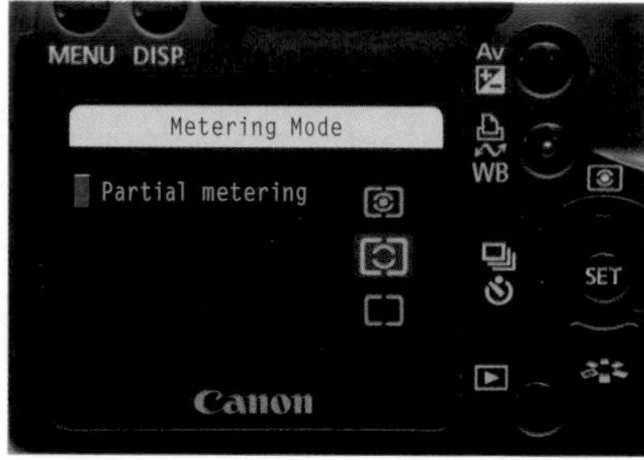

2 SET METERING PATTERN
For the greatest accuracy, set your camera to take an exposure reading using its spot or partial metering pattern (see pp.76–77).

USING A HAND-HELD LIGHT METER

An alternative to a grey card is to use a hand-held light meter. This type of exposure meter reads the light falling onto your subject (known as an "incident" reading) rather than the light being reflected off it (a "reflected" reading). The advantage of this is that the meter isn't "fooled" by how light or dark the subject appears.

3 USE A GREY CARD
Place a photographer's grey card in the scene, under the same light as your subject. Aim your camera at the grey card, so the card is under the central autofocus point (this is also the spot meter area on most cameras).

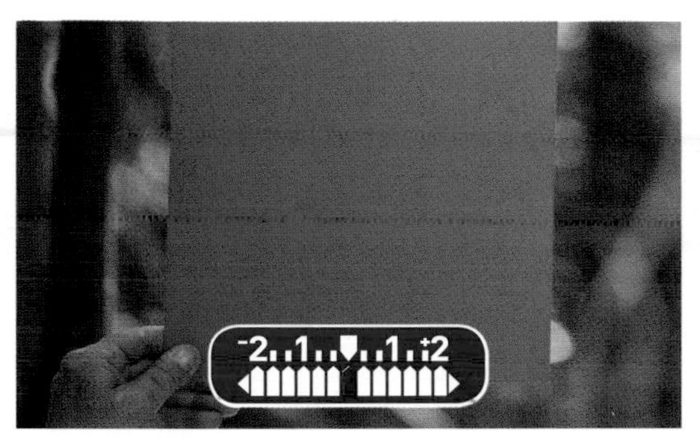

4 USE THE EXPOSURE SCALE

Use the exposure scale in the viewfinder to assess exposure. A shift towards "+" indicates overexposure, towards "-" indicates underexposure.

5 MAKE ADJUSTMENTS

Set aperture and shutter speed until the scale shows the "correct" exposure, indicated by a "0" or a triangle. Once your exposure's dialled in you can remove the grey card and take the shot.

THE RESULT

Despite the heavy backlighting and deep shadows in the background, the exposure for this challenging shot is perfect thanks to the use of a grey card and manual exposure mode.

CAMERA **SETTINGS**

WHAT ARE **METERING PATTERNS?**

Getting the exposure "right" is largely about choosing the most suitable combination of aperture, shutter speed, and ISO (see pp.44–47). However, in order to make that choice, you and/or your camera need to know precisely what's going on in terms of the light levels: unless you know how much (or how little) light there is in a scene, it's impossible to know precisely what settings are needed. Thankfully, all modern cameras have an array of exposure metering "patterns" to point you in the right direction.

IN-CAMERA

▲ The metering pattern options are usually accessed using a button on the back of your camera.

Exposure meter

The exposure metering system in your camera is an incredibly complex device, which is designed to measure the light in a scene to create an accurate exposure. However, these meters are not infallible, because they work on the basis that the subject you want to photograph would average out as a midtone, which isn't always the case. Therefore, to help you get the most accurate light readings, different metering patterns are employed, allowing you to assess the light levels from the entire frame or, if you want to exclude any overly bright or dark subject areas, just a small part of it.

▲ Which metering pattern you select depends on the subject you're photographing: for a shot like this, with tricky, contrasty lighting, spot metering would be a good choice.

PARTIAL METERING

Partial metering is found mainly on Canon cameras and can be thought of as a "large spot" area: it doesn't read as much of the scene as centre-weighted metering, but it's not as small as a true spot meter (see opposite).

METERING PATTERN

MULTI-AREA

Depending on the make of camera, multi-area metering goes under many different names: Evaluative, Matrix, Honeycomb, and Multi-segment are just a few of the names used. However, they all refer to a similar principle: the camera takes its exposure reading from the entire frame. In most instances the scene is broken down into distinct areas, or segments, which are measured independently. The camera then averages out all of these measurements to give an exposure reading. Because the whole scene is taken into account, this type of metering pattern tends to be very accurate in a wide range of situations.

CENTRE-WEIGHTED

Of all the metering patterns, centre-weighted metering is the most long-standing; some might argue that it's no longer as relevant as it used to be, especially when you consider how sophisticated multi-area metering patterns have become. However, it still features on almost all cameras, and does have its uses. Centre-weighted metering is most useful when your subject occupies the centre of the frame and is surrounded by a predominantly light or dark background – portraits are a prime example. Because the metering pattern is biased towards the centre of the frame, it's less likely to be influenced by any extreme tones towards the edges.

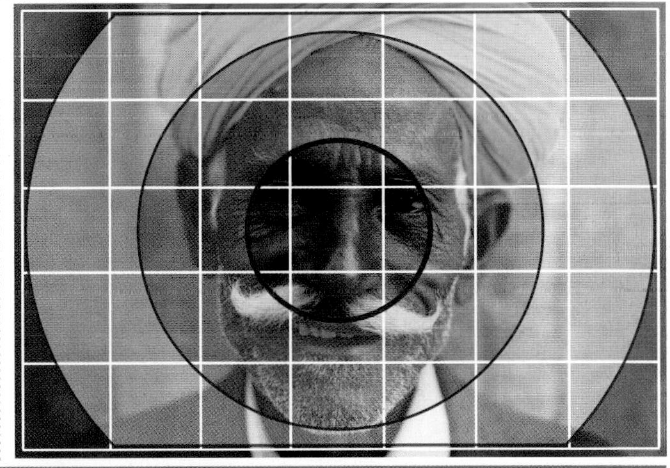

SPOT

When you switch your camera to its spot metering mode, it will take an exposure reading from a very small and precise area, usually at the centre of the frame, although sometimes it can be linked to the active focus point (see pp.90–91). The benefit of using a spot metering pattern is that it won't be affected by the surrounding area, so if your subject is very small in the frame and surrounded by a large expanse of dark or light (a figure in snow, for example), the extreme tones won't affect the exposure reading. With some high-end cameras, multiple spot readings can be taken and averaged out, and/or the size of the area used for the meter reading can be changed to make it slightly larger or smaller for even greater precision.

WHAT IS A **HISTOGRAM?**

The histograms that pop up in your camera and editing software when you review your image can initially seem rather daunting. With a little experience, however, reading a histogram becomes second nature, allowing you to see just how the tones (from light to dark) are distributed across your image. Because it relies on a graphic display, a histogram isn't affected by the light you view it under (as an LCD screen can be), so it's an incredibly effective way of checking whether your exposure is "good".

IN-CAMERA

▲ All dSLRs and CSCs allow you to call up a histogram when you review your images on the LCD screen. This is far more accurate than simply assessing the brightness of the image on screen.

UNDEREXPOSED

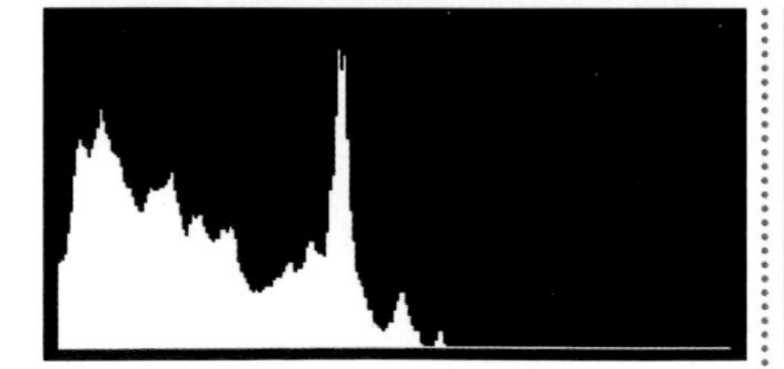

When the bulk of the histogram is towards the left of the scale it means that there are a lot of dark tones in the image. If it isn't a particularly dark scene, then the shot is almost certainly underexposed. In extreme cases the graph will "hit" the left end of the scale, indicating that some of the darkest tones are lost.

CORRECT EXPOSURE

The "ideal" histogram will have the tonal spread fitting within the ends of the graph. This tells you that you've recorded all of the detail in the scene, from the very darkest areas through to the brightest. Because a full tonal range has been recorded, this type of image responds well to further editing.

OVEREXPOSED

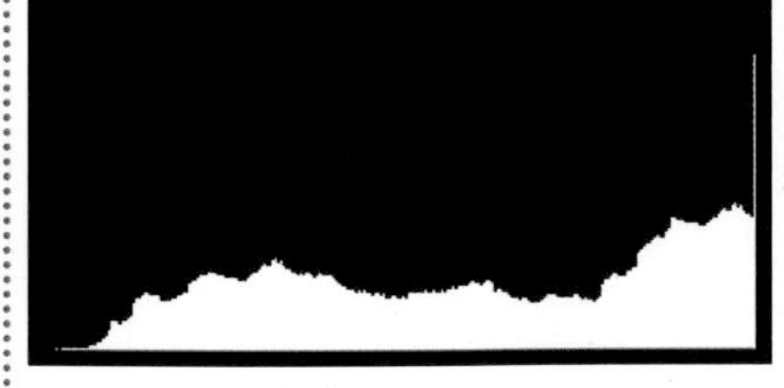

If your histogram crashes into the right end of the scale it means that certain areas are pure white, and no amount of processing will enable you to bring out any detail: it's lost for good. When the histogram suggests that this might be the case, adjust the exposure and shoot again.

How to read a histogram

Essentially, the dark tones/shadows in your image are represented at the left edge of the histogram, while the right end represents bright tones/highlights. The height of the graph shows how many pixels have a particular tone, but this can be largely ignored. What's more important is that the graph fits within the scale: if it appears to go off the scale to the right, then certain highlight areas have become pure white; if it appears to go off the scale to the left, then shadow detail has been lost. This loss is known as "clipping".

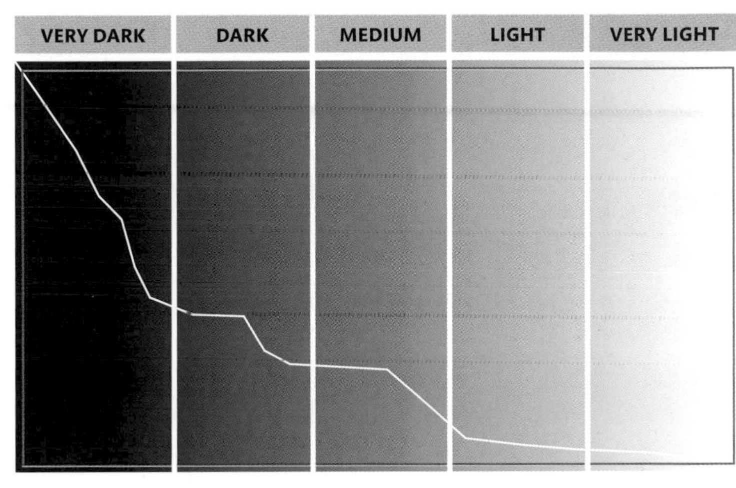

▲ SCALE OF TONES

LOW KEY

Here the histogram is shifted to the left, which would suggest that this particular image has been underexposed. However, this example shows why you can't rely purely on the histogram: the shot is of a "dark" subject, so you'd expect to see more dark tones present.

HIGH KEY

This high-key image is made up primarily of bright, light tones, with little in the way of shadow. Because of this, the histogram is shifted to the right. That's not a problem in itself, but it's a good idea to keep an eye on the end of the histogram to avoid clipping too many light areas.

SILHOUETTE

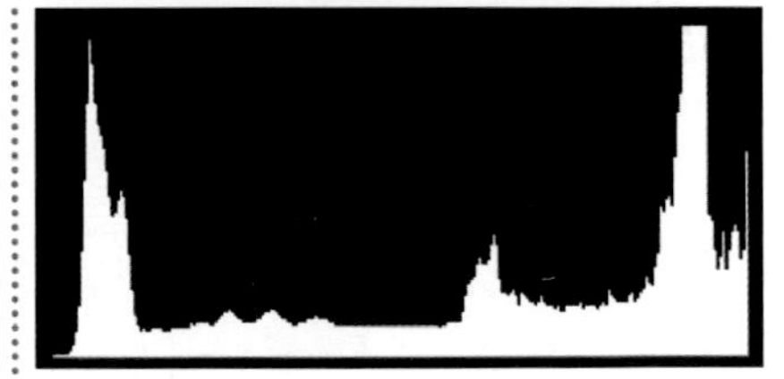

When an image is made up of a combination of very dark and very bright areas, as is the case with this silhouette, the histogram tends to appear split between the two ends of the scale. In this particular instance it doesn't really matter if the highlights or shadows are clipped.

FINE-TUNING EXPOSURE

Although your camera's metering system does a great job of getting the exposure right, it's not infallible. There will be times when a picture comes out lighter or darker than anticipated, and the most common reason will be because the scene you're photographing is primarily very dark or very bright. In this situation your camera will try to expose it as if it's a midtone (see pp.124–25), so a bright scene will appear dark and vice versa. When this happens, exposure compensation can be used: dialling in positive (+) compensation will brighten an image, and negative (-) compensation will darken it.

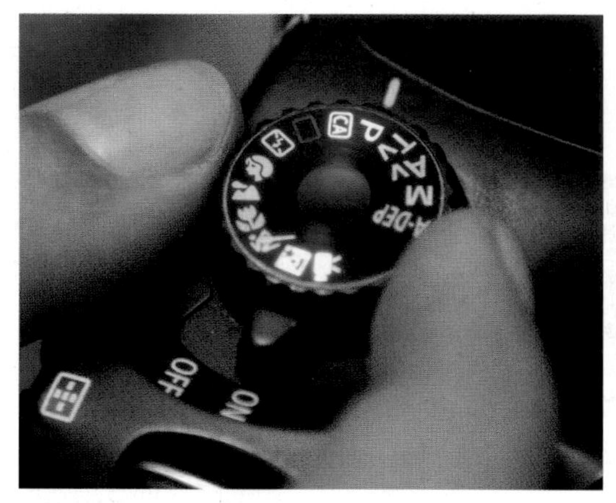

1 SELECT A MODE Exposure compensation can be applied in Program, Aperture Priority, or Shutter Priority modes. It's not usually available in Auto, Scene, or Manual modes.

2 TAKE A TEST SHOT There's no surefire way of determining the correct amount of exposure compensation to apply – and it depends on the look you're after – but taking a test shot at the camera's recommended exposure setting will give you a good starting point.

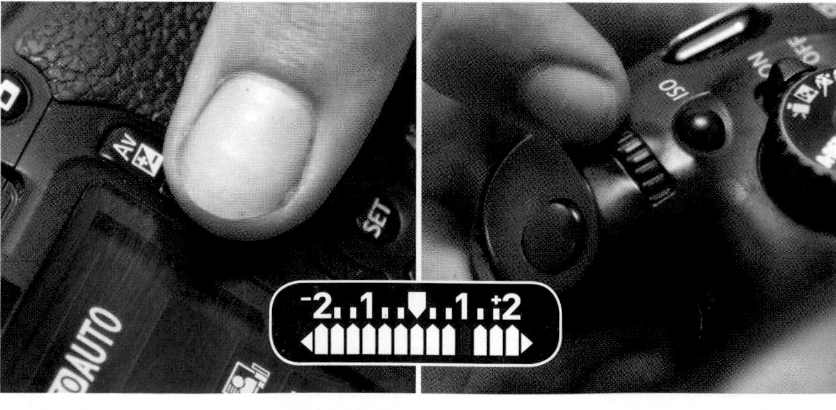

3 ASSESS YOUR IMAGE Your test shot's histogram will tell you whether your image is under- or overexposed (see pp.78–79) and give an indication of how far out the exposure is.

4 APPLY EXPOSURE COMPENSATION To apply exposure compensation, press and hold the exposure compensation button (left), and turn the main control wheel (right). If you're working in Aperture Priority mode, exposure compensation will adjust the shutter speed; in Shutter Priority mode, it will adjust the aperture.

5 TAKE A SET OF EXPOSURES
The precise level of exposure compensation needed will vary from shot to shot, even with the same subject, so it's a good idea to take a series of shots with different levels of compensation applied. Alternatively, you could start by dialling in a small amount of exposure compensation and using your camera's exposure bracketing feature (see pp.82–83).

THE RESULT

If you let the camera determine the exposure, the dominant bright tones in this scene would lead to underexposure. With a touch of exposure compensation, however, the shot sparkles.

CAMERA **SETTINGS**

USING AUTOMATIC **EXPOSURE BRACKETING**

Although you can apply exposure compensation (see pp.80–81) to tweak the camera's suggested exposure, it means taking a shot and assessing its histogram, which takes time. With moving subjects this has obvious implications, because the moment you want to record may have passed by the time you've made your changes and are ready to shoot again. That doesn't just apply to fast-moving subjects – a fleeting break in the clouds that produces a patch of light can be just as time-sensitive. In these instances, activating your camera's Automatic Exposure Bracketing (AEB) feature is the answer.

1 FRAME YOUR SHOT
It's always a good idea to set your camera up on a tripod if you've got time (and a suitable subject). When you're using AEB it's especially useful because it will allow you to fire off your exposure sequence without any movement between frames.

2 LEVEL YOUR TRIPOD
Whenever you're shooting a landscape (and by extension, a seascape), it's important to keep the horizon level, but special care should be taken when you're setting up on an uneven or soft surface such as pebbles or sand. Use your tripod's built-in spirit level to guide you.

3 SELECT A MODE
On most cameras it isn't possible to use AEB in Auto, Manual, or Scene mode, so choose Program, Aperture Priority, or Shutter Priority instead.

4 ACTIVATE AEB
AEB is found as a menu option or accessed via a button on your camera. In both cases you need to set the number of frames and an exposure gap.

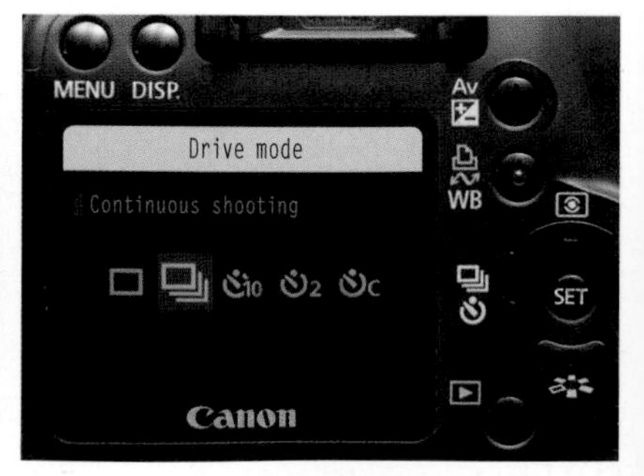

5 ACTIVATE CONTINUOUS DRIVE
When using AEB you need to take your bracketed sequence as a "burst" of shots, so set your camera's Continuous Drive mode.

6 **TAKE A SET OF EXPOSURES**
Hold down the shutter-release button to take your bracketed exposure sequence. For this image we set AEB to make three exposures at 1-stop increments. This meant that we ended up with one shot that's 1 stop darker than the camera's suggested exposure setting (-1EV), another at the suggested exposure (0), and a third that's 1 stop brighter (+1EV).

THE RESULT

When we opened the images on the computer we decided that the exposure that's 1 stop brighter than the suggested reading works best: the extra exposure really makes the water shimmer.

CAMERA **SETTINGS**

WHAT IS **HDR IMAGING?**

The "dynamic range" of a scene refers to the brightness range between the darkest shadow and the lightest highlight, or, in layman's terms, the contrast. This is important for photographers because a camera's sensor can only record a limited dynamic range: if the range of a scene exceeds the capability of the camera, the highlights, shadows, or both will be "clipped" (see pp.78–79). However, there's a practical – and creative – solution: High Dynamic Range (HDR) imaging.

Shooting for HDR

The idea behind HDR imaging is to make a number of exposures of the same scene, adjusting the exposure between shots so you have one shot that records detail in the brightest highlights; another that records all the shadow detail; and additional exposures in between. These images are then combined using HDR tools or software.

The easiest way of capturing your initial sequence is to use your camera's Automatic Exposure Bracketing feature (see pp.82–83). Setting the number of frames to 3 or 5, and the spacing between them to at least ±2EV, will be sufficient in most instances.

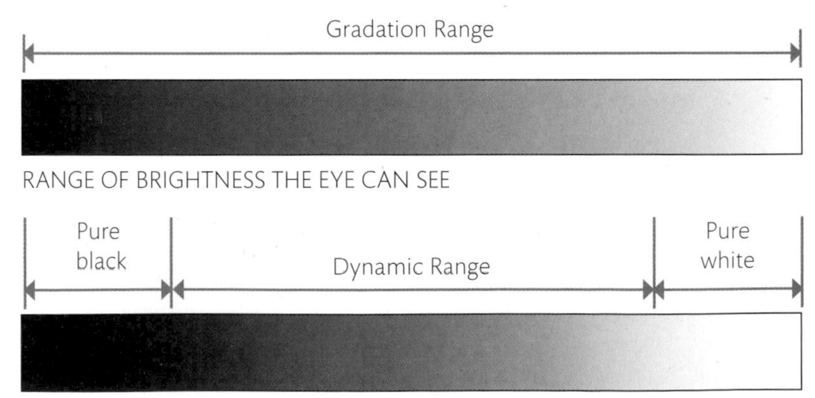

▲ Because our brain constantly adjusts for different brightness levels, we can see a wide range of tones. However, a digital camera's sensor has a fixed "dynamic range" – anything outside that range will appear as pure black or pure white.

HDR SOFTWARE

Once you've made your exposure sequence you need to use editing software to merge them using a process known as "tone-mapping". This takes the "best bits" (in terms of exposure) from each image and combines them into a single picture. Your current software package may have some sort of built-in HDR feature, but stand-alone software, dedicated to to HDR imaging, tends to produce much more sophisticated results.

EXPOSURES

HIGHLIGHTS

MIDTONES

SHADOWS

IN-CAMERA DYNAMIC RANGE OPTIMIZATION

An increasing number of camera manufacturers have developed in-camera tools to help deal with scenes of high dynamic range. These include Auto Lighting Optimizer from Canon, Active D-Lighting from Nikon, and D-Range Optimizer from Sony. Each works in a slightly different way, but the general approach is the same: the exposure is set to preserve as much detail as possible in the highlight areas, and then the shadow areas are lightened in-camera to prevent them from appearing too dark. This image shows the same scene both without (left) and with (right) in-camera dynamic range optimization.

MERGED HDR IMAGE

3 FOCUSING

FOCUSING

After exposure, focusing is perhaps one of the most important areas in photography. Most people will tolerate colours that are a little "off", or a slightly awkward composition – and these can often be corrected using editing software – but an out of focus shot will almost always look "wrong" (unless it's a deliberate creative effect). Moreover, there's very little you can do to salvage a blurred photograph, so getting the focus right is an essential skill. In this chapter you'll discover the tools your camera has to help you, and how best to use them.

Manual focus

Before Automatic Focusing (AF) systems were developed, the only way to get a sharp picture was to focus the lens by hand, manually adjusting it until the image in the viewfinder appeared to be "in focus". Although this is a much slower process than using a modern AF system, the advantage is that you can choose precisely where you want to focus.

This can be useful for a number of reasons. For example, you may wish to focus on a particular point in a scene for creative effect, or you may need to take over from the camera when low light and/or low contrast make it difficult for the AF system to lock onto your subject.

Manual focus is also the best option when you're photographing close-up subjects, or are working with a very shallow depth of field – in any situation, in fact, where you want to have absolute control over the point at which your lens is focused.

◀ Low light and low contrast are two common situations in which modern AF systems can struggle, but this is another: photographing someone (or something) through glass. The various reflections can easily throw the AF system off track, making manual focus a more reliable alternative.

Autofocus points

All cameras now have AF, and all AF systems rely on one or more focus "points", which are sensors that the camera uses to set the focus. The precise number of focus points depends almost entirely on the level of the camera you're using, with advanced models tending to have more AF points than entry-level cameras. However, the number of AF points isn't the only factor affecting accuracy: the spread of the points and the sophistication of the focusing system behind them is equally important.

ENTRY LEVEL

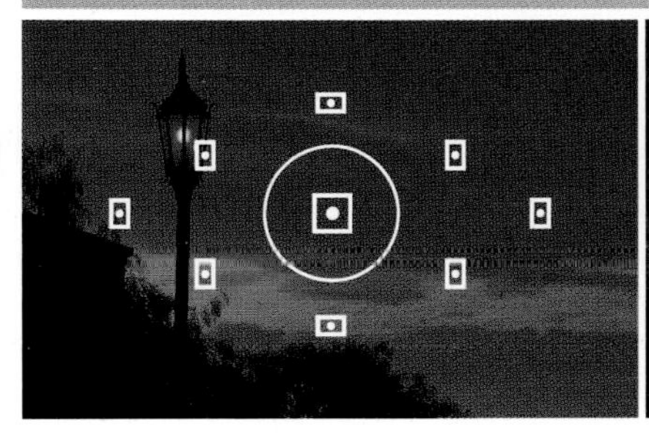

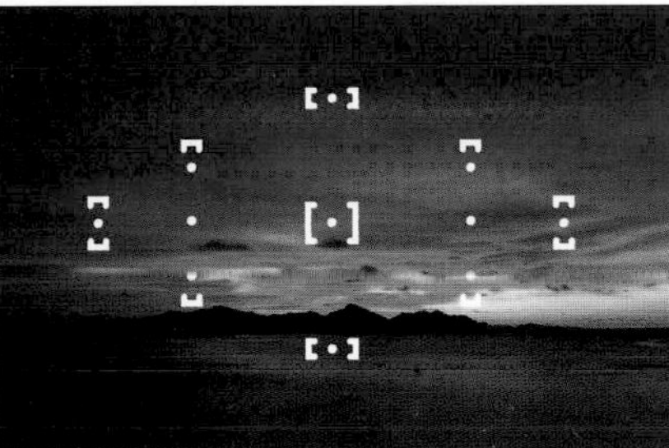

ADVANCED

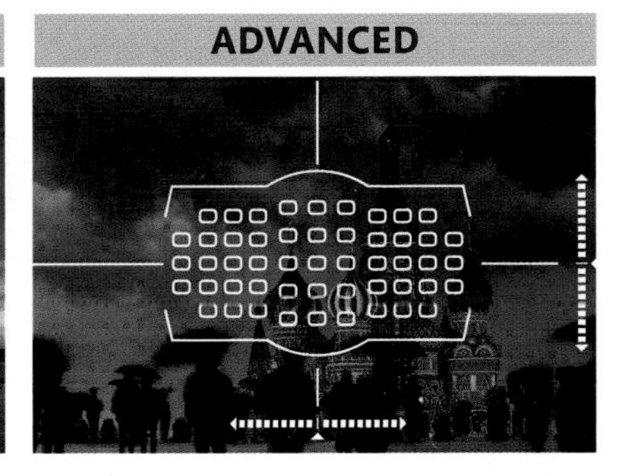

Autofocus modes

There are three AF modes that you need to familiarize yourself with if you want to get the best from your camera: One-shot (or Single-shot), Continuous, and an Automatic option. As a simple rule, One-shot AF is usually used for static subjects; Continuous AF is the better choice when your subject is moving; and Auto is the one to go for if you anticipate that your subject *might* move.

ONE-SHOT

One-shot AF is perhaps the most commonly used mode for general subjects. In One-shot AF mode you activate the focusing system and the camera uses one or more focus points to try to set the focus. Once it's locked on, it will maintain focus at that distance until you take a shot or release the AF.

CONTINUOUS

If you're shooting a moving subject, Continuous AF (see pp.96–97) may be the mode to go for. In this mode the camera will adjust the focus if it detects that your subject is moving towards or away from the camera. It will continue doing this until you press the shutter-release button fully.

AUTO

Called AF-A by some manufacturers, many cameras have a focusing option that will switch between One-shot and Continuous AF automatically. If the subject is static, then One-shot AF is used, but if the subject is moving (or starts to move), the camera will switch to Continuous AF.

USING **MULTI-AREA** AND **SINGLE-POINT AUTOFOCUS**

Most people, when they first start taking photographs, will naturally begin by placing their subject "front and centre" in the frame. The benefit of this approach is that the main point of interest will appear in sharp focus. However, while perfectly acceptable, in photography – as with many other art forms – always positioning the main subject in the centre of the frame can feel a little predictable very quickly. To introduce more dynamism into your images, consider placing your subject off-centre and then selecting the Autofocus (AF) point that you want your camera to use.

1 ACTIVATE AUTOFOCUS
Make sure that your camera is set to AF. Depending on your equipment, you may need to set this on both the camera and lens, or just the camera body.

2 SELECT ALL AF POINTS
To be sure your camera is set to Multi-area AF, press the AF point button and turn the control wheel until all of the AF points show as "active".

3 FRAME YOUR SHOT
With the camera deciding which AF point it will use, all you need to do now is frame your shot and make your exposure. But you may decide that you need more control.

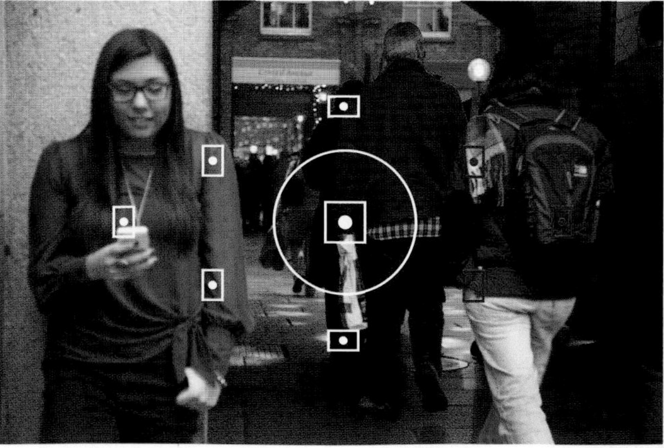

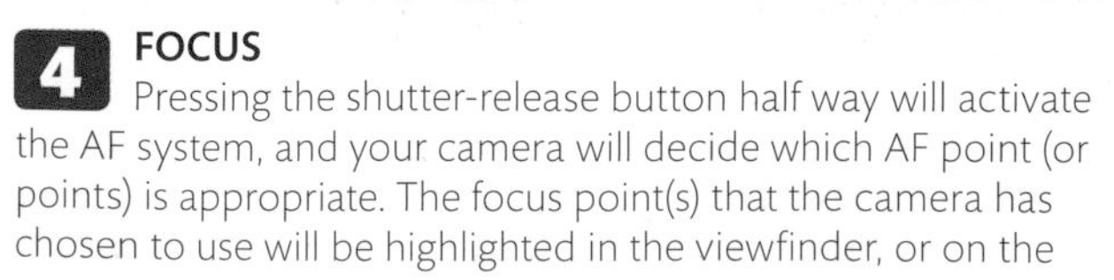

4 FOCUS
Pressing the shutter-release button half way will activate the AF system, and your camera will decide which AF point (or points) is appropriate. The focus point(s) that the camera has chosen to use will be highlighted in the viewfinder, or on the rear LCD screen if you're using Live View. This will usually (but not always) be the closest or most high-contrast area. If you're happy with the camera's choice, press the shutter-release button fully down to make your exposure.

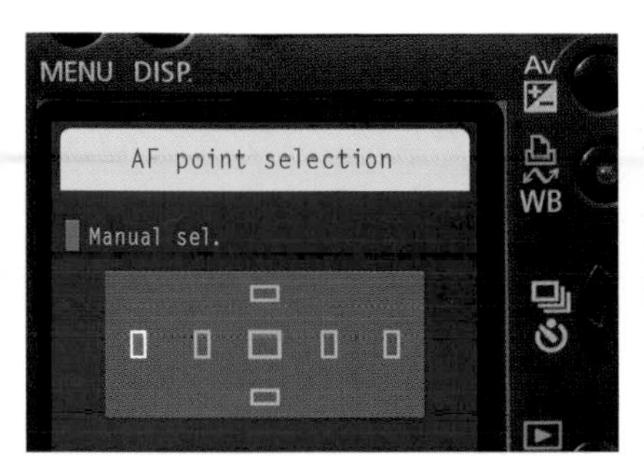

5 **ADJUST FOCUS** If you're not satisfied with the camera's choice, you can select an AF point yourself by pressing the AF point button and turning the control wheel.

6 **CHANGE POINT OF FOCUS** Here, the focus point was shifted deliberately to the figure at the left of the frame, so there was no chance of the camera picking an inappropriate AF point.

ZONE FOCUS

In addition to Multi-area and Single-point AF selection, some cameras that utilize a high number of focusing points offer "zone focusing." This allows you to choose a group of AF points (typically top, bottom, left, right, or centre), and the camera then selects a single AF point from this area. In effect, the camera is making the final decision, but you are guiding it to a specific part of the frame.

THE RESULT

To inject some energy and movement into our compostion we chose to contrast the stillness of the girl with the busy shoppers by using a slow shutter speed (see pp.62–63).

CAMERA **SETTINGS**

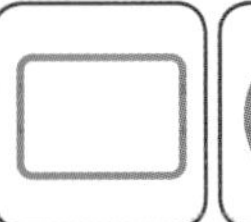

FOCUSING AND **REFRAMING**

Selecting a single Autofocus (AF) point (see pp.90–91) is often all that's needed to focus on off-centre subjects, but it's not always the most convenient way to do it. Selecting the relevant AF point takes time, especially if you have to scroll through a lot of focus point options, so it's not particularly conducive to spontaneous hand-held shooting. There's also a chance that your camera may not actually have a suitably positioned AF point to start with. In both cases, the answer is to use just one AF point and "lock" the focus before reframing the scene and taking your shot.

1 ACTIVATE AUTOFOCUS
Make sure that your lens is set to AF (with some camera models you'll need to set the camera to AF too), and that the focusing is in Single-shot mode, rather than Continuous Autofocus.

2 SELECT THE CENTRAL AUTOFOCUS POINT
Press your camera's focus point selection button and turn the control wheel to select the central AF point.

3 FOCUS
Aim your camera at your subject so the area you want to focus on is under the central AF point. Half press the shutter-release button to focus.

4 REFRAME YOUR SHOT
Keep the shutter-release button half depressed, as this will "lock" the focus (and exposure, see box opposite). You're now free to move the camera: as long as you're in Single-shot AF mode and you keep your finger on the shutter release, the camera will maintain focus at that point (shown here by the small red square). Once you've reframed your shot (as indicated by the white dotted line), press the shutter-release button fully to make your exposure.

AUTOMATIC FOCUS LOCK

As well as locking the focus, half depressing the shutter-release button will also lock the exposure. In some situations you won't want this to happen, because moving your camera to reframe your shot may mean that the exposure needs to change too (if the reframed scene is any lighter or darker). In this case, instead of using the shutter-release to lock focus, use your camera's Automatic Focus Lock (AF-L) button. AF-L usually doubles as the Exposure Lock, but you can customize it via your camera menu so that it locks only focus. This means that you can lock focus and recompose, and the exposure will change if necessary.

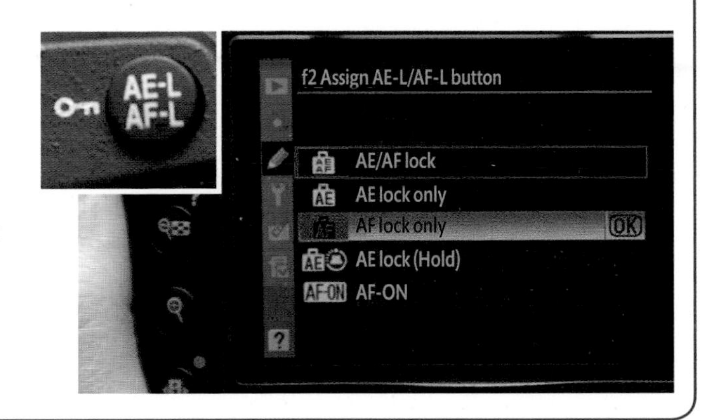

THE RESULT

The success of this slightly esoteric shot required three things: a low (ground level) vantage point; a very shallow depth of field (see pp.58–59); and precise control over the point of focus.

CAMERA **SETTINGS**

CONTROLLING YOUR **POINT OF FOCUS**

Before the advent of Automatic Focusing (AF) systems, focusing a lens by hand was the only option. In the early days of AF, many photographers still preferred to choose the point of focus for themselves, rather than relying on the camera and its then slow and unwieldy automation.

Although today's AF systems are incredibly fast and accurate compared to their predecessors, to some extent the same thinking still applies: taking full control and setting the focus manually puts you in the driving seat, and guarantees that what you want in focus in your shot is indeed in focus.

1 SELECT MANUAL FOCUS
Set your lens to Manual Focus (MF) if it has this option. Some lenses have an option that allows you to focus manually at any time, without changing the setting.

2 FRAME AND FOCUS
With your camera and lens set to Manual, you can frame your shot and choose your point of focus. Be sure to turn the focus ring on your lens, and not the zoom ring – on some lenses the two are close together.

FOCUS SETTINGS

This won't apply to all cameras, but it's important to set not only your lens to Manual Focus but your camera too, to deactivate its Autofocus motor. If you don't, you could damage the motor.

3 CHECK THE VIEWFINDER
The majority of dSLR cameras have a focus confirmation in the viewfinder display – usually a dot or asterisk that appears when focus is set (here it's the green dot). In MF mode this will still work, so you can use it as a guide to focusing if you wish to.

4 ADJUST FOCUS USING LIVE VIEW
If you have Live View available, it's likely that you'll be able to magnify a central section of the preview image to help you to focus precisely. This option varies between cameras, so check your manual.

ALSO WORKS FOR...

Choosing to use Manual Focus is usually a creative decision, but there are times when it becomes a necessity. The most common of these is when you're working in low light. To function efficiently, an AF system requires light and contrast: the more there is of each of these, then the quicker the AF will be. However, this means that your camera will sometimes struggle to lock onto your subject in low-light and low-contrast conditions, which makes Manual Focus the only reliable option.

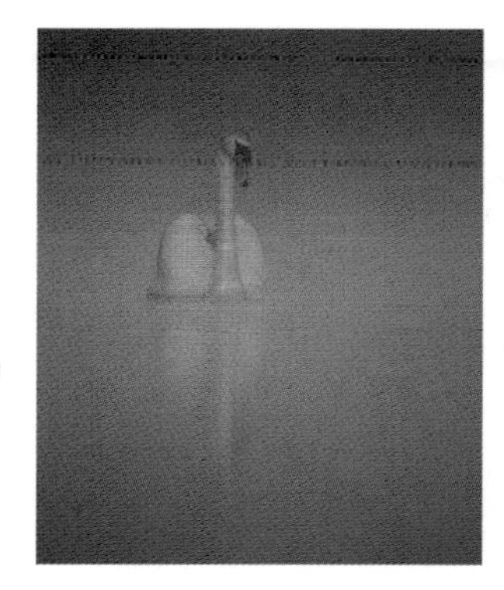

THE RESULT

For this shot we wanted to keep the farmer sharp and his produce slightly blurred, rather than showing it in graphic detail, so switching to Manual Focus was an obvious choice.

CAMERA **SETTINGS**

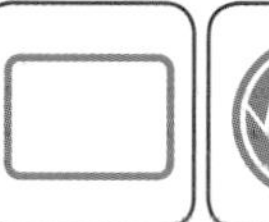

f/2.8

TRACKING A MOVING SUBJECT

Your camera's default single-shot Autofocus (AF) mode is more than a match for static subjects, but you may find that your results aren't quite as sharp as you'd like when your subject starts to move. The reason for this is simple: Single-shot AF focuses at a specific point and keeps the lens focused at that distance until you make your exposure. If your subject moves towards you or away from you before this happens, then it will start to become less focused. In these situations the answer is fairly straightforward: switch to Continuous AF mode, which allows the focus to adjust continuously until you shoot.

1 BE READY

Using your camera hand-held gives you greater flexibility when it comes to photographing a subject that could move erratically around the frame.

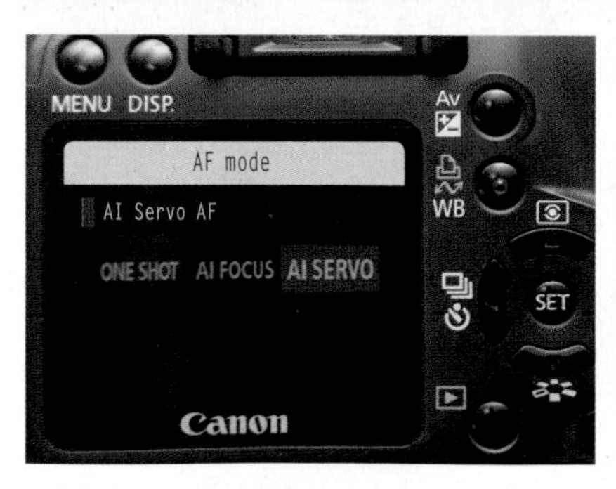

2 SELECT CONTINUOUS AF

Switch your camera to Continuous AF mode, so the focus will be adjusted automatically as your subject moves around the frame. On most cameras this is done via a button on the camera body.

3 SELECT CONTINUOUS DRIVE

Press the Drive mode button and set the shooting mode to Continuous. Be aware that some cameras have more than one Continuous setting (typically Lo and Hi).

FOCUS TRACKING

In addition to Continuous AF, some cameras offer focus tracking (also referred to as Dynamic AF). In this mode, your camera will attempt to predict how your subject will move around the frame and use different AF points to maintain focus. So, not only will it adjust the focus as the camera-to-subject distance alters, but it will also actively follow your subject.

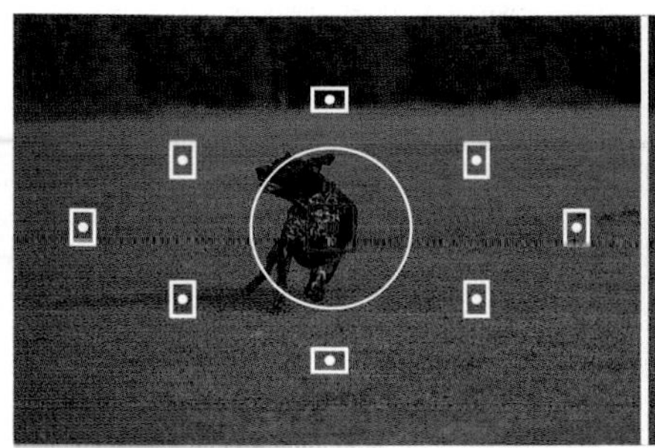
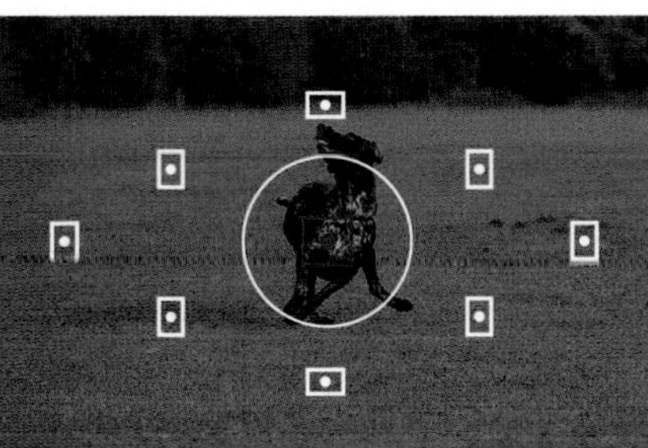

4 ACTIVATE CONTINUOUS AF

Once you have tracked your subject – in this case an excitable dog – sufficiently to get it under an AF point, half-depress the shutter-release button to activate your camera's Continuous AF system. The camera will automatically attempt to focus on your subject, and maintain focus, as long as it remains under the AF point. When the subject is in the optimum position, press the shutter-release button fully and hold it down to make a series of exposures.

THE RESULT

With both the camera's AF and Drive mode set to Continuous we increased our chances of getting that one "decisive" shot.

CAMERA **SETTINGS**

FOCUSING ON HIGH-SPEED SUBJECTS

No matter how sophisticated your camera's Autofocus (AF) system is, or how many focus points are on offer, the physical process of focusing a lens takes time. Even if it appears instantaneous, there's a fraction of a second before the lens "locks on". While this isn't a problem with the majority of subjects, it can be frustrating when you're trying to focus on something that's moving really quickly. Continuous AF will help up to a point, but it still needs a moment to identify the subject – and if it's moving at high speed, it could be gone before that's happened. In this situation, prefocusing is the answer.

1 SWITCH TO MANUAL FOCUS Although it might seem counterintuitive, when it comes to photographing fast-moving subjects you should switch to manual focus rather than relying on your camera's AF system.

2 SELECT A MODE Set Aperture Priority (see pp.54–55) if you want to control the depth of field, or Shutter Priority (see pp.62–63) to control the appearance of movement, then set the aperture or shutter speed accordingly.

3 SELECT CONTINUOUS DRIVE Switch to your camera's Continuous Drive mode (rather than Single-shot) so you can hold down the shutter-release button and shoot a burst of frames.

4 PREFOCUS Focus manually at the point where you anticipate your subject being: in this case, a particular point on a race track. The key is to try to predict where your subject will be and focus on that point.

5 WATCH AND WAIT
Just before your subject reaches the predicted point of focus, trigger the shutter, holding it down to capture a series of images.

ALSO WORKS FOR...

Prefocus can be used for any subject that moves very quickly – typically something faster than the camera's AF system can deal with – as long as you know where the action will take place. Use your camera's fastest continuous shooting mode and record JPEGs rather than Raw files, as this will enable your camera to record a greater number of frames in a burst, at a faster rate.

THE RESULT

Prefocusing can be tricky to master, but when everything comes together – focus, exposure, and timing – the reward is a tack-sharp shot, regardless of the speed at which your subject is moving.

4

LENSES

LENSES

The lens is one of the most critical components in photography, and the quality of the lens is arguably even more important than the quality of your camera: a top-of-the-range camera will never achieve the results it's capable of if it's paired with a lower grade lens, but a good lens can unlock the full potential of even the most modest SLR camera or CSC. In this chapter, you'll find out what lenses are available, and how to get the best from them.

WIDE-ANGLE FOCAL LENGTH

Wide-angle focal lengths have a wide angle of view which enables them to "get it all in", and for many photographers, that's reason enough to own one. But they can do so much more: when used for close-up work they can appear to exaggerate the distance between near and far elements, while providing an extensive depth of field that enables both to be kept in focus.

BEST USED FOR

- Wide-angle lenses are great for landscape photography when you want to record a large-scale scene (see pp.108–09).
- When used with care, wide-angle lenses can be very useful for interior shots when space is limited (see pp.110–11).

STANDARD FOCAL LENGTH

An image from a standard lens is roughly the same as we see with our eyes. Strictly speaking, the standard focal length is equal to the diagonal measurement of the sensor, which is 43mm for a full-frame 35mm sensor, but a 50mm focal length is more widely used. On cameras with APS-C sized sensors, a 35mm focal length is considered standard, while for FourThirds systems, 25mm is standard (see p.106).

BEST USED FOR

- A standard lens is a good choice when an entirely natural-looking perspective is required.
- Prime standard lenses have wide maximum apertures, so are ideal when you want to focus selectively.

PRIME LENSES

A "prime" lens is one with a fixed focal length, such as a 28mm lens, 35mm, 50mm, and so on. Although not as versatile as a zoom lens that covers multiple focal lengths, prime lenses are typically cheaper, have faster maximum apertures (which is great for low-light photography), and, most importantly, can often deliver better results than a zoom lens. This is simply because it's easier to optimize the design of a lens for a single focal length, rather than a range.

▲ 17MM

▲ 35MM

▲ 50MM

▲ 85MM

▲ 180MM

TELEPHOTO FOCAL LENGTH

A telephoto lens has a "telescopic" effect, with long focal lengths (75mm+) that enable you to get closer to distant subjects. This is useful when you're trying to photograph something that you can't get physically closer to, but you do need to take care: long focal lengths magnify movement, so use a tripod or image stabilization to avoid camera shake.

BEST USED FOR

- Traditionally, a telephoto lens is used for sports or wildlife photography (see pp.114–15).
- "Mild" telephoto lenses in the region of 75–150mm are widely considered as ideal for portraits (see pp.112–13).

MACRO FOCAL LENGTH

A macro lens allows you to focus at a much closer range than other lenses allow, so you can really fill the frame. Technically, "true" macro offers 1:1 reproduction, so a subject will appear "life-size" on the sensor. However, zoom lenses that have a macro setting don't usually offer that level of magnification: a ratio of 1:2 (half life-size) or 1:4 (a quarter life-size) is more common.

BEST USED FOR

- Small subjects such as flowers and insects (see pp.116–19).
- Although designed primarily for close-up photography, macro lenses can also be used for other subjects: a 150mm macro makes a good telephoto lens, for example.

WHAT IS **FOCAL LENGTH?**

All lenses are described by a "focal length," whether it's a single focal length for a prime lens (see p.103) or a range of focal lengths covered by a zoom lens. Put simply, the focal length of a lens gives you an indication of its angle of view, as illustrated below, so you have an idea of how "wide" it is, or how much of a telephoto effect it will have when it's attached to your camera. The focal length(s) that you use most will generally be dependent on the subjects you prefer to photograph.

IN-CAMERA

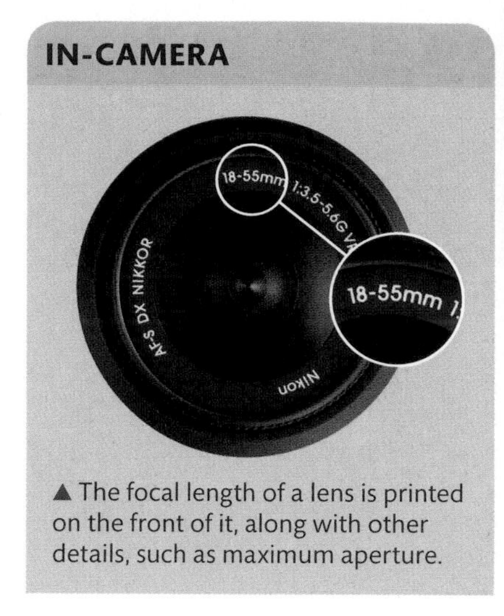

▲ The focal length of a lens is printed on the front of it, along with other details, such as maximum aperture.

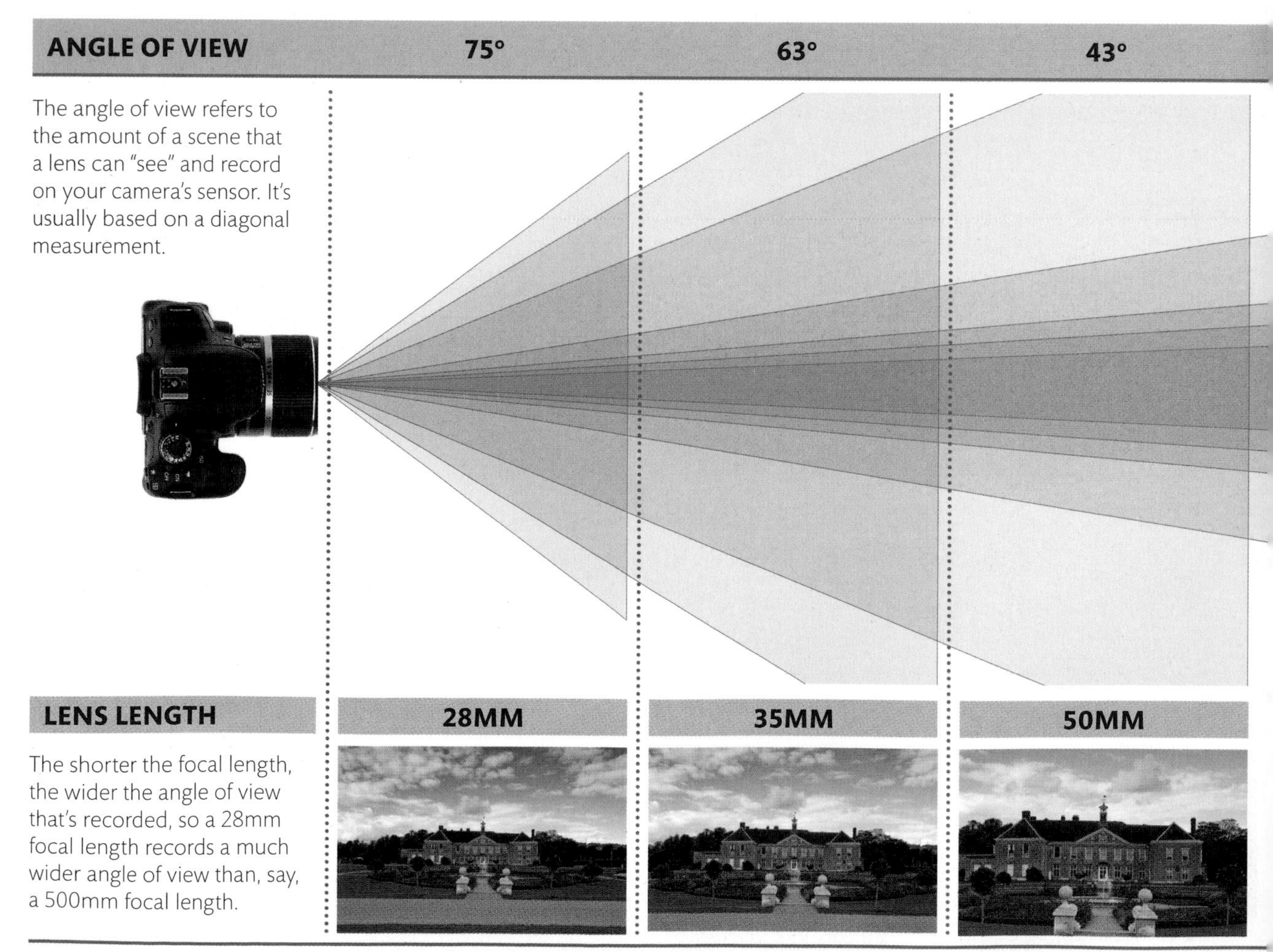

ANGLE OF VIEW

The angle of view refers to the amount of a scene that a lens can "see" and record on your camera's sensor. It's usually based on a diagonal measurement.

LENS LENGTH

The shorter the focal length, the wider the angle of view that's recorded, so a 28mm focal length records a much wider angle of view than, say, a 500mm focal length.

FISHEYE LENS

A fisheye lens is an extreme wide-angle lens, with a focal length of 14mm or less and an angle of view of around 180 degrees. There are two types of fisheye lens: circular and full-frame. As its name suggests, a circular fisheye lens produces round images on the sensor (right), which can limit its appeal for general photography, although the effect can be striking. Full-frame lenses are more popular, as they produce a rectangular image that covers the entire frame (far right).

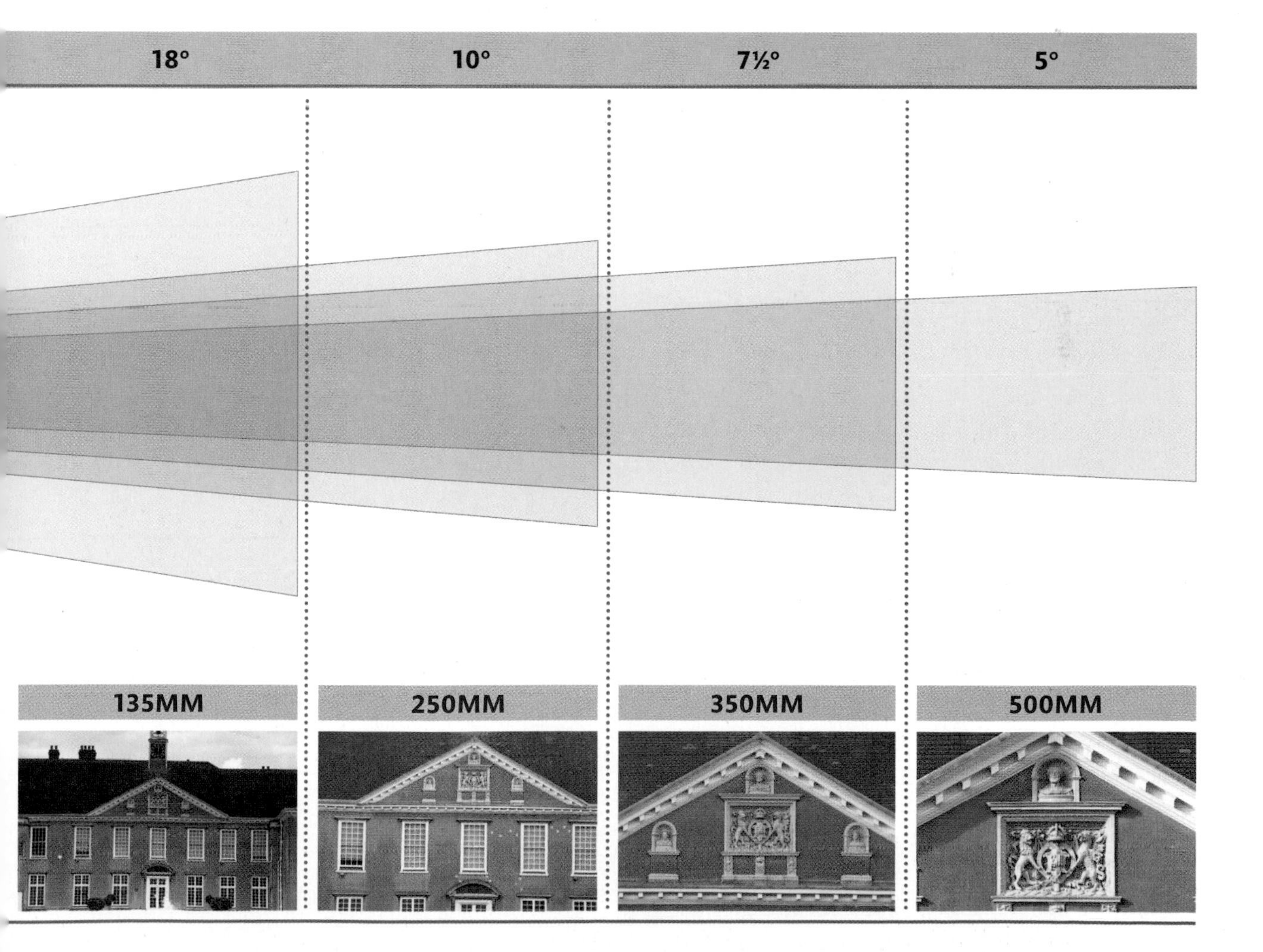

Sensor size and crop factor

If you've recently bought, or are intending to buy, a new camera, then you're probably aware that different cameras use different sized sensors. Some use a "full frame" (36 x 24mm) sensor, others use a smaller, Advanced Photo System type-C (APS-C) sensor (23.6 x 15.7mm or 22.2 x 14.8mm), and some use a 17.3 x 13mm "FourThirds" sensor. Although this doesn't change what you can photograph (or how), it does have an impact on focal length.

The example below demonstrates the effect of taking the same picture with the same focal length, but using cameras with different sized sensors. The dotted blue line shows the area that would be recorded if you were using a camera with a full-frame sensor, which is the sensor size used to measure focal lengths. The other colours shows the effect of using a camera with a smaller sensor: as the sensor gets smaller, the angle of view narrows, making the lens behave as if it were a longer focal length.

To account for this, a "crop factor", or "focal length magnifier", is used to determine the effective focal length of a lens. For example, a Nikon with an APS-C sized sensor has a crop factor of 1.5x, so a lens with a 100mm focal length will actually behave like a 150mm lens. With a crop factor of 2x, the same lens on a FourThirds camera would have an effective focal length of 200mm.

SENSOR SIZE KEY

FULL FRAME 36x24mm

APS-C Canon 22.2x14.8mm

APS-C Nikon 23.6x15.7mm

FourThirds System 17.3x13mm

Image stabilization

Camera shake is one of the most common causes of blurred images, and is guaranteed to ruin what might otherwise be a great shot. It usually occurs when you shoot hand-held, and is most often a result of your own tiny, involuntary movements.

Image stabilization is a technology built into some lenses to help prevent camera shake. It does this through the use of sensors in the lens, which can detect any camera movement. When they do, a special group of lens elements inside the lens moves in the opposite direction to compensate, which keeps the image in the same place on the sensor while you take your shot. This means you get a sharp result, even if you're a little shaky yourself.

SUPERZOOM LENS

A "superzoom" is a specific type of zoom lens that covers a wide focal length range, typically in the region of 18–200mm or 18–300mm (this example is 18–270mm). Although wide-ranging, this type of lens increases the risk of camera shake, since long focal lengths will amplify even the tiniest movement, so image stabilization is essential.

SUBJECT	WITHOUT STABILIZATION	WITH STABILIZATION
MOVING SUBJECTS Image stabilization can't prevent blur that's caused by a subject moving during an exposure, but it can help you to get a sharper result when you're shooting hand-held, without you having to change the exposure settings.		
WORKING IN MACRO Macro and close-up photography is all about magnifying small subjects so that they fill the frame. However, the slightest camera movement will be magnified too, so image stabilization is very important when it comes to this type of shot.		
USING A TELEPHOTO LENS Telephoto lenses let you get up close to distant subjects, but in doing so they exaggerate any camera movement. Ideally, you'd use a tripod when you're zooming in like this, but if you don't have one with you, image stabilization will help keep things steady.		

USING A WIDE-ANGLE LENS OUTDOORS

Wide-angle lenses and outdoor photography are a near-perfect match for each other. The great outdoors offers sweeping views and often dramatically changing weather conditions that are just begging to be captured in their entirety. However, using a wide-angle lens can sometimes reduce the impact of a scene, because distant elements appear very small in the frame and you may end up with large swathes of featureless sky at the top of your shot. So get as close as you can to your subject and think about including foreground interest to compensate if you have an empty sky.

1 SET UP YOUR TRIPOD
For landscape scenes (or any other shot, if you have the time) it's a good idea to set your camera up on a tripod to reduce the risk of camera shake.

2 FIT A LENS HOOD
A lens hood is always useful in combating flare (see pp.146–47), even on seemingly dull days. It's even more important with wide-angle lenses that have a large front lens element.

3 LEVEL YOUR CAMERA
Level your tripod so the horizon doesn't slope to one side. Although you could correct this with your editing software, getting it right in-camera is a much better option.

4 SELECT APERTURE PRIORITY
Use Aperture Priority and set a small aperture to achieve an extensive depth of field.

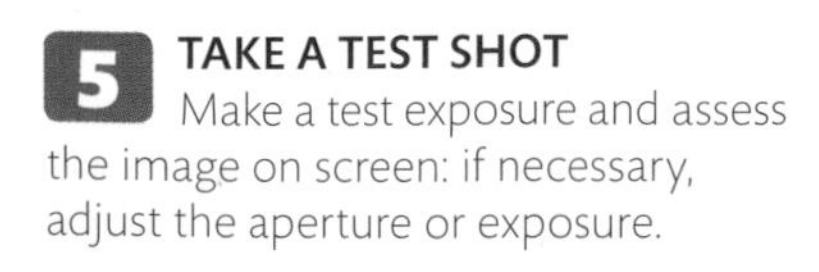

5 TAKE A TEST SHOT
Make a test exposure and assess the image on screen: if necessary, adjust the aperture or exposure.

6 **REFRAME IF NECESSARY**
Take the time to look at the framing of your shot. Most wide-angle photographs taken outdoors can benefit from having something in the foreground, so consider tilting your camera downwards slightly or lowering your tripod so it's closer to ground level.

BARREL DISTORTION

Because of their wide viewing angle, wide-angle lenses are prone to displaying "barrel distortion". As the name suggests, this distortion results in images appearing as if they have been projected onto a barrel, so the centre of the frame appears inflated. The severity of the distortion varies between lenses, but as a general rule, the wider the focal length, the more pronounced the barrelling.

THE RESULT

The wide-angle focal length allowed us to record the full span of the bridge, while the muted colours in the original scene made it an ideal candidate for black-and-white conversion (see pp.176–77).

CAMERA **SETTINGS**

USING A WIDE-ANGLE LENS INDOORS

Although wide-angle lenses are a perfect match for expansive landscapes, they're also a great choice when you're indoors and space is more restricted. In this situation the wide angle of view will enable you to record as much of your chosen interior as possible. However, there are two important things to remember. First, a wide-angle lens is likely to display barrel distortion (see p.109), so you need to take care when placing walls or other vertical (or horizontal) planes close to the edges of the frame. Second, when you aim a wide-angle lens upwards, any vertical elements in the image tend to converge.

1 CHOOSE A LENS
Attach your chosen wide-angle lens, whether it's a fixed focal length or a wide-angle zoom.

2 SELECT APERTURE PRIORITY
Aperture Priority will not only allow you to determine the depth of field in your shot, but also the shutter speed: smaller apertures result in longer exposure times.

3 SET UP YOUR TRIPOD
If you anticipate using a slow shutter speed – to blur figures moving through the scene, for example – use a tripod, or activate your camera's image stabilization, if it has this feature.

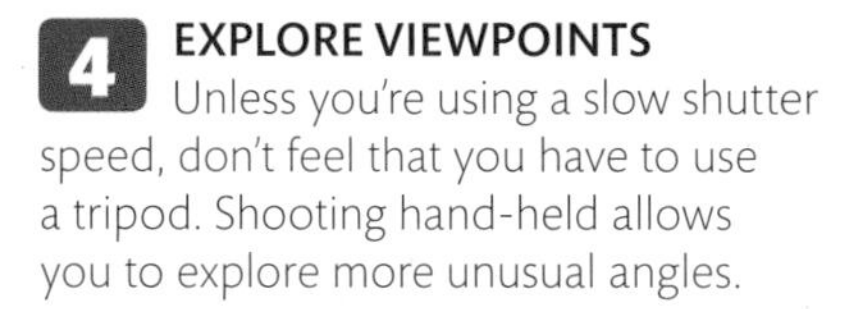

4 EXPLORE VIEWPOINTS
Unless you're using a slow shutter speed, don't feel that you have to use a tripod. Shooting hand-held allows you to explore more unusual angles.

KEEP IT LEVEL

You can minimize the effects of barrel distortion (see p.109), which makes straight lines appear to bow outwards, by keeping your camera level and as square to the subject as possible.

5 **SELECT A FOCUS POINT**
With such a wide angle of view, it's a good idea to select a single focus point yourself (see pp.90–91), so you know precisely where your camera is focusing.

ANGLES

A wide-angle focal length can offer a dramatic perspective, which is part of its appeal. Even though distortion can be an issue, don't be afraid to experiment and "work the angles".

THE RESULT

Shooting from low down and tilting the camera intentionally gives this museum interior shot a dramatic edge. The inclusion of the figure provides a sense of the scale of the building.

CAMERA **SETTINGS**

USING A TELEPHOTO LENS FOR PORTRAITS

Although there's really no such thing as a "portrait lens", there's a general (and longstanding) consensus that using a mild telephoto focal length is usually the best option when you want to take pictures of people without including vast expanses of background. There are two main reasons for this choice: it won't distort your subject's face as a wide-angle lens would, and it allows a comfortable "working distance". This is the distance you would need to be from your subject to take a head-and-shoulders portrait. A telephoto lens is also great for taking candid portraits, as the distance encourages your subject to "forget" you're there.

1 ATTACH A LENS
A focal length of around 75–135mm is ideal for portraits, so fit an appropriate prime lens, or a zoom lens that covers this range.

2 SET AUTOFOCUS
Make sure that your camera (and lens) is set to Autofocus and that image stabilization (if available) is switched on if you intend to shoot hand-held.

3 SELECT CONTINUOUS SHOOTING MODE
Continuous Shooting mode will allow you to fire a burst of shots, which will help capture the most fleeting expression.

4 FRAME WITH LIVE VIEW
Using Live View (if your camera has it) will enable you to frame your shot using the camera's rear LCD screen, allowing you to communicate with your subject, if necessary, without having a camera in front of your face.

PRIME LENSES

A 50mm prime lens (see p.103) is perfect if you're using a camera with an APS-C sized sensor, as it will give you an angle of view equivalent to a 75–80mm focal length when the crop factor is taken into account (see p.106). Most 50mm prime lenses also have a wide maximum aperture – great for blurring backgrounds.

5 FOCUS

As a general rule you should aim to focus on your subject's eyes whenever you're shooting a portrait, simply because this is the first thing that people tend to look at.

ALSO WORKS FOR...

A telephoto focal length is also a good choice for close-up photography, especially when flying insects are involved. A popular focal length for macro lenses is 105mm, as the longer focal length means you don't have to get as close to your subject, so are less likely to scare it away.

THE RESULT

A mild telephoto focal length allowed a comfortable distance between photographer and subject, so she is less self-conscious than she might have been with a camera inches from her face.

CAMERA **SETTINGS**

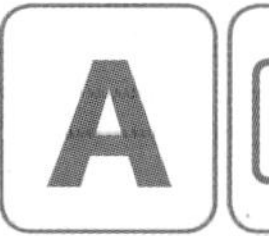

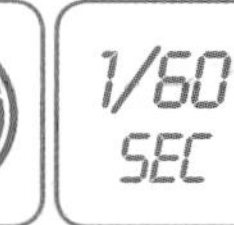

USING A TELEPHOTO LENS FOR DISTANT SUBJECTS

A mild telephoto focal length is a popular choice for portraits because you don't want to be inches away from the person's face, but with some subjects you'll need a longer lens. Most wildlife, for example, isn't going to sit and wait while you get up close and personal with your camera, and for the majority of sporting events you'll need to photograph from the sidelines. In these situations shooting hand-held is often preferable because it gives you the freedom to move the camera quickly to follow fast-moving subjects, but as the focal length increases so too does the risk of camera shake. It's therefore even more important than usual to make sure that you use your camera correctly.

1 ATTACH YOUR LENS
Fit a long telephoto lens to your camera. Something in the region of 200–400mm is ideal, whether it's a fixed focal length (prime) lens or a zoom lens.

2 ACTIVATE IMAGE STABILIZATION
Any movement will be magnified by a long lens, so switch on your camera's image stabilization, if available (see also Step 4).

3 SELECT A MODE
When you're using a long lens hand-held, it's a good idea to set the shutter speed to counter camera shake. That means using either Program or Shutter Priority modes.

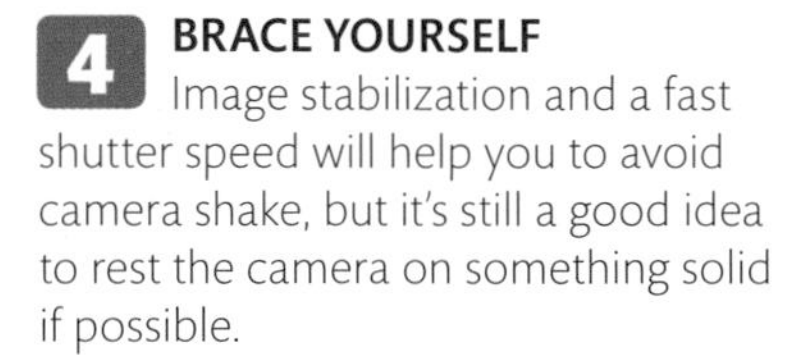

4 BRACE YOURSELF
Image stabilization and a fast shutter speed will help you to avoid camera shake, but it's still a good idea to rest the camera on something solid if possible.

SHUTTER SPEEDS

A simple rule with long lenses is to use a shutter speed that's at least 1/focal length. So with a 200mm focal length you should set your shutter speed to 1/200 sec, 1/400 sec with a 400mm focal length, and so on.

5 SELECT CENTRAL AUTOFOCUS (AF) POINT

Select the central AF point manually (see pp.94–95), choose your point of focus – in this case, the lemur's eye – then reframe your shot if necessary (see pp.92–93).

ALSO WORKS FOR...

A long telephoto lens will also appear to compress perspective, so can be used creatively to "stack" distant subjects, such as buildings.

THE RESULT

Using a 300mm focal length ensured the lemur filled the frame, but it's important that the focus is precise: for wildlife shots like this, focusing on the eyes almost always creates the most impact.

CAMERA **SETTINGS**

USING A MACRO LENS FOR STATIC SUBJECTS

A tripod is useful in most areas of photography, but it's even more important for close-up and macro work – at least if you're photographing a static subject. The reason for this is simple: the closer you are to your subject, the less depth of field there is at any given aperture setting. This means you'll often want to use small aperture settings to maximize the depth of field in your close-up shots, and a low ISO setting for image quality. However, this combination can result in a slow shutter speed that increases the risk of camera shake. The answer, of course, is to attach your camera to a tripod.

1 SET UP YOUR CAMERA
Fit your macro lens (or set your lens to its macro setting) and attach the camera to a tripod so you have precise control over the framing of your shot.

2 SELECT APERTURE PRIORITY
Use Aperture Priority mode so you can control the depth of field, but be aware that this will be severely reduced with close-up subjects (see box opposite).

WITHOUT DIFFUSER

WITH DIFFUSER

3 USE A DIFFUSER
Contrast can appear heightened when you're photographing something that's on a small scale, so it's useful to have a pop-up diffuser to hand (see p.37). Since you don't need to worry about the camera moving, you can hold the diffuser in one hand and tilt it this way and that to see what effect it's having on your subject. It's a good idea to take shots with and without the diffuser so you have a choice.

THE RESULT

We took the final shot using a diffuser to soften the hard shadows. Shooting square-on to the peeling paintwork meant depth of field was less of an issue than it might otherwise have been.

CAMERA **SETTINGS**

DEPTH OF FIELD

The shorter the distance between the lens and the subject, the shallower the depth of field becomes at any given aperture: so while an aperture setting of f/16 might give you a depth of field that can be measured in yards or metres in a landscape photograph, it can be reduced to just a few inches - or even less - when the subject is much closer to the camera.

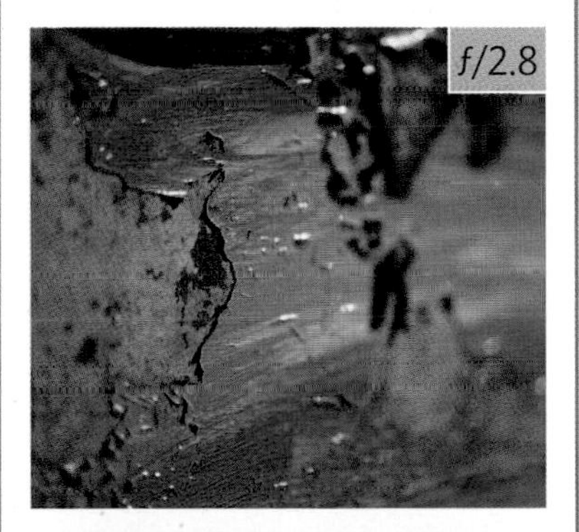

AVAILABLE LIGHT

AVAILABLE LIGHT

When photographers talk about "available", or "ambient", light they're simply referring to any light that exists in a location before they set up a flash or other lights. The available light could be artificial (tungsten, for example), natural, or a combination of these. Appreciating how best to use this light, in terms of its colour, direction, and strength, is often the difference between an average and an outstanding shot.

Quality of light

All light falls into one of two categories: "hard" or "soft". This refers to how diffuse the light is: that is, how it's dispersed. When it comes to photography it's important to appreciate the difference between the two, as they can create significantly different results; one may be better suited to a particular subject over the other. On an overcast day the light will be "soft" as the sunlight is scattered by clouds; this is perfect if you want to take portraits without heavy shadows being cast across your subject's face. However, in some situations you may prefer "hard" light, such as direct overhead sunlight, which will create dark, hard-edged shadows that are great for graphic architectural shots (see pp.138–39).

SOFT LIGHT | **HARD LIGHT**

Direction of light

As well as the quality of light, the direction from which the light is coming will also play a key part in the "look" of your photographs, via the effects you can achieve with shadows (see table, below). When you're relying on available light, your options may be more limited than when you're using a more controlled light source, such as off-camera flash (see pp.160–63). Sometimes, to obtain the result you want, you may need to move your subject (if possible), or change the position you're shooting from.

POSITION OF LIGHT		EXAMPLE
HIGH When the light is coming from above, the resulting shadows will be small and fall directly below your subject. The intensity of the shadows will depend on the quality of the light: hard light will create dark, hard-edged shadows, and soft light will give a more subtle, amorphous effect.		
LOW When the light is coming from a low angle (as it does at the beginning and end of the day), shadows are elongated. This creates a strong sense of space and mood in a photograph, and it's partly for these reasons that many landscape photographers prefer to shoot at dawn and dusk.		
IN FRONT When the light strikes your subject from the front, the illumination will be even and any shadows will be thrown behind it. This is ideal when you want to shoot shadow-free portraits, regardless of whether the light is soft or hard.	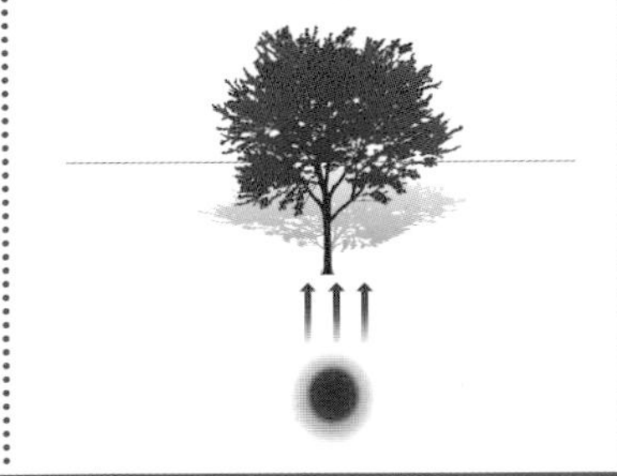	
BEHIND When the light is behind your subject it will naturally throw the side you're photographing into shadow, but this isn't necessarily a bad thing: backlighting is perfect for creating silhouettes (see pp.144–45) or producing a halo around your subject (see pp.142–43).		

WHAT IS THE **COLOUR OF LIGHT?**

All light sources have a colour temperature (see below). Our eyes and brain adjust continually to these temperatures, so that the world around us stays fairly "neutral". For example, if we enter a tungsten-lit room from outdoors, we won't perceive much change, even though tungsten light is orange and daylight is blue. Digital cameras compensate for these variations through the "White Balance" feature (see opposite).

▼ Colour temperature is measured in degrees Kelvin (K): the cooler (more blue) the light, the higher its temperature. Daylight has a nominal colour temperature of 5,500K.

TONE	TEMPERATURE	TYPE OF LIGHT	EXAMPLE
	12,000K AND HIGHER	CLEAR SKYLIGHT IN OPEN SHADE/SNOW	
	10,000K	HAZY SKY LIGHT IN OPEN SHADE	
COOLER	**7,000K**	OVERCAST SKY	
	6,600K		
	5,900–6,000K	ELECTRONIC FLASH	
	5,500K	MIDDAY	
TONE	**4,100K**		
	3,750K		
	3,600K		
	3,500K	PHOTOLAMP	
WARMER	**3,400K**		
	3,200K	SUNSET/SUNRISE	
	3,100K		
	3,000K		
	2,900K	100-WATT TUNGSTEN BULB	
	2,800K		
	1,900K	CANDLELIGHT/FIRELIGHT	

White balance

All digital cameras offer White Balance adjustment. This is the system that compensates for different lighting conditions, adjusting the colour in your images so that they appear "neutral". There are several options available, including an Automatic White Balance (AWB) setting that allows the camera to set what it calculates is the most appropriate white balance, plus a selection of preset values for specific colour temperatures (see table, left). Some cameras also have a custom setting that allows you to set your own white balance (see pp.128–29). However, as the images below demonstrate, there's not always such a thing as the "right" white balance: each one of these pictures could be seen as acceptable, depending on your personal preference.

WHITE BALANCE SETTINGS

AUTO
With Auto, the camera assesses the scene and calculates the white balance: you have no input.

DAYLIGHT
At around 5,500K, this is the ideal setting if you're shooting at midday under a cloudless sky.

CLOUDY
Your camera's Cloudy setting is slightly warmer than Daylight, making it useful for shooting outdoors on overcast days.

SHADE
The Shade setting is designed to compensate for the cool shadows created outdoors on a sunny day.

TUNGSTEN
Also known as Incandescent, this setting is good for indoor shots under regular domestic lighting conditions.

FLUORESCENT
Most cameras offer a variety of Fluorescent settings to compensate for different indoor artificial lights.

FLASH
This setting is balanced for electronic flash, which at around 6,000K is often slightly cooler than Daylight.

CUSTOM
The Custom setting allows you to set your own white balance, often by using a white or grey card (see pp.128–29).

AUTO

DAYLIGHT

SHADE

FLUORESCENT

SETTING A **CUSTOM WHITE BALANCE**

Leaving your camera's White Balance set to Auto or, better still, choosing one of its White Balance presets, is usually all you need to do to get consistently accurate results. However, there may be times when you find yourself struggling to overcome a stubborn colour cast. This happens most often when you're trying to take photographs under mixed lighting conditions – tungsten and daylight, for example – where the two (or more) light sources have very different colour temperatures (see pp.124–25). Short of removing one of the lights sources, there's often no other choice but to set a custom White Balance.

1 ASSESS THE PROBLEM
With tungsten lighting overhead and a window nearby, finding a single White Balance setting that produces a neutral result is impossible.

2 SHOOT A NEUTRAL TARGET
The precise process varies between cameras, but you'll need to shoot a neutral grey target (in this instance, a grey card) to use as the basis for your custom White Balance.

DAYLIGHT

TUNGSTEN

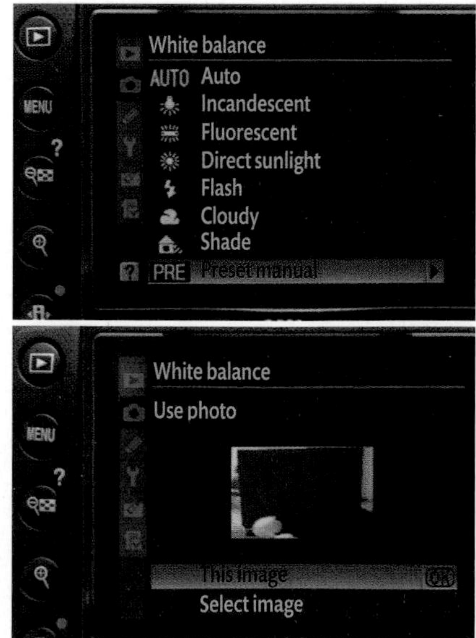

3 SET YOUR TARGET
Go into the White Balance menu and select the neutral target photograph to set your custom White Balance.

4 BEWARE OF LIGHTING CHANGES
A custom White Balance will only be accurate if the lighting remains exactly the same, so be alert to even minor changes, as this could affect your results.

WHITE BALANCE DISC

Smaller and more convenient to carry with you than a grey card, a white balance disc fits over the front of your lens in a similar fashion to a lens cap. You simply take a shot of the light source through the disc and use that to set your custom White Balance. Some manufacturers produce versions that are designed to add a little warmth to skin tones in portrait photographs.

THE RESULT

A custom White Balance has ensured that the flowers in this still life are neutral. There's still a hint of cool daylight and warm tungsten in the rest of the shot, but this just adds to the atmosphere.

CAMERA **SETTINGS**

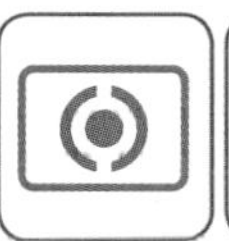

USING REFLECTORS TO ADD LIGHT

Although ambient natural light is ideal for photography, it does have one quite significant downside: you have very little control over it. However, that's not the same as having no control, and perhaps one of the simplest, cheapest, and arguably most effective ways in which you can modify ambient light is to use one or more reflectors to bounce it back onto your subject. As you'll see, a single reflector is great for filling in shadows without having to worry about flash, and by varying the direction, angle, and even the colour of your reflector, you can make quite radical changes to your shot.

1 ASSESS THE PROBLEM
With the light coming from slightly behind the subject, most of her face is in deep shadow.

2 POSITION A REFLECTOR
Holding a reflector in front of your subject will bounce light back onto her face: either ask your subject to hold the reflector (if it won't affect the shot), or get a friend to help.

3 ADJUST THE DISTANCE
You can effectively control the amount of light that's reflected back onto your subject by varying the distance between your subject and the reflector: the shorter the distance, the stronger the fill. This is where it's useful to have an assistant, as it will be easy for them to vary the distance and angle at which they hold the reflector.

4 TRY DIFFERENT REFLECTORS

A white reflector isn't your only option: most kits come with other colours too. Gold will give your subject a warm glow, while a silver reflector can be used for a "harder" fill.

DIFFUSERS

As well as reflecting light to fill in shadows, you can soften it before it reaches your subject by using a diffuser (see pp.132–33). A diffuser positioned between your subject and the light source will scatter the light and make it less harsh.

THE RESULT

Using a reflector has helped lift the dark shadows that were originally affecting this portrait, so we can now see details of the subject's face. It's a subtle difference, but an effective one.

CAMERA **SETTINGS**

USING A DIFFUSER
TO SOFTEN LIGHT

Although a reflector can be used to "fill in" shadows in photographs taken in direct sunlight (see pp.130–31), it has one slight drawback – it effectively adds a second light source to your shots. Sometimes this isn't what you want, and rather than creating a second light source, you just want the overall light to be softer. In this situation the tool you require is a diffuser, which uses a translucent material to scatter the light passing through it. Commercial versions of these are widely available and often have a "pop-up" design similar to reflectors, which allows them to be folded up when they're not needed.

1 SELECT A MODE
Because a diffuser affects the light falling onto the subject it's entirely up to you which exposure mode you use: even Auto will work in this instance.

2 POSITION YOURSELF
Diffusers are most useful when the light is bright and behind you. Fortunately this will also mean that the subject is lit from the front, which is usually desirable.

3 DEPLOY THE DIFFUSER
Position your diffuser between the light source (in this case, the sun) and your subject.

4 CHECK THE VIEWFINDER
You can see immediately what effect the diffuser is having on your subject, and it often helps if you look through the viewfinder or use your camera's Live View mode.

5 REPOSITION THE DIFFUSER
Move the diffuser around until it's having the desired effect. This is much easier to do when your camera is mounted on a tripod or you have someone with you who can hold the diffuser for you.

CLOUD COVER

If you don't have a diffuser to hand, you may be able to make use of nature's own diffuser. The image on the left shows the flower in full direct sunlight, while the one on the right was taken when the sun disappeared behind a cloud for a moment.

THE RESULT

With delicate subjects such as flowers, diffusing the light can have a significant impact on the image. Here it has minimized the shadows, which prevents the shot from appearing too "hard" and contrasty.

CAMERA **SETTINGS**

AWB

▼ SHOT WITHOUT DIFFUSER

WORKING IN **LOW LIGHT OUTDOORS**

Photography is all about exposing your camera's sensor to light, so you might wonder why you would bother taking pictures when the light levels are low: surely that would just make things difficult? In a way you'd be right, since exposure, focusing, and white balance all become a little trickier when light levels drop. At the same time, however, your subject can be transformed if you shoot in the early evening or at night, especially if you're photographing outdoors: floodlit buildings, light trails from cars, and even the colour of a twilight sky can produce stunning shots that are just not possible during daylight hours.

1 USE A TRIPOD
If you're working outdoors with a static subject there's no excuse not to use a tripod: your photographs will be much better for it.

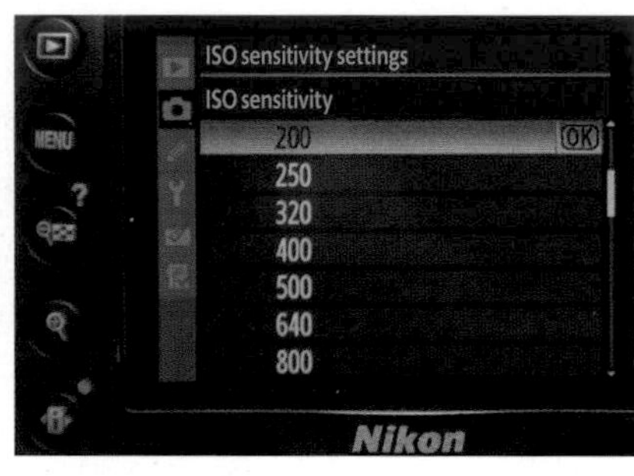

2 SET ISO
With your camera on a tripod you can use a relatively low ISO to minimize noise. Something in the region of ISO 200–400 will work well.

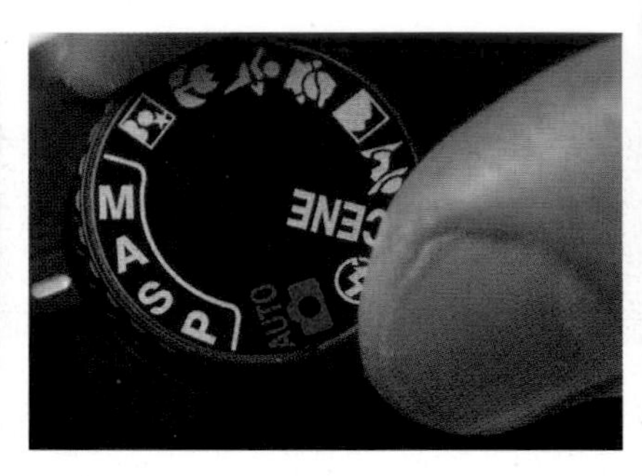

3 SELECT APERTURE PRIORITY
To get a reasonable depth of field requires a relatively small aperture, so set the camera to Aperture Priority and dial in an aperture setting of around f/8.

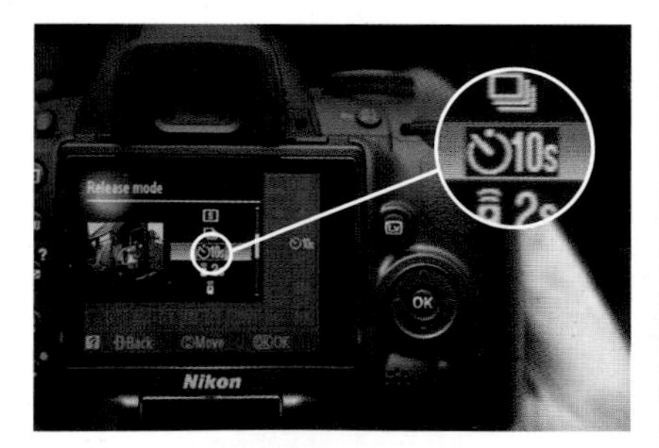

4 TRIGGER WITH SELF-TIMER
Unless you have a remote release, use your camera's self-timer to trigger the shutter. This reduces the risk of camera shake when you press the shutter.

5 ASSESS THE IMAGE
Play back the image and call up the histogram (see pp.78–79). If the bulk of the histogram is shifted to the left (as it is here), the image might be considered underexposed; a shift to the right would suggest overexposure.

LESS LIGHT **EXPOSURE** MORE LIGHT

6 SET EXPOSURE COMPENSATION

Depending on the look you're after, dial in positive (+) exposure compensation to increase the exposure and brighten your image, or use negative (-) compensation to darken it (see pp.80–81). You might also want to consider bracketing your exposures (see pp.82–83) so you have a number of different options to start with.

THE RESULT

The optimum exposure reveals plenty of detail in the building, but the exposure isn't so bright that the shot appears to have been taken in broad daylight.

CAMERA **SETTINGS**

6 SEC

WORKING IN **DIMLY LIT INTERIORS**

Unless you're taking pictures in a glasshouse, or somewhere with vast windows, photographing indoors will almost inevitably involve low ambient light levels. Of course, you can use flash if you want to (and are permitted), but more often than not you'll simply have to rely on what light is available to you. This not only raises issues regarding exposure, but also with colour balance, since you may be dealing with incandescent and fluorescent light sources, sometimes mixed with daylight. However, low light indoors doesn't have to be a challenge: your camera has all the tools you need.

1 USE A TRIPOD IF YOU CAN
When the light levels are low, shutter speeds naturally get longer, even if you use a wide aperture and high ISO setting. Set up a tripod if it's possible to do so where you are.

2 IF YOU CAN'T USE A TRIPOD, BRACE
If setting up a tripod is impractical (or simply not permitted), then steady the camera by resting it on or against a solid surface. If there's nothing suitable, then using Live View and adding tension to your neck strap will help.

3 SELECT APERTURE PRIORITY
Switch to Aperture Priority and set a relatively wide aperture. An aperture of around f/5.6 will let in plenty of light but still provide a modest depth of field.

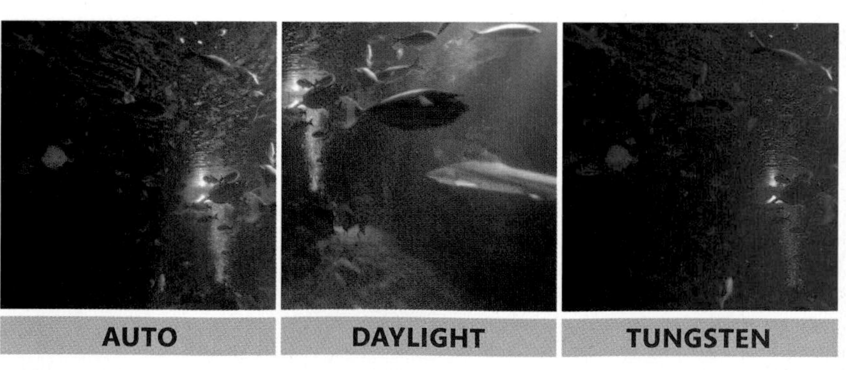

4 SET WHITE BALANCE
The White Balance setting you use will depend on the prevalent light source. In this aquarium there was a mix of fluorescent and tungsten lighting, making the correct option hard to determine. However, by shooting a number of test shots it's possible to get the look you're after.

5 SET ISO
Increase the ISO until the camera suggests a shutter speed of 1/60 sec: this will reduce the risk of camera shake with focal lengths up to around 100mm.

THE RESULT

The combination of a wide aperture and high ISO allowed us to use a "safe", shutter speed that works when shooting hand-held. The image may be a little noisy, but it's also sharp, which is more important.

CAMERA **SETTINGS**

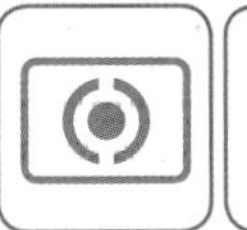

EXPLOITING **LIGHT AND SHADOW**

Many experienced photographers – especially those with a keen interest in landscape photography – advise against taking pictures when the sun's high in the sky and the light's particularly harsh. To a certain extent they're right, as the hard shadows cast by a noon sun aren't always flattering to either landscapes or portraits. But that doesn't mean you can't take any photographs at all – you just need to pick the right subjects. Architecture is a great place to start, since you can use shadows to your advantage, exploiting them to define crisp edges and create striking graphic images.

1 ASSESS THE LOCATION
Although you can dive straight in and start shooting, it's worthwhile taking a bit of time simply to look at your subject and decide what it is you want in shot.

2 ATTACH A LONG LENS
Using a telephoto lens for architectural shots is a great way of isolating part of the building, but it will magnify the slightest movement so it's a good idea to use a tripod.

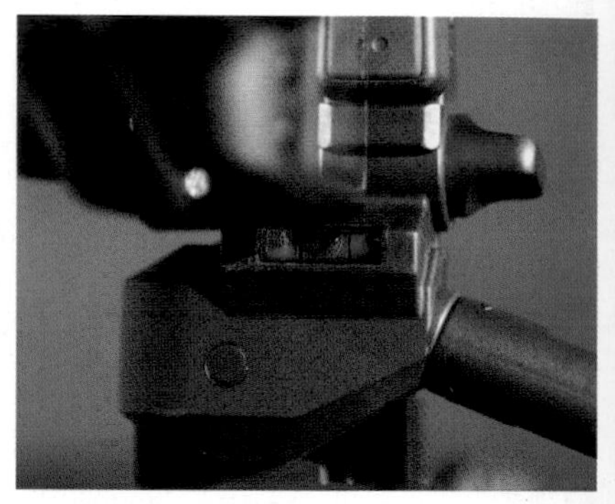

3 KEEP IT LEVEL
You can adjust your images in your editing software (see pp.168–69), but it will save you a lot of time if you get straight lines in-camera, so level your tripod before you shoot.

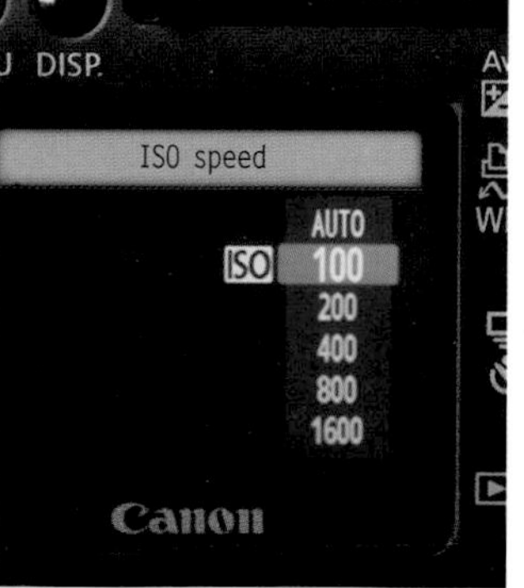

4 CHOOSE YOUR SETTINGS
Set your camera to Aperture Priority so you can control the depth of field, and choose a low ISO setting (ISO 100–200). If there's movement in the shot that you want to control (people in front of a building, perhaps), then you may want to choose Shutter Priority instead.

5 SET THE METERING MODE
Switch to your camera's spot metering pattern (see p.77) and aim the camera at a sunlit area of the building to take your exposure reading: grey concrete is perfect for this.

6 REFRAME
Hold the Auto Exposure Lock button or shutter-release button to lock the exposure while you reframe your shot.

ALSO WORKS FOR...

The heavy shadows created by harsh light can be used creatively for a wide range of subjects. However, as the shadows will generally conceal detail, a bold, graphic shot should be your aim. Converting to black and white (see pp.176–77) often enhances this effect.

THE RESULT

A tight crop has reduced this modernist architecture to simple grey shapes, but the dark, blocky shadows add essential contrast. The clear blue sky is the perfect backdrop.

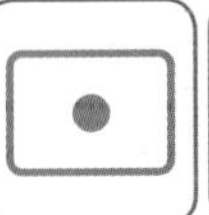

EXPOSING FOR **THE HIGHLIGHTS**

In some ways, the sensor in a digital camera is very similar to transparency, or slide, film. Don't worry if you're not familiar with this type of film – all you need to know is that it's much easier to reveal detail in the shadow areas of a digital image than it is to extract detail in highlight areas that are overexposed. The technical reason for this is that once the camera has recorded part of an image as "white", it's as bright as it can possibly be: it won't have any detail, and even your editing software can't bring out what isn't there. So, when you're faced with a high-contrast scene and are wondering how to expose it, the answer's simple: expose for the highlights and sort out the shadows later (see pp.172–73).

1 FRAME YOUR SHOT
For this technique you'll probably need to take several shots, so if the framing is critical you'll have to set up your camera on a tripod.

2 SELECT A MODE
Set the exposure mode to something other than Auto, Manual, or a Scene Mode as you'll need to apply exposure compensation (see pp.80–81).

3 TAKE A TEST SHOT
Take a shot at the exposure suggested by the camera and review it on screen. Call up the histogram so you can see the tonal range (see pp.78–79).

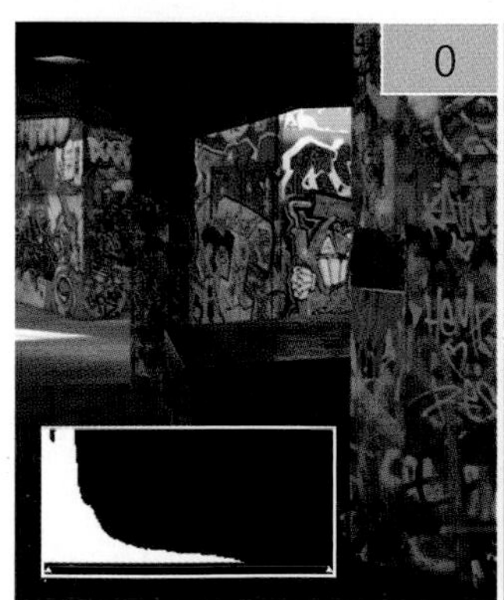

LESS LIGHT — **EXPOSURE** — MORE LIGHT

4 DIAL IN EXPOSURE COMPENSATION
Assuming your test exposure doesn't clip the highlights, dial in positive exposure compensation (see pp.80–81) and shoot again. Start at +1 stop and assess the image's histogram, paying close attention to the right (highlight) end of the graph. The aim is to get the histogram to end as close to the right edge as possible, but without going off the scale. Here, +1 stop was sufficient.

5 ADJUST THE SHADOWS

The final step happens when you've got the image on your computer. Use your editing software's Levels tool (see pp.170–71) to adjust the shadow areas without affecting the highlights. It's entirely up to you whether you make the shadows lighter or darker.

LIVE VIEW

Some cameras allow you to have a histogram "live" on-screen when you use the camera's Live View mode. If your camera allows this then there's no need to play back your image and assess its histogram – use the Live View histogram as a guide instead.

THE RESULT

Our final shot maximizes the detail recorded in the brightest areas of this high-contrast scene, but without sacrificing the shadows.

CAMERA **SETTINGS**

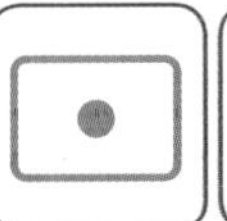

CREATING A **HALO OF LIGHT**

When Kodak launched its Box Brownie camera at the beginning of the 20th century, the advice they gave to the new breed of enthusiast photographers was to always take pictures facing away from the sun, never towards it. To some extent that advice is still valid today: if you photograph with the sun in front of you there's a very strong chance that your images will suffer from lens flare (see pp.146–47), and whenever your subject is lit from behind there's the risk that it will appear as a silhouette (see pp.144–45). If you're careful, however, lighting your subject from behind can also produce stunning results.

1 SELECT A MODE
It's likely that you'll need to adjust the exposure from the camera's recommended reading, so choose something other than Auto or a Scene mode. Aperture Priority (see pp.54–61) is best for a close-up shot like this as it allows you to maximize the depth of field.

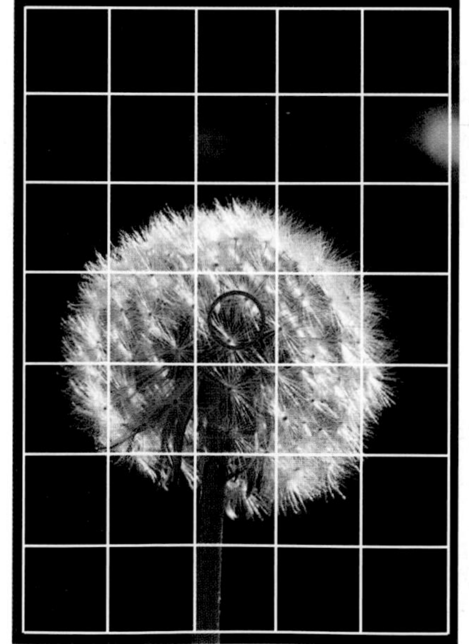

2 TAKE AN EXPOSURE READING
Use your camera's spot meter (see pp.76–77) to take an initial exposure reading from a midtone area of your subject. Alternatively, you could take a reading from a grey card (see pp.74–75).

3 TAKE A TEST SHOT
In challenging lighting conditions it can be hard to get the exposure right first time, so it's a good idea to take a shot and call up the histogram on playback (see pp.78–79). Here the exposure is a touch too bright and the highlights are clipped slightly as a result. With a detailed subject like this, this isn't ideal.

4 ADJUST THE EXPOSURE

To reduce the exposure, dial in negative (-) exposure compensation (see pp.80–81). For this shot, -1 stop of compensation was needed to prevent the highlights from being blown out.

BACKLIT PORTRAITS

Backlit portraits can work fantastically well, with the light adding a beautiful halo to hair. However, with the light coming from behind your subject there's always the risk that the face will be in shadow. To counter this, consider using a reflector (see pp.130–31) or fill-flash (see pp.154–55). Here, a gold reflector was used to add a warm glow to the skin tones.

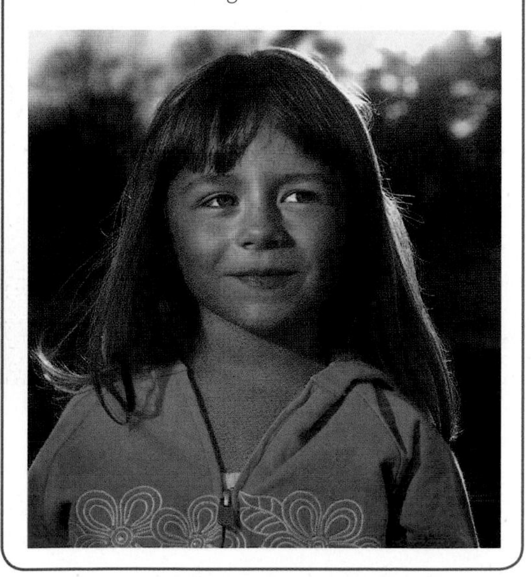

THE RESULT

Shooting from a low angle and choosing a dark background helps this dandelion seed head to stand out, but it's the strong backlighting that makes the image really glow.

CAMERA **SETTINGS**

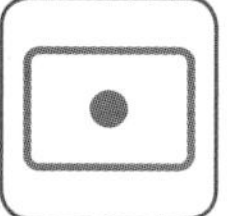

CREATING A **SILHOUETTE**

Although many people think that specific lighting conditions are needed to create a silhouette, this isn't necessarily true – any subject that can be photographed against a bright background has the potential to be transformed into a silhouette. The key is to look for recognizable subjects that can be "read" without relying on every last detail: plants, people, and architecture can all work well. Strong graphic shapes become the most important element in the shot, but colour should be a consideration too – do you want to create an almost black-and-white image, or use background colour to set off your subject?

1 CHOOSE A VIEWPOINT The strongest silhouettes have a plain, uncluttered background, so look at your subject from different angles to see where you'll get the best shot.

2 SELECT A MODE You need to be in control of your exposure when you're shooting silhouettes, so use Program, Aperture Priority, Shutter Priority, or Manual modes. For this shot Shutter Priority was selected because the breeze was disturbing the grasses and seed heads, so a fast shutter speed was needed.

REFLECTED LIGHT

You don't have to shoot towards an obvious light source, such as the sun, to create a striking silhouette: light reflecting off glass, metal, or water, can just as readily provide the strong backlight that you need.

3 SELECT SPOT METERING Switch your camera to its spot metering pattern (see pp.76–77) and take an exposure reading from the bright background. This will ensure that your subject is underexposed.

4 LOCK EXPOSURE AND RECOMPOSE Lock the exposure by holding down your camera's Automatic Exposure Lock (AE-L) button and then reframe your shot. You may need to access your camera's menu to make sure that the AE-L button doesn't lock the focus too (see pp.92–93).

ALSO WORKS FOR...

Dawn or dusk are perhaps the best times for creating silhouettes. The low angle of light provides the perfect backlit conditions, and there's also the increased chance of capturing some striking colours in the sky. Shooting with the "wrong" White Balance setting (see pp.126–29) can also produce interesting results.

THE RESULT

The striking pattern formed by these seed heads and the barbed wire works well in silhouette. We shot from a low angle looking upwards, so that the sky, rather than the field beyond, formed the background.

CAMERA **SETTINGS**

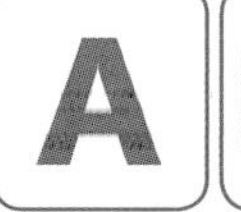

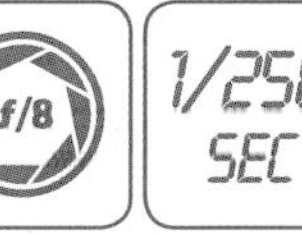

1/250 SEC

HOW DO YOU WORK WITH **LENS FLARE?**

You've probably seen plenty of photographs that have been affected by lens flare, whether it manifests as coloured "blobs" that emanate from a source of light (typically the sun) or simply as an overall loss of contrast. Camera lenses are made up of numerous glass "elements" that are designed to control, direct, and focus light onto your sensor. However, when you take a photograph with your lens pointed towards a light source, some of the light can reflect off the various elements, rather than passing through them, resulting in flare.

Avoiding lens flare

The most obvious way to avoid lens flare is to aim your camera away from the light source, so you take the picture with the light behind you. Although effective, this can be restrictive – if you slavishly stick to this "rule", then all of your photographs will be lit from the front. There will also be shots that you'll miss out on, due to the position of your subject in relation to the sun or other light source.

Instead, it's far better to be aware of flare (and its causes) and understand the ways in which you can work around it. This can be done by blocking the light source with your subject or another element in the scene, or using one of the techniques below.

HOW IT HAPPENS

Flare is caused by non-image-forming light (either in the scene being photographed or out of shot) reflecting off various parts of the lens and reaching the sensor.

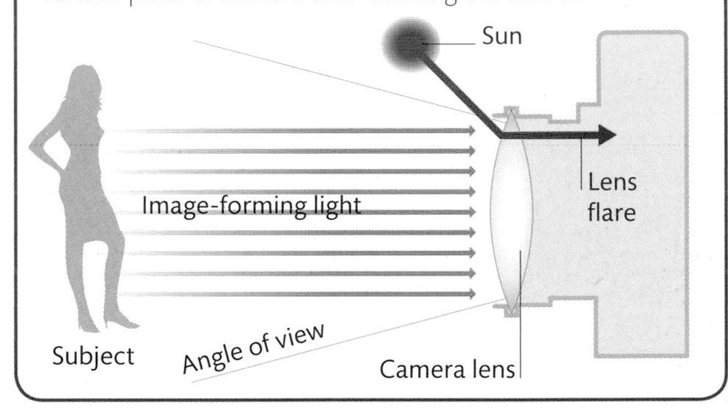

LENS HOOD

▲ A lens hood is designed to "shade" the front of your lens and minimize the amount of light that can hit it from the side, reducing the chance of flare.

SHIELD WITH YOUR HAND

▲ If you can hold the camera steady you can use one hand to shield the front of your lens. You can do this in addition to using a lens hood.

MAKESHIFT SHADE

▲ Not all lenses come with a lens hood, but you can use items such as magazines or maps to make an effective impromptu lens shade.

Using flare creatively

Although lens flare is often seen as an undesirable addition to a photograph, it's not always all bad. In some situations flare can actually have a positive impact on a picture, enhancing the atmosphere and giving an impression of dazzling sunlight or adding a splash of colour to an otherwise subdued scene.

Some photographs work best when you include the source of the flare (the sun, for example) in the frame. This not only enhances the flare, but also means that anyone viewing your picture will see that including it was a conscious decision on your part, rather than a mistake.

▼ The flare in this shot is subtle, yet effective. It demonstrates that you don't always need to include the light source in the frame to use flare creatively.

▲ The starburst effect of the low sunlight filtering through the trees is an integral part of this shot, and is as much the "subject" as the woodland itself. Without it the atmosphere would be entirely different.

▲ Flare doesn't have to dominate a photograph to have an effect. In this urban scene it imparts a sense of the heat of the day on this busy city street, but it doesn't overpower the detail in the lower half of the image.

6 FLASH

FLASH

After a lens, a flash is the most popular add-on accessory for dSLRs and CSCs (and some high-end compacts as well), augmenting the built-in unit found on most cameras. As you'll discover in this chapter, the versatility of today's flashes can really broaden your photographic capability, regardless of whether you simply use your camera's pop-up flash or decide to invest in an external hotshoe flash. The table below describes some of the most useful (and creative) flash modes.

RED-EYE REDUCTION

Red-eye occurs most often when you're photographing people (or animals) in low-light situations and they're looking directly at the camera. It's caused by light from your flash entering your subject's dilated pupil and reflecting off the blood vessels at the back of the eye. Red-eye reduction works by firing a pre-flash (or several pre-flashes) before the main flash, which causes your subject's pupils to contract before you take the shot.

WHEN TO USE IT

- For taking pictures of people in low-light situations
- For low-light pet portraits
- When photographing wildlife at night

SLOW SYNC

In some modes your camera will set a fairly fast shutter speed when you use flash, and while this will expose your subject correctly, it may not let enough light into your camera to expose the background, especially at night. Slow sync tells the camera to use a slower shutter speed to capture ambient light, in addition to firing the flash. Slow sync is linked directly to 1st and 2nd curtain sync (see right), so activating one of these modes automatically initiates slow sync too.

WHEN TO USE IT

- For recording ambient background light
- When you want to record background movement blur while keeping your main subject sharp

FLASH COMPENSATION

Just as you can use exposure compensation (see pp.80–83) on your camera to make an image brighter or darker, so you can compensate your flash exposure too. This increases or decreases the power of the flash, either to balance it with the ambient light, or simply to change the intensity of the flash for creative effect. Flash exposure compensation is usually activated via a button on the camera body and is adjusted in ½- or 1-stop increments.

1ST/2ND CURTAIN SYNC

With a "regular" shot, the flash fires as soon as the shutter is fully open. This is known as "1st curtain" sync (see p.153). It works well for static subjects, but if you're using slow sync flash (see left), any movement after the flash has fired will be recorded as a blur, with the trails in front so that moving elements appear to be going backwards (above left). Switching to "2nd curtain" sync fires the flash at the end of the exposure, creating a more natural look, with movement trails behind the subject (above right).

WHEN TO USE IT

- For static subjects, 1st curtain sync is ideal
- Use 2nd curtain sync to record movement blur in your subject, while keeping the subject itself sharp

HI-SPEED FLASH

Hi-speed flash, or "high-speed sync", is typically found on high-end external flashes. It enables you to use shutter speeds that are faster than the camera's sync speed (see p.152), so you can use flash at 1/1000 sec, 1/2000 sec, or even faster. It achieves this by firing a series of very rapid flashes. The flashes are so close together that they effectively create a "continuous" light source that guarantees the entire frame is exposed, despite the very fast shutter speed.

WHEN TO USE IT

- On bright days, to provide fill-flash
- When you're using very fast shutter speeds
- When you're using a wide aperture and/or a high ISO

WHAT ARE **SYNC SPEEDS** AND **GUIDE NUMBERS?**

Perhaps the most important concept to understand when it comes to using flash is "sync speed" (short for "synchronization speed"). Your camera's "flash sync speed" is the fastest shutter speed at which the sensor is exposed to light in its entirety. This is the point at which a flash can be fired, and that brief burst of light will expose the whole frame. If you use a faster shutter speed, then the sensor is only being exposed to a slit of light, so you end up with a partial image. The sync speed on most cameras is around 1/200 sec.

▼ Flash synchronization is based on the way in which camera shutters work. With fast shutter speeds (usually faster than 1/200 sec), the sensor is exposed to a travelling slit of light, rather than being exposed in its entirety, so the resulting image is "cut off".

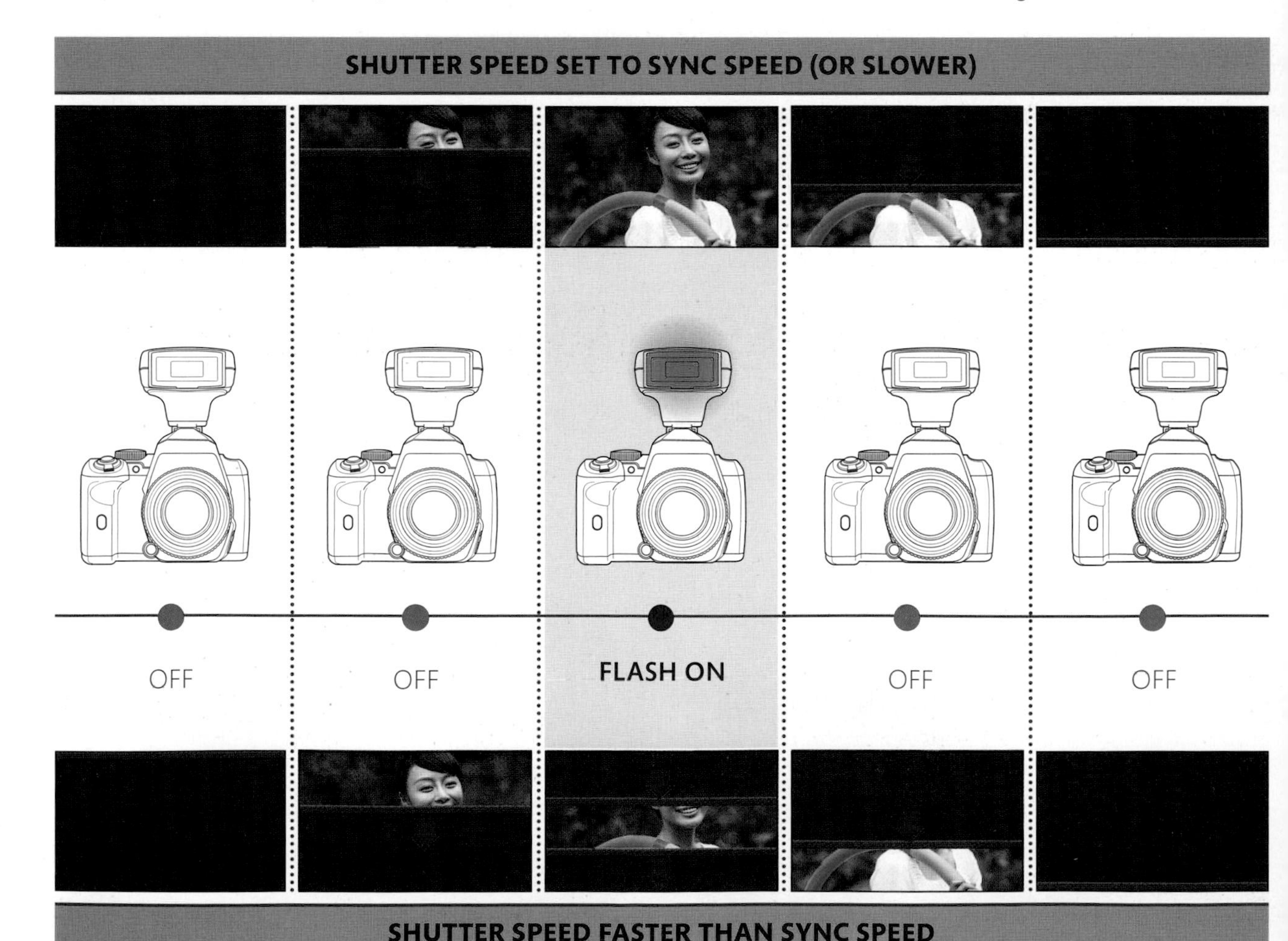

How a shutter works

To understand flash sync speeds you need to know how a camera's shutter works. A shutter is comprised of two "curtains". When you press the shutter-release the first curtain opens, exposing the sensor to light. After a predetermined amount of time (which is the shutter speed), the second curtain closes to end the exposure. Your flash needs to be triggered when the first curtain is fully open and the second curtain has yet to start closing. However, with fast shutter speeds this moment doesn't actually happen: the second curtain starts to close before the first is fully open. So, if you fire a flash, you'll record the closing shutter, as shown below.

GUIDE NUMBERS

The flash guide number is effectively an indication of its power. In the past, knowing the guide number was essential, as you needed to use it in conjunction with the flash-to-subject distance and the aperture setting to determine the correct exposure. However, it's no longer quite so necessary. Through-the-lens (TTL) flash control means that the camera can now make the exposure calculations for you, and you may view your image immediately, so you know whether you need to tweak your settings. The guide number is no longer an accurate indication of a flash's power, either. In an attempt to make their flashes appear more powerful (at least on paper), some manufacturers have taken to measuring flash power at longer telephoto lengths and/or high ISO settings: both of which inflate the guide number.

1/200 SEC

1/250 SEC

1/320 SEC

1/500 SEC

USING **FILL-FLASH**

Your camera's built-in flash can be both a blessing and a curse, especially for portraits. On the one hand it can be invaluable when you're shooting in low-light conditions, but it can just as easily ruin your shots as its direct light creates deep shadows and can result in red-eye. However, it doesn't have to be this way. Often, it's not so much the flash itself, but the way in which it's used that's the problem, and making a few basic changes to your flash settings can transform your results.

1 SELECT APERTURE PRIORITY Aperture Priority will give you control over the depth of field, so you can throw the background out of focus if you want to.

2 ACTIVATE FLASH Press your camera's flash button to pop it up or lift it manually – it depends on your camera model (but don't force it).

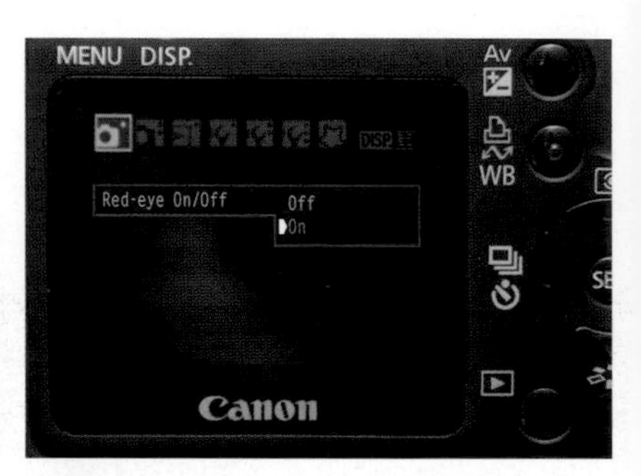

3 ACTIVATE RED-EYE REDUCTION The default setting for red-eye reduction is usually Off, but you can change this on most cameras by using the flash button and control wheel.

INDOOR PORTRAITS

The simplest option for indoor portraits is to activate red-eye reduction as described above and use your camera's built-in flash in Program mode. You'll be able to adjust the exposure pairing to use a wider or smaller aperture (to change the depth of field), although the shutter speed won't go past the camera's maximum sync speed (usually around 1/200 sec). The aperture range will also be limited by the power of the flash, but don't forget that you can change the ISO if you need to. Increasing the ISO will allow you to use a smaller aperture setting and/or increase the effective range of the flash.

4 TAKE A TEST SHOT
Make an exposure and check the result on your camera's LCD screen. If you need to, you can fine-tune the flash compensation to make the flash more or less obvious (see p.151).

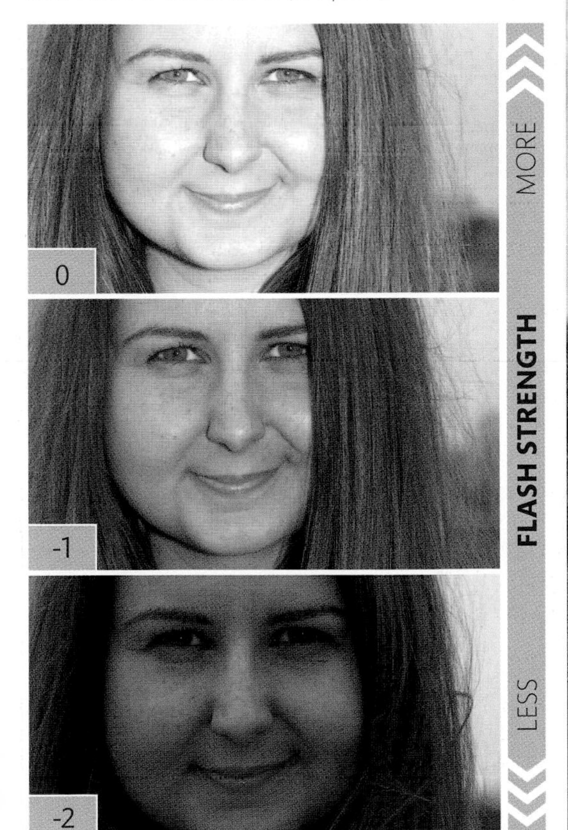

5 ALTER THE FLASH STRENGTH
Decreasing the flash power by 1–2 stops will let the flash act as a fill light, rather than the main light source. On most cameras this is achieved by pressing the flash compensation button and turning the control wheel.

THE RESULT

Fill-flash has prevented any hard shadows being cast across our subject's face, which not only lifts the shot as a whole, but also adds sparkle to her eyes.

CAMERA **SETTINGS**

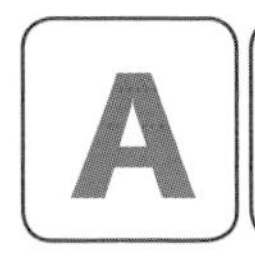

BOUNCING THE FLASH

In addition to offering you more in the way of power, a key difference between your camera's built-in flash and a good external, hotshoe-mounted unit is the ability to tilt and possibly rotate the flash head. Not all external flashes offer this, but it's worth investing in a model that does have this feature, even if it means spending a little more. This is because a hotshoe flash allows you to bounce the light off a ceiling or wall, which effectively spreads it and makes it much "softer." As a result, your photographs won't suffer so heavily from the hard, unattractive shadows associated with direct flash.

1 ATTACH YOUR FLASH Fit your flash and lock it. Switch it on and set the flash to TTL (through the lens) so the camera will be controlling the flash output.

2 SELECT A MODE Set your camera to Program, Aperture Priority, or Shutter Priority. Here Aperture Priority was selected to allow control over depth of field.

3 ACTIVATE FLASH SETTINGS To balance the flash with the ambient light you may need a slow shutter speed, so use slow sync, setting either 1st or 2nd curtain sync (see pp.151).

4 TILT THE FLASH HEAD To bounce the flash you need to tilt the flash head upwards: the flash will probably have a lock that stops you doing this accidentally, so don't force it if it doesn't tilt easily.

5 TAKE A TEST SHOT As your camera and flash are set to TTL metering, the camera will automatically try to compensate for the added distance the flash has to travel (to the ceiling and back again, rather than simply straight), but it is worth firing a test shot, just to be sure the exposure is adequate.

6 ADJUST THE FLASH If the lighting in your test shot isn't quite how you want it, adjust the flash compensation to make the flash appear more or less obvious, and shoot again.

HOTSHOE ACCESSORIES

There are many accessories designed to soften flash light. Diffusers fit over the flash, while others use an angled white card to bounce the light (so you lose less power, and it can be used outdoors). Other gadgets "split" the flash, so some light is directed upwards, and some at your subject.

THE RESULT

Direct flash resulted in very harsh, artificial-looking illumination, but by bouncing the flash off the ceiling – effectively creating a much larger light source – we were able to produce a more natural-looking light.

CAMERA **SETTINGS**

▼ DIRECT FLASH

USING **FLASH AT NIGHT**

When you're photographing at night, or under any low-light conditions, you have several options when it comes to getting the exposure right. You could use a slow shutter speed, which might result in blur; set a wide aperture, which will restrict your depth of field; or you can increase the ISO, which will make your images more noisy. None of these approaches is necessarily "wrong", but using a hotshoe flash may be the best solution as it will give you much more control over the exposure. This, in turn, will give you a greater level of control over the overall look of your photograph.

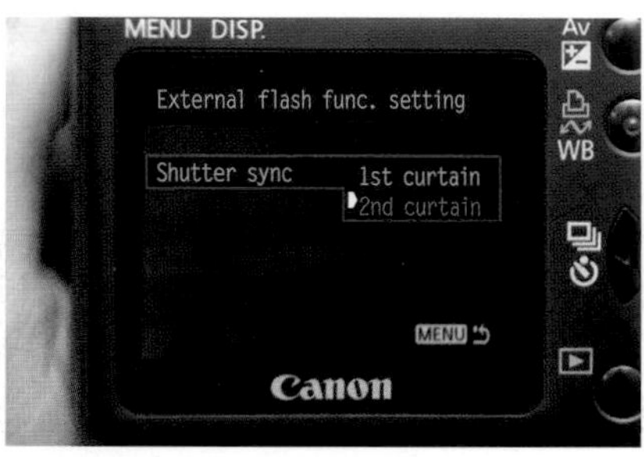

1 SET UP YOUR TRIPOD
If you want to retain some of the ambient light, you'll need to use a slow shutter speed, so a tripod is essential – unless you have a solid surface that you can sit the camera on.

2 SET SHUTTER SYNC
Once you're set up, set the sync mode on your camera. For static subjects, use either 1st or 2nd curtain sync. If your subject is moving, 2nd curtain sync is the better option (see p.151).

3 SELECT APERTURE PRIORITY
To use a slow shutter speed while keeping control over the depth of field, select Aperture Priority and set the aperture to f/8, which will keep the background fairly sharp.

NORMAL FLASH

NO FLASH

4 LET THE CAMERA DECIDE
The camera will set a fairly slow shutter speed because of the low light and relatively small aperture setting. With "normal" flash, your subject is well exposed, but the background is barely visible (above left). If you use a slow shutter speed without flash, you see the background but the ambient lighting isn't enough to light your subject properly (above right). Setting the camera to slow-sync gives you the best of both worlds; the slower shutter speed captures ambient background light, while the aperture controls depth of field and flash power to ensure your subject is well-lit.

IMPROVING FLASH

Using a hotshoe-mounted flash (or built-in flash) in low-light conditions is almost certain to produce red-eye if your subject is looking directly at the camera. Avoid this by activating Red-eye reduction (see p.150). Direct flash is a "hard" light source, so invest in a diffuser that slides over the flash head (see p.157). Alternatively, you'll find instructions for making various ingenious DIY flash diffusers online.

ALSO WORKS FOR...

Slow-sync flash also works indoors, when you want to expose for your main subject but retain a sense of "place." You need to be aware, however, that although the flash will freeze your subject at the moment the flash fires, the slow shutter speed can cause movement blur trails. This effect can work well for some shots, but act as a distraction in others.

THE RESULT

The final shot combines a well-lit subject with a background exposure that gives a sense of place. The warm colours from the streetlighting and light trails from the moving traffic impart an urban "edge".

CAMERA **SETTINGS**

1 SEC

USING A **SIMPLE LIGHTING SET-UP**

Wireless flash control is an increasingly common feature on hotshoe-mounted flashes and dSLR cameras and CSCs, and one that allows you to start exploring "professional" lighting set-ups with minimal fuss. Even if you don't have wireless flash you may be able to take your flash away from the camera using a dedicated through-the-lens (TTL) lead or remote triggering system. The main benefit of off-camera flash is simple: you're no longer limited to flat, frontal lighting. These opens up a whole world of creative options, starting with this simple one-flash set-up that's perfect for portraits.

1 SET UP YOUR FLASH
Because you'll be using the flash away from the camera, you need something to hold it in place. Lightweight stands like the one shown here are inexpensive and perfect for the job, but you could use a tripod with a suitable hotshoe adaptor.

REMOTE CONTROL

Remote triggering systems are available for a wide range of cameras that don't have wireless control as standard. These triggers consist of a transmitter that sits in the camera's hotshoe, and a receiver under the flash that together provide you with full TTL wireless flash control.

2 SWITCH TO TTL
Set your hotshoe flash to its TTL mode, so the camera can control how powerful the flash is, depending on the exposure settings you're using. That way, if you change the aperture, the flash will compensate.

3 POSITION A REFLECTOR
Adding a reflector (see pp.130–31) opposite the flash will help fill in any potentially hard shadows created by the flash. For portraits this softer light is almost always preferable.

4 SELECT A MODE
As your camera will be controlling the flash output automatically, you can set the shooting mode to Program, Aperture Priority, or Shutter Priority. But be sure not to exceed the camera's flash sync speed (see pp.152–53).

SHADOWS FILLED

5 TAKE A TEST SHOT AND EXPERIMENT
Until you take a test shot, you won't know for sure what effect your flash will have. Make sure that you don't have any exposure warnings indicated in the viewfinder (if you do it's probably because the aperture's too wide), and be prepared to move the reflector around to fill any hard shadows.

THE RESULT

Getting your flash away from the camera avoids the harsh, front-lit look you'd get from a built-in or direct hotshoe flash. This instantly produces more professional-looking results.

CAMERA **SETTINGS**

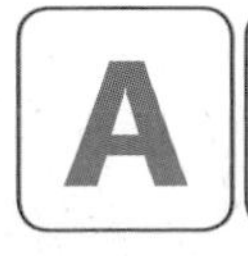

PAINTING WITH LIGHT

With off-camera flash you can create truly unique night-time images by "painting with light". The basic technique is fairly easy to grasp: set a long exposure time on your camera and fire your hotshoe flash multiple times to illuminate your subject. Assuming your exposure time is long enough, it's possible to light an entire building in this way (if you wish to), but there are a couple of things to be aware of. First, you need to work in total darkness and wear dark clothes so that the long exposure doesn't record you as a "ghost". Second, you have to be patient; it takes practice to get consistently stunning results.

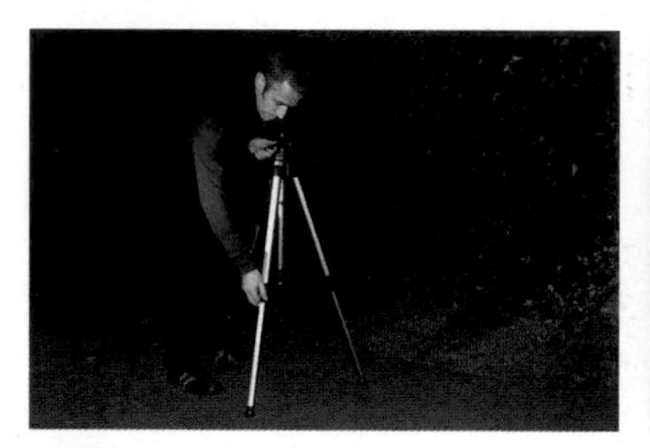

1 SET UP A TRIPOD
A tripod is essential for light painting: you'll be holding the shutter open for a while, so your camera must be steady.

2 SELECT MANUAL
Set your camera to Manual mode and dial in a shutter speed of 30 seconds (usually the camera's maximum automatic setting). As a starting point, choose the lowest ISO, an aperture of f/8, and set the White Balance to Flash or Daylight for neutral colours.

3 SET YOUR FLASH TO MANUAL
Set your flash to manual and zoom it to its widest zoom position so you get the greatest spread of light. Start with the power set at 1/16.

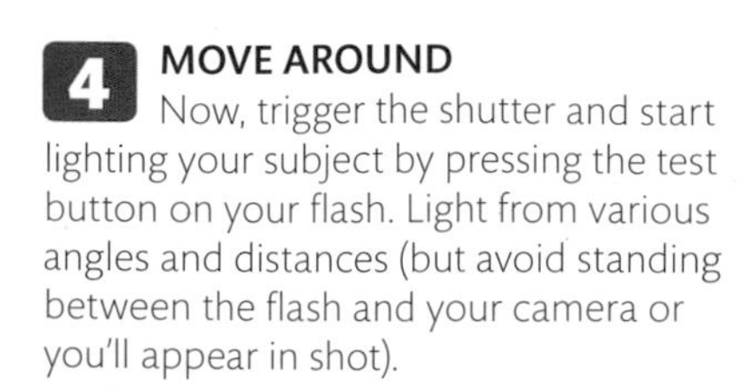

4 MOVE AROUND
Now, trigger the shutter and start lighting your subject by pressing the test button on your flash. Light from various angles and distances (but avoid standing between the flash and your camera or you'll appear in shot).

5 ASSESS THE SHOT Check the exposure. If it's too bright, try reducing the flash power, firing fewer flashes, and/or setting a smaller aperture. If it's too dark then the opposite applies: increase the flash power, fire more flashes, and/or use a wider aperture setting until you get the result you're after.

COLOURED LIGHT

You don't have to restrict yourself to "straight", daylight balanced flash. Coloured lighting gels can be used to transform the light from your flash, simply by holding them in front of the flash as you fire it.

THE RESULT

The long exposure has lightened the residual orange glow in the sky, but it's a single flash fired from multiple angles that has illuminated the facade of this ruined gatehouse.

CAMERA **SETTINGS**

M

IMAGE
ENHANCEMENT

IMAGE ENHANCEMENT

Although it's by no means essential, the majority of digital photographs will benefit from a certain level of post-production work, or "image enhancement", whether that means simply tweaking the exposure or completely deconstructing and reassembling an image. Between these two extremes are the steps that will ensure that every photograph you take looks as good as possible, and in this chapter you'll discover just how easy and effective these adjustments can be.

Working with layers

When it comes to choosing editing software, "Layers" should be considered an essential feature. In the simplest sense, layers can be thought of as clear sheets of acetate that you place over your image. You can then make any changes you wish on that layer, and your underlying digital image will be protected. If things go wrong at any time, you can simply get rid of the layer, rather than the original photograph. Using multiple layers enables you to make complex groups of changes, which can then be blended together, giving you even greater control over your images.

▲ Adjustment layers allow you to make changes to an image that can be reversed and fine-tuned without degrading the original.

SUGGESTED WORKFLOW

DOWNLOAD

The first step is to get your images onto your computer, either by connecting your camera to your computer, or by putting your memory card into a card reader.

OPEN IMAGES

All editing software will allow you to open your images individually, but some will also let you apply changes to multiple images at the same time.

CROP & STRAIGHTEN

Rogue elements creeping into the edges of frame and sloping horizons are very common problems and should be fixed before you do anything else (see pp.168–69).

SET EXPOSURE

Even if you get the exposure "right" in-camera, it's worth tweaking it on screen to see if there's any room for improvement (see pp.170–71). Before you start, create an adjustment layer.

ANATOMY OF A TOOLBAR

All image-editing software differs to a greater or lesser degree (the anatomy here shows Photoshop Elements), but certain features are shared by most: selection tools, brush tools, the ability to add text, and one or more retouching tools that will help you edit out unwanted blemishes, for example. These tools are generally found in a toolbar at the top or side of the screen. Additional features that call up a separate window or dialog box are usually accessed from the main menu bar.

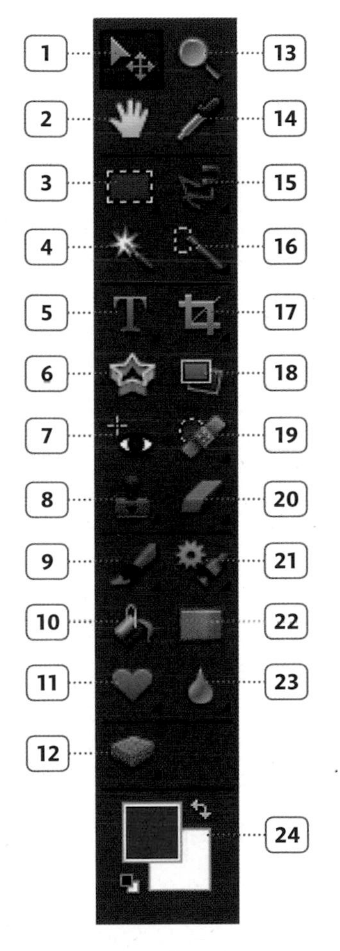

KEY

1 **Move tool** For moving selected parts of an image from one place to another

2 **Hand tool** For dragging your image around the screen to see different areas

3 **Selection tool** A variety of regularly shaped selection tools

4 **Magic wand tool** Uses colour to select areas of an image

5 **Type tool** Allows you to add text to your digital images

6 **Cookie cutter tool** Creates quirky cutouts from your image

7 **Red-eye removal tool** Corrects red-eye in portraits taken with flash

8 **Clone stamp tool** For removing dust and scratches manually

9 **Brush tool** Used to "paint" onto your digital images

10 **Paint bucket tool** For filling large, flat areas with a single colour

11 **Custom shape tool** Adds predefined shapes to your pictures

12 **Sponge tool** Lets you selectively increase or decrease saturation

13 **Magnifier tool** Used to zoom in and out of your image

14 **Eye dropper tool** Allows you to "sample" (pick) colours from anywhere on the screen

15 **Lasso tool** Selection tools for choosing irregularly shaped parts of an image

16 **Quick Selection tool** Uses edge contrast to quickly select parts of an image

17 **Crop tool** A quick and efficient way to trim your images

18 **Straighten tool** Helps correct sloping horizons and converging parallel lines

19 **Healing brush tool** Removes defects and blemishes with a single click

20 **Eraser tool** Allows you to delete areas from a layer

21 **Smart brush tool** Allows you to paint creative effects onto your image

22 **Gradient tool** Allows you to add a gradient effect to your image

23 **Blur tool** Used to selectively blur parts of an image

24 **Color swatch** Used to set the current foreground and background colour

ADJUST CONTRAST

If your image is looking a little flat and lacklustre you can boost the contrast between light and dark to make it appear more vibrant and "3-D" (see pp.172–73).

COLOUR

From highly saturated colours, to subtle tints, to black-and-white, colour – or the lack of it – has a huge impact on how we perceive an image (see pp.174–79).

SHARPEN

Once you've made any other adjustments, ensure that small details and edges in your image are crisply defined (see pp.180–81).

OUTPUT

The final stage in your digital image workflow is to save and output your adjusted image, whether to print or the web.

CROPPING FOR IMPACT

In an ideal world it would be possible to have your camera locked on a tripod and carefully levelled for every shot you take, with a full range of focal lengths at your disposal so you can get as close to your subject as you wish. However, often you will be shooting hand-held, rather than with a tripod, and sometimes you simply won't have a lens that's long enough. In these situations, take the shot and use your editing software's crop and rotate tools to improve the image in post-production.

1 ADD A GUIDE
Most editing software allows you to add guidelines, which are horizontal or vertical lines superimposed over the image. Drag a horizontal line to the horizon to determine whether it's straight; if not, this gives you a target for alignment.

2 ROTATE YOUR IMAGE
The Rotate feature is most commonly a menu option, and when activated it will select the entire image area. Use the "handles" at the corners of the image to rotate the image by clicking and dragging them.

3 SELECT THE CROP TOOL
The Crop tool usually sits as an option on the main toolbar of your editing software. The icon, as shown here, often depicts a pair of traditional "cropping Ls".

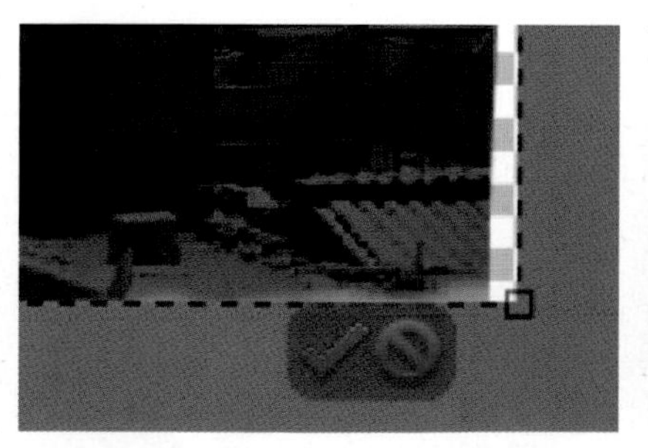

4 SELECT THE WHOLE IMAGE
With the Crop tool activated, click and drag from one corner of your image to its diagonal opposite (top left to bottom right, for example). This will select the entire image area.

5 RESIZE THE CROP AREA
As with the Rotate tool, handles will appear at the corners of the area selected. Drag these inwards to set the crop area. Here, the area that will be cropped out is shown in red: the full-colour area is the new crop.

ALSO WORKS FOR...

There are two main reasons why you might crop an image. The first is to make your subject appear bigger in the frame; the second is to remove distracting elements, such as someone stealing the limelight in the background.

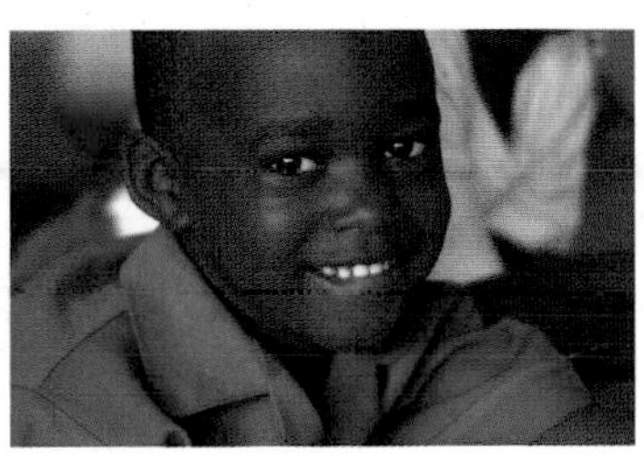

THE RESULT

Rotating the image has levelled the horizon, but it's the fairly severe crop that's had the most effect by focusing attention on the floodlit building and removing several unnecessary elements from the foreground.

CAMERA **SETTINGS**

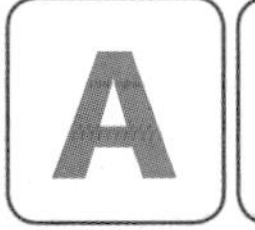

▼ BEFORE CROP AND ROTATE

CORRECTING **EXPOSURE**

With so many different exposure modes and exposure metering patterns built into your camera, you may wonder why you'd ever need to adjust the exposure of a shot in your editing software. But sometimes you may feel that an image would look better a little lighter or darker than shot, or your camera will have been "fooled" by tricky lighting conditions. Whatever the reason, your editing software will have tools to help you, ranging from simple exposure sliders through to the more advanced Levels, a histogram-based tool which gives you greater control.

LESS LIGHT **EXPOSURE** MORE LIGHT

1 APPLY EXPOSURE COMPENSATION

The Exposure tool is the simplest way to correct exposure, and it works in a similar way to the exposure compensation found in your camera (see pp.80–81). Increase the exposure level (+) to brighten an image, or decrease the exposure level (-) to darken it. As with in-camera exposure compensation, adjustments are usually made in "stop" increments, although editing software is usually more precise.

2 USE LEVELS

While Exposure allows you to make universal changes to your images, Levels lets you control the shadows, highlights, and midtones independently. It does this by using an editable histogram (see pp.78–79).

3 SET THE BLACK POINT

At the left end of the histogram (the shadows) is a black slider control. Move this to the right to darken the shadows in your image without affecting the highlights.

4 SET THE WHITE POINT

At the right end of the histogram (the highlights) is a white slider that controls the brightness of highlights. Move the slider to the left to brighten light areas without affecting the shadows.

5 SET THE MIDPOINT

At the centre of the Levels histogram is a grey, midtone slider (known as the "gamma" slider). This controls the overall brightness of the image and can be used to make universal exposure changes. Slide it to the right to brighten your image, and move it to the left to darken it.

THE RESULT

Adjusting the midtone and highlight areas with Levels quickly corrected the exposure in this shot. A subsequent colour boost (see pp.174–75) and some sharpening (see pp.180–81) further improved the shot.

CAMERA **SETTINGS**

▼ BEFORE EXPOSURE CORRECTION

ADJUSTING **CONTRAST**

When photographers talk about contrast, they're usually referring to two extremes: low contrast and high contrast. Neither of these is necessarily bad or wrong, but sometimes a shot feels a little "flat" or too "contrasty". It's generally much better to deal with high contrast when you're actually taking the picture (see box, below), but your editing software is the perfect solution to the problem of flat-looking, low contrast images. The best tool for adjusting contrast is Curves, thanks to the high level of control it offers: shadows, highlights, and midtones can all be locked and manipulated independently.

1 OPEN CURVES

When you open a Curves dialog box, you'll see a straight line running across a box from bottom left (shadows) to top right (highlights). The aim is to change the line into a "curve" to modify the shadows and highlights.

2 ADJUST THE HIGHLIGHTS

In its simplest sense, adding a control point to the top right end of the curve allows you to adjust the highlights in an image. When you move the curve upwards, they brighten; when you move the curve downwards, they darken.

3 ADJUST THE SHADOWS

The same process applies when adjusting shadows, except this time you need to add a control point to the lower left end of the curve. Drag the point downwards to darken the shadows, or drag it upwards to lighten them.

HIGH CONTRAST

While low-contrast images can often be improved in your editing software, the same isn't true with high contrast. Many programs have a Shadow/Highlight Recovery tool (or similar), but this won't help when the shadows or highlights in an image are "clipped" (see pp.78–79), as is the case here. In the original image (left), the highlights on the child's face are pure white, and they remain so after adjustment (right). You simply can't recover what isn't there to begin with, which is why high contrast is best tackled in-camera, either by using a reflector (see pp.130–31) or diffuser (see pp.132–33), or by shooting for HDR (see pp.84–85).

4 APPLY AN S CURVE

The simplest way to boost contrast is to create a shallow S shape, as shown here. This deepens the shadows and brightens the highlights without losing detail, which can occur with other contrast adjustment tools.

LEVELS VS. CURVES

You can use Levels (see pp.174–75) to adjust contrast: moving the black slider to the right and the white slider to the left to darken shadows and lighten highlights. However, with Curves you can usually add multiple control points, allowing you to finesse your results, should you need to.

THE RESULT

The original image felt a little washed out. Applying an S curve has made a significant difference – the increased contrast has made the colours appear more vibrant, and the flower now leaps from the picture.

CAMERA SETTINGS

▼ BEFORE CURVES ADJUSTMENT

BOOSTING **COLOUR**

The meaning of "colour" in photography doesn't just relate to the colour temperature of the light (see pp.124–25) or the white balance (see pp.126–29) – it can also refer to the intensity and level of colour in an image. In this sense, colour can be subjective, with no "right" or "wrong" result. For instance, by boosting colour you can can rescue photos taken on overcast days, when colours tend to appear drab and uninspiring. In abstract photography, colour and shape are often more important than the ostensible subject – and improvements in post-production can lift this effect to a whole other level.

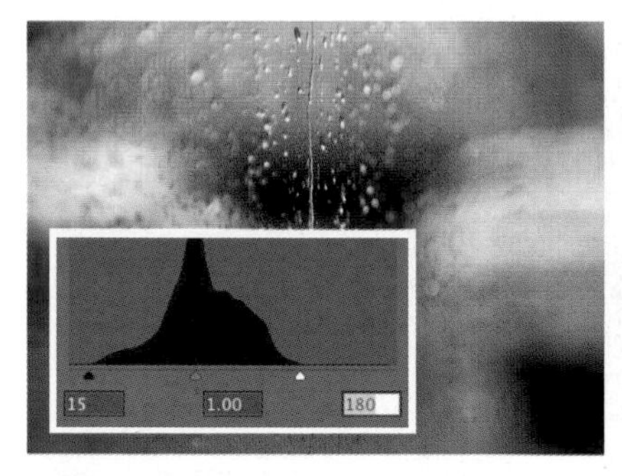

1 SET LEVELS
Before you start adjusting the colour, use Levels (see pp.170–71) to get the exposure right: overexposed images appear washed out, while underexposed images may look over-saturated.

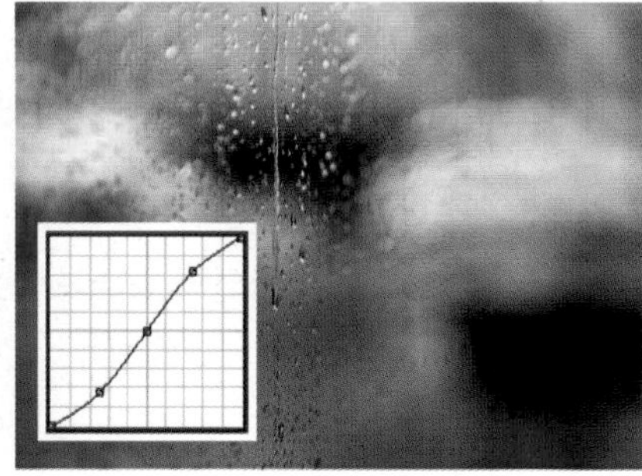

2 ADJUST CONTRAST
Contrast can also have an impact on colour: low-contrast images appear flat, while colours tend to stand out when the contrast is higher. Use Curves (see pp.172–73) to fine-tune the contrast.

CORRECTING COLOUR CASTS

If your image has an overall colour cast (that is, it appears overly cool or blue, or it has an orange tint), then you need to make an equal and opposite colour adjustment. Look for a Colour Balance or Colour Variations tool in your editing software, as these are usually a little more refined than Hue/Saturation in this instance. However, set the exposure and contrast before you make any adjustments.

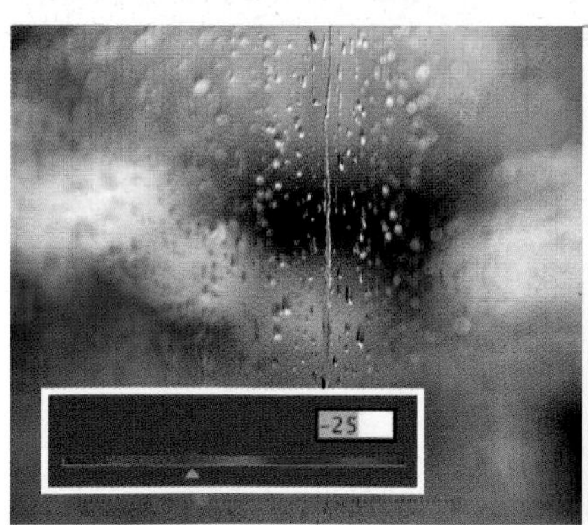

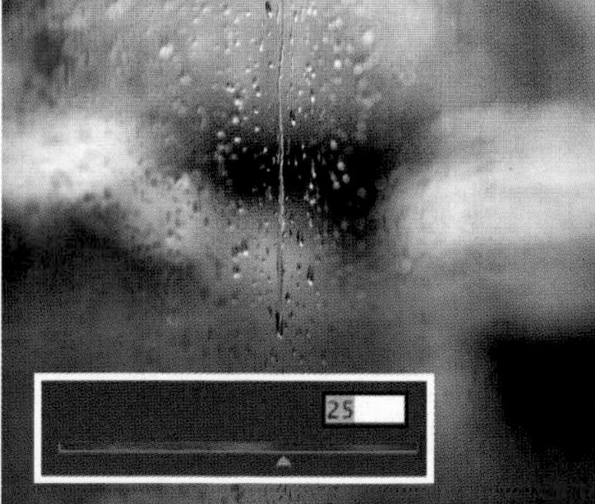

3 ADJUST HUE
Once the exposure and contrast have been set you can make changes to the colour. A Hue/Saturation tool can be found in most editing software, and the first step is to see whether changing the Hue will improve your image. Adjusting the Hue slider shifts the overall colour bias of an image, from green through blue, red, yellow, and all colours in between. A small adjustment usually creates a significant overall visual effect.

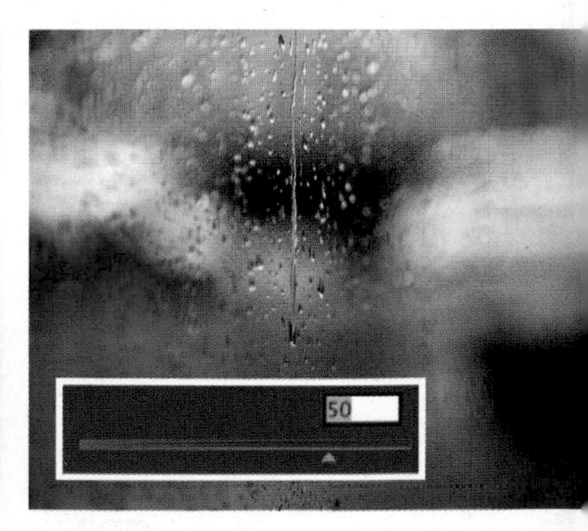

4 ADJUST SATURATION
While Hue alters the colour itself, Saturation determines its intensity, usually from a scale of 0 (fully desaturated/shades of grey) to 100 (heavily saturated colour). Even small shifts in the Saturation slider can have a major impact on the image.

ALSO WORKS FOR...

Hue and Saturation adjustments can be used to transform your pictures, either by changing one of the parameters or changing them both together. A popular method is to brighten up shots containing people, as this instantly makes this type of photograph more appealing: warmer tones suggest a happier mood.

THE RESULT

A combination of exposure, contrast, and colour adjustments has transformed this dreary, nondescript shot of a rain-spattered window into a pleasingly vibrant and eye-catching abstract.

CAMERA **SETTINGS**

▼ BEFORE COLOUR BOOST

CONVERTING TO **BLACK AND WHITE**

All image-editing software offers a simple Desaturate or Greyscale option (or similar), which will remove the colour from your photograph at the click of a button. However, this won't give you any control over the appearance of the final image. It's the same as if you were to set your camera to capture in black and white: a straight conversion can result in a flat-looking image, without contrast or dynamic range. So, unless it's your only option, it's not the most effective route to take. Instead, check to see whether your software has a more sophisticated black-and-white conversion tool.

PORTRAIT **LANDSCAPE**

INFRARED

NEWSPAPER

1 EXPERIMENT WITH PRESETS

To begin with, try each of the available presets to see their effects. The images above show a variety of presets available in Photoshop Elements, demonstrating how the notion of "black and white" isn't as straightforward as it seems.

INCREASED RED

INCREASED GREEN

INCREASED BLUE

2 EXPLORE COLOUR FILTERS

Some software offers colour adjustment in addition to (or instead of) preset styles. Through the use of sliders for red, green, and blue (and possibly more colours), these can also control how different colours appear in black and white. Increasing one slider generally means reducing the strength of other colours to compensate.

3 FINE-TUNE THE RESULT

If appropriate, you can apply an S curve to finesse the image (see pp.172–73). In this case, a boost in contrast has accentuated the modern feel.

USING DIGITAL COLOUR FILTERS

Digital colour filters replicate the effect of lens filters, traditionally used in black-and-white photography to, for example, create dramatic, high-contrast skies in landscape images. The way they work can seem confusing at first, but there's a simple way to remember the effect they'll have on your image. A colour filter will lighten areas of the subject that are the same colour (or similar), and darken opposite colours. For example, when you convert to black and white, a red filter will lighten red areas (and, to a lesser extent, orange and yellow areas) of the image, while at the same time darkening blue-green areas.

THE RESULT

Converting portrait and wedding pictures to black and white is a great way of giving them a timeless yet contemporary look. Removing the colour can often enhance the romantic mood of an image like this.

CAMERA **SETTINGS**

▲ BEFORE BLACK AND WHITE CONVERSION

TONING THE IMAGE

Before colour photography was invented, toned black-and-white prints were relatively common. Initially, this wasn't so much a creative decision as a technical one, as various photographic pioneers experimented with different chemicals in an attempt to extend the life of their delicate prints. However, even after it became possible to produce a stable black-and-white print, toned images remained a popular means of adding colour and atmosphere to an otherwise greyscale image. The practice is still used today, although now the tones are more often applied using software, rather than toxic chemicals.

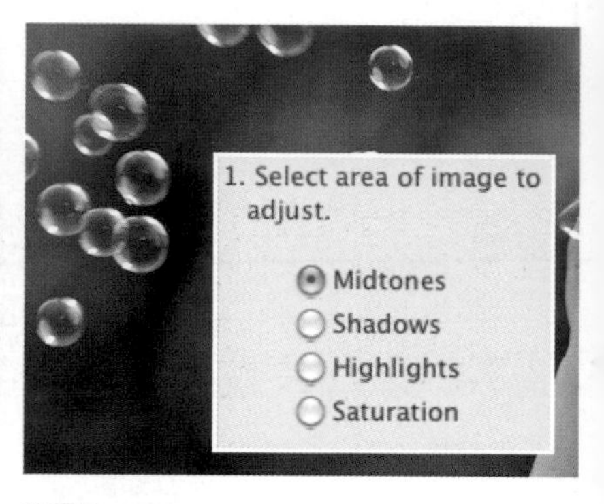

1 REDUCE CONTRAST

Toning works best when it's applied to a slightly "flat" (low contrast) image, so rather than boosting the contrast, consider reducing it using Shadows/Highlights (or similar) before you begin (see pp.172–73).

2 REMOVE COLOUR

The basis for any toned image is a black-and-white "original", so you need to remove the colour. Convert the image to black and white (see pp.176–77) without increasing the contrast.

3 ADJUST TONE

Using the Color Variations (or just "Variations") tool allows you to tone the shadows, midtones, or highlights, and you can also set the adjustment intensity from a mild tint through to a strong tone.

INCREASED RED

DECREASED BLUE

LIGHTENED

4 EXPERIMENT

The adjustment buttons give a "live" preview, so it's simply a case of clicking on an adjustment button and the "After" image will be updated to show how your picture's looking. For a "straight" toned image it's a good idea to leave the area set to Midtones, but you can change the intensity of the colour adjustment, if you wish. Clicking on Increase Red, Decrease Blue, and Lighten results in a subtle, sepia-toned look.

5 MAKE FINAL ADJUSTMENTS

When you're happy with the tone you've created, click on OK to apply it to your image. Then, if necessary, tweak the brightness and contrast (see pp.170–73), and sharpen (see pp.180–81) ready for printing or sharing online.

SPLIT TONE

You can add a "split tone" to your images by toning the shadows with a different colour to the one you've used for the highlights. This is usually done with "opposite" colours – adding a blue tone to the shadows and making the highlights more yellow is a classic combination.

THE RESULT

This was an incredibly straightforward process, yet the picture has been completely transformed: the warm sepia tone gives it an "antique" appearance that enhances the quiet, contemplative nature of the image.

CAMERA **SETTINGS**

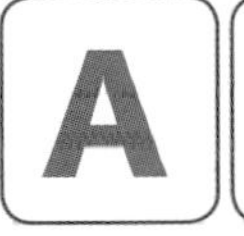

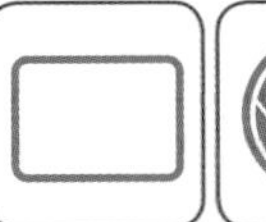

▼ BEFORE TONING

ACHIEVING **CRISP DETAILS**

If you've spent a fair amount of money on a camera and an accompanying lens (or lenses), you might wonder why you'd ever need to sharpen your photographs with editing software: surely your camera will deliver a sharp image? Well, yes and no. Your lenses have a significant impact on how sharp your pictures will be, but all digital photographs can benefit from additional digital sharpening. This is essentially because of the way in which digital camera sensors work – it's unavoidable, and not a camera fault – but your editing software is more than capable of putting things right.

1 DUPLICATE THE IMAGE LAYER

You'll need software with Layers for this technique (see p.166). First, duplicate your image so you have a copy of it on a second layer (the "adjustment layer"). This will be at the top of the Layers palette, with your "master" layer beneath.

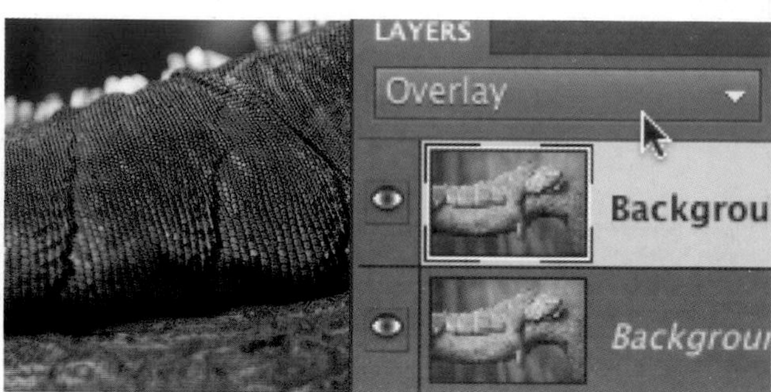

2 SET THE BLENDING MODE

Using the drop-down menu in the Layers palette, change the Blending mode for your duplicate layer from Normal to Overlay. Don't worry if the image looks overly saturated and contrasty at this point.

SHARPENING FILTERS

Most editing software incorporates several sharpening filters, ranging from simple Sharpen options that don't give you any control at all, through to advanced sharpening tools such as Unsharp Mask (USM). USM is an incredibly powerful (and complex) sharpening tool, but should be used with caution: it's easy to overdo it and end up with an unattractive, over-sharpened result (see detail below, right).

3 APPLY THE HIGH PASS FILTER

Although you want to sharpen the image, you won't be using one of your editing software's sharpening filters. This may seem strange, but these filters tend to be either rather crude or overcomplicated in their approach (see box, left). Instead, apply the High Pass filter to your duplicate layer. Adjust the filter amount so that the details in the image appear crisp.

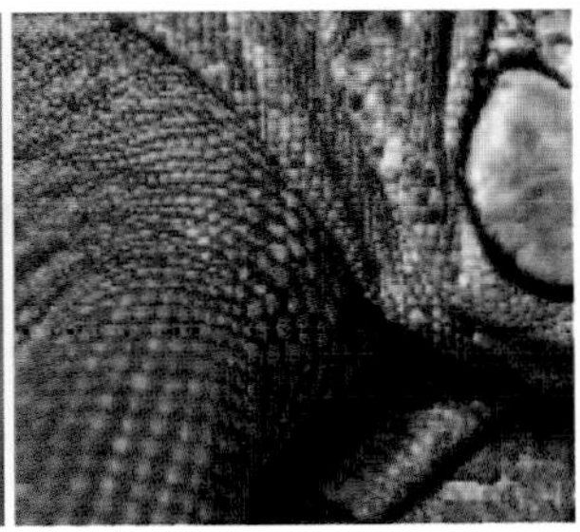

4 ADJUST OPACITY

Fine-tune the effect of the High Pass filter by adjusting the Opacity of your adjustment layer. Decreasing the opacity allows the master layer below to show through. Although this effectively reduces the sharpening effect slightly, you should be able to keep the edges nice and crisp, without any halos appearing along them: this would be a sure sign that the image is over-sharpened.

THE RESULT

With a subject that contains a lot of fine detail, such as this scaly iguana, sharpening is essential, especially if you plan to print your image. It also boosts colour and contrast slightly, which further enhances the shot.

CAMERA **SETTINGS**

▼ BEFORE SHARPENING

GLOSSARY

(words that appear bolder *in the entries also have their own entry)*

aberration Unwanted defect in an image, typically caused by the camera lens.

AE-L (Automatic Exposure Lock) A camera feature that allows you to lock the **exposure** set by the camera, usually so you can reframe a shot.

AF-L (Automatic Focus Lock) A camera feature that holds the **focus** at a set distance.

ambient light Existing light in a scene, such as daylight.

angle of view The amount of a scene imaged by the camera. Usually given as a diagonal measurement.

aperture A variable opening in the lens that allows light to pass through to the sensor. The main control over **depth of field**.

Aperture Priority A semi-automated **exposure** mode: the photographer sets the **aperture** (and **ISO**), and the camera selects a shutter speed that will give the "correct" **exposure**.

APS-C A discontinued film format, measuring 25.1mm x 16.7mm. The size closely matches that of the **sensor** found in many dSLR cameras and CSCs and results in a 1.5x or 1.6x **focal length magnification**.

artifact An unwanted defect in a digital image, such as sharpening halos or **noise**.

Auto (exposure) Exposure mode in which the camera sets the **aperture**, shutter speed, and **ISO**, in addition to the **white balance**, and most other camera settings.

autofocus A system that uses sensors to assess the subject and focus the camera lens automatically.

AWB (Automatic White Balance) A camera feature where the camera assesses the scene and sets the correct **white balance**.

backlighting Lighting situation where the primary light source is behind the subject, pointed towards the camera.

blending mode A feature in digital image editing software that enables you to change the way one **layer** interacts with other layers.

bracketing Making a number of exposures of the same scene at different **EV** settings to ensure that one is correctly exposed, or to create an HDR image.

brightness The intensity of light in an image.

centre-weighted metering An exposure metering pattern with a bias towards the centre of the image.

clipping When detail is lost in either the **highlight** and/or shadow areas of an image.

CMYK (Cyan, Magenta, Yellow, Key) The primary colours used in printing, where "Key" is black.

colour cast An overall colour shift in an image, typically caused when the incorrect **white balance** is set.

colour temperature A measure of the temperature of light, given in degrees Kelvin (K).

compression Typically used in reference to image files and the way in which they are saved. **JPEG** files use "lossy" compression to produce small file sizes, with some data loss. Some **Raw** files are uncompressed.

Continuous Autofocus (AF) Mode that allows the camera to constantly adjust the **focus** of the lens to compensate for a moving subject.

contrast The range between the brightest and darkest parts in an image. Contrast can be low or high.

crop To remove unwanted areas from an image, usually using image-editing software.

depth of field The area of an image in front of and behind the point of focus that appears acceptably sharp.

diffusion The scattering of light particles, which softens the light and shadows cast by it.

digital manipulation To make changes to a digital image using image-editing software.

display Part of a device that can show a digital photograph on a screen, such as a computer monitor, rear LCD screen on a camera, tablet, or smartphone.

distortion Commonly refers to a lens **aberration**, whereby straight lines appear curved, especially towards the edges of the frame.

dpi (dots per inch) Used as a measure of print **resolution**: the greater the number of dots (of ink) per linear inch in a print, the higher the resolution.

dynamic range The difference between the brightest and darkest parts of a scene that a camera can record information in. Usually given as a range of **stops**.

EFL (Effective Focal Length) Used to describe the **angle of view** shown by a lens when it is used on a camera with a sub-**full-frame** sensor (see **focal length magnification**).

EV (exposure value) A single number given to the permutations of **aperture**, shutter speed, and **ISO** that all produce the same overall **exposure**. A change of one EV is the same as a change of one **stop**.

evaluative metering A metering pattern that assesses the scene as a whole, sometimes by dividing it into zones. Also known as Matrix, Multi-area, and Multi-segment metering.

EVF (electronic viewfinder) A viewing system common to bridge cameras and CSCs that uses a small, eye-level LCD screen to provide the photographer with a through-the-lens view of a scene.

exposure The fundamental process of allowing a specific amount of light to reach the camera's **sensor** for a specific amount of time to create a digital photograph.

exposure compensation Camera feature that allows you to adjust the **exposure** from that given by the camera, usually in 1/3, 1/2, or 1 **EV** increments.

f/number (f/stop) Term used to refer to the size of the **aperture** in a lens. Expressed as a fraction of the **focal length**; f/4, f/11, f/22, etc.

fill-in Using flash or a reflector to lighten ("fill") any shadows falling across your subject. Commonly used in portrait photographs.

filter (1) A piece of glass or resin, often coloured, that is put in front of the lens to modify the light entering the lens. (2) A software feature that changes an image (or part of an image), sometimes to emulate a lens filter.

flare An **aberration** that manifests as either distinct coloured polygons, or as an overall "haze" that reduces **contrast**. Caused by non-image-forming light reaching the sensor.

focal length The distance between the optical centre of a lens and a sharp image of an object at infinity projected by it. Usually measured in millimetres.

focal length magnification Magnification factor applied to a lens used on a sub-**full-frame** camera to give its full-frame equivalent focal length. With **APS-C** sized sensors this is 1.5x or 1.6x; with **Micro Four Thirds** cameras it is 2x.

focus The point at which the light rays are brought together to produce the sharpest image.

full-frame A sensor size that matches the traditional size of a 35mm film frame; approximately 36mm x 24mm.

greyscale A monochrome digital image made up of shades of grey.

highlight The brightest or lightest parts of an image.

histogram Graph showing the distribution of tones in an image, from pure black to pure white. Can be used to determine **exposure** accuracy and clipping.

hotshoe A fitting found on the top of most digital SLR cameras and some CSCs that allows a flash to be attached to the camera.

ISO An international standard film rating, denoting a film's sensitivity to light. Now used in digital cameras, although changing ISO boosts the signal amplification, not sensitivity.

image stabilization Lens-based or **sensor**-based technology that typically uses sensors and gyros to sense and counter camera shake.

JPEG (Joint Photographic Expert Group) One of the most popular file formats for recording and saving digital photographs. It uses **compression** to reduce file sizes, although the compression process loses some of the information. This data loss is cumulative, so more data is lost every time a JPEG file is resaved as a JPEG.

Kelvin (K) Scale used for measuring **colour temperature**.

landscape (format) When used to refer to an image format, signifies that the longest side of the rectangular frame is horizontal (as opposed to **portrait** format).

layer A feature of image-editing software that allows some elements of an image to "float" above others, thereby allowing adjustments to be made selectively.

LED (Light Emitting Diode) The display technology behind the vast majority of camera screens and flat-screen televisions.

Levels A feature of image-editing software that is based around a **histogram**. Allows you to adjust the black and white points (shadows and **highlights**), as well as the **midtones**.

light meter A tool used to measure light and produce an **exposure** reading. All cameras feature a built-in light meter that takes reflected light readings, but you can buy handheld light meters that take both reflected and incident light readings.

macro Specifically refers to close-up photography at a magnification ratio of 1:1 or greater, so the subject appears at least "life size" on the **sensor**.

macro lens A lens designed specifically for **macro** photography.

manual exposure An **exposure** mode that gives you full control over the **aperture**, shutter speed, and **ISO** settings.

memory card The solid-state storage device used by virtually all digital cameras and smartphones. The most common type in current use is SD (Secure Digital). Some cameras use CF (Compact Flash).

metadata Information about an image that forms part of the image file itself. Metadata can record the location, time, and creator of an image, amongst other things, as well as camera, lens, and exposure details. Some metadata can be edited, allowing you to add copyright information and keywords to your images.

Micro Four Thirds A digital standard developed jointly by Panasonic and Olympus and popularized by their G-series and PEN compact system cameras respectively. Based around a **sensor** size of 17.3mm x 13mm, giving a **focal length magnification** of 2x.

midtone A tonal area in an image that is equidistant between pure black and pure white.

monochrome Any image made up of a single colour, typically black.

multiple exposure A camera feature that allows you to take several shots and combine them into a single image. The effect can be created with image-editing software using **Layers**.

noise Random variations in digital images. There are two types of noise – chroma noise and luminosity noise. The former exhibits as coloured patches or speckles; the latter as an underlying texture. Noise has two main causes: heat (as a result of long exposures) and high **ISO** settings. Most cameras and image-editing software offer some form of noise reduction system.

opacity Used in digital imaging as a measure of how transparent a **layer** is. Typically shown as a percentage value where 0% is entirely transparent and 100% represents total opacity.

optical viewfinder A camera feature that uses an optical system to view a scene, rather than relying on the camera's LCD screen or an electronic viewfinder (**EVF**). All dSLRs use an optical viewfinder.

overexposure When too much light is received by the **sensor**, resulting in an overly bright image, most often with a loss of detail in the **highlight** areas.

panoramic (format) Used to describe a picture format where the image is letterbox-shaped.

partial metering Metering pattern used by Canon. Measures at the centre of the frame, using an area that is larger than a **spot meter** pattern, but smaller than **centre-weighted metering**.

pixel Short for "picture element"; the smallest unit of digital imaging.

pixellated Appearance of a digital image in which the individual pixels are clearly discernible.

portrait (format) When used to refer to an image format, signifies that the longest side of the rectangular frame is vertical (as opposed to **landscape** format).

ppi (pixels per inch) A measure of a digital image's **resolution** based on the number of **pixels** per linear inch.

prefocusing A technique where the focus is set (usually manually) in anticipation of the subject arriving. Suitable for fast-moving subjects.

prime lens A lens with a single, fixed **focal length**.

Program An **exposure** mode where the camera sets both the **aperture** and shutter speed. Differs from **Auto** in that the photographer can set the **ISO**, and can also "shift" the exposure pairing to prioritize **depth of field** or shutter speed.

Raw Image file format that records the data from the camera "as shot", with little or no processing. Processing is then carried out on the computer.

red-eye An effect created when light (usually from an on-camera flash) reflects off the blood vessels at the back of the subject's eye, making their pupil appear red in an image.

red-eye reduction A feature of a camera flash that attempts to prevent red-eye by firing a series of pre-flashes to dilate the subject's pupil.

resizing Changing the size of a digital photograph, either making it smaller to use online, for example, or increasing the size to produce an enlarged print. Increasing the size of an image reduces its quality.

resolution (1) Of a lens, is a measure of its ability to record fine detail clearly. (2) Of a digital image, refers to the number of pixels per inch (ppi) or, in the case of a print, the dots per inch (dpi).

rim lighting Lighting technique where the subject is lit in such a way that it is outlined with light. Usually results in the subject falling into silhouette unless fill-in is used.

RGB (Red, Green, Blue) The primary colours used in the recording and viewing of digital images.

rule of thirds A traditional composition "rule". Based on the idea of dividing the frame into three equal segments, both horizontally and vertically, using imagined lines. Key elements of the image should be placed along these lines, or at their intersection, for greatest effect.

saturation The intensity of colour.

scanning The process of digitizing a printed image, film frame, or document using a scanner.

Scene mode A set of pre-programmed exposure modes optimized for use with specific subjects – for example, Landscape, Portrait, and Sports.

sensor The light-sensitive imaging chip inside a digital camera.

sepia Traditional colour tone applied to monochrome images to give them an "antique" look.

shutter The mechanism inside a camera that determines how long the sensor is exposed to light. The time the shutter stays open for is the shutter speed.

Shutter Priority A semi-automated exposure mode in which the photographer sets the shutter speed (and ISO), and the camera chooses an aperture that will give the "correct" exposure.

silhouette Effect in which the subject appears as a black shape, usually against a brighter background. Can be caused by or created with strong backlighting, and avoided through the use of fill-in lighting.

Single-shot Autofocus (AF) Mode where the lens is focused and the focus distance will not change until an exposure is made or the shutter-release button is released. Ideal for static subjects.

SLR (single-lens reflex) A viewing system that uses a prism and mirrors to transmit the light passing through the lens to an optical viewfinder. Now used to describe a type of camera that uses that viewing system: for example, a digital SLR.

spot meter Very precise metering pattern that reads the light in a very small area of the frame.

stop A change in exposure equal to a halving or doubling of the amount of light. Can be used to refer to exposure in general, or any one of the exposure controls: aperture, shutter speed, and ISO.

sync speed The fastest shutter speed at which the camera's sensor is exposed to light in its entirety. At faster speeds the sensor is exposed to a travelling slit of light.

telephoto A focal length with a narrow viewing angle, typically 35° or smaller.

TIFF (Tagged Image File Format) Widely used image file format for saving processed Raw files. Produces high quality files that are either uncompressed, or use lossless compression algorithms.

TTL (through-the-lens) Any camera system that receives information via the lens, such as a viewfinder, exposure meter, or autofocus system.

underexposure When not enough light is received by the sensor, resulting in an overly dark image, most often with a loss of detail in the shadow areas.

white balance A camera feature used to adjust the colour of an image to match the prevalent colour temperature of the light.

wide-angle A focal length giving a wide angle of view, usually at least 50°.

zoom lens A lens covering a range of focal lengths.

INDEX

A

B

C

G

H

I

J

L

U

W

Z

ACKNOWLEDGMENTS

DK would like to thank:

Gerard Brown and John Munro for the photography and Thomas Morse for retouching. Many thanks also to our models: Rhiannon Carroll, Hannah Clark, Satu Fox, Joe Munro, Priscilla Nelson-Cole, John Owen, Farmer Sharp, Duncan Turner, and Angela Wilkes (also Lotus the pug and Piper the pointer).
For their kind permission to photograph we're very grateful to: Borough Market, Brands Hatch Racing Circuit; The British Museum; Drusilla's Animal Park; and Earnley Butterflies, Birds and Beasts.

The publisher would like to thank the following for their kind permission to reproduce their photographs:

(Key: a-above; b-below/bottom; c-centre; f-far; l-left; r-right; t-top)

2 Corbis: Staffan Andersson / Johnér Images. 3 Corbis: (cl). 4-5 Corbis: Guido Cozzi / Atlantide Phototravel. 6 Corbis: Nabiha Dahhan / Westend61 (tl); Yves Marcoux / First Light (tc). Getty Images: The Image Bank / Peter Adams (tr). 7 Corbis: Imaginechina (tl). 8 Corbis: Chris Collins (tl); Frank Lukasseck (tr); Tim Fitzharris / Minden Pictures (cra); Tabor Gus (cb); Tim Graham (fcr). Getty Images: Blend Images / JGI / Jamie Grill (c); Ricardo Cappellaro / Flickr Open (cl). 12-13 Getty Images: E+ / kgfoto. 16 Courtesy of Nikon. 17 Courtesy of Canon (UK) Ltd: (b). Pentax UK Ltd: (ca). Sony Corporation: (tc). 18 Courtesy of Canon (UK) Ltd: (tr). Courtesy of Nikon: (b). 19 Courtesy of Canon (UK) Ltd. 20 Courtesy of Canon (UK) Ltd: (br). Courtesy of Nikon: (bl). 21 Courtesy of Canon (UK) Ltd: (bl, br). Courtesy of Nikon: (cl, cr). 24 Olympus.co.uk: (cl, cr). Panasonic: (bl, br). 25 Olympus.co.uk: (cl). Panasonic: (bl). 26 Courtesy of Canon (UK) Ltd: (bl, br). Courtesy of Nikon: (cla, cra). 27 Courtesy of Canon (UK) Ltd: (bl). Courtesy of Nikon: (cla). 32 Tamron Co. Ltd. 34 Manfrotto: (r). 35 Manfrotto: (tr, bl). 36 Courtesy of Canon (UK) Ltd: (cl, cr). 37 LumiQuest®: (bl, bc, br). Manfrotto: Lastolite (cr). Courtesy of Nikon: (tr). Image Courtesy of Sigma Imaging (UK) Ltd: (tc). 38 Crumpler: (cla). Hoya Filters: (clb, bl). LowePro / DayMen International Limited: (fcla). Manfrotto: Manfrotto Bags / KATA (cra). Peli Cases: (fcra). 39 Courtesy of Canon (UK) Ltd: (fcr). Courtesy of Nikon: (cr). SanDisk Corporation: (tc, tr). Sony Corporation: (ftr). 40 Getty Images: Taxi Japan / Ryuichi Sato (c). 42-43 Getty Images: Photodisc / Arthur S. Aubry. 48 Corbis: Nabiha Dahhan / Westend61 (macro/close-up / l); Photosindia (portrait / l); Bruno Morandi / Hemis (portrait / r); (landscape / l, landscape / r); Randy Faris (child / l); Isaac Lane Koval (sports / l); Patrick Seeger / EPA (sports / r); Frank Lukasseck (macro/ close-up / r). Getty Images: Riser / Sean Justice (child / r). 50 Corbis: Guido Cozzi / Atlantide Phototravel (auto / l); Hero (program / l); Rob Taylor / Loop Images (program / r); Frank Lukasseck (shutter priority / l); Henrik Trygg (shutter priority / r); Martin Puddy (aperture priority); Martin Sundberg (aperture priority / r); Kenji Hata (manual / l); Bruno Ehrs (manual / r). Getty Images: Monkey Business Images / the Agency Collection (auto / r). 57 Getty Images: Arctic-Images / The Image Bank (tr); Daniel Osterkamp / Flickr (tc). 59 Getty Images: blue jean images (cra); Imagemore Co, Ltd. (crb). 62 Corbis: Michael Durham / Minden Pictures (water); Michael Truelove / Cultura (sports); Helen King (night lights); James Hager / Robert Harding World Imagery (wildlife). 63 Corbis: Tim Fitzharris / Minden Pictures (wildlife); Paul Souders (tr); Image Source (sports); Lawrence Manning (night lights); Frank Krahmer (water). 67 Corbis: Tim Davis (tc); Radius Images (tr). 73 Getty Images: Martin Harvey (tc). 76 Corbis: Tim Graham (bl); Reed Kaestner (br). 77 Corbis: Kent & Charlene Krone / SuperStock (br); Hugh Sitton (cr). Getty Images: Photodisc / Dennis Flaherty (tr). 78 Corbis: Rudy Sulgan (cl, c, cr). 79 Corbis: Roy Hsu (cl); Frank Lukasseck (cr). Getty Images: Photonica / Geir Pettersen (c). 84-85 Chris Gatcum. 86-87 Getty Images: Ricardo Cappellaro / Flickr Open. 88 Corbis. 89 Corbis: Guido Cozzi / Atlantide Phototravel (ca); Odilon Dimier / PhotoAlto (cla); Jon Hicks (cra). Getty Images: Blend Images / JGI / Jamie Grill (clb); Digital Vision (cb); BLOOMimage (crb). 95 Corbis: Ted Levine (tr); Andrew Parkinson (tc). 99 Jurek Biegus: (b). Corbis: Koji Aoki / Aflo (tr). 100-101 Corbis: Frank Lukasseck. 102 Corbis: Frank Krahmer (cr). Courtesy of Nikon: (crb). Tamron Co. Ltd: (fclb). 103 Corbis: John E. Marriott / All Canada Photos (cl). Getty Images: The Image Bank / Darrell Gulin (cr). Courtesy of Nikon: (cla, ca, cra, fcra). Olympus. co.uk: (fcla, fclb). Tamron Co. Ltd: (cb). 105 Corbis: Leslie Richard Jacobs (tr); Oanh / Image Source (tc). 106 Getty Images: The Image Bank / Peter Adams. 107 Corbis: Tim Graham (bc, br). Getty Images: Photodisc / Ursula Alter (cb, crb). Tamron Co. Ltd: (tr). 113 Getty Images: Taxi Japan / ICHIRO (tr). 115 Corbis: George Hammerstein (bl). 117 Corbis: Staffan Andersson / Johnér Images (tr). Getty Images: Digital Vision / Frank Krahmer (tc). 120-121 Corbis: Chris Collins. 123 Corbis: Peter Dressel / Blend Images (crb); Yves Marcoux / First Light (cr); Jim Zuckerman (br). Getty Images: Iconica / Stephen Simpson (cra). 124 Corbis: Blaine Harrington III (candlelight); Radius Images (clear skylight); Sara Wight (overcast sky); Myopia (midday). Getty Images: OJO Images / Le Club Symphonie (sunset). 127 Corbis: Julian Calverley (tr); Jeremy Woodhouse / Blend Images (tc). 134–135 Andy Mitchell and Joe Munro.139 Getty Images: Photographer's Choice / Richard Boll (tr). 143 Corbis: Daniel Smith (bl). 145 Getty Images: Photonica / EschCollection (tr); Visuals Unlimited, Inc. / Adam Jones (tl). 147 Corbis: Tabor Gus (cr); Gerolf Kalt (clb); Matt Mawson (br). 150-151 Getty Images: Tom Merton / OJO Images. 150 Corbis: Caterina Bernardi (cr, fcr); Tim Hall / Cultura (fcl, cl). 151 Corbis: Awilli (cr). 152 Getty Images: Lane Oatey / Blue Jean Images (c, cl, cr, bl, bc, br). 153 Getty Images: Blend Images / JGI / Jamie Grill (cl, cr, bl, br). 159 Getty Images: Stockbyte / George Doyle (tr). 164-165 Getty Images: Photodisc / David De Lossy. 169 Corbis: Anthony Asael / Art in All of Us (tc, tr). 176 Getty Images: The Image Bank / Byba Sepit (fcl, cl, cr, fcr, fclb, clb, crb, fcrb). 177 Getty Images: The Image Bank / Byba Sepit (cla, br). 178 Corbis: Imaginechina (cla, ca, cra, clb, cb, crb). 179 Corbis: Imaginechina (b, cra, tl).

At the other end of the scale one consultant records the example of a study involving an analysis of British industry by size of establishment and by product groups. The questionnaire was long by any standards—28 pages—and, moreover, required several people to answer it completely. However, of the 6000 questionnaires sent out, 5520 were usable when returned—a response rate of 92 per cent.

The reasons for the wide disparity in response pose several questions:

(a) What is the quality of the preparation that has gone into each questionnaire?

(b) Do the low responses affect the validity of the results?

(c) How can the response rate be increased to a level where non-response becomes relatively unimportant?

Provided sufficient control data has been available at the sampling stage or arises from the answers themselves then a low response rate may not invalidate the results. For example, when seeking to identify types of users of a product, an otherwise unsatisfactory response of say 20 per cent might prove adequate provided suitable control data is used to weight the answers.

3.2.8 Non-response

Why should the user of postal questionaires be so concerned in getting a high response? In the first place the cost of each usable reply will diminish as the numbers received go up. This is true whether direct or total costs are considered. Second, the investment in time is spread over a greater return. Third, it adds to the confidence of both researcher and client in the results. Fourth, it ensures that bias has not crept in and affected the apparent results.

However, the main reason for the concern with non-response when using the postal questionnaire is that the reason for non-response is not known. With a personal or telephone interview an impression can be formed, or even a reason obtained, for non-cooperation. With the postal method a wall of silence is all that remains. This creates the uncertainty that, in spite of great care in drawing up the sample frame, the replies received may not, after all, be typical of the Universe.

It is useful to distinguish different types of non-response. Non-receipt is a cogent reason for non-response; however, the proportion this forms of total non-response is usually very small, as indeed should be the case if adequate preparation has been given to the sample frame. In the case of one survey where separate records were kept, the total number sent out was 497 of which 9 (2 per cent) were returned 'not known here', 'gone away', or 'dead'.

A further type of non-response might be designated 'inadequate response'. The extent of this problem can be gauged from examples in Table 3·2 of surveys in the paper, packaging, and electrical industries.

Table 3.2

P.Qs sent	Returns %	Effective %	Non-Effective %
1 110	13	12	1
38	34	29	5
122	19	17	2
593	19	17	2
252	39	35	4
300	45	40	5
393	30	30	—
2 500	21	20	1

The arithmetic mean of these results is about 2 per cent non-effective replies.

3.2.9 Reasons for non-response

It is generally believed that the main reason for non-response is a lack of interest in the subject by the recipient. He cannot see really why he should fill in and return the questionnaire. Too much should not be made of this: it does not explain why a reminder produces such an increase in response, if the subsequent follow-up offers no greater incentive than the initial approach. Nevertheless, lack of identification with the purpose of the survey is felt to be the most important single reason for non-response.

Another reason for low response is the fact that the recipient is not only unwilling, but unable to answer. He may just not have the information for which he is asked. It may be that this information is not kept in an appropriate way, or that information is simply not recorded.

A further cause of low response is ambiguous questions. This is common to all forms of reseach but doubly so with postal questionnaires where no interpeter is available.

The length of the questionnaire is held by some to affect response: a long questionnaire gives the impression that much time and trouble is likely to be involved.

Apart from length, other aspects of presentation appear to have some bearing on response. A poorly printed or typed letter, a questionnaire on cheap paper, ill-considered wording, all make an impression on the recipient that is not conducive to obtaining his response.

3.2.10 Methods of overcoming non-response

The main weapons used in overcoming non-response have been touched on by implication. They are now dealt with in more detail.

(i) An adequate reason

The respondent must be encouraged to feel that he or his company will gain something from the survey. Surveys connected with new products, or products new to a particular industry, will generate more interest and response than products which have become so heavily pushed that buyers are rather tired of hearing about them. 'The respondent is likely to be particularly uncooperative if he feels that the researcher is tackling with apparent enthusiasm something which to him is old hat', to quote one authority. One consultant makes a practice of offering, with the original questionnaire, to send a summary to respondents of those findings of the survey which are relevant to their particular industry, and claims that this doubles the response rate.

(ii) The appropriate respondent

Considerable care is necessary in deciding which person in an organization is best able to provide the required information. Traditionally the buyer has been the most frequent contact, but nowadays others come within the orbit of the researcher, e.g. works engineers, organization and methods staff, operational researchers, accountants, even marketing researchers themselves!

One method that various practitioners have found helpful is to make the initial request to the managing director, chairman, or other high level appointment. A simple letter and an abbreviated questionnaire can be sent together with the request, 'Who should we contact for this information?' An adaptation is to send several copies of the full questionnaire with the original letter and request that they be passed on to the appropriate staff. This method has worked well with, for example, Town Clerks to Local Authorities where various departments possess the required data.

One problem of course is that re-routing may take some extra time and more than one follow-up. With a complex questionnaire, research by the respondent is necessary and some will take longer than others to complete this. Indeed, it is possible that the later information may be more accurate through superior effort.

(iii) Presentation and layout

Not the least important feature of the questionnaire is its first impression on the recipient. A neatly printed sheet of easily read typeface will create a better impression than a badly duplicated page of coarse paper.

The presentation falls logically into two parts:

The covering letter. This should be individually typed as well as addressed. If the former is impossible by reason of sheer numbers, then a substitute such as power-typed copies can be acceptable with carefully matched addresses. The cost may be significantly higher than a printed one, but the better results obtained are considered to be bell worth this extra expense.

The principle of establishing a personal contact as soon as possible is well illustrated by the following practical application. A study of small boat owners was conducted with the use of Lloyd's Register. Where the covering letter was addressed to the owner of the boat a 50 per cent response was achieved. However, a subsample included, with the owner's name, that of his boat; the result was a leap to 93 per cent response.

The letter must be checked by the researcher's own organization—probably a technical salesman—before piloting. This applies not only to the technical accuracy but also the appropriateness of the terms from the recipient's standpoint.

The promise of confidence can hardly harm the response rate and may improve it. Once made it must be scrupulously observed. The offer of anonymity may appear less necessary, but more objective. If the offer of anonymity may increase response, then surely it is reasonable to make it: increasing the effective rate by 10 per cent could be important.

The questionnaire. The length of the questionnaire may have a bearing on the response. Wherever possible the questionnaire should be limited to four sides of paper. One way to reduce length is to avoid asking for data that can be checked in other ways.

There is a grave danger, in seeking brevity, of cramping the questionnaire to make it appear short: the effect, in fact, is to make it obscure and difficult to fill in.

It is considered good practice to include a spare copy of the questionnaire.

The comments made above regarding the technical accuracy of the letter apply with even greater force to the questionnaire. Clear and unambiguous questions that have been carefully tested will avoid frustration and disappointment. If the recipient thinks it possible that the reply will be misleading, he is likely to join the ranks of non-respondents.

(iv) Follow-up

Of all the steps taken to increase response or reduce non-response, the follow-up or reminder is the one most likely to produce a significant result. The effect of the follow-up can be graphically illustrated, as in Figure 3·1.

The customary effect of a reminder is to produce a sudden upsurge in replies, followed by a levelling or plateau effect until the next follow-up is sent out.

Factual evidence is provided by a recent example from France. The sample covered users of certain types of steel. Two follow-ups were used at 14 days intervals with the following results. Of the total response the figures were:

Initial letter	40 per cent
1st reminder	67 per cent
2nd reminder	77 per cent.

The drawback of the follow-up is, of course, the extra time and cost it involves. If 10–14 days elapse between reminders then each will add between three and four weeks to the survey's duration when adequate time for reply has been allowed. Perhaps this serves to emphasize the value of adequate preparation of the questionnaire in the first place in order to produce the maximum response without follow-up.

(v) The effect of premiums

The use of premiums in consumer goods promotion is well known, if not accepted. When it comes to industrial surveys, opinion seems rather sharply divided. As one authority has put it: 'these do not work to improve the return of uninteresting surveys and are quite unnecessary otherwise.'

Concrete evidence on this issue, as with so many others, is scant. However, certain instances have been recorded which suggest that the use of the gift increases the response to a questionnaire. Two surveys were conducted among road haulage vehicle operators. The first took place in 1962: some 500 questionnaires were sent out to a random sample being split into two equal parts. The approach was identical save that even numbers received a ballpoint pen, which fact was referred to in the covering letter. Of the total replies received 55 per cent were from even numbers within the sample who received pens, and 45 per cent from those not receiving pens. The second postal survey was conducted in 1967. The sample was doubled to 1000 and again half were sent out with a gift—this time a small pocket knife with the company's name inscribed. The final total response was 45 per cent, compared with 72 per cent in the first case. Of the 454 replies no less than 58 per cent were from those receiving the pocket knife; when the non-effective responses were eliminated this proportion rose to 61 per cent.

3.2.11 Conclusions

The postal questionnaire as a technique for data collection for industrial market researchers has been abused and misused. There is no doubt that for the reasons discussed it will continue to be a useful tool in the marketing reseracher's chest of techniques.

3.2.12 References

1. International Chamber of Commerce (1963). *Industrial Marketing Research*, Paris. Gives a fuller discussion of horizontal and vertical market structures.
2. Pearce, F. T. (1966). *The Parameters of Research*, Industrial Marketing Research Association, Lichfield.

3.2.13 Suggestions for further reading

Bird, G. F. and Bird, K. (1958). Increasing the Response of a Mail Questionnaire. *Journal of Marketing (U.S.A.)*, October, p. 186.

Clansen, J. A. and Ford, R. N. (1947). Controlling Bias in Mail Questionnaires. *Journal of the American Statistical Association*, **42**, 497–511.

British Psychological Society (1956). Who Doesn't Answer?—A symposium on the problems of bias through non-returns in questionnaire surveys and follow up conducted by post. *Bulletin of the British Psychological Society*, **29**, 33–34.

Frankel, L. R. (1960). How Incentives and Sub-samples affect the Precision of Mail Surveys. *Journal of Advertising Research*, **1**, 1–5.

Goldstein, H. A. and Kroll, B. H. (1957). Methods of Increasing Mail Responses. *Journal of Marketing*, **22**, 55–57.

Scott, C. (1961). Research on Mail Surveys. *R.S.S. Journal, Series A*, **124**, Part 2. An important work in this field.

Shankleman, E. (1962). The Use of Postal Surveys in the Assessment of certain Characteristics of Non-Consumer Markets. *XVth E.S.O.M.A.R. Conference*, Evian.

Sergean, R. (1958). The Response of Industrial Firms to an Approach by Letter and Questionnaire. *Occupational Psychology*, **32**, 78–85.

Jackson, P. (1966). Case History Evidence of Errors associated with Non-Response in Industrial Market Research. Paper read at *Market Research Society Conference*, Eastbourne. (Private Papers).

Heads, J. and Thrift, H. J. (1966). Notes on a Study in Postal Response Rates. *Commentary*, **8**, No. 4.

Simon, R. (1967). Responses to Personal and Form Letters in Mail Surveys. *Journal of Advertising Research*, **7**, No. 1.

Cox, W. E. (Jr) (1966). Response Patterns to Mail Surveys. *Journal of Advertising Research*, **3**, No. 4.

Stanton, F. (1939). Notes on the Validity of Mail Questionnaire Returns. *Journal of Applied Psychology*, **XXIII**, No. 1.

Isaacson, H. L. *et al.* (1967). Mail Survey Research in Britain; an Experiment in Incentives. *Commentary*, November edition.

le Roux, A. A. (1968). A method of Detecting Errors of Classification by Respondents to Postal Enquiries. *Applied Statistics*, **17**, No. 1.

Swain, G. R. (1968) *Postal Questionnaires*. Industrial Marketing Research Association, Lichfield.

Baur, R. K. and Meissner, F. (1963). Structures of Mail Questionnaires: Test of Alternatives. *Public Opinion Quarterly*, **27**, 307–311.

Ognibene, P. (1971). Correcting Non-response Bias in Mail Questionnaires. *Journal of Marketing Research*, **8**, 233–235.

3.3 TELEPHONE AND PERSONAL INTERVIEWING

Throughout this section respondents have been considered to be men and interviewers to be women. This is not a manifestation of sex discrimination but in the interests of simplicity!

3.3.1 Telephone interviewing

(i) Telephone interviewing is used extensively in industrial market research, not only as an alternative interviewing method to the personal interview, but also as a preliminary to it:

To establish quickly and economically whether the sample criteria (see Chapter 4) apply or not. The type and size of a company, the type of equipment installed and details of 'end products' are examples of the information which can be obtained speedily by means of a telephone call. On the basis of this, companies can be rejected or retained in the sample for subsequent contact—either by telephone, personal interview, or by post.

To ascertain, before a postal survey (see previous section), the name and areas of responsibility of the appropriate decision maker to whom the questionnaire should be addressed and perhaps also to tell him that such a questionnaire is on its way, and encourage him to complete it when it arrives. Another effective use in postal surveys is in 'following up' non-responders. It is often possible by doing this to effect a considerable increase in the response rate.

To identify the applicable respondent and fix an appointment for a subsequent interview.

(ii) *It has many advantages*, notably:

It is much cheaper than a personal interview though more expensive than a postal survey. In addition to the fact that telephone charges are less than travel costs, the interviewer can carry out very many more telephone interviews than personal interviews in a day, because no travel time is involved.

A geographical 'spread' of interviews can be achieved without undue increase in costs, particularly if the telephone interviews are located in different regional centres thus reducing the number of trunk calls.

People can be located by telephone, and interviewed if an appointment has been made, who would be difficult to contact for a personal interview. For example, if they are mobile and working on scattered factory or other sites. Such people are of course less likely to reply to a postal enquiry.

The interviewer is able to take copious notes without the respondent seeing her doing so, and without the necessity of looking up from the notes and her interview guide or questionnaire.

The respondent can look at confidential material, or look up references during the course of the interview, which would be more difficult for him to do if the interviewer was present.

Probing to extend and clarify responses can be done, as in a personal interview. It is not of course possible to obtain such a wealth of information by such means in a postal survey.

It is possible to reach virtually all commercial and industrial establishments by telephone. This is of course not the case in consumer marketing research in the United Kingdom. Telephone calls are part of the way of life for businessmen, and although some respondents occasionally seem to be annoyed or impatient about being approached in this way, the majority enjoy it and are flattered that they have been chosen. The ringing of the telephone bell nearly always takes precedence over people in the room and therefore it is a very powerful and important technique.

(iii) *Its limitations are:*

The interview length is more restricted than in a personal interview.

Although it is reported that some structured telephone interviews lasting 40–50 minutes have been conducted they usually average about 20 minutes.

The impossibility of supplementing the information from the interview by walking round the plant and observing actual processes and machines.

The use of visual aids is not easy. Some success has been obtained by sending out carefully designed stimuli after making an appointment for a telephone interview, and asking the respondent to have them on hand during the interview.

The interviewer is not aware of all the aspects of the interview situation. For instance she does not know whether there are other people in the room, which might be causing some bias in the responses. She is also unable to be sure that the respondent is concentrating solely on the interview or whether he is doing something else at the same time.

The empathy produced by the face to face interaction of respondent and interviewer is removed. All that can be relied on is the magnetism of her voice to establish and maintain rapport and hold the respondent's interest. She cannot look him in the eye and encourage further response, and silences as probes cannot be used—respondents may think that they have been disconnected!

(iv) *Dos and don'ts*

DO get the name of the appropriate respondent at once—from the switchboard operator or by being put through to the wrong person and getting it from him.

DO stress confidentiality and IMRA/MRS Code of Conduct (See Appendix) if challenged.

DO Keep up the tempo and avoid pauses.

DO ensure that you make it possible for a call back to be made to clarify any points or to elicit more details should they be required at a later stage. Such call backs can also be used as an interviewer quality control.

DON'T give any details about the survey until you 'get your man'.

DON'T allow secretaries to put you off—be persistent and ask to 'speak to Mr. X personally'!

3.3.2 Personal interviewing

The personal interiew is the richest source of data for survey research. Carefully constructed, well-piloted questionnaires or 'checklists' of questions and, above all, well trained and adequately briefed interviewers are essential for their maximum cost effectiveness.

(i) Preliminaries to the Inteview

Briefing. Interviewers should always be personally briefed with background information and also possibly a visit to the client's factory, or pictorial or actual displays of products and equipment. All this is particularly important when the interviewers are not 'in-house', and is, of course, in addition to instruction on sampling procedures and on the questioning techniques to be used for the specific questions. It is advisable for clients, whenever possible, to attend briefings for their surveys. They often enjoy role-playing a respondent in a 'dummy' interview.

Fixing the appointments. In order to identify the appropriate decision-maker within the organization and make an appointment to interview him, it is necessary as we have seen, to make telephone contact. It is *not* usually advisable to go to an interview 'cold', that is without an appointment. The first task in appointment-making is to get the *name* of the required respondent as soon as possible. This can often be obtained from the switchboard operator. The interviewer then asks to be put through to 'Mr X' *by name.* Usually, his secretary answers the telephone and the interviewer's skill then comes into play in 'by-passing' the secretary. The best approach is usually to say, 'I must speak to Mr. X personally.' When asked, 'What's it about?' the less said to the secretary the better. A good reply is, 'It is important that I speak direct to Mr X—when will he be in?' By persisting at this stage it is usually possible to make direct contact with him. After having done this, Mr X is asked if he will grant an interview at a time and date *to suit him.* This request should be made by the interviewer in a positive, not apologetic, tone. At this stage as little as possible should be revealed about the subject of the survey. Sometimes it is necessary to say a little, but only enough to titillate his appetite for the actual interview. Sometimes, Mr X may say, 'Oh, it's not me you really want at all—its Mr Y.' In this case the interviewer apologizes and asks the switchboard to connect her to Mr Y. Once she gets through to Mr Y or his scretary, she should say, 'Mr X said that you would be able to help me, and I would like to come and see you as soon possible'—and then fix the appointment with him. Such 'referrals' are excellent introductions and are also useful when it is necessary to interview more than one decision-maker in an establishment.

Use of Authority Letters Very often, authority letters are provided for the interviewers, either by the research company or by the client. These should contain an assurance of anonymity and confidentiality in accordance with the IMRA/MRS Code of Conduct. (See Appendix). Such assurances should also be given by the interviewer whenever necessary.

If these *are* provided, the interviewer can mention this when contacting the potential respondent by telephone. Usually it is sufficient for her to bring the letter along when she comes to carry out the interview. Respondents will often ask interviewers of course, how long the interview will take. They are very busy, their time is valuable, and this is a reasonable request. The interviewer should never mislead the respondent about the possible duration of the interview. For example, if she knows that the interview length will average 40 minutes she should say it will take at least 30–40 minutes and she should *not* say, 'It will just take a few minutes of your time.' This would cause great annoyance and very possibly prevent the respondent from ever again agreeing to be interviewed.

The research company for whom the interviewer is working should provide the interviewers with visiting cards to present to the reception office. They are much more preferable than the ordinary interviewer-authority-card for this purpose. If an authority letter is brought, this should be given personally to the respondent rather than handing it in at the reception office.

(ii) General interviewing procedures

The initial approach to the respondent should be pleasant, friendly, relaxed, and one which will immediately make him feel at ease. The interview should be introduced in a businesslike way and the respondent motivated to co-operate to the utmost.

The use of tape recorders for recording interviews is a debatable issue. Experience has shown that a small cassette tape recorder is usually acceptable when it is correctly introduced. This can easily be done by saying, 'I really can't write quickly enough to get all you say down, and it will save a lot of time if I can use this. I *do* assure you that everything you say is completely confidential and the tape will only be used as an "aide-memoire".' The recorder is very soon forgotten, and the tempo and flow of the interview is greatly improved when responses do not have to be written down. The main problem is the cost of transcribing the interviews, rather than the non-acceptance of the tape recorder by the respondent or its effect on responses.

As the interview proceeds it is essential for the interviewer to maintain the respondent's interest and to avoid any sign of strain developing. Encouragement should be given throughout the interview without being patronizing. When the interview ends, whether it has been tape-recorded or not, the interviewer should close up her file and thank the respondent warmly and then very often a story will be told. This can be the respondent's real opinions which may have been suppressed, possibly because of the restraint of the technique used. This is known as the 'closed book' technique. Sometimes the story is told as the respondent escorts the interviewer into the lift, or over a cup of coffee at the end of the interview. If so, then the interviewer hurries to her car and records it!

(iii) Types of interview

In Section 3.1, the types of questionnaire used in industrial marketing research have been described. The fully structured interview is rarely used except for postal surveys, although it is frequently used in large-scale surveys in consumer marketing research. It can become a 'strait jacket' when obtaining information in some depth and complexity. On a highly technical topic, respondents certainly do not enjoy being constrained in this way. It is important to note, however, that the degree of interviewer variability is proportional to the amount of structuring. The more structured the interview, the less interviewer variability, but of course, the more structured the interview, the less rich will be the resulting data.

(iv) Use of probes in the semi-structured interview

The order and wording of the questions are predetermined in the semi-structured questionnaire. Factual questions, e.g. number of employees, turnover, etc., may be pre-coded but most of the questions are open-ended.

Non-directive probes are used to expand and clarify responses. A probe can be defined as 'any stimulus, other than a prompt, which is applied in order to obtain a response from a respondent or a more extensive or explicit expression of it.' Probes can be divided into 'expanders' and 'clarifiers'. Expander probes are destined to expand and get more extended information. These are the usual ones: 'That's interesting, can you tell me more about it?', 'What else?', 'Anything else?'.

The use of silence is a very powerful probe and it is one which interviewers find most difficult to use. After a silence very often extremely pertinent responses are obtained. Expectant noises: 'uh, huh' which can sound differently when put over by different interviewers are also useful expanders. They let the respondent know the interviewer is still listening and encourage him to enlarge on his previous response.

It is possible to use a summary as an expander: for example, 'You've been telling me this, this, and this, what else do you think ...?' The 'playback' is also a useful expander probe. This involves the repeating of the respondent's last few words in an interrogatory tone of voice. Playbacks may also be used by repeating words used earlier by the respondent, 'You were saying ..., what else can you tell me about that?'

Clarifying probes are necessary when vague responses are given. The simplest form of clarifying probe is to repeat the question in its entirety. This has to be done when the respondent has obviously not understood the question or the response he gives does not answer the question. In industrial interviewing, care has to be taken when doing this so that the respondent is not annoyed. Other clarifying probes which can be used are, 'in what way ...?' or 'I wonder what you mean by ...?'

Some of the questions on a semi-structured questionnaire are often pre-coded, for example factual ones about the number of employees, amount of turnover, and so on. Even so, interviewer variability is very much greater in this type of interview than in the purely structured one.

(v) Use of probes in the depth or focused interview

In the depth interview the interviewer is provided with a guide listing topics to be covered, and she formulates her own questions. The interview can begin at any point but it is preferable that the first question should be a very general one which is likely to arouse the respondent's interest and motivate the respondent to communicate and discuss his feelings freely and fully. The interviewer should then become a passive listener guiding the respondent through the interview, listening attentively throughout and reacting to cues. The respondent should be allowed to talk at length, if possible, for as long as possible without interruption. Some points which may need amplification and expansion could come up in answer to the opening question, but the flow should not be interrupted and the interviewer should take them up later in the interview if they have not by then already been developed and explored. A useful way of bringing them out at that stage is by repeating the previous actual words of the respondent with a rising inflection and then a pause, 'You said ....' The unstructured interview should never be allowed to develop into a 'question and answer' process. Allowing the respondent to continue with his answer to the first question, without interruption, helps to ensure this. Continuity in the interview can be assisted by the interviewer merely saying 'uh, huh', which is neutral. It does, however, provide encouragement to the respondent.

In order to maintain the flow and tempo of the interview the interviewer should avoid new subjects, but the respondent should be given every opportunity to bring them up himself. It is necessary for the interviewer to 'recap' on important points directly related to the research objectives detailed in the interview guide which may not have been sufficiently developed. The question, 'Why?' should be avoided. It is usually possible to do this by using one of the probing techniques already described. These can also be used where appropriate in group discussions, which will be described later (Section 3.4).Clarification of vague responses should also be carried out, but a suitable break in the flow should be used for such elucidation to avoid breaking the respondent's train of thought.

In unstructured interviews, as in group discussions, the less the interviewer says, and the fewer interruptions there are, the more fruitful the results are likely to be. After each topic has been thoroughly explored other leads can be taken up, clarifying, and, where necessary, validating the information already given. This may be done indirectly perhaps by asking the question in a different way. Inconsistency should be challenged, but not in an aggressive, interrogatory way. A useful way of challenging inconsistencies is to say, 'Oh, I'm very sorry, I must have misunderstood you, I thought you said ....'

It is necessary in this type of interview for the interviewer to interpret the information as she goes along, listening for cues and influencing the next progression without appearing to control the interview in any way. This type of interview is the one which is most commonly used by 'in-house' interviewers. Their knowledge of the market is a great advantage, enabling them to have a detailed discussion with the respondent on common ground. The possibility of a 'threat' situation, of course, in these cases, is possible, but most 'in-house' interviewers are aware of this and many of the people they interview are familiar with their company and are fully aware that the interviewers *are* technical specialists. The informality and freedom of such interviews tends to minimize strain or anxiety which might arise in some interview situations and creates a more relaxed atmosphere. The interviewer is also able to be much more flexible than in more structured interviewing and can change direction quickly and approach subjects from a different angle if the respondent seems to be having difficulty in understanding or in verbalizing his ideas. The main disadvantage, apart from the problem of actually writing down all the responses if they are not tape recorded, is that there is the danger of bias and interviewer variability.

(vi) Dos and don'ts

DO hand in a visiting card to the receptionist on arrival, giving the authority letter, if provided, to the respondent.

DO make your initial approach friendly and relaxed.

DO then introduce the interview in a businesslike, positive way.

DO motivate the respondent to cooperate fully from the outset.

DO hold the respondent's interest and attention by keeping up the tempo and flow.

DO encourage the respondent.

DO ask the respondent at the end of the interview if you may telephone him if necessary to confirm points for the report.

DO thank the respondent at the end of the interview, close your folder—and wait—a further 'story', hitherto suppressed, may then emerge.

DO send a 'thank you' letter to the respondent.

DON'T say 'Do you mind' OR HE WILL!

DON'T mislead the respondent about the duration of the interview.

DON'T ever break an appointment or arrive late.

DON'T indicate your own views.

DON'T be patronizing—or opinionated!

DON'T pause unnecessarily between questions.

3.3.3 Suggestions for further reading

MacFarlane Smith, J. (1972). *Interviewing in Marketing and Social Research*, Routledge and Kegan Paul, London.

Zattman, G. and Burger, P. C. (1975). *Marketing Research—Fundamentals and Dynamics*, The Dryden Press, North Elm, Hinsdale, Illinois.

3.4 GROUP DISCUSSIONS AND THEIR VALUE IN IMR

Group discussions can be described as 'the interviewing of a number of people at the same time where the response of individuals resulting from their association is sought.' They are used very often in consumer research as a preliminary to a quantified survey by indicating the language actually used when discussing the topic informally and facilitating the construction of a questionnaire for piloting and pre-testing. Sometimes they are used as an end in themselves and may result in a decision not to proceed with the research. Experience has shown they are also valuable in industrial research. Ideas are brought out in the dynamic group situation which cannot be elicited by other methods. Examples of their use include:

For 'internal' company or group attitude research studies concerning:
- personnel selection and executive recruitment;
- internal group and house publications.

For 'external' attitude research studies concerning:
- company image;
- existing and proposed services;
- technical and professional media;
- new product development;
- industrial advertising, e.g. awareness;
- copy testing—new campaigns.

Stimuli (range of existing and new products and/or adverts) are produced at end of discussion.

The method of recruitment is usually first a telephone fact-finding call, then a telephoned invitation followed up by a confirmatory written invitation, and then a telephone call on the day of the discussion. An incentive is offered—usually a bottle of sherry or spirits!

Group discussions are usually held in the early evening—lunchtime ones being less satisfactory because of the time constraint. Drinks, buffet food, or sandwiches are served on arrival and every effort is made to create a relaxed atmostphere. A room in a hotel either in a city centre or close to a large industrial area is the most suitable venue.

The group leader, who should be a skilled and experienced 'outside' practitioner, is provided with a list of topics to be covered. He controls and guides the discussion unobtrusively. The pace of the discussion soon increases, and the leader is forgotten.

Group discussions are usually tape recorded and may be video-taped. The group leader should stress confidentiality and that the tape will be used only in the compilation of the final report.

3.5 USE OF 'IN-HOUSE' PERSONNEL VERSUS OUTSIDE FIELDWORK AGENCIES FOR INTERVIEWING

The decision on the use of internal company personnel or outside fieldwork agencies is often one of the most controversial, and certainly critical, in undertaking marketing research surveys which require fieldwork.

A typical situation requiring this decision would be one in which the 'in-house' market research unit is required to undertake a market survey, involving an extensive fieldwork exercise, for a product which it is intended to market in more than one country. The 'in-house' market research unit usually has sufficient expertise to:

(a) Draw up and agree with management the terms of reference for the survey.

(b) Undertake the desk research from both internal and external records.

(c) Construct a sample frame.

(d) Prepare a questionnaire and test it on a small sample of say 6 or less, depending on the sample size.

At this juncture it is unlikely that the average medium sized industrial company has a large enough market research department to undertake a survey which requires 40 or more in-depth personal or telephone interviews in the time allotted, particularly when the survey requires overseas travel and/or linguistic abilities. There are of course medium sized industrial companies which are subsidiaries of larger Corporations where the parent company offers a 'Group Marketing Research' service to the subsidiary companies. These are classed as 'in-house' personnel although they may act as consultants to the subsidiaries on a fee-paying basis.

Wholly 'in-house' surveys, which require extensive fieldwork, can only be contemplated by the larger companies who have invested sufficient funds in their own IMR function. Even these 'in-house' marketing research units have limitations or considerations which may necessitate the use of external fieldwork agencies.

The following points should be evaluated by the internal marketing researcher before arriving at the final decision to use internal or external fieldworkers.

(a) *Product/industry knowledge* Undoubtedly the industrial 'in-house' marketing researcher will have a far better understanding of his company's product range and possibly the competitors' product ranges, since part of the 'in-house' function on an on-going basis is the evaluation of his company's strengths and weaknesses measured against the competition. Included under the heading 'product knowledge' is the supporting knowledge and expertise, often technical in nature, which includes the understanding of jargon and terminology used by both the manufacturer and customer to describe the product and its applications. Care is required, however, not to overwhelm the respondent in the interview situation with excessive technical knowledge. The respondent may feel he is being criticized or even being made to feel inferior, and this may cause him to withhold important information.

Against this, fieldwork agencies often specialize in undertaking work on particular groups of products or industries and hence acquire this knowledge from a wide range of manufacturers.

(b) *Market knowledge* The experienced 'in-house' marketing researcher should have a good background knowledge of the market within which his company operates: with established contacts at major customers, relevant Trade Associations, and competitors. This, combined with an understanding of government and national statistics covering the market, leads to a strong position, compared with that of an external agency, when new work is being contemplated.

However, the specialist external agency can usually offer a greater knowledge of the market than the 'in-house' researcher when dealing with new products/markets and diversification studies. Also when undertaking multi-national surveys the agencies can offer the added advantage of linguistic capabilities.

(c) *Bias* This is one of the strongest arguments in favour of the use of external agencies and consultants generally. The need to eliminate bias is often expressed by management as a need for an independent or alternative survey in addition to, or instead of, an 'in-house' company survey.

The market researcher, be he employed 'in-house' or by agencies/consultants, should at all times remain objective; but there is no doubt that there is more pressure and opportunity to introduce a bias into market surveys when they are undertaken 'in-house'. Certainly the use of untrained, inexperienced 'in-house' personnel to undertake fieldwork should be avoided at all times, no matter how great the pressure from management to 'cut costs and utilize available internal non-marketing research personnel'.

Indeed, where salesmen have been used as interviewers they have tended to avoid asking questions to which the customer would think that the salesmen would already know the answer. Instead the salesmen answered the questions themselves! This illustrates the fact that the role of salesman–customer is very different from that of the interviewer–respondent.

(d) *Time* In situations where there is no urgency or short deadline for a survey the 'in-house' marketing research unit can usually cope. Quite often though the 'in-house' unit is overloaded or there is some urgency for a large market survey. From experience, most fieldwork agencies have the capacity to respond quickly to requests for major fieldwork exercises on short deadlines which would tie up the 'in-house' unit for a long period. In addition, the agencies have interviewers who are strategically located.

(e) *Anonymity and confidentiality* There are two aspects to anonymity. Firstly, the non-disclosure of the company's name: for instance where there is research to be undertaken on a new product or in an acquisition study. This makes it virtually impossible for the 'in-house' unit to conduct fieldwork, whereas an agency may achieve results. However, it must be remembered that the request for anonymity does restrict the response rate and level of cooperation which can be expected from the fieldwork. Thus it will introduce a significant statistical bias to the sample.

The second aspect is the unwillingness of respondents to disclose information to 'in-house' marketing researchers, particularly concerning consumption of competitive products. On the other hand the respondent may disclose such information to an agency providing that it is only used to derive totals and that specific company consumption detail is withheld. However, this also is a two-edged argument, since from experience many respondents are often prepared to talk in more detail and more freely to a representative of a reputable supplier believing that his comments may help to improve the product supply situation and improve supplier–customer goodwill.

(f) *Cost* It must be remembered that external agencies are in business to make a profit, and good marketing research is not procured cheaply. (See Section 11.2 for points to watch out for when commissioning an outside agency/consultant.)
With the majority of surveys it is usually cheaper to undertake survey work utilizing 'in-house' personnel. However, if the company can acquire the desired information by participating in a multi-client survey (see Section 11.3) then the cost of the information is often below that of the 'in-house' level.

(g) *Control* Many companies make a great deal of the fact that they have control of 'in-house' personnel, whereas an external interviewer is 'on his own'. In fact, once the interviewer is in the field and provided the IMRA/MRS Code of Conduct is followed there is little difference between the two.

So summarizing, the advantages of using an outside fieldwork agency are:

They can offer special skills and trained interviewers speaking the required languages.

They have the capacity to cope with larger-scale projects.

The locations of their interviewers are geographically spread.

Their assurance of confidentiality and anonymity may be more convincing.

They should obtain more truthful and critical answers and will certainly be less biased.

They are more readily perceived, parti' answers.
There are, however, disadvantages:

Their cost in terms of direct 'out of pocket' expenditure.

They may have little or no specific product/industry knowledge.

The lack of day to day control by the commissioning company.

These then are the points to be resolved and, depending on the nature of the project, the workload at the time, the state of the budget, etc., a decision will be made whether to opt for an outside agency or carry out the work using resources from 'in-house'.

Chapter 4

Sample Surveys in Industrial Markets

In the last chapter we dealt with the techniques used in surveys. To be strictly correct, we should use the term 'social surveys' to emphasize the fact that we are gathering information from people who will supply the data required either by returning a questionnaire or by answering questions on the telephone or at a personal interview. It has not been necessary so far to distinguish between a survey where the whole population is questioned (also called a 'census') and a survey where only a part of the population is questioned (also called a 'sample survey').

In this chapter we shall be making this distinction because the technique of sampling is useful and sometimes necessary in conducting IMR.

4.1 INTRODUCTION

Most people have an intuitive grasp of the principles of sampling, based on their everyday experience. 'Shake the mixture before use', for instance, is good advice to ensure that the sediment is evenly distributed, and that the tablespoonful when taken is in the same proportions as the prescription made up by the chemist. In statistical language, the sample should be truly representative of the population. Another example is the drawing of numbers from a hat to decide a winner. The hat is given a good shake to ensure that each number has the same chance of being drawn. Each entrant, therefore, has an equal probability of winning the prize. Also, to eliminate bias, the person making the draw is blindfolded so that he cannot see his own number and thus take an unfair advantage.

In these few sentences, then, we have already stated some of the basic principles of sampling. What we need is to discuss the subject in a logical and quantified manner so that it may be used in marketing research. If we do not do this, we may draw the wrong inferences from our procedure. If, for instance, from a list of 100 companies we select one and find that it uses ceramic tool tips, we are not entitled to assume that they all use ceramic tool tips. But if we select 10 companies at random (shaking the hat) and find that 5 use ceramic tool tips, we are entitled to assume that 50% of the 100 companies do use them, give or take a few. It is that last phrase that causes the difficulty, 'give or take a few'. We need to quantify our procedure.

4.2 WHY SHOULD WE SAMPLE?

We should sample for the same reason that we do anything else in life, either because we have to or because we expect some benefit.

If we send out a questionnaire and we get an $x\%$ response then, whether intended or not, we have taken a sample of $x\%$ from the people to whom we sent the questionnaire. Since few questionnaires give a 100% response (at least by mail) we can generalize by saying that questionnaires usually involve us in unavoidable sampling. We shall see later what kinds of error thus arise.

As for the advantages of sampling, it is rather obvious that it saves time and money. In some cases it can give a more accurate answer, in other cases it can give a quicker answer, and in even more cases a cheaper answer. The technique of sampling, then, should be familiar to marketing researchers, even though they may not in practice master the technique or use it.

It is a fact that many industrial surveys (perhaps the majority) do not use a formalized sampling technique. Marketing researchers often use the '80–20' rule, which is a generalization that in many markets 20% of the firms produce or consume 80% of the product. The researcher uses his judgment to select the vital 20%, which may be no more than a dozen firms, and concentrates his survey on those only, reasoning that he can thus cover 80% of the market more thoroughly than if he attempted to survey all the firms in the market. This is a judgment, or selective sample, and in the right hands can give results equally as satisfactory as random sampling, in which each firm has a known chance of being selected. However, only the latter method is amenable to statistical analysis.

4.3 PRINCIPAL STEPS IN A SAMPLE SURVEY

This list of steps in designing and executing a sample survey is drawn primarily from Cochran.[1] Most of the steps are also applicable to a complete enumeration or to a judgment survey. Some of the terms used in sampling theory will be defined.

4.3.1 Objective of the survey

A survey should begin with a lucid statement of the objective, such as, 'How many firms use ceramic tool tips?'. This will involve discussions with informed and interested parties, a review of the relevant literature, of existing statistics, and the requirements of the sponsor. This may need much re-formulation of the objective, such as, 'How many firms in the U.K. use ceramic tool tips?' or 'How many firms in the U.K. use disposable ceramic tool tips?'. Mastery of the technology of the subject is imperative at the earliest stage lest important factors are overlooked.

4.3.2 Population to be sampled

Statisticians are usually precise in their use of words as well as numbers. However, the literature does not seem to be agreed on the meanings of the terms 'Universe' and 'Population'. Some authors think they are synonymous, others think that Universe is an obsolete term for Population, while still others drop the term Universe and use instead Physical Population and Statistical Population.[2] However, marketing researchers could well adopt the definitions given by Ostle[3] because they emphasize a very important concept. In these definitions, the Universe is a specified group of 'objects', such as people, households, or firms, from which a Population of numbers can be extracted. For instance, a Universe of 6000 selected firms in the U.K. (which is not the total number of firms in the U.K.) can give many different populations of numbers, such as the number of employees in each firm, the annual turnover, the capital employed, etc. When a sample is drawn, it may be drawn either from the Universe or from the population of numbers which has already been derived from the Universe. Whether the sample is drawn from the Universe or the population, there will be no difference in the results. The drawing of the sample from the one or the other is merely dependent on whether the elements comprising the Universe have been 'measured' before of after the sample is drawn.

A simple illustration makes this clear. If we compile a list of addresses of all the elements in the Universe (this defines 'list') which in this case will be 6000 companies, and we then sample 100 of them, we can then question the 100 firms to obtain the sample data. Alternatively, if the data pertaining to the 6000 companies are already available on file, we can sample the population of numbers by selecting 100 pieces of data from the file. Obviously, one would adopt that procedure which minimizes effort. In the one case we do not need to compile a list of 6000 companies because the 6000 pieces of data are already on file, and in the other case we do not extract 5900 pieces of data which will never be used. If this point is agreed, we can henceforth use the phrase 'sampling the population' to cover both methods, it being understood that either method can be used as a matter of practical convenience. It also simplifies matters as all textbooks commonly use this phrase.

The statistician thinks of a population as a population of numbers (attributes will be discussed later), from which a sample of numbers will be drawn, in a similar manner to our previous illustration of drawing numbers from a hat. Given the population of numbers, the sample, and the method by which it was drawn, the statistician can use highly elegant theories to arrive at probabilistic conclusions, but if there is an imperfect correspondence between the Universe and the population, the results will be unrealistic. As an example, there has been endless trouble in trying to assess national R&D expenditures. The Universe of firms is known, but the population of numbers is extremely difficult to define because each firm seems to have its own idea of what constitutes R&D, and what expenditure should properly be attributed to it.

If there were to be a division of labour, it would be the marketing researcher's job to define the Universe, compile the list, and extract a homogeneous population of numbers which correspond exactly to what he wants to know about the Universe. The statistician would then be concerned with devising a method of sampling which gave the required precision for the minimum cost, and for analysing the results, drawing the conclusions, and testing them.

4.3.3 Data to be collected

Care is needed to verify that all the relevant data are included and no essential data omitted. One may, for instance, wish to specify 'all ceramic tool tips costing less than £10', or 'all ceramic tool tips purchased directly from the manufacturer'.

4.3.4 Degree of precision required

The degree of precision obtainable in a survey is a combination of the statistical error and the systematic error. Systematic error is also called bias. Many authorities believe that the error due to bias is larger than the statistical error due to sampling, but this will be treated in greater detail later. The last word on the degree of precision required must rest with the sponsor of the survey, and the issue must be placed squarely before him at the planning stage.

4.3.5 Methods of measurement

By this we mean 'how do we extract the data required from the sample drawn from the list?'. We may for instance sample 500 addresses from the list of 6000 and then get the data from those 500 firms. The primary measuring instrument is the question, although other indirect methods may be used. The marketing researcher can be expected to be familiar with mail questionnaires, telephone interviews, and visits.

4.3.6 The list

This has already been defined. The term 'Frame' is sometimes used rather than 'List' as having a slightly less restricted connotation—for example, maps can be used as sampling frames. The compilation of a list is work that is frankly dull, exacting, and frustrating, but nevertheless of cardinal importance since the list is the foundation on which the whole survey stands.

4.3.7 Method of selecting the sample

This is the only area which is almost exclusively the province of the statistician. Various methods will be described later. It is this topic which often appears most baffling to the beginner, but it must be remembered that this is a branch of applied mathematics which has been developed by long and frequent usage in scientific disciplines such as agriculture and medicine. If it is any consolation to the marketing researcher only an elementary understanding of these principles is required. Anything deeper should be left to the statistician.

4.3.8 The pre-test

This may be necessary in order to get some information for the statistician if nothing whatever is known about the population beforehand. It may also be a pilot run for the main survey, designed to show up ambiguities in questions, and test the methods of coding and analysis.

4.3.9 Organization of the fieldwork

These problems are mainly administrative, but competent organization of the fieldwork can give useful reductions in cost.

4.3.10 Summary and analysis of the data

The completed questionnaire must be edited both to amend obvious recording errors by the respondent and if possible to detect erroneous data resulting from misunderstandings. It will sometimes be necessary to refer to the respondent and ask questions such as, 'Are you sure these were your annual sales and not your monthly sales?' The disadvantage of an anonymous questionnaire is immediately apparent. It is imperative to check the input data.

4.4 PRECISION OF THE SURVEY

The precision of the survey is made up of the sampling error (statistical) and the systematic error (bias). Figure 4.1 shows in an illustrative way how the cost of a survey varies with the precision required. A typical survey, as represented by the line AD, shows that as the accuracy increases the cost also increases. The total error is the

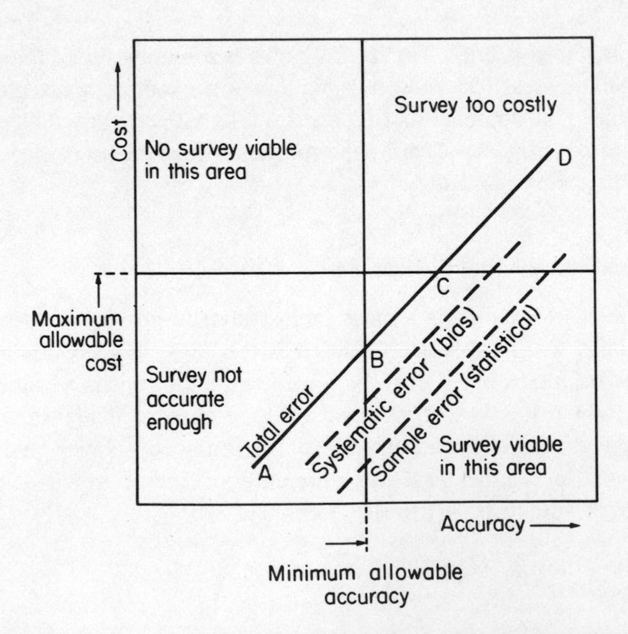

Figure 4.1 Sample surveys are viable only in the bottom right-hand quadrant. AB—survey can be done but no use; CD—survey useful but too costly; BC—survey useful and possible

sum of the systematic error and the sample error. The systematic error is shown as larger than the sample error because many authorities believe that systematic error is always the larger of the two. The diagram can be divided into four quadrants by a vertical line giving the minimum allowable accuracy and a horizontal line giving the maximum allowable cost. In the top left-hand quadrant no survey would be viable because it would be too costly and insufficiently accurate. In the bottom left-hand quadrant the survey is within the cost limit but still not accurate enough. Only in the bottom right-hand quadrant is the survey both useful and possible. This corresponds to the portion BC of the line AD. We can see therefore that the reduction of both types of error can make a survey viable, and we will therefore discuss in turn systematic error and sample error.

4.5 BIAS IN SAMPLING (SYSTEMATIC ERROR)

This section is drawn primarily from Edwards-Deming.[4] Twelve factors are listed which could affect the ultimate usefulness of a survey.

(i) Variability in response

There are two kinds of variability in response: (*a*) that which is given by the same person at two different times; and (*b*) that given by different persons. Both kinds of error are often much greater than is ordinarily supposed. An example of the second kind of variability in response is the discrepancy between duplicate reports of the occupations of workers, one report coming from the worker himself and the other coming from the worker's employer. Edwards-Deming points out that this type of error is one of the reasons why even 100% coverage cannot give absolute accuracy. This latter term is, in fact, non-definable. If one were to make two surveys, both of them having 100% coverage, the variability of response would make the results of one survey differ from its identical succeeding one.

(ii) Differences between different kinds and degrees of canvass

Differences are obtained between postal, telephone, and interview canvasses. The problem is not whether differences exist but how great are the differences and why they do exist.

(iii) Bias and variation arising from the interviewer

Variation attributable to the interviewer arises from many factors: the political, religious, and social beliefs of the interviewer; his economic status, environment, and education. Another source of bias arises in the interviewer having a lack of understanding of the subject under investigation and its purpose, without which the interviewer cannot evaluate a situation or properly record the respondent's statements.

(iv) Bias caused by the sponsor's 'image'

It is also well recognized that both government and private organizations sometimes attempt to hide their identities by subcontracting the collection of data, so that the respondents will be unaware of the sponsoring agency.

(v) Imperfections in the design of the questionnaire and tabulation plans

Faulty design of the questions, which can be a considerable cause of bias, often arises from lack of knowledge of the subject matter and the possible different replies from the respondent. Many jokes are based on deliberately ambiguous questions! Ambiguity often arises from misguided attempts at brevity.

(vi) Changes that take place in the Universe before tabulations are available

One may be assessing the market-share for product X, but if during the survey another competitive product Y reaches the market, the assessment will be in error.

✓ *(vii) Bias arising from non-response*

It is curious how many fail to see that non-response can cause a very large bias. Why do people not return questionnaires? One cause has already been discussed under (iv). Another cause of non-response is the failure to address the questionnaire to the appropriate source of data in the firm. This may cause a bias due to a late return (see viii). It is not sufficiently appreciated that a 70% response on a complete coverage may be unusable, whereas a 95% response on a 10% sample can be quite useful.

✓ *(viii) Bias arising from late returns*

See also item (vii). This form of non-response is not strictly speaking attributable to the non-respondent but to the inability to process delayed reports because of the necessity for a 'cut-off'.

(ix) Bias arising from an unrepresentative selection of data for the survey, or for the period covered

The problem here is one of seasonal variation in purchasing, such as for airline tickets which peak during the holiday season. It is probably of most relevance to researchers estimating derived demand where the derived demand is seasonal in nature.

(x) Bias arising from an unrepresentative selection of respondents

This can arise from the inability to compile a satisfactory list of the Universe. Another possibility is an unrepresentative choice of respondents which often arises as a matter of convenience to the interviewer, or his inability to cover the whole list, e.g. those at home and abroad. It often arises also in the 'invitation questionnaire' where a patron of the goods or service is supplied with a questionnaire asking for comments. The returns show only the extremes in satisfaction or vexation, and that only from the articulate.

(xi) Processing errors

These may range from a simple error in recording to a major difference of opinion between the respondent and the coder. Two coders working on the same set of schedules will give different sets of results.

(xii) Errors in interpretation

Errors and differences in interpretation often arise from a misunderstanding of the question, either on the part of the interviewer or the respondent.

4.6 STATISTICS OF SAMPLING AND SAMPLE SIZE

We turn now to the other source of error described in Figure 4.1 : statistical error due to sampling, and also the determination of the optimum sample size. Before going any further it should be pointed out that the use of analytical methods of determining the optimum sample size may not be possible because they require: (a) some foreknowledge of the population; and (b) the sponsor to state the degree of accuracy required and to justify his requirement for that accuracy. Also, it is necessary to distinguish carefully between the different methods of sampling, because the statistical treatment varies between one method and another.

All methods of sampling can be classified into either 'random' or 'non-random'. Only random methods are amenable to statistical analysis. Non-random methods are called judgment, or selective samples, because, unlike the drawing of numbers from a hat, the sample is selected with a purpose in mind. This does not imply that there is no rationality in selective sampling, or that it is not done in a highly organized way. In quota sampling, for instance, each interviewer is given a quota of firms to interview, e.g. so many engineering firms, so many textile firms, so many chemical firms, etc. The choice of which particular firm to interview is then left to the interviewer. This method is usually more economical than other sampling methods, firstly because it is easier to administer, secondly because each interviewing expert can deal with his own particular industry, and thirdly because there are fewer follow-ups. It will however give biased samples and it is impossible to apply statistics to calculate sampling errors. It is a method, however, which may have to be used if one is doing an international survey.

4.6.1 Random sampling

Random sampling does not mean haphazard sampling. It is a term used by the statistician to mean that each member of the population has a calculable and non-zero probability of selection. We need to distinguish between three different methods of random sampling.

(i) Sampling without replacement from an infinite population

The term "infinite population' refers to one which is inexhaustible. If for instance we were to sample a uniformly distributed population of the single digit numbers from 0 to 9, taking as a sample one digit at a time, it is clear that the population is inexhaustible, and therefore, as a concept, infinite. As another example, the population may be so large that it can be regarded for the purposes of the survey as being infinite, although in fact it is not so.

(ii) Sampling with replacement from a finite population

As an example, let us consider the sampling of a pack of playing cards, one card being drawn at a time as a sample, its denomination noted, and the card then returned to the pack before the next card is drawn. It is clear that the population being sampled is always 52 playing cards, and for no matter how long the sampling is continued the population remains constant, or inexhaustible. The population is therefore, as a concept, infinite, and the same statistical treatment can be applied as in case (i) above. However, it may be thought that the sample will not be representative of the population, because the same card, e.g. the Queen of Hearts, could be drawn more than once, yet the cards in the pack each have a unique identity. It must be remembered that although we are physically sampling from a finite population of 52 cards, we are effectively sampling from an infinitely large pack of cards which contains an infinite number of Queens of Hearts. There is really no difference here from the previous example of selecting single digits from 0 to 9, where each digit is written on a card, and the card after sampling is returned to the population.

The term 'representative' can cause a great deal of philosophical argument, and yet most people have an intuitive grasp of what it means. It is that the sample shall be a microcosm, or miniature, of the population, in which each part of the population is present, or 'represented', but not 'over-represented'. As applied to parliamentary democracy, the term is quite clear. Each electoral constituency has one, and only one, representative in Parliament.

Because of this difficulty of representativeness, the marketing researcher is not recommended to use the method of random sampling with replacement, although, as a method, it is based on impeccable statistical theory. It is better to retain the intuitive concept of representativeness but use the modified theory of sampling without replacement.

(iii) Sampling without replacement from a finite population

In using this method, we select a sample from the population and retain it so that it cannot be selected again. If for instance we have a long list of firms and we randomly select one firm from the list, we then delete that firm from the list before taking the next sample.

However, it can be argued that once again we may not get a representative sample because a complete sector of the population may be omitted, purely by chance. This is undoubtedly correct, and is one of the reasons for adopting stratified random sampling. This is a variant in which the population is stratified before sampling, e.g. into SIC (or NACE) classification, and each stratum, or classification, is then sampled independently. In this way we ensure that all sectors in the population are represented in the sample. A further refinement is that the statistician can sometimes arrange the procedure so that stratification can increase the precision.

Simple random sampling is a technical term used for any random sampling method in which each member of the population has an equal chance of being selected. 'Simple' is not used as an adjective in the ordinary sense of the word, i.e. the opposite of complex.

Clearly, sampling methods (i) and (ii) above are simple random methods, whereas (iii) is not, and, therefore, the latter is properly referred to as 'random sampling'. However, method (iii) is no more complex in practice than the other two methods.

4.6.2 Random sampling (without replacement) from the list, using random numbers

Let us assume we have defined the Universe and that we have compiled a satisfactory list. Let this list of firms be numbered serially from 0 to N, where $(N + 1)$ is the number of firms on the list. The firms on the list may be arranged in any order, e.g. alphabetically or geographically, etc. We need to sample the numbers, each of which represents a particular firm.

Physically, there are many different ways of sampling a population of numbers from 0 to N. All of them have disadvantages. We may for instance write each number on a slip of paper, each slip of paper being of the same size, weight, colour, and texture, and we may put all of these slips of paper into a rotating drum to mix them thoroughly before drawing one at random. Or we could perhaps use a 10-sided die, or a roulette wheel, or a spinning pointer. Each method depends for its freedom from bias on the exactitude of mechanical construction, which is never perfect. Each method, before use, should be thoroughly tested to ensure the sample is strictly random. Such methods are lengthy and time-consuming.

It is for these reasons that we choose to select the sample by selecting, or generating, random numbers from 0 to N. When a random number in the specified range is selected, the firm on the list which has that number is selected for the sample (if more than one in the sample) and the same firm is then deleted from the list. We can use random numbers from tables such as *A Million Random Digits* (The Rand Corporation, 1955), in which case tests for randomness will have been made on the tables, and they are therefore termed 'true random numbers'. Alternatively, random numbers can be generated using mathematical functions, in which case, although believed to be random, they have not been tested for randomness, and hence are termed 'pseudo-random numbers'. In practice there is no perceptible difference between the two, although the statistician would naturally prefer to use only tested methods.

4.6.3 Two procedures for obtaining integer random numbers in the range 0 to N

(i) True random numbers can be obtained from tables. To obtain an integer random number in the range 0 to N, select a series of digits from the table to make a number which has the same number of digits as N itself. Express this random number as a decimal fraction. Multiply the decimal fraction by $N + 1$ and take the integer part of the result. The number so obtained will be that which is required.

Example To find an integer random number in the range 0 to 1700.

(a) Select 4 digits to form a 4 digit number. Say 3824.

(b) Express this as a decimal fraction, 0·3824.

(c) Multiply 0·3824 by 1701.

(d) The result is 650·4624.

(e) The integer of this number is 650, which is the number required.

(f) Repeat for as many random numbers as required. They will all lie within the range 0–1700.

(ii) Alternatively, with an electronic calculator generate the uniformly distributed pseudo-random number using the previously generated number X_i using:

$$\text{decimal portion}\left[\left(X_i+\frac{11}{87}\right)\times 87\right].$$

a pseudo-random seed between 0 and 1 is needed to initialize the procedure. A typical seed is $1/\pi$. The seed should contain as many digits as in R (the random number) itself, although as a precaution it is best to take a seed with $(R + 1)$ digits and discard the last digit of the random number in case there is any tendency for it to be cyclic. Then, as above, to obtain an integer random number in the range 0 to N, multiply the decimal portion by $(N + 1)$ and take the integer part of the result. This will be an integer pseudo-random number in the range 0–N. The whole calculation can be set up in less than 200 steps on a programmable calculator. It is available on a cartridge for the Tektronix 31 programmable calculator.

4.6.4 Statistical theory of random sampling (without replacement)

(i) Sampling a continuous variable

Let us take an example of 1000 firms using ceramic tool tips. The Universe is 1000 firms, the population is the 1000 numbers representing their weekly usage of tool tips, the average of these 1000 numbers is μ and their variance is σ^2. The standard deviation of the population is σ.

The population parameters of concern to us here are therefore:

$N = 1000$

$\mu = ?$

$\sigma = ?$

If the population of numbers were known, we could calculate μ and σ from:

$$\mu = \frac{\sum X}{N}$$

and

$$\sigma^2 = \frac{\sum \Delta^2}{N-1}$$

where X is any of the 1000 numbers and Δ is the deviation of X from the population mean μ. The variance of a finite population is usually expressed with a divisor of N instead of $(N-1)$, but the convention of using $(N-1)$ has been used by those who approach sampling theory by means of the analysis of variance.[1] Its advantage is that most results take a slightly simpler form. This convention of using a divisor of $(N-1)$ is adopted here, and provided that the same notation is maintained consistently, all results are equivalent in either notation.

Now we do not know μ and σ, and we wish to estimate their values by taking a sample. Having estimated μ and σ, we can find the total market demand, $D = N\mu$ and we can estimate the precision of D.

Let us take a random sample of 100 firms, and let this number be n. Let the average m of these 100 numbers be 9 say, and let the standard deviation s be 3 say.

The corresponding sample statistics are therefore:

$n = 100$

$m = 9$

$s = 3$.

These values are calculated in the same way as for the population above, i.e.

$$m = \frac{\sum X}{n}$$

and

$$s^2 = \frac{\sum \Delta^2}{n-1}$$

where X is now any of the 100 numbers in the sample and Δ is the deviation of any of these numbers from the sample mean m.

When the population parameters and the sample statistics are calculated in this way, statistical theory tells us:

(*a*) m_i is an unbiased estimator of μ. By this statement, we mean that if a large number of samples are taken, the samples having means of m_1, m_2, m_i, etc., it will be found that the average of the m_i is, in the long run, equal to μ. We may also note that as we increase the size of n towards its maximum value of N ($n \Rightarrow N$) the value of m converges to μ. It is obvious that in the limiting case when $n = N$, m_i must equal μ. This second property is known as consistency.

(*b*) s^2 is an unbiased estimator of σ^2. This statement has an exactly analogous meaning to that given above. Strictly speaking, this second statement is only applicable to s^2 and σ^2; for s and σ it is only approximately true—the degree of approximation depending on the sample size.

Let us now take many different samples of size 100 from our population of 1000 numbers. We now have another set of numbers denoted as above by m_1, m_2, m_3, etc. Let the number of samples taken be ν. The maximum number of distinct samples that we can take is simply the number of ways in which n can be selected from N, given by:

$$\nu_{max} = \frac{N!}{n!(N-n)!}.$$

In our sample of the means we have, therefore, ν numbers with a·mean of say M and a variance V^2. We now have another set of statistics pertaining to the sample of the means:

ν

M

V.

The sampling distribution of a sample statistic such as the sample mean can only be obtained by taking infinitely many samples from the population, although, as said above, only $N!/n!\,(N-n)!$ will be distinct. However, the important point here is that as ν tends to infinity, M converges to μ, and V^2 converges to

$$\sigma^2(1/n - 1/N).$$

That is

$$\nu \rightarrow \infty$$

$$M \rightarrow \mu$$

$$V^2 \rightarrow \frac{\sigma^2}{n}(1-f)$$

where the approximation

$$f = (1/n - 1/N) = n/N$$

is used. f is known as the sampling fraction.

So far we have not discussed the shape of the sampling distribution. For this purpose we can use a form of the central limit theorem which states that for an infinite population the shape of the sampling distribution tends, as the sample size increases, to be that of the normal distribution, whatever may be the shape of the population distribution. This can easily be demonstrated[3] by taking a rectangular uniform distribution, which is of course non-normal, and sampling it repeatedly with a varying sample size n. The sampling distribution of the sample means rapidly approaches normality as n increases. Further, the nearer the population to be sampled is to normality, the more quickly does the sampling distribution approach normality as n increases.

Given that the sampling distribution is normal, we can make the following series of statements about the sample means:

(*a*) 67% of all the possible values will be within plus or minus one standard deviation from the population mean μ.
(*b*) 95% will be within ± 2 standard deviations.
(*c*) 99·7% will be within ± 3 standard deviations.

The above statements, as they stand, are simply statements about the sample mean, but with a little manipulation they may be converted into what appear to be statements about the population mean μ. For example, statement (*b*) implies that, in repeated sampling, the sample mean m will in the long run satisfy the condition $\mu - 2V < m < \mu + 2V$ in 95% of all samples. Now the condition $\mu - 2V < m < \mu + 2V$ is satisfied the condition $m - 2V < \mu < m + 2V$ is satisfied. It follows that, in repeated sampling, the statement $m - 2V < \mu < m + 2V$ will be true, in the long run, on 95% of all occasions. In other words, if after drawing a sample we make the assertion that μ lies in the interval $(m - 2V, m + 2V)$, we stand 19 chances in 20 of being correct (or, to put it another way, 1 chance in 20 of being wrong). The interval $(m - 2V, m + 2V)$ is called a 95% confidence interval for μ, or alternatively a 5% significance level. $(m - 2V)$ and $(m + 2V)$ are known as the upper and lower 95% confidence limits respectively. Similarly, $(m - V, m + V)$ is called a 67% confidence interval for μ, $(m - 3V, m + 3V)$ is called a 99·7% confidence interval for μ, and so on. The factors 1, 2, 3, etc. in front of V are called percentage points of the normal distribution and are denoted by Z. Tables are available for these points, the main ones of use being summarized in Table 4.1.

Table 4.1 Z table

Required confidence level	Confidence level factor (Z)
67%	1·0
95%	2·0
99·7%	3·0

In general, replacing V by $[\sigma^2(1-f)/n]^{\frac{1}{2}}$, the confidence limits for μ corresponding to any chosen percentage are:

$$\mu_{\text{LOWER}} = m - Z\sqrt{\left(\frac{\sigma^2(1-f)}{n}\right)}$$

$$\mu_{\text{UPPER}} = m + Z\sqrt{\left(\frac{\sigma^2(1-f)}{n}\right)}.$$

Again, in general, σ^2 is unknown, but for large samples, say $n \geqslant 30$, it may be replaced without serious error by its unbiased sample estimate, namely s^2. However, if n is less than 30, it would be better in a sample survey where n is not predetermined to set $n = 30$ as the minimum sample size. Alternatively, and strictly, one must use Student's 't' distribution table instead of the Z table given above. [1,2,3]

Note that the above treatment assumes that the sampling distribution of m is normal. Strictly speaking, this can never be so when we are sampling without replacement from a finite population, although it will usually be approximately so when N is large and f is small ($\leqslant 0{\cdot}1$), subject to the condition $n \geqslant$ about 30.

Now since m is an unbiased estimator of μ, we can state:

$$\mu = m \pm ZV$$

where Z has been set by the confidence level we arbitrarily selected. Hence:

$$\mu = m \pm Z\left[\sigma^2 \frac{1}{n}(1-f)\right]^{\frac{1}{2}}. \tag{4.1}$$

But when taking a sample, we use s as an unbiased estimator of σ, hence:

$$\mu = m \pm Z\frac{s}{n^{\frac{1}{2}}}(1-f)^{\frac{1}{2}}.$$

Now the upper value of μ is given by:

$$\mu_{\text{UPPER}} = m + Z\frac{s}{n^{\frac{1}{2}}}(1-f)^{\frac{1}{2}}$$

and the lower value is given by:

$$\mu_{\text{LOWER}} = m - Z\frac{s}{n^{\frac{1}{2}}}(1-f)^{\frac{1}{2}}.$$

Hence the width of confidence interval, $\mu_{\text{UPPER}} - \mu_{\text{LOWER}}$, which we can denote by $2H$, is given by:

$$2H = 2Z\frac{s}{n^{\frac{1}{2}}}(1-f)^{\frac{1}{2}}$$

which, on re-arrangement, gives:

$$n = \frac{Z^2 s^2}{H^2}(1-f). \tag{4.2}$$

We can now continue with our example of the survey on ceramic tool tips as follows.

We have a population of $N = 1000$, a sample size of $n = 100$, a sample mean of $m = 9$ and a sample standard deviation $s = 3$. Then f, the sampling ratio, is 0·1.

Let us now select a confidence level of 95%, and from the Z-table find the confidence level factor $Z = 2$. Inserting these values in equation (4.1) we obtain:

$$\mu = 9 \pm \frac{2{\cdot}0 \times 3}{(100)^{\frac{1}{2}}}(1-0{\cdot}1).$$

That is:

$$\mu = 9 \pm 0{\cdot}54.$$

Hence our total market demand $D\ (= N\mu)$ is:

$D = 9000 \pm 540.$

Since sample error is frequently expressed as a percentage of the mean, we can write the following explicit relationship:

$$H\% = \frac{H}{m} \times 100 \tag{4.3}$$

where H is the half-width of the confidence interval as defined above.

We have therefore, in the above example, determined the market demand with a sample error of:

$$H\% = \frac{0{\cdot}54}{9} \times 100$$

$$= \pm 6{\cdot}0\%.$$

Having made a survey by taking a sample of 100 firms, let us now assume that the required sample error is to be ± 3% at the 95% confidence level, and that the further sampling is done in such a way that we can still use the data from the original 100. How many more firms must be sampled?

We use equation (4.3) and the previously determined value of $m = 9$ to obtain H:

$$H = \frac{m \times H\%}{100}$$

$$= \frac{9 \times 3}{100} = 0{\cdot}27.$$

We insert Z and H into equation (4.2). (Z remains unchanged.) We assume that f will not change appreciably from its previous value of 0·1.

Hence:

$$n = \frac{(2)^2 \times (3)^2}{(0{\cdot}27)^2}(1-0{\cdot}1)$$

$$\doteq 444.$$

However, the value of f has now changed too much for our assumption to hold, so we repeat the calculation using the new estimate of $f = 0{\cdot}444$, hence:

$$n = \frac{(2)^2 \times (3)^2}{(0.27)^2}(1-0{\cdot}444)$$

$$= 275$$

and repeat again using a new value of $f = 0{\cdot}275$, giving:

$$n = 358$$

and if we repeat again we get $n = 317$.

The reader will see that this is an iterative procedure where the value of n finally settles to about 300. We therefore need to sample a further 200 firms. It will be noticed that we have exceeded our arbitrary limit of $f = 0{\cdot}1$, and therefore it may be considered desirable to widen the confidence limit in order to reduce f.

Although we have achieved our objective of determining the sample size, it can be seen that it is not a straightforward analytical procedure. It involves a double iteration for finding n and f. It also needs an understanding of some rather sophisticated mathematical concepts and the relationships between the variables. For the sake of clarification, these relationships are shown in tabular form in Figure 4.2.

Much of the effort involved in determining sample size can be reduced if we have some prior information about the population of numbers to be sampled.

(*a*) If the specified sampling error is quoted as a percentage, we need an approximate estimate of the population mean so that the half-width of the confidence interval H can be calculated.

(*b*) If we know the range and the likely distribution of the population, we can roughly estimate the population variance from Table 4.2.

If the '80–20' rule seems applicable to the market being sampled, then the distribution is definitely skewed and is best classified in Table 4.2 as a right triangle. If all the firms seem to be roughly the same for the variable being assessed, then the distribution is approximately rectangular, or uniform. If one can guess that the distribution has a peak with a tail on each side, then the isosceles triangle would be a rough fit.

(ii) Sampling an attribute

The sampling of an attribute, as distinct from a continuous variable, is another important type of survey which is often used. We have already discussed the

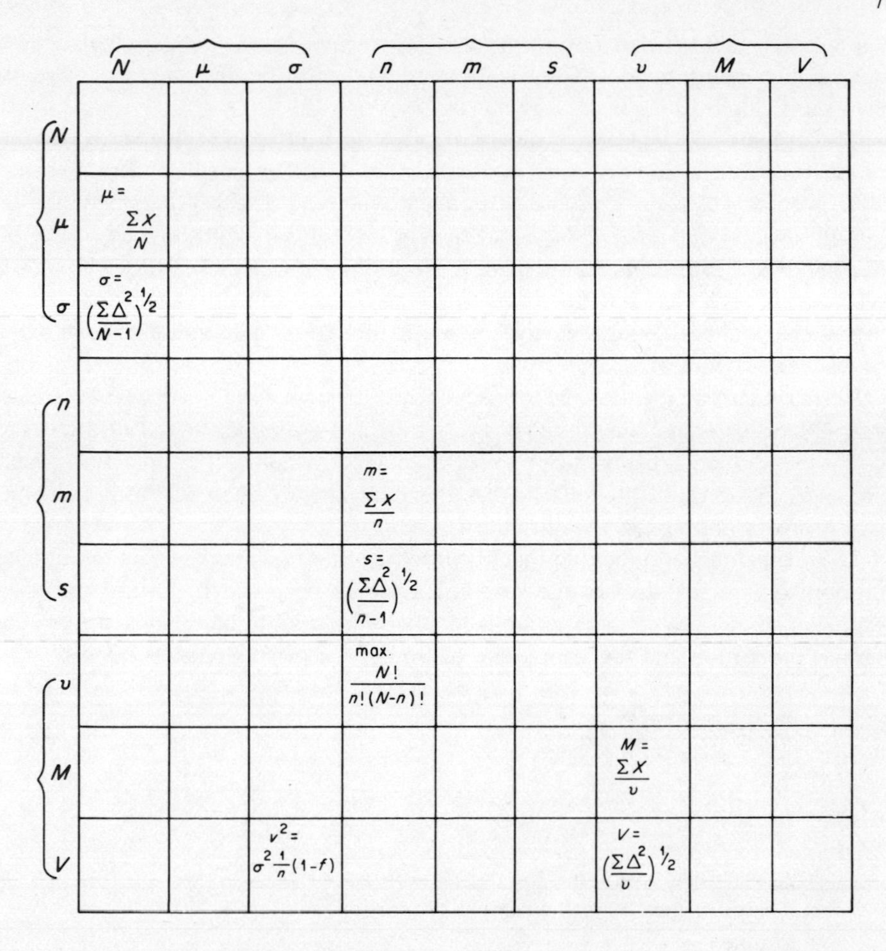

Figure 4.2 Random sample surveys: the relationships between the variables

Table 4.2 Range–variance table for some distributions

Type of distribution	Variance (σ^2)
Binomial (a proportion p of the observations at one end of the range and a proportion q at the other end)	pqR^2 (max. value $0.25R^2$)
Rectangular (uniform)	$0.083R^2$
Right triangle	$0.056R^2$
Isosceles triangle	$0.042R^2$

example of finding how many tool tips each company uses. We could however ask the simpler question of whether each company uses tool tips, the answer being 'yes' or 'no' irrespective of the quantity each firm uses.

The answer is not now a continuous variable, but a dichotomous, or two-valued variable. It is said to be an attribute because any member of the Universe will or will not possess the attribute. The two values are, and must be, mutually exclusive. A firm cannot both use tool tips and not use tool tips.

The attribute may appear in a variety of forms, such as 'red' or 'blue' (provided the product is marketed in only those two colours) or 'large' or 'small', where the same proviso applies. For a given journey between two towns, the travellers may 'fly' or 'not fly'. Motorists buying replacement engines for their cars will either buy 'new' or 'reconditioned', although many engines are of course repaired without buying a replacement. The reconditioned engine may be bought 'from the manufacturer' or 'from other sources'. Books may be bought 'hardback' or 'soft-bound'. The number of examples is endless.

The attribute can therefore be defined as a variable which can take the two values 1 or 0, these corresponding to the possession or non-possession of the attribute. Let us use the population parameter π to represent that fraction of the population which possesses the attribute. It follows that the remaining fraction of the population, $(1 - \pi)$, does not possess the attribute.

Using a parallel argument to that given for a continuous variable, let the sample proportion which possesses the specified attribute be p. Then p is an unbiased estimator of π. The confidence limits for the estimates can be calculated from the sample proportion and the sample size assuming $n\pi \geqslant 15$ (see below). Thus:

$$\pi = p \pm Z\frac{[p(1-p)]^{\frac{1}{2}}}{(n)^{\frac{1}{2}}}(1-f)^{\frac{1}{2}} \tag{4.4}$$

where

π = a parameter specifying the population proportion.
p = a statistic specifying the sample proportion.
n = sample size.
Z = confidence level factor.
f = sampling fraction.

Rearranging the equations, and introducing as before H as the half-width of the confidence interval, we obtain:

$$n = \frac{Z^2 p(1-p)(1-f)}{H^2}. \tag{4.5}$$

Unless $n \geqslant 30$, the normal approximation does not hold for small sample sizes, and unless $\pi = 0{\cdot}5$, the confidence interval estimate will be asymmetric about the mean. These conditions are likely to arise if we are sampling for a very scarce attribute, such as the number of animals with dissimilar coloured eyes in a large population. In these cases, instead of using the normal approximation to the binomial, one should use the Poisson approximation to the binomial.[3] As a rough guide, Table 4.3 gives the smallest values of n for the normal approximation to hold, the values being arrived at empirically.

Table 4.3 Approximating the binomial with the normal

Use equations (4.4) and (4.5) if $n >$ 30 and π approximates to 0·5
Use equations (4.4) and (4.5) if $n >$ 30 and π approximates to 0·4 or 0·6
Use equations (4.4) and (4.5) if $n >$ 80 and π approximates to 0·3 or 0·7
Use equations (4.4) and (4.5) if $n >$ 200 and π approximates to 0·2 or 0·8
Use equations (4.4) and (4.5) if $n >$ 600 and π approximates to 0·1 or 0·9
Use equations (4.4) and (4.5) if $n >$ 1400 and π approximates to 0·05 or 0·95

As before, $$H\% = \frac{H}{P} \times 100.$$

Once again we cannot calculate n unless we know π, which is still an unknown quantity. We must therefore make an educated guess as to the likely value of π. Let us say that $\pi = 0{\cdot}25$, i.e. 25% of the firms use ceramic tool tips. Let us specify a 95% confidence level, hence from the 'Z' table $Z = 2{\cdot}0$, and let us specify a precision of $\pm$ 25%, i.e. $H\% = 25\%$. Using equation (4.6) we find that $H = 0{\cdot}0625$. Now, assuming that $f = 0$,

$$n = \frac{(2{\cdot}0)^2(0{\cdot}25)(0{\cdot}75)}{(0{\cdot}0625)^2}$$
$$= 192.$$

Iterating the calculation by using a value for f of 192/1000,

$$n = \frac{(2{\cdot}0)^2(0{\cdot}25)(0{\cdot}75)(1-0{\cdot}192)}{(0{\cdot}0625)^2}$$
$$= 155$$

and a further iteration for n using a value of $f = 0{\cdot}155$ gives:

$n = 162.$

If therefore we took a sample of about 160 firms, and our guess of $\pi = 0{\cdot}25$ were nearly correct, our sampling error of $\pm$ 25% would be achieved. If the value of π as determined from the sample were very much different from 0·25, then the precision would be over- or under-achieved, in which case we would either have to increase the size of the sample or accept the fact that we have over-sampled. In practice, the situation is not so obscure as it may seem because n is more sensitive to H than it is to $p(1-p)$. Hence it is more important not to over-specify the required precision than it is to set π quite arbitrarily at a value of 0·5, which is what one would have to do if no better prior estimate for π were available. If we had used a value of $\pi = 0{\cdot}5$ in the above example, n would be 204, and if in fact π were found to be 0·25 we would have over-sampled by $(204 - 162) = 42$ firms.

4.7 WHERE SAMPLING ERROR IS IMPORTANT

The foregoing discussion has emphasized the importance of systematic error over sampling error. Systematic error is not only important but also insidious because it often remains undetected. In the laboratory, systematic error is investigated by measuring the variable to be assessed in many different ways and comparing the results, but this procedure is rarely available to the marketing researcher, who must do the best he can by intuition and experience.

However, in IMR, sampling error would be important where we are doing repeated surveys, month after month or year after year, in order to monitor some parameter of the market, such as the rate of penetration with time. Obviously, in order to draw valid conclusions between one sample and the next, the sampling error must be less than the change of the parameter with time, otherwise we would not be able to detect the trend because of random variation. This is where the theory outlined above can be used, because the survey previous to the one being conducted can be used as the pilot survey, and the sample size can be adjusted as the series of surveys proceeds. There is another type of survey when sampling error is important, and that is in election polls, where the result is critically dependent on the accuracy of the 'yes' or 'no' answers. If there are 50·1% 'yes' and 49·9% 'no', the forecast can be 100% wrong if the total error exceeds 0·1%. Fortunately, however, this is not IMR.

4.8 SAMPLE SURVEYS AND FORECASTING

It is instructive to classify sample surveys into those which are retrospective and those which are prospective, the latter being the ones which will be involved with forecasting. The two kinds of error, statistical and systematic, occur in both types of survey, but the magnitude of the total error in forecast sample surveys can be so enormous that the sampling statistical error becomes trivial, provided of course that the sample size is not itself ridiculously small.

As an example, there is a case which is known, but not published, of an industrial marketing survey undertaken by consultants of international repute who estimated the market demand 5 years ahead at £50m. As the product was of a highly sophisticated technological nature, a second survey was commissioned from different but equally distinguished consultants who reached substantially the same conclusion. The forecast market demand proved to be in error by a factor of 50, involving the manufacturing firm in an eventual loss of £10m. The difference in scale between errors of this magnitude and those in the examples discussed earlier makes one wonder whether a difference of principle is involved, but this is not so. The error was due to systematic bias in the assessment.

One can easily see how such a situation can arise by considering the difference between the two questions 'Did you purchase product A last year?', and 'Will you purchase product A when it reaches the market 5 years hence?' Future demand is not of course assessed in such a simplistic way. Extrapolation methods, for instance, are used, except where a new product with no historic data is to be marketed. Now, it can be argued that all forecasts are to some extent conditional, being based for instance on relative price changes, or changes in real net disposable income, etc. When these conditions are not fulfilled, the forecast is in error. These errors are systematic because, unlike the sampling error, they do not decrease in magnitude as the sample size increases. The marketing researcher would do well to bear this point constantly in mind, because, as has been stated earlier, the sample error could well be the least of his worries.

4.9 STEPWISE PROCEDURE FOR DETERMINING SAMPLE SIZE IN RANDOM SAMPLE SURVEY

4.9.1 Sampling a continuous variable

Step 1 Precision. Decide on the required half-width of the confidence interval. If this is expressed as a percentage of the mean, decide roughly what the mean is likely to be and then use equation (4.3) to find H.

Step 2 Confidence level. Decide on the required confidence level and then use the Z-table (Table 4.1) to find the confidence level factor, Z.

Step 3 Estimate very roughly the population variance. If this is unknown, decide what type of distribution the population of numbers will have, and the approximate range, then use the range-variance table (Table 4.2) to obtain the approximate variance.

Step 4 Assume $f = 0$ and use equation (4.2) to obtain a trial value of n.

Step 5 Use this trial value of n to calculate f.

Step 6 Return to Step 4 and repeat the trial calculation of n. Repeat this cycle until n remains reasonably constant.

Step 7 If n is less than 30, either take the value $n = 30$ or use a 't' distribution table to find Z. If the latter, return to Step (2) and repeat, using the 't' value instead of the 'Z' value.

Step 8 If n is too large, given the limited resources of the survey, return to Step 1 and choose a lower precision and/or confidence level.

Step 9 If satisfactory values for precision, confidence level, and sample size cannot be found from the above procedures then the survey is not viable.

Step 10 If the survey is viable, take the random sample of size n, but be prepared to increase the sample size, or to repeat the survey with a bigger sample size, if the required precision is not achieved.

4.9.2 Sampling an attribute

Step 1 As Step 1 in (4.9.1), except use equation (4.6) instead of (4.3).

Step 2 As Step 2 in (4.9.1).

Step 3 Make a guess as to the value of , the proportion of the population possessing the attribute. Use this as a trial value of p.

Step 4 Assume $f = 0$ and use equation (4.5) to obtain a trial value of n.

Step 5 Use this trial value to calculate f.

Step 6 Return to Step 4 and repeat the trial calculation of n. Repeat this cycle until n remains reasonably constant.

Step 7 Check that n is within the limits for normal approximation. Otherwise use equations for the Poisson approximation. (See reference in text.)

Step 8 As Step 7 in (4.9.1).

Step 9 As Step 8 in (4.9.1).

Step 10 As Step 9 in (4.9.1).

Step 11 As Step 10 in (4.9.1).

Procedural flow sheets for both types of survey are given at the end of this section.

4.10 REFERENCES

1. Cochran, W. G. (1963). *Sampling Techniques*, Wiley, London.
2. Brabb, G. J. (1968). *Introduction to Quantitative Management*, Holt, Rinehart, and Winston, London.
3. Ostle, B. (1969). *Statistics in Research*, Iowa State University Press.
4. Edwards-Deming, W. (1944). On errors in Surveys, *Am. Soc. Rev.*, **9**, 359.
5. Fox, R. A. (1976). Sampling for Industrial Marketing Research. In *Handbook of Industrial Marketing and Research*, Handbook Editor: I. MacLEAN. Kluwer-Harrap, London.
6. McIntosh, A. R. and Davies, R. J. (1970). The Sampling of Non-Domestic Populations. *J. Market Res. Soc.* 12, 217.

Procedural Flow Sheet for Sample Surveys

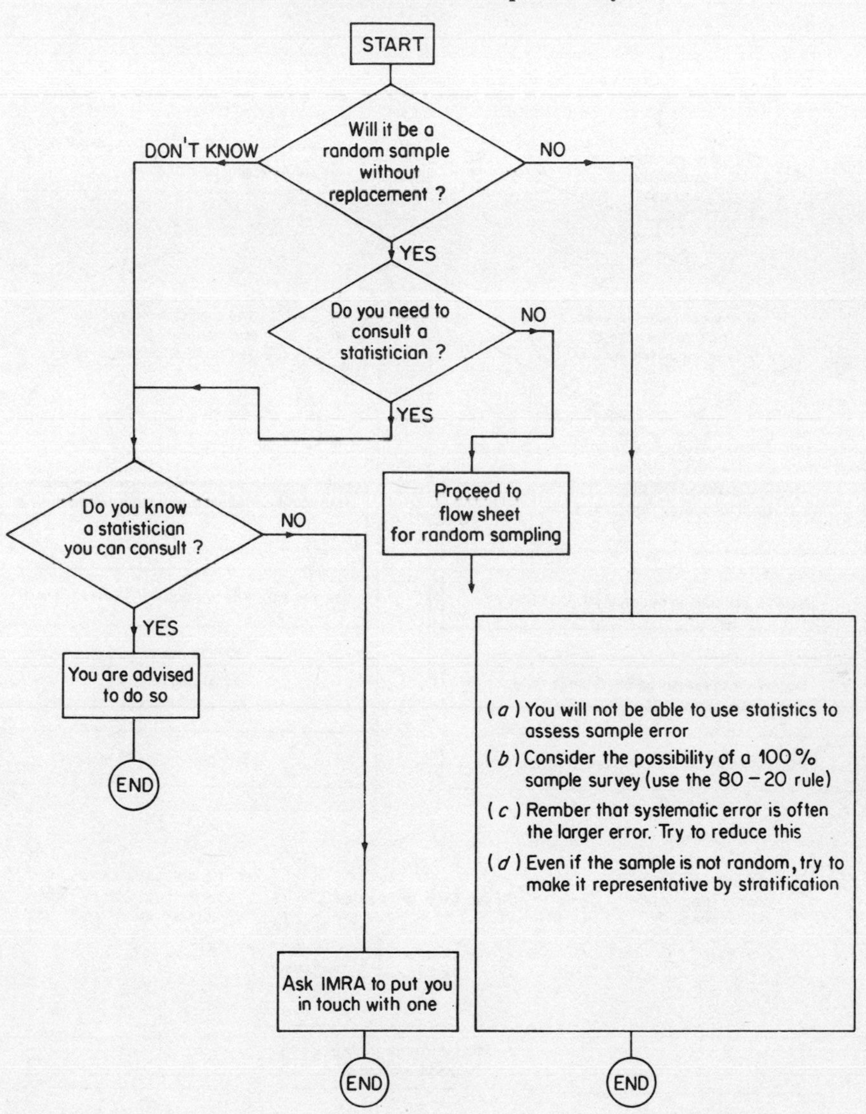

Procedural Flow Sheet for Random Sampling (Sheet 1)

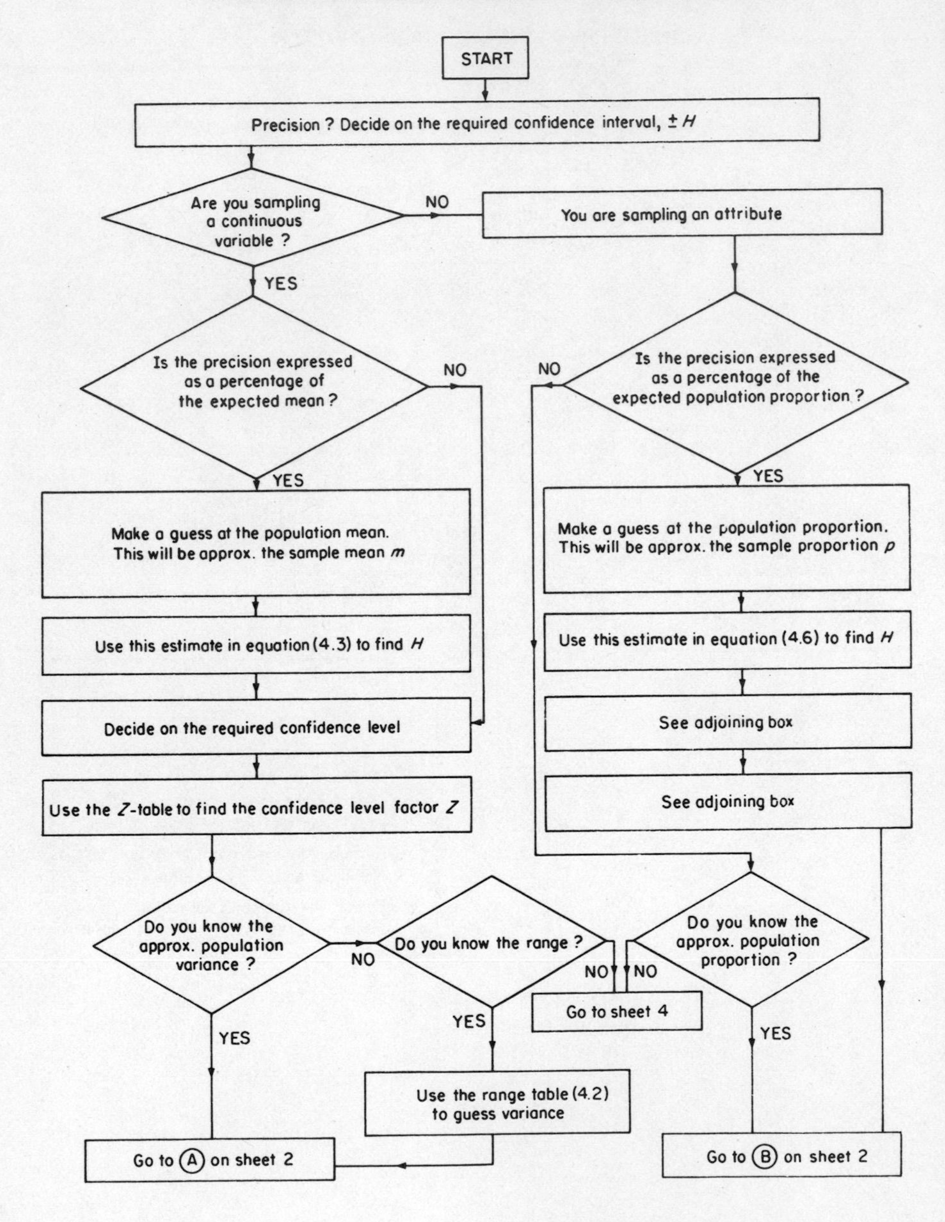

Procedural Flow Sheet for Random Sampling (Sheet 2)

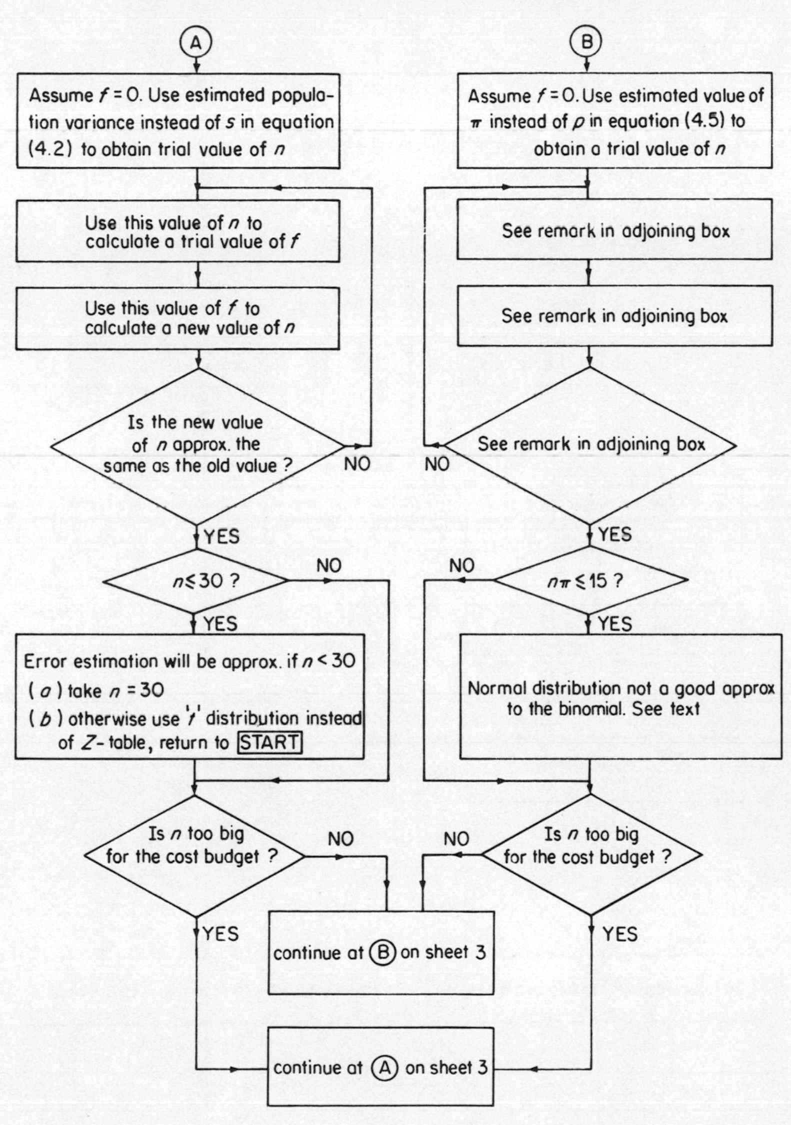

Procedural Flow Sheet for Random Sampling (Sheet 3)

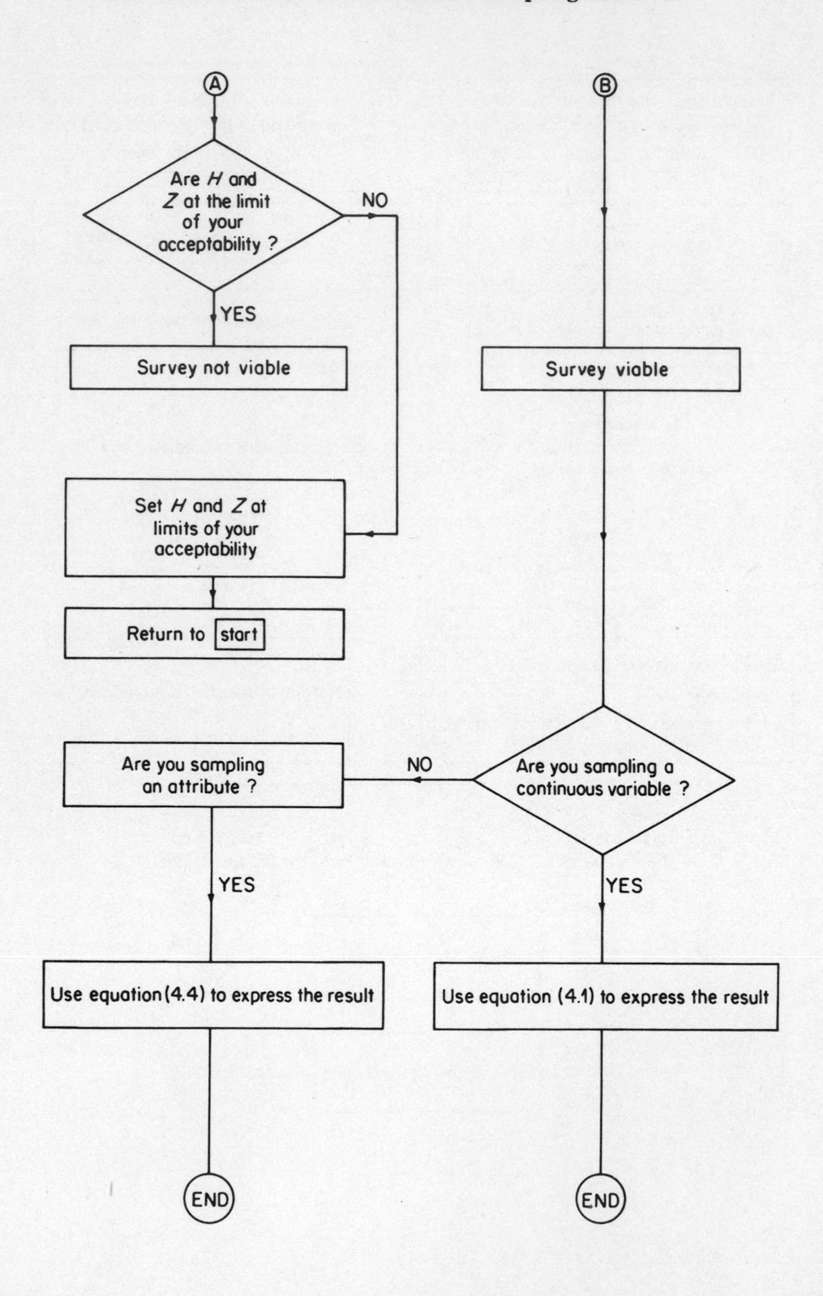

Procedural Flow Sheet for Random Sampling (Sheet 4)

You do not have enough information about the population to find the optimum sample size.

You will have to do a trial survey. This may by chance give you the required sample precision, but if it does not, you will have to consider this a pilot survey and be prepared to do a main survey.

If you are very unlucky, the pilot survey will give you the necessary initializing data, but you may then find that the main survey is not viable. There is no way of avoiding this hazard.

(a) Select a sample size according to your cost budget

(b) Take a random sample without replacement

(c) Calculate the sample variance if a continuous variable, or the sample proportion if an attribute

(d) Now follow the procedures outlined in the flow sheets

Chapter 5

Forecasting

5.1 DEMAND FORECASTING—SHORT AND MEDIUM TERM

Market measurement and forecasting is concerned with developing quantitative estimates of demand, an essential part of marketing research and planning. There are many techniques available to us, but selecting the most suitable method depends on:

Accuracy of past data.

Availability of historical data.

Final application of forecast and degree of error that can be tolerated.

Number of time periods for which forecast is required.

Time available for the preparation of the forecast.

Before describing the basic techniques it is worth considering how the above effect our choice.

If we are aware from previous research that the past data contains some inaccuracies which cannot be eliminated, then it is wasteful to expend effort on a precise mathematical technique. Similarly, it is useless to contemplate using a sophisticated technique requiring a run of data when only five or six periods are available.

It is important to make the best use of our data, but at the same time to keep within the limits of acceptable accuracy. It is worth noting, at this stage, that it is the 'art of forecasting' which is being described and that where predicted results are in conflict with known data we should adapt our conclusions accordingly.

5.1.1. Opinion surveys

Estimates of future demand, as determined for instance by the probability of getting a particular order, may be made by senior sales personnel in close contact with the market over the next time period (usually a year or less). Salesmen are, of course, in a position to make such estimates due to their intimate knowledge of their markets, and hence it is relevant to consider their role in the forecasting system.

These individual forecasts may then be reviewed by a senior executive and the overall picture may be adjusted to give a balanced view.

This method is particularly useful where the very nature of the object of the forecast does not readily lend itself to any form of mathematical analysis. Excellent examples are to be found in the heavy capital goods industry and in the civil engineering industry where the timing of large projects is very important, but can only be estimated subjectively.

One of the chief dangers encountered when using this method is that a particular salesman may consistently rate his company's chances of getting a job much higher than they really are. This weakness may be largely overcome if that salesman's actual performance is monitored against his forecasts and the degree of bias determined. Then his future forecasts may be down-rated accordingly. No matter how many adjustments for bias are made, however, the resulting forecast is still subjective and may be severely criticized on these grounds alone.

5.1.2. End-use analysis

This is a popular method of estimating market demand, particularly for companies who are concerned with the potential for a new industrial product.

The approach involves identifying the end-uses for the product, finding the market segments in which these end-uses will exist, and then making an estimate of the demand for the product within each segment. The total market is then simply the sum of the demand in each of these segments. In carrying out the third step, one or more market factors or usage factors have to be identified that relate logically to demand from each market segment. For example, an oil company wishes to determine the market potential for its industrial lubricants in a particular county. From an analysis of countrywide sales it was discovered that three industries accounted for the majority of the consumption of industrial lubricants. By mailing a simple questionnaire to a sample of firms in the industries concerned, it was possible to determine the average amount of lubricant used per employee in a given year. The results obtained were:

Engineering Industry	380 litres per employee
Transport Industry	210 litres per employee
Agricultural Industry	60 litres per employee

From these usage factors the market potential was calculated for the county area by using the Department of Employment's detailed area statistics of employment by industry. The calculations are shown in Table 5.1.

5.1.3. Time series analysis

A time series is a set of data which shows the behaviour of a variable over regular intervals of time, e.g. monthly or quarterly company sales statistics. The main objective of time series analysis is to identify measurable regularities and patterns in

Table 5.1

Industry	No. of employees in the county	Litres of lubricant per employee	Market potential in the county
Engineering	22 634	380	8 600 920
Transport	6 421	210	1 348 410
Agriculture	8 962	60	537 720
Annual market potential			10 487 050 litres

This figure for the market potential would, of course, be rounded to 10 million litres in order not to give a false sense of accuracy

the past data which can be assumed to recur in the future, and thus provide some clues for forecasting the future fluctuations of the series.

In any time series it may be possible to identify up to four variable components:

General trend, T

Seasonal variation, S

Cyclical variation, C

Irregular variation, I.

By the *general trend* of the graph we mean the general direction in which the time series appears to be going, over a long period of time. The trend may be a straight line, as in Figure 5.1(*a*), but it is just as likely to be curved. *Seasonal variation* refers to the identical—or nearly identical—patterns which a time series appears to follow during, for example, corresponding months of successive years. Such variations normally follow yearly cycles and especially so in industrial marketing, but may be monthly, weekly, or even daily. An example of this kind of variation is the increase in the sale of industrial heaters during autumn and winter and a subsequent fall in spring and summer.

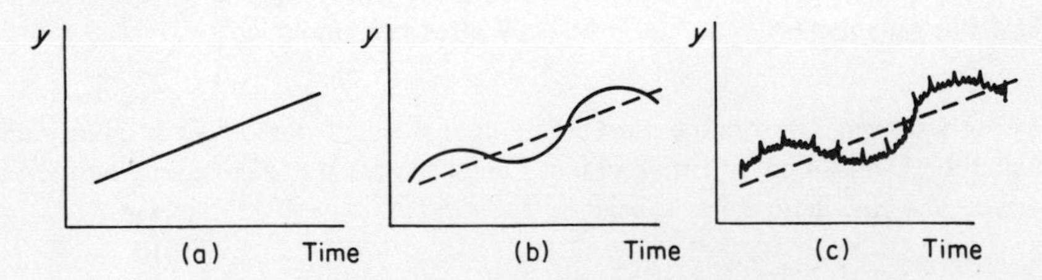

Figure 5.1 (*a*) Long-term trend; (*b*) trend and cyclical variations; (*c*) trend, cyclical, and seasonal variations

Cyclical variation is the term applied to longer-term patterns of demand. For example, statistics of the chemical and processing industry have shown that there has been a fairly regular rise and fall in demand over 4–5 yearly periods. Such variations about the trend line are shown in Figure 5.1(*b*), while Figure 5.1(*c*) shows the seasonal variations as well.

Irregular variations are unpredictable changes in demand, e.g. the fall in the sales of oil fired heating systems as a result of fuel price increase due to the world oil crisis in 1973.

It is important to realize that whilst all four kinds of variations may occur in any time series, they need not do so. Cyclical variations, for example, occur infrequently and, even when they do, need not necessarily be found if the data do not extend back over a large enough period of time.

The role of time series analysis is to break the data into these four components, where they exist. It is then possible to forecast the way each component will develop on the basis of the past patterns, and hence resynthesize them into a single forecast for the series as a whole.

When resynthesizing the different elements we may do so in two ways.

(*a*) If the four elements T, S, C, and I appear to be unrelated, i.e. a change in one element does not affect any of the others, we can say that:

$$\text{Observed value} = T + S + C + I$$

and the data conform to an 'Additive model'.

(*b*) If the four elements appear to show some inter-relationship—e.g. the difference between extreme values in a seasonal cycle, known as the 'amplitude' of the seasonal variation, frequently increases as the trend increases—we can say that:

$$\text{Observed value} = T \times S \times C \times I$$

and the data, this time, conforms to a 'Multiplicative model'.

It is important to realize that the additive model assumes that the three components S, C, and I are unchanged throughout the period being studied. Whilst this may be a fair assumption over a short period of time, over a longer term we normally find that the second situation is more likely. Consequently the multiplicative model is the one most often used.

To isolate the different elements

(i) Trend

There are four main methods for finding the trend line. These are:

Freehand curve fitting.

'Semi-averages'.

'Moving averages'.

Mathematical curve fitting ('Least squares')

Table 5·2 Sales in £ 000s

	1975	1976
Jan.	1·68	1·60
Feb.	2·37	2·59
Mar.	4·06	3·43
Apr.	6·24	6·13
May	5·58	6·28
June	6·01	5·79
July	5·64	6·11
Aug.	5·17	4·66
Sept.	3·11	3·55
Oct.	3·18	2·67
Nov.	1·45	1·28
Dec.	1·26	1·89

Sometimes combinations of one or more of these methods are used, and, of course, there are a variety of ways of making each one more sophisticated and, hopefully, more accurate. For most purposes, however, one or other of the methods given is sufficiently accurate (but for some of the refinements see Section 5.1.6, 'Suggestions for further reading').

Freehand curve fitting In this the researcher merely finds the line or curve which best fits the data: sometimes called the 'line of best fit'. Obviously this method is a subjective procedure and different observers would fit somewhat different lines. This method is normally used only as an aid to finding which other method is most appropriate, as in itself it is too inaccurate to make any further analysis of the S, C, and I elements worthwhile.

Semi-averages In this method the data are split into two parts—preferably equal—and the arithmetic mean of each group found. The data are split so that, for example, the first 5 years of 10 years of data go into the first group and the second five into the second group. A straight line is then drawn through the two means when they are represented by points on a graph. (N.B. The points are plotted at the mid-time of each group—i.e. at the third year of each group in our example.) This method can only be used when the trend approximates to a straight line, and therefore has limited use.

Moving averages This is a much more popular and accurate method than the two described so far. Essentially it is a method which attempts to iron out the effects of the cyclical, seasonal, and irregular variations from the graph.

Suppose we have a series of n observations, equally spaced in time. In the moving averages method we find the arithmetic mean of, say, the first three terms, then of the second 3 terms—i.e. the 2nd 3rd and 4th terms—then of the third 3 terms and so on till we find the mean of the $(n-2)$th to nth terms. In this case as three terms are used for each mean we call it a 'three point moving average'. If each mean used six terms of the series we should be using a 'six point moving average'.

Table 5.3

	Sales in £000s	5 month totals	5 point moving averages	12 month totals	12 point moving averages	12 point centred moving averages
1975						
Jan.	1·68					
Feb.	2·37					
Mar.	4·06	19·93	3·99			
Apr.	6·24	24·26	4·85			
May	5·58	27·53	5·51			
June	6·01	28·64	5·73			
July	5·64	25·51	5·10	45·75	3·813	3·81
Aug.	5·17	23·11	4·62	45·67	3·806	3·82
Sept.	3·11	18·55	3·71	45·89	3·824	3·80
Oct.	3·18	14·17	2·83	45·26	3·771	3·77
Nov.	1·45	10·06	2·12	45·15	3·763	3·79
Dec.	1·26	10·08	2·02	45·85	3·821	3·81
1976						
Jan.	1·60	10·33	2·07	45·63	3·803	3·79
Feb.	2·59	15·01	3·00	45·10	3·758	3·74
Mar.	3·43	20·03	4·01	44·59	3·372	3·74
Apr.	6·13	24·22	4·84	45·03	3·753	3·73
May	6·28	26·74	5·35	44·52	3·710	3·74
June	5·79	27·96	5·59	44·35	3·779	3·76
July	5·11	25·39	5·08	44·98	3·748	
Aug.	4·66	21·78	4·36			
Sept.	3·55	17·27	3·45			
Oct.	2·67	14·05	2·81			
Nov.	1·28					
Dec.	1·89					

Let us suppose the data in Table 5.2 gives the monthly sales for the years 1975–76 in £000s of a firm making ventilating equipment. If the points are plotted as they stand, there is an irregular line which appears to have a 12 month seasonal cycle (see Figure 5.2). Suppose we work out 5 point and 12 point moving averages for the data (see Table 5.3).

It is important to note that when we work out the five month moving average, that average is plotted against the middle month—the third—of that set of five months. There is no difficulty in deciding where to plot the value when an 'odd' numbered moving average is calculated. However, when the moving average is even numbered, as in the twelve month moving average, there are *two* middle months. We therefore plot the point mid-way between the two months. In Table 5.3 we placed the first of our twelve month moving averages halfway between June and July, the second average between July and August, and so on. If for some reason it is essential to plot the points exactly on the months (or whatever unit of time is being used) we can do a 2 point moving average of the moving averages! In this case we would do a 2 point moving average of the results in column 5 of the table. Such 2

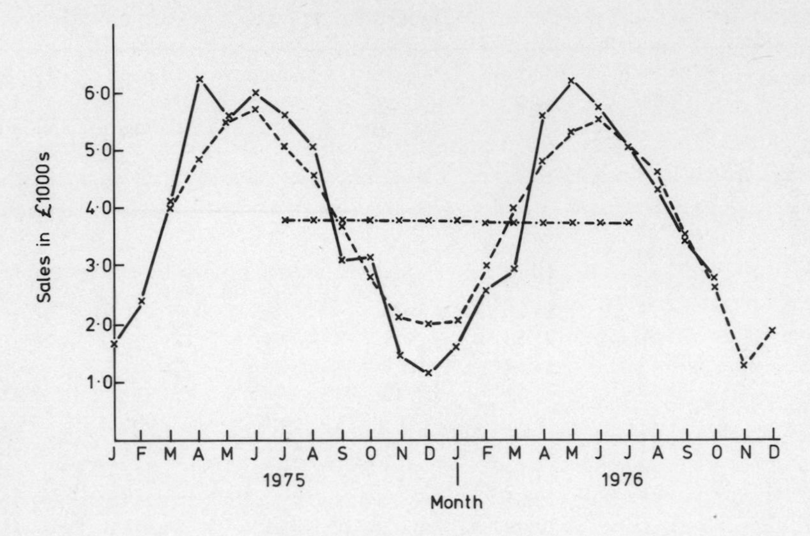

Figure 5.2 —— data; - - - - five point moving average; ·—·— twelve point centred moving average

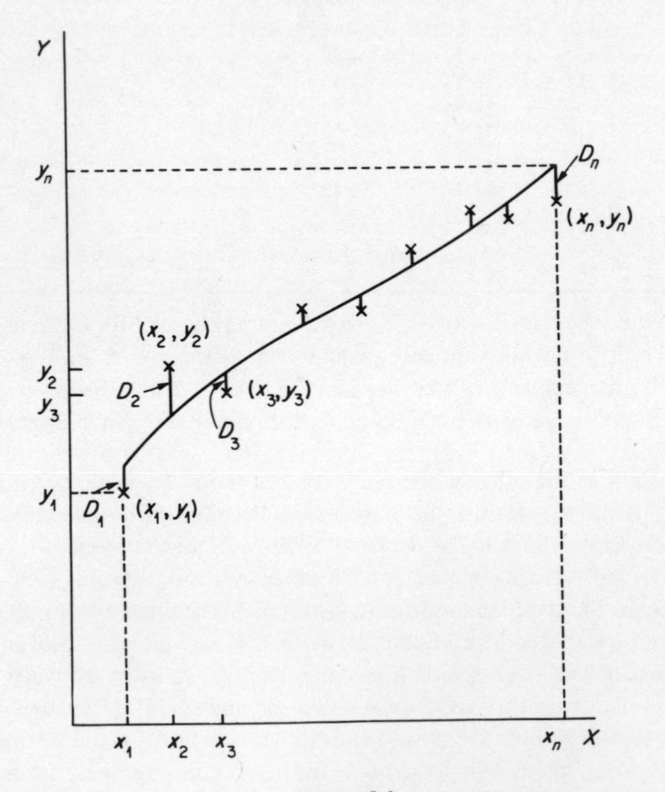

Figure 5.3

point moving averages are shown in column 6 and the averages are now back on the original month lines. The results in column 6 are said to be 12 point *centred* moving averages.

The five point moving averages and twelve point centred moving averages, have all been plotted in Figure 5.2. You will see that whilst the five point average makes the seasonal variations less extreme, the twelve point centred moving average is a considerable improvement and is a good approximation to the general trend of the graph.

We find that the longer the period of each average (in other words, the higher the value of n in the expression 'n point moving average') the less it follows any cyclical swings. A further improvement results if the length of the period of the moving average approximates to the average cycle length of the variable under study (or a multiple of the cycle length).

The moving averages method is a popular one because of its simplicity and its effectiveness in smoothing out the variations. However, there are certain disadvantages in its use. The first of these should be obvious from Table 5.3, and is that in order to get any useful trend line a considerable amount of data is required. We have said that the longer the period of each average, the smoother and more accurate the trend line—but even to get 12 points on a twelve point centred moving average we used 24 items of data. Such an amount of data is not always available. Further, the last point on the moving averages line is several months in arrears. In our 12 point centred moving average it was six months behind—and whilst we can project our moving averages trend line freehand, to bring it up to date, we cannot be sure that the trend line has not changed in that time.

The other main disadvantage is that early data has as much influence on the trend line as recent data. If the trend line is to be used for forecasting then more recent data ought to carry more weight.

The method of '*exponential moving averages*'[1] does exactly this. Weights are assigned to data in indirect proportion to their age. This method can be used for projecting trend lines found by simple moving averages, but must be continually updated and is only suitable for short term forecasting.

Mathematical curve fitting If we are proposing to do any medium or long-term forecasting, none of the methods so far are adequate. In this case we need to find a mathematical relationship which will fit the overall trend. The method of 'least squares' is then appropriate. The idea behind the 'least squares' technique is that, in order to find the best fitting line, or curve, through a set of points, we have to minimize, in some way, the deviations $D_1, D_2, D_3, \ldots, D_n$ of the points from the curve (see Figure 5.3). To overcome the fact that some deviations are positive and some negative we find the curve which makes $D_1^2 + D_2^2 + D_3^2 + \ldots + D_n^2$ a minimum.

However, before we can apply this method we must have an approximate idea of what the trend line looks like. This can be done freehand or by moving averages.

The types of trend we can identify mathematically, their names, and mathematical equations are shown in Figure 5.4.

If the general trend approximates to a straight line its mathematical equation is:

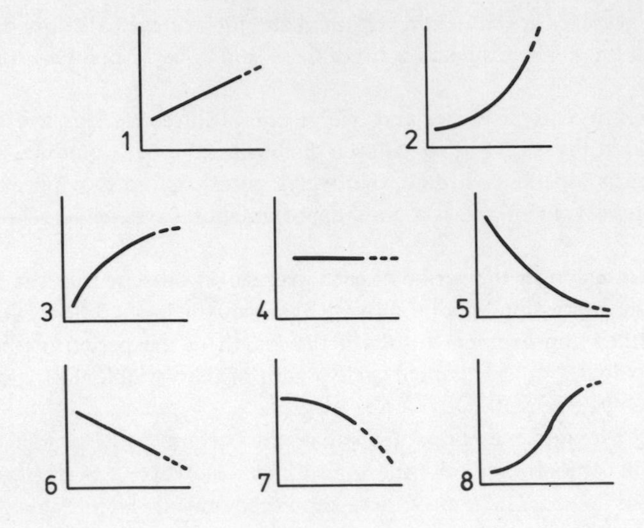

	Straight Line $Y=a+bx$	Basic Exponential $Y=ab^x$	Logarithmic Parabola $Y=ab^xc^{x^2}$	Quadratic or Parabolic $Y=a+bx+cx^2$	Modified Exponential $Y=k+ab^x$	Gompertz $Y=ka^{b^x}$	Logistic $\frac{1}{Y}=k+ab^x$
1	b+ve						
2		b+ ve		b+ve c+ve	a+ve $b<1$		
3			b+ve c+ve	b+ve c−ve	a+ve $b<1$	a+ ve $b<1$	a+ ve $b<1$
4	b = 0						
5				b−ve c+ve	a − ve $b<1$	a+ve $b<1$	$a>0$ $b<1$
6	b−ve						
7				b−ve c−ve	a− ve $b<1$		
8						a+ ve $b<1$	a+ve $b<1$

Figure 5.4 Types of trend

$Y = bX + a$ where b is the gradient of the line (i.e. the rate at which it is increasing or decreasing) and a is the intercept on the Y axis (i.e. where the line cuts the Y axis). The values of a and b are calculated by the 'least squares' method from the formulae:

$$a = \frac{(\sum Y)(\sum X^2)-(\sum X)(\sum XY)}{n(\sum X^2)-(\sum X)^2} \tag{5.1}$$

$$b = \frac{n(\sum XY)-(\sum X)(\sum Y)}{n(\sum X^2)-(\sum X)^2} \tag{5.2}$$

where the coordinates of the n points on the graph are (X_1,Y_1), (X_2,Y_2), (X_3,Y_3), ..., (X_n,Y_n), and

$$\sum Y = Y_1 + Y_2 + Y_3 + \ldots + Y_n$$
$$\sum X^2 = X_1^2 + X_2^2 + X_3^2 + \ldots + X_n^2$$
$$\sum X = X_1 + X_2 + X_3 + \ldots + X_n$$
$$\sum XY = X_1Y_1 + X_2Y_2 + X_3Y_3 + \ldots + X_nY_n.$$

We will apply this method to the sales figures for a period of eight years given in Table 5.4. When the points are plotted in Figure 5.5 the trend would appear to approximate to a straight line and we can use the formulae above.

Table 5.4

	Time point X yrs.	Sales Y £000s	X^2	XY
1968	0	8	0	0
1969	1	19	1	19
1970	2	20	4	40
1971	3	20	9	60
1972	4	26	16	104
1973	5	33	25	165
1974	6	32	36	192
1975	7	39	49	273
Totals	$\sum X = 28$	$\sum Y = 197$	$\sum X^2 = 140$	$\sum XY = 853$

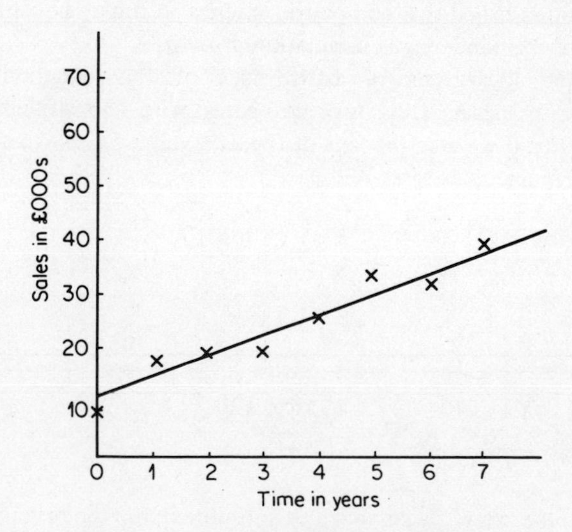

Figure 5.5 Sales for the years 1968–75

We have taken 1968 as year 0, 1969 as year 1 and so on. These are the $X_1, X_2, X_3, \ldots, X_8$ of the formulae. The sales values are the $Y_1, Y_2, \ldots, Y_8$.

In Column 3 of Table 5.4 are X_1^2, X_2^2, etc. and in Column 4 are the values of $X_1Y_1, X_2Y_2, \ldots, X_8Y_8$. As there are 8 items of data, $n = 8$. Thus

$$a = \frac{197 \times 140 - 28 \times 853}{8 \times 140 - 28^2}$$

That is $a = 11$

$$b = \frac{8 \times 853 - 28 \times 197}{8 \times 140 - (28)^2}$$

That is $b = 3{\cdot}89$.

Therefore the relationship is $Y = 3{\cdot}89X + 11$ or

sales in year $t = 3{\cdot}89t + 11$

where $t =$ Year $-$ 1968.

The method is very quick to use with the aid of an electronic calculator, and, in fact, several are pre-programmed for this calculation.

So far we have only considered straight line trends, but curved ones are just as likely. Let us now consider these exponential-type trends.

Many industries and business firms have a long-term tendency to grow geometrically—i.e. by a constant percentage—rather than by a constant amount. Such curves are shaped as in Example 2 of Figure 5.4, and the general equation is $Y = ab^X$. It is often called the 'compound interest formula' as compound interest growth is also of this kind—as is population growth.

By taking the logarithms of both sides of this equation we get $\log Y = \log a + X \log b$. This now compares with the straight line formula $Y = a + bX$. Thus if we take the logs of the data values (Y) we can then apply the least squares formulae as before. We use

$$\log a = \frac{(\sum \log Y)(\sum X^2) - (\sum X)(\sum X \log Y)}{n(\sum X^2) - (\sum X)^2}$$

and

$$\log b = \frac{n(\sum X \log Y) - (\sum X)(\sum \log Y)}{n(\sum X^2) - (\sum X)^2}$$

from which a and b can be calculated and substituted into the original formula $Y = ab^X$.

It can be seen from Figure 5.4 that sometimes the curve in Example 2 may be better approximated to a parabola with an equation of the form $Y = a + bX + cX^2$. Such an equation can also describe curves like Examples 3, 5, and 7. The least squares method for finding a, b, and c is to solve the simultaneous equations:

$$\sum Y = na + b\sum X + c\sum X^2 \quad (5.3)$$

$$\sum XY = a\sum X + b\sum X^2 + c\sum X^3 \quad (5.4)$$

$$\sum X^2 Y = a\sum X^2 + b\sum X^3 + c\sum X^4. \quad (5.5)$$

If you have access to a computer, packages are available for this, as for least squares approximations to the other curves. It should perhaps be mentioned here that there are formulae and packages for fitting higher order polynomials, e.g. of the form $Y = a + bX + cX^2 + dX3$, which may fit the same curves—as well as the 'S' shaped curve, Example 8—quite well. However, they should not be used if the trend is to be used for long-term forecasting, as they give ridiculous results. The logarithmic parabola may also fit curves of the type shown in Example 2. Its equation $Y = ab^X c^{X^2}$ may be transformed to $\log Y = \log a + X \log b + X^2 \log c$ in the same way that we transformed the simple exponential curve. This is now parabolic and we can apply the method above using values of $\log Y$ instead of Y.

The three modified exponential curves, i.e. simple modified exponential, Gompertz, and Logistic, are appropriate when the curve appears to be approaching either an upper or lower limit. For example, many industries find that there would appear to be an upper limit or maximum market saturation point for their products. The three equations are:

Simple modified exponential $\quad Y = k + ab^X$

Gompertz $\quad Y = ka^{b^X}$

Logistic $\quad \dfrac{1}{Y} = k + ab^X.$

They are all treated in the same way. There is a version of the 'least squares' technique known as Gomes method using specially prepared tables. The disadvantage of Gomes method is that the tables existing at present are limited to 10 sets of data and the method also requires continuous (i.e. unbroken) data. If the data for some years are missing it is necessary to estimate some for the missing years. A computer package is recommended if Gomes method is used.[3]

There is also an alternative method to the Gomes method known as the 'Three Point Method' which is also in common use.[3] This is much simpler to calculate but is not suitable if there is an obvious cyclical or seasonal trend.

Given that we have several types of curve to choose from, we now have the problem of deciding which one is the best for our purposes. One answer is to try all of the possibilities and find the correlation coefficient for the data on each curve. (Time sharing computer packages are available, or see Spiegel.[2]) The equation which gives the highest coefficient is the most suitable one. Alternatively there is a method by which each curve is characterized by its gradient.[3]

Before leaving the discussion of mathematical curve fitting it must be pointed out that we often find that a curve is only consistent with the data for part of the period studied. Since we are proposing to use the curve for forecasting it must fit *the most recent* data. If a curve is not consistent with the data for a substantial part of the time the curve is not suitable unless it can be shown that the inconsistency can be explained by changes in market factors.

(ii) Seasonal variations

When we are isolating the seasonal factor S in our original observed data $TCSI$ or $T + C + S + I$ equations, we find an index which fits corresponding time points in each cycle for each of those time points. The index may use a monthly average for the year as base, or points on the trend line—found by any of the methods mentioned earlier. The alternative method of Link Relatives[2] is used much more rarely.

How these indexes are found is most easily shown by an example. The methods demonstrated are:

Method 1. Using the 'monthly average' as base.

Method 2. Using 'moving averages' trend points as base.

To use any other trend lines as base we work in a similar way to that in Method 2—merely substituting the appropriate trend points for the 'moving average' points.

Suppose that Table 5.5 represents the sales data for a firm for the years 1971–75. Twelve point centred moving averages and monthly averages have been calculated for each year.

Method 1 We divide the sales for each month in each year by the monthly average for that year and multiply by 100—giving the percentage of the monthly average for the year. We then average the indexes for corresponding months in each year, e.g. we can find the mean of the January indexes to give an overall index for January. If the indexes for corresponding months cover a wide range it may be more appropriate to use the median or even the mode as the average.

Method 2 This time we divide each month by the moving averages trend value for that month, and multiply by 100 to give the percentage. We then average corresponding indexes (e.g. the January indexes) as before. When the indexes have been worked out they should total approximately 1200. If they do not, we multiply each index by the factor $1200/x$ where x is the actual total.

Tables 5.6 and 5.7 show the calculation of the seasonal indexes by Methods 1 and 2 respectively.

Table 5.5

	1971		1972		1973		1974		1975	
Month	Sales	MA	Sales	MA	Sales	MA	Sales	MA	Sales	MA
Jan.	320		345	288	370	307	395	330	423	354
Feb.	284		311	290	330	309	352	332	381	356
Mar.	278		303	291	325	311	345	334	374	358
Apr.	252		271	293	290	312	313	335	337	360
May	233		252	294	272	315	292	337	317	363
June	219		240	296	252	317	276	339	299	366
July	227	278	244	298	262	319	286	341	308	
Aug.	249	280	265	299	287	321	308	343	332	
Sept.	271	282	290	301	313	323	331	346	359	
Oct.	305	284	324	303	348	325	367	348	400	
Nov.	329	285	346	304	369	327	391	350	425	
Dec.	350	287	367	306	397	328	420	352	455	
Year totals	3317		3558		3815		4076		4410	
Monthly average	276		297		318		340		368	

The columns headed MA represent the 12 point centred moving average.

Table 5.6 Seasonal indexes using Method 1

Month	1971	1972	1973	1974	1975	Average
Jan.	116	116	116	116	115	116
Feb.	103	105	104	104	104	104
Mar.	101	102	102	101	102	102
April	91	91	91	92	92	91
May	84	85	86	86	86	85
June	79	81	79	81	81	80
July	82	82	82	84	84	83
Aug.	90	89	90	91	90	90
Sept.	98	98	98	97	98	98
Oct.	111	109	109	108	109	109
Nov.	119	116	116	115	115	116
Dec.	127	124	125	125	124	125
					Total	1199

Table 5.7 Seasonal indexes using Method 2

Month	1971	1972	1973	1974	1975	Average
Jan.		120	121	120	119	120
Feb.		107	107	106	107	107
Mar.		104	105	103	104	104
Apr.		92	93	93	94	93
May		86	86	87	87	87
June		81	79	81	82	81
July	82	82	82	84		82
Aug.	89	89	89	90		89
Sept.	96	96	97	96		96
Oct.	107	107	107	105		106
Nov.	115	114	113	112		114
Dec.	122	123	121	119		121
					Total	1200

(iii) Cyclical and irregular variations

For most forecasting purposes, cyclical patterns—the C factor—are relatively rare, and since irregular variations are unpredictable by nature, knowledge of the trend and seasonal indexes is usually sufficient.

However, if it is required to isolate the cyclical and irregular patterns we first deseasonalize the data by multiplying the data by 100 and dividing by the appropriate seasonal index. We then eliminate the trend factor by dividing the deseasonalized data by the trend values found by any of the given methods.

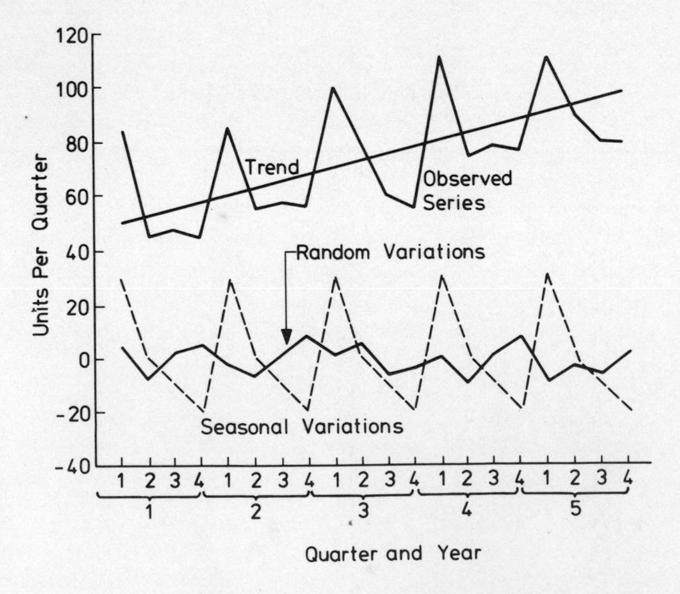

Figure 5.6 Decomposition of a time series (additive model)

If these final values are plotted on a graph they should oscillate about zero. The random variations will be obvious and so should any cyclical patterns. If a cyclical pattern does occur then we can find cyclical indexes from our deseasonalized/detrended graph, in a similar way to finding the seasonal index.

Figure 5.6 shows a typical breakdown of the time series for an additive model. For a multiplicative model we should expect an overall growth in the seasonal elements. Note that to simplify the diagram the seasonal indexes have been divided by 100.

To reassemble the elements when forecasting

(a) If the model is additive we merely add the seasonal element (*Seasonal Index*/100) and cyclical element—if there is one—to the trend values. We can make no allowance for irregular variation, and assume, in effect, that the sum of the irregular variations is zero.

(b) For the multiplicative model we multiply the same elements together. In this case, we are assuming that the product of the irregular variations is 1.

5.1.4. Hints in demand forecasting

A few further practical points worth noting are:

(*a*) The historical time series to be analysed must be self-consistent, in that there must be no change in the basis of data collection or computation throughout the series. (In this connection, statisticians view the change in the U.K. from SIC (Standard Industrial Classification) to the Common Market NACE system with profound suspicion, as it could well cause an unbridgeable discontinuity in the time series of U.K. industrial data.)

(*b*) A subjective judgment must be made about the extent of extrapolation when forecasting. One must obviously be reasonable about this, balacing the desire for long projections against the need for accuracy. There is no hard and fast rule which can help us, although some experienced forecasters would regard an extrapolation of more than 10% as risky.

(*c*) The problem of how to deal with random variation, or 'noise' as it is known in technical jargon, has received extensive treatment. We have already discussed the simpler moving average methods, but it should be noted that there are more complex methods such as multi-linear regression Box–Jenkins and X-11,[4] which use vast amounts of data and can only be realistically attempted using computer routines.

(*d*) Demand forecasting for a completely new product to be introduced to the market would seem a more difficult task because of the lack of historical data. There are two clues to guide us, however.

First, nothing is ever really new, in that it satisfies a new human need. Therefore, the 'new' product will be either extending, modifying, or cheapening an existing product, or group of products, however unlikely it may appear. For instance, paper replaced clay tablets, printing replaced handwritten scripts, microfilm is replacing books, etc.

Secondly, national economics vary in their rate of transfer technology i.e. some will lead in a particular process or product while others will lag. If we can find a leader to pair with the market for which a demand forecast is required, and can obtain data to deduce the lead time together with the rate of adoption of the technology by the leader, we can make an attempt at a forecast, allowing for the effects of scale and the current economic climate. An example is colour television, where sales in the U.S.A. have been used to predict sales in the U.K.

(*e*) Finally, no matter how sophisticated our mathematical techniques may become, forecasting is still more a craft than a science in that there is no analytical procedure which guarantees success. All computed forecasts should be subjected to close scrutiny and may be modified in the light of our experience of market forces, etc.

5.1.5. References

1. I.C.I. Monograph No. 2 (1964). *Short Term Forecasting*, Oliver and Boyd, Edinburgh.
2. Spiegel, M.R. (1961). *Theory and Problems of Statistics*, Schaum, New York.
3. I.C.I. Monograph No. 1 (1964). *Mathematical Trend Curves. An Aid to Forecasting*, Oliver and Boyd, Edinburgh.
4. Wheelwright, S. C. and Makridakis, S. (1973). *Forecasting Methods for Management*, Wiley, New York.

5.1.6. Suggestions for further reading

Lewis, C. D. (1971). *Industrial Forecasting Techniques*, Machinery Publishing, Brighton

Pearce, C. (1971). *Prediction Techniques for Marketing Planners*, Associated Business Books Ltd, London.

Robinson, J. N. (1972). *Planning and Forecasting Techniques*, Weidenfield and Nicholson, London.

Morrell, J. G. (1969). *Business Forecasting for Finance and Industry*, Gower Press, London.

Chambers, J. C. Mullick, S. K., and Smith, D. D. (1971). How to Choose the Right Forecasting Techniques. *Harvard Business Review*, July/August pp.45–74.

5.2 TECHNOLOGICAL FORECASTING

T.F. (to use the jargon!) has been defined as the probabilistic estimate of the future rate of technology transfer. Although this sounds like jargon, it is in fact a carefully worded statement about what technological forecasting can and cannot do, and is worth closer examination. The first and perhaps most important point is that the use of the term 'technology transfer' necessarily implies that the forecast must be related to that technology which is already known. The forecast cannot predict 'new' discoveries because it is a contradiction in terms to know about the knowledge which has yet to be discovered. It can, however, point to areas (particularly in scientific fields) where further advances (or breakthroughs) are most likely to occur. But those people who attempt to exploit technological forecasting as a substitute for scientific research will be disillusioned, because only scientific research can extend our existing knowledge of the real world.

Secondly, the definition specifies a 'probabilistic estimate' as a feature of the forecast, i.e. the rate at which technology is transferred must be specified in probability and time. As an example, we have known since the 1940s that supersonic flight was possible, but it was not until the 1970s that an airliner capable of supersonic flight was built. Hence a technological forecast in the 1940s would have specified that there would be a 50% chance of a 'Concorde' by 1970, a 75% chance by 1975, and a 90% chance by 1980.

The technological forecast is obviously very important to the demand forecast, especially in high technology industrial markets. A technological development may shorten the lifetime of some products, but lengthen that of others, depending on whether the development is a substitute product or an improvement to an already existing process or product. In either case the life-cycle is altered, and thus can have disturbing effects on a wide range of associated industries.

The methodology of technological forecasting has been widely discussed and the suggestions for further reading at the end of the section will enable you to delve into the subject as deeply as you wish. Suffice to say for our present purposes, that there are two distinct classes of methods: exploratory and normative. Exploratory technological forecasting starts from today's assured base of knowledge and attempts to predict the future, whereas normative technological forecasting first assesses future goals, needs, objectives, etc. and works back to the present. The two sets of techniques are, however, compatible and often a combination of both approaches is required to produce a satisfactory forecast.

5.2.1. Exploratory techniques

In this class we have both quantitative (see methods i–iii) and qualitative methods (iv–viii).

(i) Model building

Although this subject is dealt with at greater length in the next section of this chapter, in the context of market modelling, we should remember that wherever a situation is influenced by several different factors (usually called 'causal factors' in modelling jargon) that can be expressed mathematically then the technique of modelling can be applied.

The building of the model may give the forecast directly or it may be used to break a complex situation down into smaller and, we hope, simpler problems. Simplification arises out of the separation of the controllable and uncontrollable variables (respectively endogenous and exogenous variables in econometric terms). By investigating the different effects of the various factors we can choose those which cause the larger changes to the final outcome for closer study. Thus model building structures the forecasting process by enabling systematic discussion of each causal factor.

(ii) Estimation of uncertainty in forecasts and probability of occurrence of events

Uncertainty is always present in any estimate or forecast whether it is of events or figures. Thus it is useful to quantify the uncertainty surrounding each event in order that we may combine their effects in a rational manner.

To quantify this uncertainty we should adopt an interrogation procedure, as people do not often realize that they can quantify the uncertainty of their estimates. From answers to questions aimed at narrowing down the interviewee's views on the changes of occurrence of an event, we can draw a histogram having probability as the x-axis and probability density (or chances of occurrence) as the y-axis. By likening this histogram to one of the well known statistical distributions we can read off the interviewee's best estimate, from the tallest column, together with the degree of confidence he has in his estimate.

This method is very useful in assessing judgment on a range of technological forecasts which have been canvassed from experts in their field. One particular use is the narrowing down of dates by which events are most likely to occur.

(iii) Statistical methods

These rely on the availability of data in the form of time series, etc. The methods used are similar to those we have already discussed under 'Demand forecasting'.

When quoting results from these methods, which rely on extrapolation, remember to quote the goodness of fit either as a standard error in regression analysis or as a degree of correlation in curve fitting.

(iv) Delphi method

Named after the Oracle of Delphi in Greek Mythology, this approach aims to obtain the most reliable consensus of opinion of a group of experts regarding a future event. The consensus is reached according to Helmer[1], by using a series of questionnaires interspersed with indications as to how opinions differ (or feedback). An essential element in the process is the complete anonymity of the individual estimators.

Briefly the method starts with choosing the experts, the number of which can vary widely, from six to hundreds, depending on the nature of the T.F. exercise. The questionnaires are very important in the promotion of 'best estimates', hence their preparation is a skilled job. The number of rounds of questionnaires can be determined case by case by judging how quickly the estimates are approaching consensus.

Shortcomings of this method are:

(*a*) Collusion between the 'experts', who may discuss the exercise between themselves and therefore not give an independent opinion.

(*b*) The refusal of some experts to modify their view in the light of the feedback, thereby negating the consensus-forming process.

Although the Delphi method has achieved popularity, it has also achieved notoriety for the reasons discussed above. The biggest objection to its use, however, is that there is no such thing as an 'independent expert' because, by the nature of their training, their continued attendance at conferences and their reading of the literature, they tend to adopt consensus views or to adopt polarized attitudes in matters of common debate, such as the adoption of new technologies like nuclear energy.

(v) Brainstorming

This technique is similar to 'group discussions' in concept (see Section 3.4) in that a group of people are guided by a leader, but here they discuss the future. In this situation, all manner of speculation is encouraged no matter how unlikely the ideas generated may appear. The final result is a list of possible events which could happen and which can be used as the basis for further analysis.

(vi) Scenario writing

Pioneered by Herman Kahn,[2] this technique involves identifying the environment necessary to support an event. The range of the scenario is, inevitably, much wider than that of the individual company, and it is usually carried out by a University or Specialist Institute. As with brainstorming the results of scenario writing can form the basis for other T.F. processes.

(vii) Morphological analysis

Claimed to be derived from Plato and Aristotle, morphological analysis aims to foresee the likely form of future developments in technology. Its approach is to generate all possible combinations of the characteristics of the foreseen development prior to subjecting them to more detailed analysis.[3]

For example, a particular development could be: wheel supported; wheel guided; manually controlled; have multiple ground contact; be internally powered; driving through the ground; with a mechanical power source whose fuel is in the liquid state. This, in fact, is a description of the conventional motor car.

The method is comprehensive, but not all combinations of the possible alternatives are feasible, hence the efficiency of the method is low.

(viii) Envelope extrapolation

This method aims to exploit the property that the achievement of improvements in performance through time can be described by a single smooth curve. This curve is derived by enveloping several similar curves, each of which represents the contribution of individual technologies.

The result of plotting the progress of an individual technology against time is usually an S-shaped or logistic curve. If a complete technology can be represented by a set of such S-curves, e.g. the progress made in the efficiency of converting energy into illumination, then an all-embracing curve can be drawn utilizing the steeply rising parts of the S-curve of the individual technologies. Often more sense can be made if logarithmic scales are used, but beware of extrapolating the trend to infinity as, in the above case, there is a theoretical maximum efficiency of conversion beyond which technology cannot be expected to progress.

5.2.2. Normative techniques

(i) Relevance trees

Relevance trees aim to show the subgoals which must be reached before the major overall objective can be achieved.

The shape of the tree is broadly pyramidal with the number of end points of branches increasing in number as one goes down the tree. Many trial trees may have to be constructed to encompass the event in order to embrace all likely advances of technology necessary to achieve the final objective. A striking example of the use of this technique was the indication of the subgoals necessary to achieve the landing of man on the moon by 1970.

The relevance tree serves another useful role in that it enables us to check the forecast of the final objective. All subgoals must be achievable by the time the final objective is forecast to occur, i.e. it is a form of critical path analysis.

(ii) Cross impact matrix methods

The aim of this fairly complex technique is to analyse the inter-relationships between events. Firstly the chance or probability of the occurrence of a particular future event is estimated. Then the effects of the occurrence of other events on the first event are considered and the probability of this first event is modified accordingly.

By specifying the events to be considered, and estimating their initial probabilities of occurrence, and then estimating the effect each event would have on the occurrence of each other, we can build up a table, or matrix, of probabilities. This table is known as the 'cross impact matrix' and use is made of computer routines to calculate the probabilities because the occurrence of one event is dependent on others and hence the probabilities of whole chains of events have to be calculated. The results are expressed as probability distributions for particular events which may not necessarily agree with our intuitive feelings.[4]

5.2.3. Technological forecasting in the marketing context

The above are some of the better known T.F. techniques which we could use when estimating the long-term future of our industry, its processes, and products. However, the main problem when T.F. is applied to the competitive environment of private enterprise is the constraint on the free flow of information between competitors. This is very marked between nations regarding military security and defence systems. It is this constraint which ultimately restricts the usefulness of the method to specific techniques such as envelope extrapolation, where theoretical maxima can be deduced.

5.2.4. References

1. Helmer, O. (1968). Analysis of the Future: The Delphi Method. In Bright, J. R. (Ed.), *Technological Forecasting for Industry and Government*, Prentice Hall, Englewood Cliffs, N. J.
2. Kahn, H. and Wiener, A. J. (1969). *The Year 2000*, Macmillan, London.
3. Ayres, R. U. (1969). *Technological Forecasting and Long Range Planning*, McGraw-Hill, New York.
4. Gordon, T. J. and Hayward, H. (1968). Initial Experiments with the Cross-Impact Matrix Method of Forecasting. *Futures*, 1, No.2, 100–116.

5.2.5. Suggested further reading

Arnfield, R. V. (Ed.) (1969). *Technological Forecasting* Edinburgh University Press, Edinburgh.

Jantsch, E. (1967). *Technological Forecasting in Perspective*, OECD, Paris.

Wills, G.S.C., Ashton, D, and Taylor, B. (Eds) (1969). *Technological Forecasting and Corporate Strategy*, Bradford University Press, Bradford.

Wills, G.S.C., *et al.* (1972). *Technological Forecasting*, Penguin, Harmondsworth.

Linneman, R. E. and Kennell, J. D. (1977). *Shirt-Sleeve Approach to Long-Range Plans*, Harvard Business Review, March–April 1977. Details a multi-scenario approach to long term planning for the smaller company.

5.3 MARKET MODELLING

First, let us be clear what we mean by 'model'. This word has several meanings, and many people are not sure which meaning is being used in which context. When a scientist uses the term 'model' he means any simulation which describes the behaviour of the system he is studying. A model aircraft, for instance, is a physical model in which the dimensions have been scaled down. This would be necessary in order to make studies in a wind tunnel. Similarly, model ships are used in large tanks, and model bridges are used to study the effects of various loads. The other large class of models are mathematical models in which equations are used to simulate the behaviour of the system. They need not be complicated. A car, for instance, travelling at a constant speed of v kilometres per hour will cover a distance s in t seconds where $s = vt$. This equation is a model. It describes the uniform motion of an object, in this case a car. The marketing researcher has always used mathematical models in some form, and these will be the only kind described here. But remember, there are other models besides mathematical equations, such as physical models and electrical models, though these have not so far found any use in marketing research!

Next, how does modelling fit into the overall scheme of marketing research? Let us briefly review the steps the marketing researcher takes in his assignments to see where and why modelling is used.

5.3.1. The market model

A market model is an equation, or set of equations, which represents the system known as 'the market', which helps us understand and explain what the real market is like and how it works. It will contain a dependent variable, usually but not always appearing as the left-hand side of the equation, and one or more independent variables and constants on the right-hand side. These symbols are indiscriminately called parameters, even though the dictionary definition of parameter is a quantity constant in the case considered, but varying in different cases. By way of a simple, familiar, and much used example, if an industrial market is divided into N segments—say different industrial sectors—and there are X consumers in each segment, each consumer buying a quantity Q_i, then in the first segment the total sales (S_1) will be:

$$S_1 = X_{11}Q_{11} + X_{12}Q_{12} + \dots + X_{1n}Q_{1n}$$

and in the Nth segment there will be:

$$S_N = X_{N1}Q_{N1} + X_{N2}Q_{N2} + \dots + X_{Nn}Q_{Nn}.$$

This series of equations is an $n \times N$ matrix which can be summarized by:

$$S = \sum_{\substack{i=1 \\ j=1}}^{\substack{j=n \\ i=N}} X_{ij}Q_{ij}$$

where S represents the total sales.

This is one starting point for an industrial market model which could be developed in a variety of ways. For instance, if it were permissible to use the concepts of the average number of consumers in a sector ($\overline{X}_j$) and the average quantity purchased in each sector ($\overline{Q}_j$), then the expression (model) could be simplified to give:

$$S = \sum_{j=1}^{j=n} \overline{X}_j\overline{Q}_j.$$

The dependent variable is S, which is giving the information we require and the independent variables are $\overline{X}_j$ and $\overline{Q}_j$. As a mathematical model of an industrial market this could be quite adequate, despite its simplicity. It is not, however, very informative because it tells us nothing of how the market works.

Primarily, a model formalizes one's thinking about a system in a way which others can comprehend without misinterpretation. In doing this it will often make explicit certain assumptions, or enable one to deduce such assumptions, which were previously taken for granted or not even perceived, thereby reducing a frequent cause of misunderstanding. Secondly, a model can be viewed as an information processor whose output is more readily usable than its input. Thirdly, the model may be descriptive and/or predictive, by which is meant that the model may be designed

purely to give a better understanding of the market, e.g. consumer preferences, market shares, etc., or it may be used for making projections into the future, e.g. sales forecasting, changes in consumer preferences, etc. The model may be designed to answer a specific question at one point in time, and thereafter discarded, or it may be used on a continuous basis for monitoring and forecasting. Whatever its use, therefore, the model is a 'socket' into which the data must be 'plugged'.
Generally speaking, models are of two kinds, either deterministic or statistic. Both could be used in market research. A deterministic model is one where the laws of behaviour are completely understood, and the model can be written exactly without reference to the data. A well known example is the time of oscillation of a simple pendulum in a gravitational field, where the period T is given by:

$$T = 2\pi \sqrt{\frac{l}{g}}$$

where the length of the pendulum is l, and g is the acceleration due to the gravitational field. If however we are thinking of the Earth's gravitational field, then g would be given by:

$$g = a(l + b \sin^2 \phi - c\sin^2 2\phi) - \mathrm{d}H$$

where ϕ is the latitude of the point on the Earth's surface where the measurement is being made, H is the height of this point above sea-level, and a, b, c are numerical constants. This equation contains the essence of several hundred thousand measurements over many years. It is a statistical model. The mathematical function and the constants have been derived from the data.

5.3.2 Building the model

It has been said that model building is an art which, like chess playing, is gained by long experience. It has much to do with the ingenuity of the modeller and his selection of the most appropriate technique.

The first step is the specification of the output of the model, or the information which it will be designed to produce. This is sometimes called 'formulation of the problem'. The required information may be market share, influence of advertising expenditure, projected sales, etc.

The next step, and perhaps the most difficult one, is to decide the least number of variables which must be included to derive the result, what these variables are, and what functional relationship holds between these variables. An additive relationship, for instance, assumes that the independent variables do not interact. This is an essential requirement for multi-linear regression analysis. The relationship may be logistic (S-curve function) which is frequently presumed to hold for market penetration. There is obviously an infinite number of possibilities, several of which may be suitable.

The third step is the validation, or testing of the model using real—as distinct from simulated—data. Here there are two possibilities:

(*a*) The use of historic data.

(*b*) The provenance of new data not at present available.

The danger of using historic data is that the model could be 'forced' to fit data which are not relevant to future conditions. One way of overcoming this is to split the data into two sets, one set being used for building the model and the other for validating it, a procedure only possible if sufficient data are available. The second method, that of providing new data, avoids this difficulty, and could be more economic because one only collects the specific data required, but if the model eventually proves a failure it could also prove frustrating and expensive. There is no 'golden rule' to follow here.

The fourth step is 'tuning' the model, by which is meant modifying it to make it as realistic, or as best fitting, as possible, The dangers here are those of complication and specification. A simple example of the latter is polynomial curve fitting. Given n points, a polynomial of $(n-1)$ degrees will be a perfect fit, but the results of even a short extrapolation could be startling.

The last step is one not often mentioned—returning to the beginning and starting again!

5.3.3. General applications in industrial markets

There are crucial differences between consumer and industrial markets such that the models used in the former are not necessarily applicable to the latter. Briefly, some of these differences are:

(*a*) Industrial firms may buy in very much larger and varying quantities. Hence, 'poll-counting' techniques are no indication of market size.

(*b*) Industries 'buy forward', especially for commodities, and may buy under long-term contracts. Hence industrial markets are generally more stable with time.

(*c*) Reciprocal trading is another factor which tends to stabilize industrial markets.

(*d*) The buyer(s) in an industrial market may be difficult to identify. This obscures the buying decision and may obscure attempts to elucidate the qualities of the most sought-after product.

(*e*) The demand for an industrial product may often depend on the subsequent demand for the consumer product. Hence estimation of consumer demand can be a leading indicator of industrial demand ('derived demand').

The techniques, however, may be common to both consumer and industrial markets.

5.3.4. Case-study of a statistical model

An econometric model to forecast the sale of fork-lift trucks (FLT) used the well-known technique of multiple linear regression.[1] This technique[2] expresses the relationships between a dependent variable X_1 and a number of independent variables X_2 to X_N:

$$X_1 = A_1 + A_2X_2 + A_3X_3 + \dots + A_NX_N.$$

The equation is derived from the data using the method of least squares which is employed by many available computer programmes. (Desk top programmable calculators can handle 12 or more variables.)

The variables used were as follows:

X_1 = FLT sales in year t.
X_2 = The lagged index of manufacturing industrial production (year 1955 = 100).
X_3 = A constructed index of the lagged price image of industrial trucks (year 1955 = 100).
X_4 = The lagged Department of Employment and Productivity Index of Wage Rates (annual) of manual workers (year 1955 = 100).
X_5 = The lagged value of gross trading profits of companies and public corporations.
X_6 = The increase in X_5 over the preceding year.
X_7 = The increase in X_1 over the preceding year.
X_8 = The lagged stock of FLTs in existence.
X_9 = The increase in X_2 over the preceding year.
X_{10} = The increase in X_9 over the preceding year.

At least 15 annual observations were available on all of the variables, and a series of equations were derived giving the value of X_1 in terms of one or more of the 9 independent variables. The total number of possible equations is obviously 9! (factorial 9) hence some intuitive selection of the variables was made. A typical equation was:

$$X_1 - 344 + 0{\cdot}153X_8 + 217X_9 + 151X_{10}.$$

Statistical tests were used to assess which hypothesis (equation) best fitted the data. It was noticeable how similarly the various hypotheses fitted the data, and, in fact, because of multi-collinearity, discrimination between them was difficult. 'Occam's razor' was therefore applied, i.e. take the simplest hypothesis:

$$X_1 = -14311 + 203X_2.$$

This is of course a simple linear regression, which nevertheless 'explains' about 92% of the variation in FLT sales. Hence, using alternative growth rates for the lagged index of manufacturing industrial production ranged from 2% to 4%, the model was used to derive the following conditional forecast:

	2%	3%	4%
1975	14 000	15 000	16 000
1980	17 000	19 000	22 000

This forecast was combined with other data on the market to give a forecast of 25 000 annual sales of FLT and in the UK in 1980.

Although, for other reasons, the forecast may prove incorrect, the principles in building a model have been demonstrated.

5.3.5. References

1. Goldstone, L. A. and Kay, A. (1972). Long-term Forecasting in the U.K. Fork-lift Truck Market. *IMRA Journal*, 8, No. 2.
2. Wheelwright, S. C. and Makridakis, S. (1973). *Forecasting Methods for Management*, Wiley, New York.

5.3.6. Suggestions for further reading

Leeflang, P. S. H., Naert, P. A., and Koerts, J. (1975). *Modelling Markets*, MKG Marketing Books and Monographs, Bradford.

Mulvaney, J. E., and Mann, C. W. (1976). *Practical Business Models,* Heinemann, London.

Chapter 6

Presentation of results

In previous chapters we have dealth with how the research is commissioned, how the data are collected, and then how they are processed. This chapter now deals with the transmission of the prepared information.

The most usual method of transmitting information from the marketing researchers to the sponsor is by a written report and/or verbal presentation: although audio-visual means, such as sound cine films, are increasingly being used where the sponsors of the report do not speak the same language as the research team.

Where the researchers and sponsors speak the same language the written report is quite satisfactory, but it must be carefully broken down into Sections and Subsections, with a good Index, so that it can be used for reference purposes after the original reading.

6.1 REQUIREMENTS OF THE REPORT

The requirements of any report are determined by who is the reader and what we want to convey to him/her.

Let us identify four different types of reader, and their requirements from a marketing research report.

6.1.1 The Marketing Researcher

This is usually the person who is the day to day point of contact in the organization commissioning the research. We may term the person the 'professional reader' who will want to pass on the information and conclusions in some form to a third party—a decision-maker.

For the professional reader, it is necessary not only to give the facts, but also to show the way they were derived. Most of all it is important that any limitations and assumptions made regarding the data presented are spelt out.

An example of this may be taken from the presentation of forecasts. Often a forecast is expressed as the upper and lower limits of a range of possibilities which may or may not have an equal probability of occurring. If these limits have been arrived at by making a best estimate, and the range is the degree of statistical confidence appropriate to the estimate, then this must be stated exactly so that our professional reader can judge the degree of reliance he can place on the forecast presented.

6.1.2 Marketing Management

Although interested in the data and the way in which it was collected and processed, Marketing Management will be looking for the factual analyses which led to the conclusions and recommendations of the report.

Thus a report concerned with hydraulic hose for earth moving equipment will have to contain not only a forecast of hose sales, but also the calculations on which this forecast is based, e.g. forecast sales of earthmoving equipment, average number of metres of hose per unit of equipment, working life of hose in relation to the working of the equipment, and technical developments in hose design which may affect its use and life. Only with this information can Marketing Management evaluate the effect of alternative marketing strategies.

6.1.3 Research and Development

The requirements of Research and Development Management are very similar to those of Marketing Management. The same analysis of the hydraulic hose market, as in the example given, is required if the engineers are to meet the changing needs of the equipment manufacturers and interpret them to their company's advantage.

6.1.4 Senior Management

Senior managers rarely read the detail of marketing research reports. They require not more than two pages near the front of the report entitled 'Summary of Findings' or 'Executive Summary', which gives the terms of reference, conclusions, and recommendations of the report as concisely as possible.

6.2 BREAKDOWN OF THE REPORT

The terms of reference which have been used during the research will usually stipulate the Section headings required in the report.

Although circumstances alter cases very widely, a typical example of the contents list could be:

Section 1 Terms of Reference.

Section 2 Summary of Conclusions.

Section 3 Marketing Recommendations.

Section 4 The size and structure of the current United Kingdom market for Product X.

Section 5 Emergent trends and dynamic factors impinging on the future market for Product X.

Section 6 The user industries for Product X.
The purchasing decision makers.
Price and quality considerations.
Delivery considerations.
After-sales service and spares requirements.

Section 7 The competitors. Their market share, marketing and product strengths and weaknesses. Their reaction to the entry of Product X onto the market.

Table 1 The market for Product X broken down among user industries.

Table 2 The market for Product X broken down among suppliers.

Figure 1 The future market for Product X.

Appendices

6.3 WRITING THE REPORT

6.3.1 Dos and don'ts

DO provide a comprehensive contents page to enable the reader to locate important points easily.

DO use a comprehensive numbering system which is consistent throughout the report for ease of cross-referencing. Main sections, subsections and minor subheadings should be numbered.

DO indent any lists of points within the narrative, e.g. the five major competitors, the seven important markets, etc.

DO use figures wherever they clarify the point being made, and avoid using inexact phrases such as 'just over a half' or 'a clear majority'. Confine the use of algebraic symbols to the section presenting the mathematical argument, or you are likely to discourage all but the most determined of your readers.

DON'T change the basis of the analysis half way through a report. It not only confuses the reader, but may also give a completely wrong impression if he fails to read the whole report.

DON'T as a rule write the report in the chronological sequence of the research. Be guided by your brief and lay the report out to satisfy its objectives.

DON'T use marketing research jargon without a full explanation, as it does not impress the reader. He is more likely to think that something is being concealed.

DON'T be afraid to use technical terms related to the subject of the report, however. It is likely that the reader will be familiar with the terms and, in any case, it may be difficult and lengthy to describe a particular process without using them. In such cases it would always be useful to supply a glossary as an appendix for the less informed reader.

6.3.2 Style

Each organization has its own 'housestyle', whether it be a formal or informal discipline. A few simple pointers may be in order, however:

(*a*) Be as concise but as explicit as possible. There is nothing to be gained in length for its own sake.

(*b*) Although marketing research often deals with less than precise facts, over-qualification should be avoided. As marketing researchers, we have a professional duty to state the limitations of our forecasts, but we cannot evade the responsibility of drawing conclusions from them and making recommendations.

(*c*) Elegant variation or the attempt to liven up repetitious material by changes in terminology should be used with care. The report is not intended to be a literary essay, but at the same time should attempt to hold the interest of the reader. Provided there is no loss in clarity of the report, there is no reason why some variation of phrase of terminology may not be used.

6.4 PREPARATION OF FIGURES AND TABLES

Probably as much as 95% of statistical data in marketing research reports may be expressed in the form of time series or frequency distribution tables, but it is useful to remember that other methods can help to break up the monotony of the report and also aid in its clarification. Among these are:

Line graphs—which express inter-relationships between two continuous variables, e.g. time series. (See Figure 6.1.)

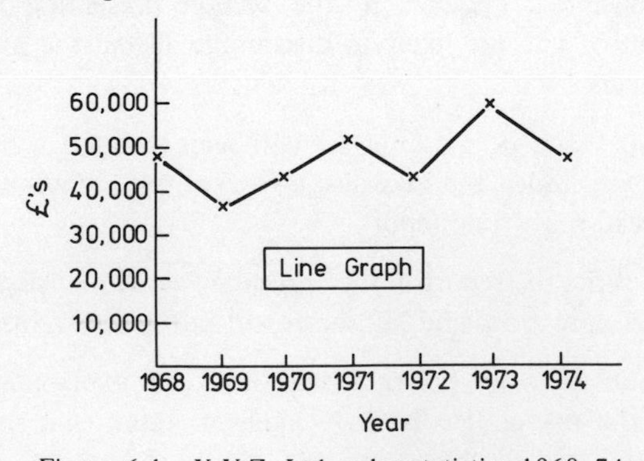

Figure 6.1 X.Y.Z. Ltd: sales statistics 1968–74

Histograms—which depict the frequency of occurrence of events with the height of each column giving the frequency. (See Figure 6.2.)

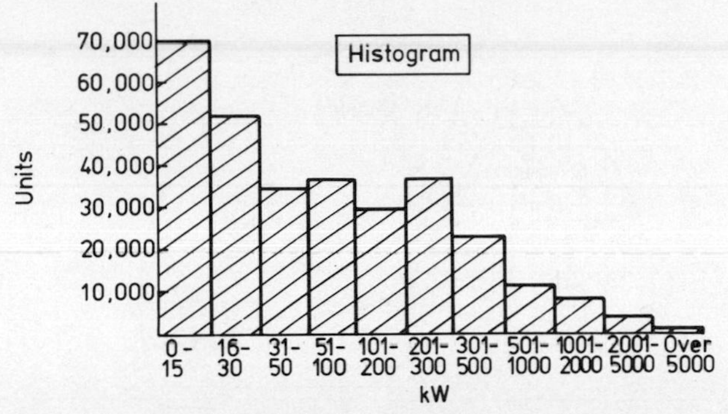

Figure 6.2 X.Y.Z. Ltd: analysis of sales 1974

Frequency polygons—which are graphs where points representing frequencies of events are joined by straight lines. This gives an outline of the distribution only, and since the information here is discontinuous, no assumptions can be made regarding intermediate points. (See Figure 6.3.)

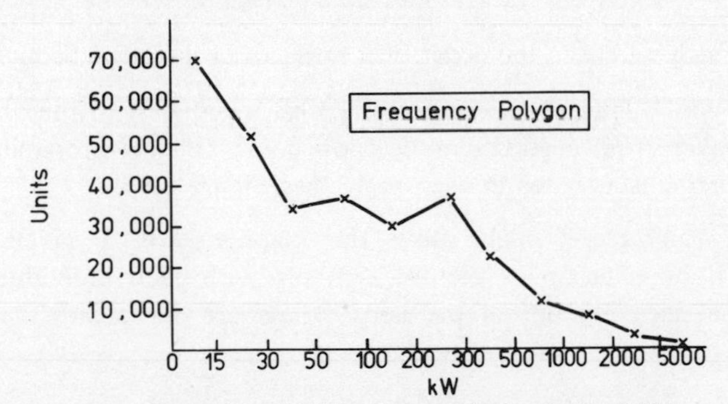

Figure 6.3 X.Y.Z. Ltd: analysis of sales 1974

Ogives or cumulative frequency curves/polygons—which, as their alternative name indicates, express the cumulative frequency above or below a given value. (See Figure 6.4.)

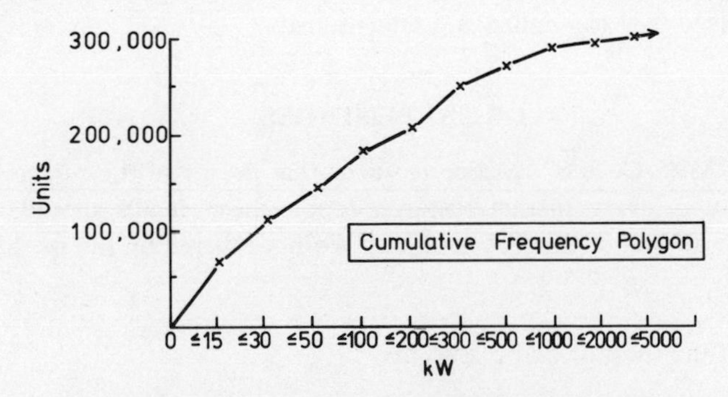

Figure 6.4 X.Y.Z. Ltd: analysis of sales 1974

Pie charts—which depict the whole by a circle and its constituent parts by portions or sectors where the angle represents the proportion of the part to the whole. (See Figure 6.5.)

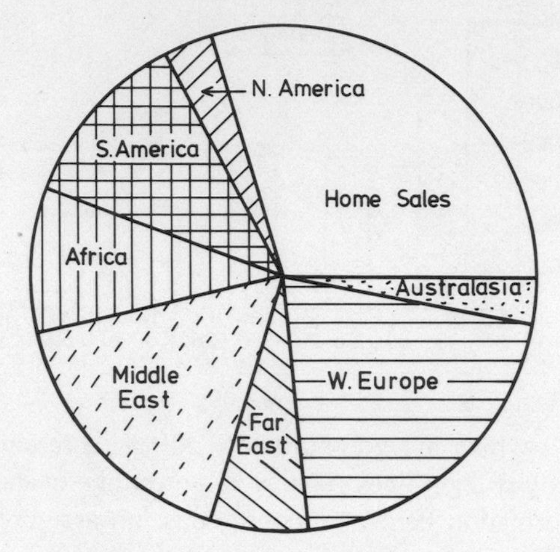

Figure 6.5 X.Y.Z. Ltd: sales by region 1974

Flow charts—which set down the order of a series of events. (See Section 3.2.)

Decision trees—which illustrate the different paths, together with their outcomes, that can be taken from a particular decision point. Often a probability of the outcome occurring is assigned to each path. (See Figure 6.6.)

Pictograms or ideographs—which show the magnitude of a given item by representing it by a group of picture symbols with each individual symbol standing for a fixed amount of the item. These are particularly suitable for presentations to the non-technical reader.

Graphical presentations, like tables, should be unambiguous, simple (concerned with one subject only), and legible. They should illustrate a trend, either over time or between variables, which is less apparent from a table or written text. Too often graphics are used to cover up deficiencies in data, or in the logic of the report, but used to advantage they can enhance it enormously.

6.5 APPENDICES

As the IMRA/MRS Code of Practice requires that details of the research method used be set out in every market research report these details should, wherever possible, be the subject of the first appendix. Points covered by the method should include:

The identity of the sponsor and researcher.

How the data were collected and by whom.

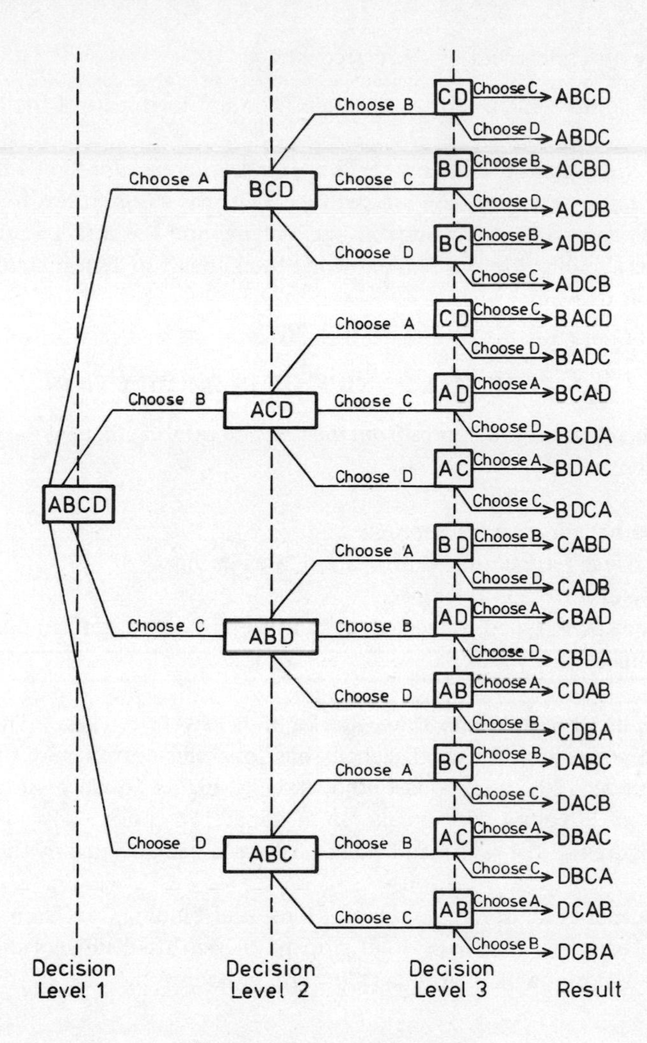

Figure 6.6 A decision tree

Date of the research.

Published sources used.

Sampling methods, if any.

Methods used for analysis: grossing up to national levels, etc.

Subsequent appendices may be used for:

Statistical data which are not quoted or used directly in the text.

Questionnaires, checklists, and raw material for the research project.

Verbatim or summary reports of individual interviews.

Bibliography and references to sources consulted.

Coverage of points which, though of interest, do not form part of the brief.

However important the contents of the appendices, great care should be taken not to give the impression that they are the report. It may be judicious to present the body of the report and its findings in one volume and the detailed appendices in another, thus avoiding the criticism of having been unable to discriminate from what is, and is not, relevant.

6.6 THE MECHANICS OF REPRODUCTION

By extracting all tables and figures from the text and printing them at the back, many advantages ensue:

They always have a page to themselves.
If a section needs retyping the tables and figures do not.
They are useful for ready reference.
They can be drawn, typed, stencilled, or compiled by other staff simultaneously in another office.

Reprographic processes have changed a lot in the past fifteen years. The agonies of reading and correcting Gestetner stencils has long since given way to Xerox for quantities under 20, with offset-litho having higher quality and becoming worthwhile at 20 copies with breakeven at about 150 copies. Nowadays pull-out tables and figures on the right-hand side of A3 are usually printed by the offset litho process.

There are merits for some purposes in loose-leaf binding, but from about 1965 either the plastic ring binder or solid strip have been used universally except for multi-client reports which are usually rigidly bound by one of the adhesive processes.

6.7 PERSONAL PRESENTATION

Presenting a report in person is not a substitute for, but an addition to, the written report. The most common procedure is for the written report to be issued to the sponsors in advance, so that the researchers can be questioned in detail on the findings, and further action can be discussed.

As with the readership of a written report, it is not always possible to select the audience for a personal presentation: in most cases, the audience imposes itself. It is therefore impossible to tailor the presentation exactly to the audience, since the needs of the different members will probably be as varied as those of the many readers of a written report. A simple and infallible rule is that the smaller the audience for a first presentation, the better.

Subsequent presentations to a sales force, or board of directors, may be as diffuse as you like: but the more people who think they may be involved in a decision process arising from the research findings, the more likelihood there is that the decision will take adequate account of the research.

6.7.1 Visual aids

It is just as important to illustrate your talk as it is to use graphics in your report in order to make the arguments and results as clear as possible. The principal aids available for doing this are:

Flip charts

These are effective for an audience of 5–25, but are difficult to make bold enough for a larger gathering. Flip charts are essential in locations where no facilities exist for electrical display: otherwise they have few advantages.

Overhead projectors

Charts can be readily prepared photographically from plain paper copy, or even from typewritten copy, and can be shown on an overhead projector to an audience of up to 200. The equipment is fairly portable and it is usually possible to find a white wall or sheet if no portable screen is available. The versatility of this method is further increased if a roll of transparent film is placed over the lens as it can then be used continuously by just winding on the unwanted illustration. Used in combination with pre-prepared transparencies the film allows on-the-spot additions or amendments without spoiling the original, if the film is laid on top of the transparency. This medium is ideal for the quick thinker and the instructive teacher, but those who are less sure of themselves should beware of the risks of under-preparation.

Slides

Slides are the most convenient, durable, and portable of all visual aids, but they take a long time to prepare. Unfortunately, the projector operator often loses the order of the slides or has trouble with the focus with the result that the audience's concentration is broken and interest is lost. Their optimum use is at international conventions.

Issued tables

If you do not trust electric gadgetry and your audience numbers over 25 then you should opt for a set of tables issued to the audience in advance of the presentation. The main advantage of this method is that everbody gets the chance of reading the illustrations, but unfortunately many are doing so at the most critical point of your argument!

Films

The ultimate in visual aids, films may only be justified on very large projects such as international multi-client research.

6.7.2 Informal presentation

Quite often the presentation consists of the researcher sitting at a table with his "audience", going through the report informally. Care should be taken, however, not to spend too much time on minor points, but on explaining the findings of the research and how they lead to the conclusions and recommendations. It is only in marketing action that the work of the marketing researcher finds its justification; everything else is merely academic.

Chapter 7

New Techniques

For too long the Industrial Marketing Research profession has been primarily concerned with techniques and developments that can, in some mysterious way, be considered the sole and exclusive province of IMR teams. This view has two very unfortunate drawbacks:

(*a*) It restricts the use of marketing skills and research methods to traditional areas.

(*b*) It restricts the techniques available to marketing researchers by classifying methods of operation of other company functions as non-marketing and hence the evolving techniques are at best overlooked and at worst considered invalid in the marketing research field.

The purpose of this chapter is to break down those self imposed barriers on the range of techniques available to us. No matter how well prepared this Manual is, it cannot be, and is not intended to be, the last definitive work on IMR techniques. Many more techniques will be found outside the covers of this book. It might mean taking the hitherto unusual step of discussing marketing research problems with other functional areas in the Company to find out how they tackle their problems. An hour with production, work study, or the accounts department can be informative, stimulating, and extremely valuable. The new techniques needed to solve our problems are often right under our noses. It is up to us to look: indeed, industrial marketing researchers should be 'technique scavengers'.

7.1 RESTRICTED VIEW OF THE PROBLEM

Ever since the marketing concept became accepted, IMR departments have focused their attention principally on the customer and competitors. In our great desire to shrug off the charge of Theodore Levitt[1] that we suffer from 'marketing myopia' we have convinced ourselves that customers and competitors are the only areas of relevant research. However, if we place too great an emphasis on either of these areas in the IMR field they may prove self-defeating. Over-emphasis on customer research often results in outcomes that are desirable from the customer's point of view, but not from the company's. For example, a very detailed market research programme by a steel panel radiator manufacturer had one real conclusion—

produce 'invisible' radiators. This conclusion, whilst very interesting, bore no relation to the skills and expertise of the company: a golden opportunity exists for some practical scientist with H. G. Wells' Invisible Man formula, but until that scientist emerges in the company, the marketing research work is redundant.

An increasing emphasis must be made in creating marketing strategies with the maximum degree of overlap between market requirements and the firm's skills. Every organization operates in an environment of 'publics'. Kotler[2] defines a public in the following way:

A public is a distinct group of people and/or organizations that have an actual or potential interest in and/or impact on an organization. That is:

Customers

Shareholders

Financial Institutions

Employees.

Industrial marketing researchers must be concerned with the whole of the Company's publics in developing new techniques and research skills.

Over-emphasis on competitors can be disastrous. It leads to a 'me-too' attitude and produces in IMR departments skills which are too narrow and specialist. Most IMR departments do a maintenance job rather than a development job. Visits to IMR departments are as predictable as they are monotonous, each department seeming to emphasize:

(*a*) Advanced statistical forecasting normally linked to the computer.

(*b*) Detailed computer analysis of actual sales.

(*c*) An extensive set of files on competitors which are dusted down annually!

(*d*) A magazine 'clipping' service.

(*e*) A host of charts.

The result is that the bulk of the time is spent mechanically up-dating the information they already have. Questions like, 'Why are we collecting this information?' are rarely, if ever, asked. This attitude of constantly asking 'Why?' is essential for IMR practitioners. In fact, 'why-meetings' should be held twice a year when every mechanical aspect of the department's work, every carefully maintained file, should have an in depth why-scrutiny, and be graded accordingly, e.g.:

A. Essential to maintain.

B. Don't really know, but could be useful.

C. Waste of time—cut out.

If a file has three consectuve B ratings it automatically gets a C rating and is cut out. It is surprising the number of files that are maintained for no purpose whatsoever. When an IMR department allows itself to operate in a stereotyped manner it is hourly reducing its effectiveness. In a time of rapid and, at times, bewildering economic and technological change, any department that considers itself unmoved is simply not fulfilling its role.

7.2 RESEARCH ORIENTATION

The one common element in those publics demanding the researcher's attention is people. The human aspects of IMR are often forgotten. Attitude and motivation research, whilst commonplace in consumer marketing research fields, is seldom used in IMR.

For some unknown reason an image has been built up that industrial publics consist of dispassionate and unemotional individuals who make all their decisions on objective and rational grounds. Do we really believe that:

Professional buyers always buy against a fixed set of rational criteria?
City investors do not make decisions on hunches?
Shop floor workers are not influenced by the amount of involvement they have in designing the product?

Those who do should ignore the next section, which is aimed at making a brief input to the solving of this type of problem.

The various early streams of thought have now crystallized into modern social sciences of sociology, social anthropology, and social psychology. Common to them is the view that man's attitudes and behaviour are influenced by several levels of society; Kotler[3] lists the following levels:

(*a*) Culture.

(*b*) Subculture.

(*c*) Social Class.

(*d*) Reference Groups.

(*e*) Face to Face Groups.

(*f*) Family.

The challenge for IMR is to determine which of these social levels are most important in influencing the company's publics.

Several *IMRA Journal* writers have, in the past, tried to assist us with guidance and help. The following points should be noted, with reference to professional buyers, shareholders, and employees.

7.3 PROFESSIONAL BUYERS

Kellogg[4] suggests that in the U.S.A. purchasing managers are held responsible by their companies for the following points:

(*a*) Consistent product quality.

(*b*) Dependable delivery.

(*c*) Practical, helpful, technical service.

(*d*) Accurate information on new products.

(*e*) Correct packaging.

(*f*) Acceptable terms of sale.

(*g*) Prompt, and correct, customer account service.

(*h*) Favourable price.

(*i*) Prompt and competent after-sales service.

(*j*) Good value overall.

Let us assume that this is the case in the U.K. (Students at Hull College of Commerce have completed several investigations which seem to justify this assumption.) The question that must now be posed is: what are the other behavioural factors which affect their buying decisions?

This information is normally obtained by depth interviews, conducted by suitably trained experts. It is unlikely that the research budget will be large enough to allow this sort of in-depth work. However, a suitably designed matrix form, to be completed by the sales force, can be particularly valuable in highlighting group influences in the company.

Each salesman should be given a check list against which he can comment on his contacts. Hudson[5] suggested that the following points could be researched:

(i) *Customer—Vital data on the company*

Capital.
Number of employees.
Number of divisions or subsidiaries.
Size of product range.
Markets served.
Credit rating.
Purchasing policies.
Chief contact.
Call frequency.
Products bought or used.
Last order value.
Service needs.

(ii) Buyers and executives—data on people

Names (with job title).
Characteristics.
Motivation.
Buying patterns.
Likes/dislikes.
Needs.
Entertainment.

(iii) *Competitive activities*

Identification of competition.
Competitive activities.
Customer acceptance.
Innovative reputation.
Product quality Pricing.
Product design (reliability).

(iv) *Are there any other needs and wants*?

Hird[6] suggested that IMR should concern itself with an approach built on the concepts of organization theory. The interested reader will find many good texts on this topic. Hird's checklist is as follows:

(i) *The organization's buying behaviour*

Task orientated, i.e. rational: do they buy against some logical model e.g. minimum price, lowest total cost, reciprocal buying, etc?; or

Non-task orientated, i.e. irrational: do they buy for illogical reasons e.g. ego enhancement, perceived risk, self-aggrandisement?

(ii) *Kinds of environmental influences*

Physical.
Technological.
Economic.
Political.
Legal.
Cultural.

(iii) *Organizational variables*

Communication processes.
Authority systems.
Status systems.
Technology.

Rewards.
Centralization.

(iv) *Group roles*

Users.
Influences.
Buyers.
Deciders,
Gatekeepers.

(v) *Individual factors*

Personality.
Motivation.
Prescribed role.
Cognition.
Learning.

A primary task for the researcher is to devise the most suitable form or matrix to ascertain the information really needed. It may comprise some points from Hudson's list or from Hird's, or be a purely tailor-made form devised from experience. One further advantage of this approach is that, by entrusting to the sales-force an extra responsibility, it becomes a most effective way of training them in the objective collection of data.

7.4 SHAREHOLDERS—THE CITY

Redwood[6] suggests that management have a tendency to assume that shareholders know little and care less about the company's activities. But who are the shareholders? The answer to this question is easy to find: the company should thoroughly analyse its shareholders' register.

In 1969 Fisons Ltd went a step further and completed attitude surveys of the private and institutional investor. An interesting result of this work was the judgment of management performance. This was a 'prompted' question in that respondents were asked to pick and grade the four criteria which they regarded as the most important, from a list presented to them. The lists shown to institutional and private holders differed somewhat but gave similar emphasis to the balance between financial and non-financial criteria.

The results showed the following preferences, graded in order of their importance to each type of shareholder:

Private	*Institutions*
1. Management capability.	1. Growth of earnings per share.
2. Increasing sales.	2. Management capability.
3. A safe investment.	3. Return on capital.
4. Widening international interests.	4. Widening international interests.

The highest rating was given by the Institutions to 'growth of earnings per share'. By contrast, neither of the main financial criteria submitted to private holders, i.e., 'net profits' or 'appreciation in the share price', reached the leading scores. Nor did 'appreciation in the share price' receive a particularly high score with institutional respondents.

From surveys such as these much of relevance can be found. The great problem is that many companies ignore their shareholders until too late.

7.5 STAFF SURVEYS

Attitude surveys of members of staff are becoming more widely accepted. The advantages are enormous: in most marketing situations quality is a vital ingredient, and good quality springs from a genuine concern from each operative. Many industrial sociologists believe that involving the staff in marketing decision-making processes will lead to a greater sense of belonging and a higher degree of concern. In Industrial Marketing the after-sales service aspect plays an important role; because of this the customer comes in contact with a wide variety of company personnel: receptionist, R&D, Accounts department, Transport department, Service department, Shop floor, etc. A unanimity of purpose is highly desirable.

Fortunately, this is probably the easiest area to research. The company has immediate access to an up to date sampling frame, i.e. lists of employees, thus postal questionnaire methods are much more easily controlled via the facility of the 'in-house' mail system.

However, the major problem with attitude measurement work is the questionnaire design, and much work has been done in an attempt to solve this problem. In practice we try to measure attitudes by means of attitude scales and related techniques such as semantic differential scales. Those interested should refer to the work of Likert,[8], Guttman,[9], Thurstone[10] and Kelly.[11] Much of this work may sound very complicated, but the onus is very much on the industrial marketing researcher to simplify and adapt the ideas as much as possible.

One technique which is particularly suitable for staff surveys is sequential analysis. Anderson, Tudor, and Gorton[12] have adapted this technique to market research problems. The following section gives a brief outline of this method.

7.6 SEQUENTIAL ANALYSIS: BASIC PRINCIPLES

Essentially, sequential analysis is concerned with a cumulative, simple analysis of results as they are obtained, rather than—as in conventional techniques—preselection of a number of respondents and completion of field research before attempting a full analysis. Sequential analysis enables field research to be terminated when sufficient evidence has been accumulated to validate a particular inference.

This approach has in the past been applied to a variety of problems, especially in medical research where it is essential to draw reliable conclusions from a minimum of data.

Sequential analysis is particularly suitable for application to problems which may be regarded as a dichotomy. For example, we may wish to distinguish between preferences for two alternatives A and B. The conclusions which may be drawn are: (i) A is preferred to B; or (ii) B is preferred to A; or (iii) the evidence is insufficient to enable a distinction to be made between A and B.

7.6.1 Application of sequential analysis

In applying the above method, randomly selected respondents are asked in turn to state a preference for either A or B. Preferences are then plotted sequentially on the appropriate chart, 'no preference' replies being ignored for purposes of analysis. The investigation is terminated when the sample path, which has been plotted, hits one of the significance boundaries.

Two situations can arise in marketing research: (i) where it is important to determine which alternative is preferred (is A preferred or B or no preference?); (ii) where the researcher is concerned only whether A is preferred and other possible results, i.e. no preference, or a preference for B, are of less interest.

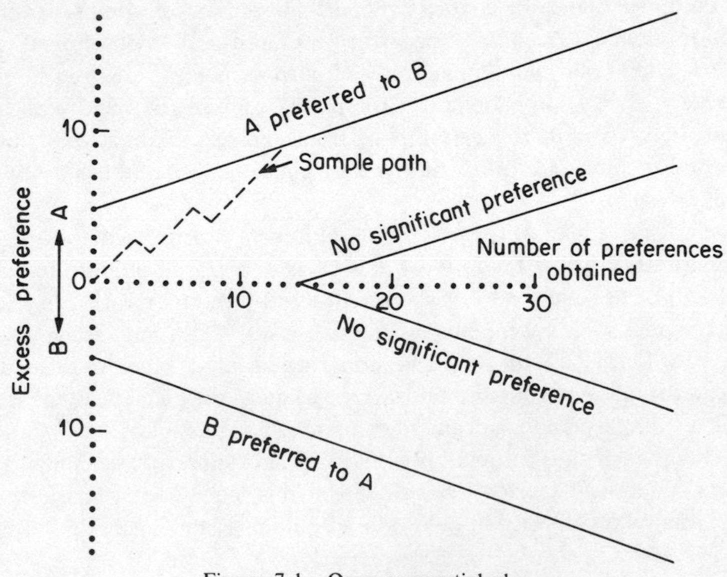

Figure 7.1 Open sequential plan

Slightly different approaches are adopted in each case, as described below.

(i)Symmetrical designs

These are used for determination of absolute preferences. The exact choice of chart design depends upon balancing the desire to make the test as sensitive as possible with a desire to economize in time and expense. One possible chart is shown in Figure 7.1.

The sample path shown as an example corresponds to the sequence of preferences AAABAAABAAAAAA.

At this stage after 14 preferences have been recorded, the sample path crosses the 'A preferred to B' significance boundary, at which point the investigation would be terminated. The significance boundaries shown in Figure 7.1 are diverging pairs of parallel straight lines; the procedure illustrated is said to be open because there is no limit to the distance that the sample path may travel between either limit of the significance boundaries. This is clearly a disadvantage in terms of economy, and several authors have described truncated or 'closed' designs in which a decision boundary must be reached eventually. An example is shown in Figure 7.2.

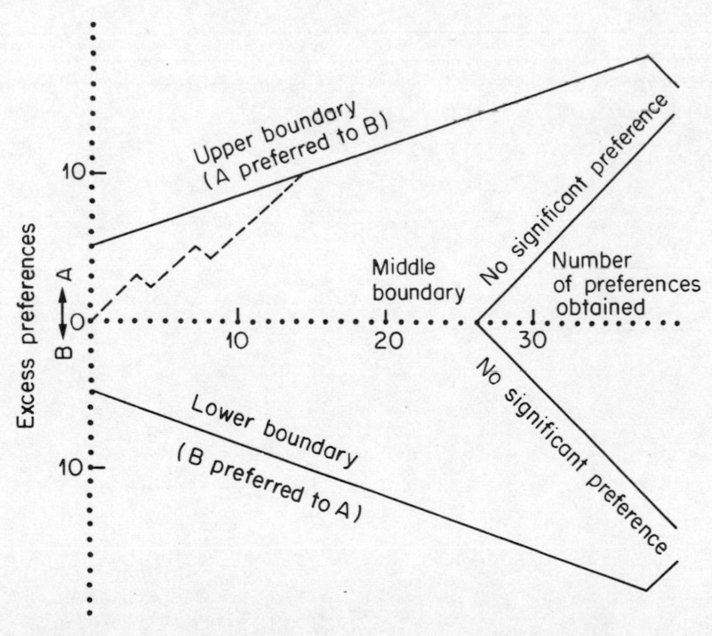

Figure 7.2 Closed sequential plan

Of the many closed designs described in literature the one that is recommended for IMR is Bross's Plan B.[13] This recommendation is made on the grounds that the Bross plan combines simplicity with the best compromise of sensitivity and economy. This plan is shown in Figure 7.3; the specification is given in Table 7.1 which enables the boundaries to be drawn.

Table 7.1 Specification of boundary points for Bross's Plan B

Number of preferences	Excess preferences y		Number of preferences	Excess preferences y	
	Upper boundary	Lower boundary		Middle boundary	
8	8	−8	58	12	−12
11	9	−9	57	11	−11
14	10	−10	55	11	−11
17	11	−11	54	10	−10
20	12	−12	52	10	−10
23	13	−13	51	9	−9
26	14	−14	49	9	−9
28	14	−14	48	8	−8
30	14	−14	46	8	−8
32	14	−14	45	7	−7
35	15	−15	43	7	−7
37	15	−15	42	6	−6
39	15	−15	40	6	−6
41	15	−15	39	5	−5
43	15	−15	37	5	−5
45	15	−15	36	4	−4
47	15	−15	34	4	−4
49	15	−15	33	3	−3
51	15	−15	31	3	−3
53	15	−15	30	2	−2
55	15	−15	28	2	−2
57	15	−15	27	1	−1
58	14	−14	25	1	−1
			24	0	
			22	0	
			20	0	

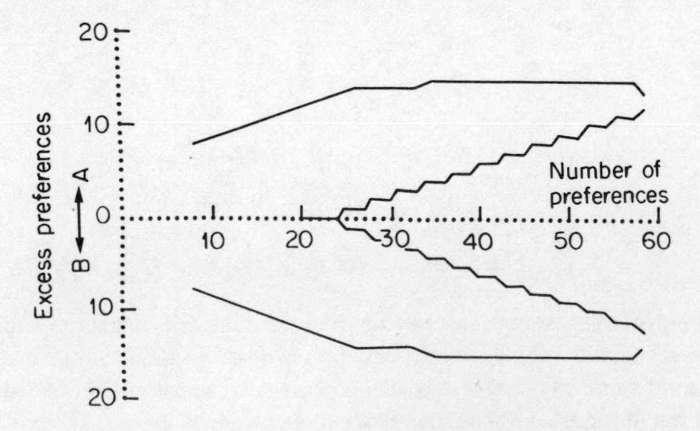

Figure 7.3 Bross's Plan B (shown in Armitage's convention)

(ii) Skew designs

These are used for determination of selected preferences. So far only those situations where we wish to know whether A or B is preferred, or if there is no preference, have been discussed. Occasions will arise when we shall merely wish to establish if A is preferred, other alternatives being of little interest.

An example might occur when a possible change to an existing product is under consideration. The change would be made only if the test product (A) were significantly preferred to the standard product (B).

In this instance a new middle boundary is drawn in the lower segment of the chart. Figure 7.4 shows the new boundary drawn at an angle of 45° from point X, as the ordinate and abscissa scales are equal.

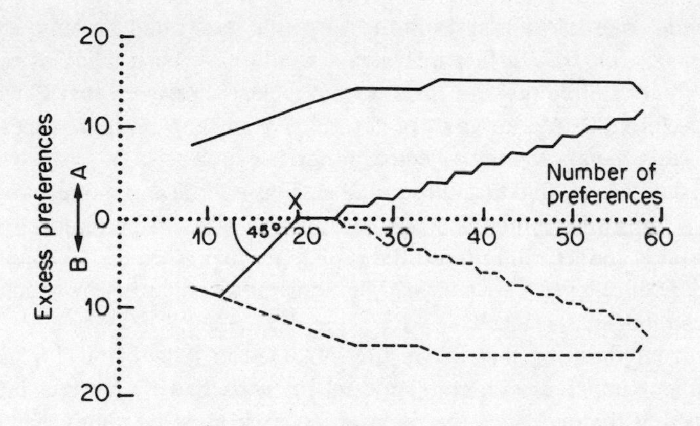

Figure 7.4 Modified Bross Plan B

Should the path intersect either with the lower boundary or with the new middle boundary, it is clear that under no circumstances could A be significantly preferred. The test can then be terminated.

7.6.2 In-use procedures

All marketing research practitioners know the frustration of being commissioned on projects in which essential objectives have not been explicitly defined at the outset. Sequential analysis, however, puts an onus on the commissioner of any research to identify clearly the dichotomy under investigation, and the extent of the funds available to solve that dichotomy.

A thorough understanding of this concept can create a synergy of purpose, which epitomizes the major advantage of this technique.

Practically, the method is simplicity itself:

(*a*) Clearly identify the dichotomy under investigation.

(*b*) Draw up the decision boundaries on graph paper according to the scheme used. Data are given in Table 7.1 for construction of Bross' Plan B. Identical proformata can then be used for future trials.

(*c*) Plot references obtained from randomly selected respondents in a sequential manner on the appropriate chart.

(*d*) The investigation is terminated as soon as a boundary line is reached. We are then assured of a statistically significant result.

7.6.3 Validating exercises

Numerous studies utilizing conventional analysis have been conducted over a period of years and these have been checked using the sequential technique. This was possible because the completed questionnaires had been numbered consecutively.

Five tests were re-examined by the sequential technique and the results are outlined in Table 7.2 and shown graphically in Figures 7.5–7.9

Tests 1 and 5 plot into a non-decision 'no man's' area; had we used sequential analysis, it is possible that further interviews would have been taken as significant preferences might still be possible. It is certainly clear, however, that B would not have been preferred to A and X not preferred to Y since in both instances the line plotted intersects the appropriate selected preference area.

In tests 2, 3 and 4, we find that substantial savings in time and money would have been achieved using sequential analysis: the more positive a preference, the more rapidly a result is confirmed. In test 3 the preference expressed is significant even at the 99% confidence level. Test 4 clearly demonstrates a situation in which the 'no preference' boundary is reached.

It is worth emphasizing that the results obtained in tests 1 and 5 would have shown savings compared with conventional methods had the correct dichotomy been identified at the outset i.e. the research sponsor must be quite clear as to his objectives to gain the maximum effectiveness from the technique.

Table 7.2 Summary of results

Test No.	Results using conventional analysis		Resulting using sequential analysis		
	Conclusions drawn	No. of interviews	Conclusions drawn	No. of interviews Required	Saved
1	No significant difference	30	Uncertain: further interviews could be useful as preferences are possible; B is *not* preferred	30	—
2	U preferred to V	31	U preferred to V	26	5
3	S preferred to R	30	S preferred to R	18	12
4	No significant difference	33	No preference	20	13
5	No significant difference	29	Inconclusive: X is *not* preferred	29	—

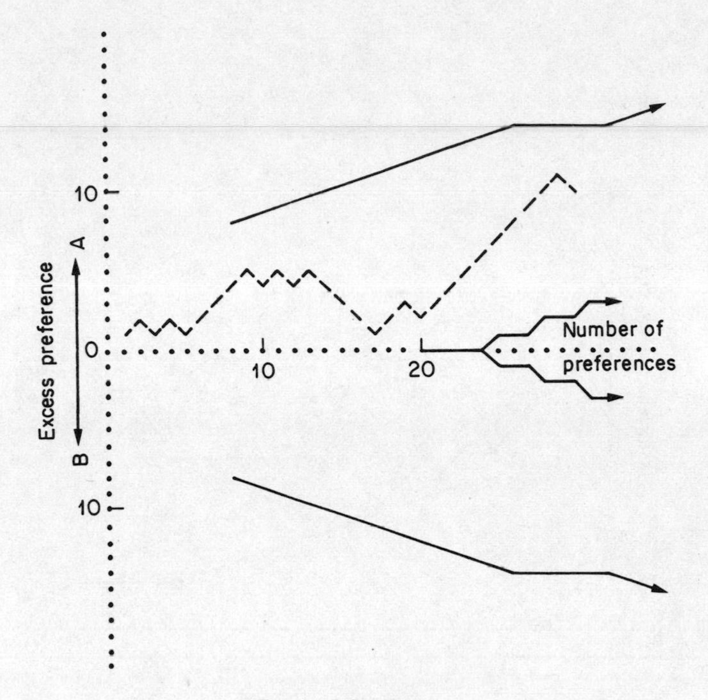

Figure 7.5 Test 1

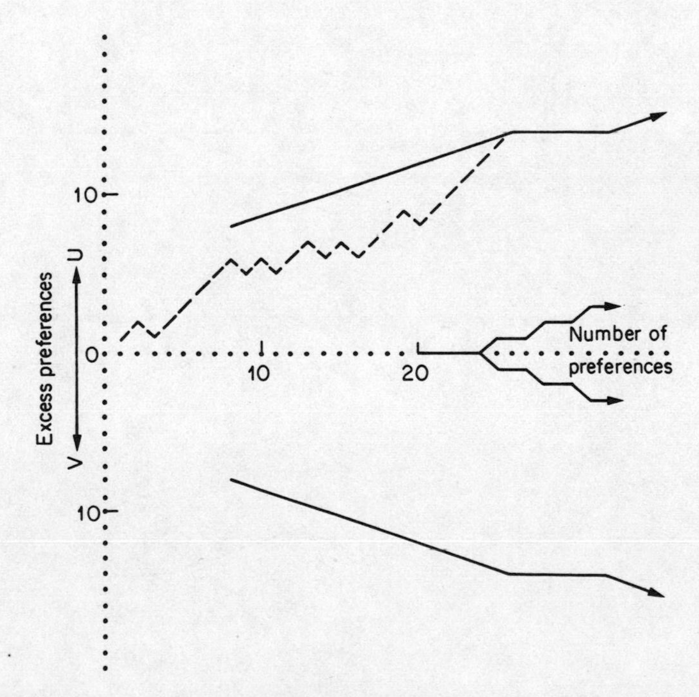

Figure 7.6 Test 2

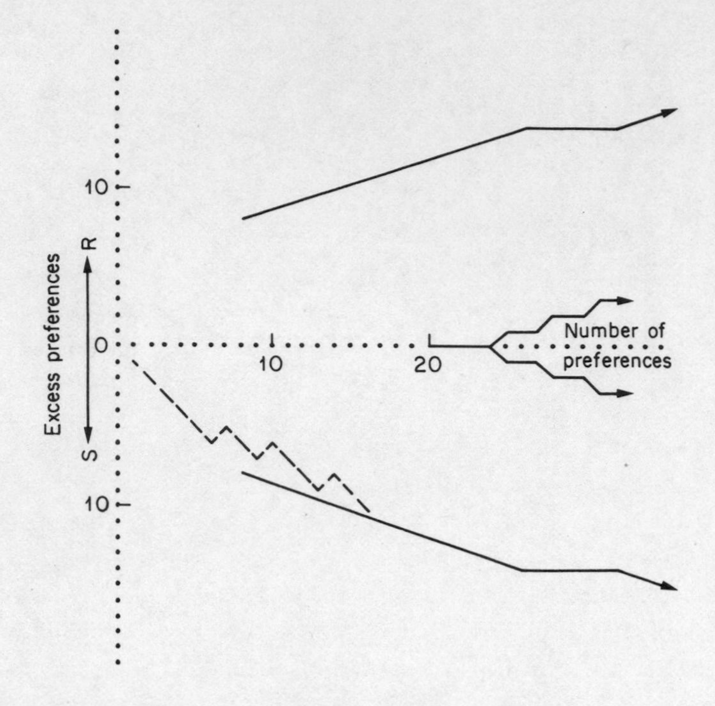

Figure 7.7 Test 3

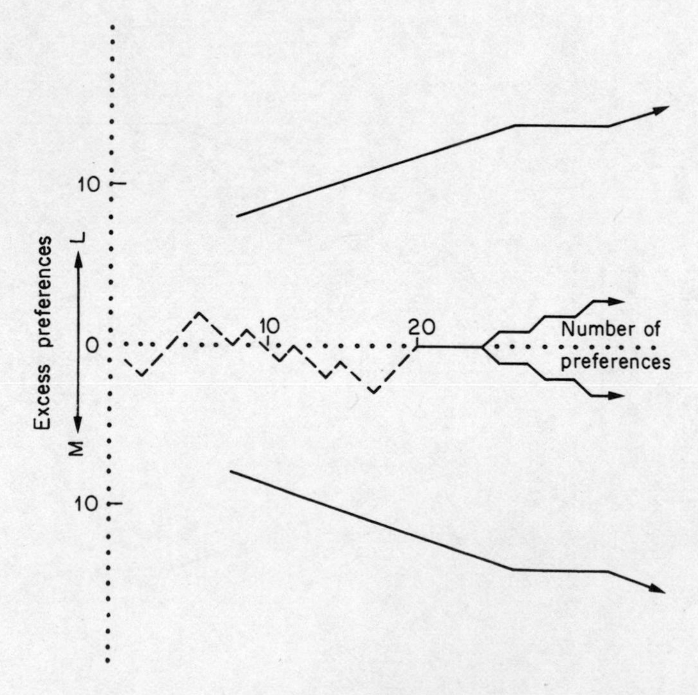

Figure 7.8 Test 4

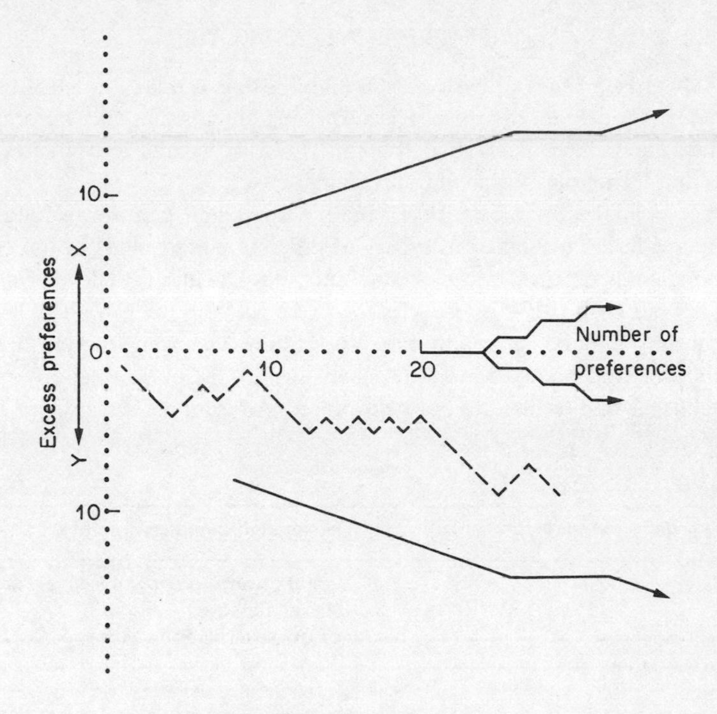

Figure 7.9 Test 5

7.6.4 Applications

So far, we have discussed the uses of sequential analysis to conventional marketing research programmes.

Consider for example any management decision dichotomy in which an opinion from employees would be helpful: for example on a trivial level, selection of the day for an extra holiday, or more seriously, the choice of a preferred bonus scheme. Currently management has four alternatives: (*a*) a census; (*b*) consultation with members of consulting bodies; (*c*) no consultation at all; (*d*) a 'conventional' survey.

Sequential analysis could readily be applied to the opinions of a random sample of employees to establish more quickly than other methods whether a preference exists, and if so precisely what it is.

Imagine trade union leaders using this method to establish whether they should recommend industrial action!

Although we have only considered dichotomous situations, there is no reason why the method should not be applied to those multi-choice situations which can be considered as a multiplicity of dichotomies, e.g. preference for A/no preference for A, preference for B/no preference for B, preference for C/no preference for C, etc. The only note of discord in this particular instance is that the prime strength of the technique is its supreme simplicity and any confusion which arises from a multiple dichotomy could defeat this advantage.

7.7 CREATIVE ASPECTS

One of Edward de Bono's[14] basic assumptions is that people, i.e. all of us, are far more creative than we ever realize. The surprising thing is that once an organization has gained experience of creative thinking it easily adapts and creates its own methods and techniques for solving problems.

In order to make the most of the creative approach, venture technique teams should be set up consisting of members of different departments in the company: production, management services, accountants, etc. The idea is to develop synergy of talent from our own existing resources.

One meeting may be chaired by the Work Study Manager with an input, 'How work study methods could solve IMR problems'. A list of work study methods is soon established and techniques can be explored. An example is shown in Table 7.3.

Table 7.3

Work Study Dept. Methods	Triggered Techniques for IMR
Value analysis	Venture teams looking objectively at problem-solving methods
Critical path analysis	Direct use in planning surveys
Critical examination	'Why' meetings
Form design	Questionnaire work
Stock models	Decision tree analysis, etc.
Simulation models	Various model applications

On one occasion we took *Alice in Wonderland* as a base for suggestions. The bizarre idea of 'unbirthdays' put forward by the Mad Hatter triggered 'unprogress meetings'. These meetings were specifically designed to bring to light those areas of the companies activities where IMR had made no contribution at all. Such meetings held bi-annually were a revelation!

The important point of this chapter is that the Industrial Marketing Researcher should realize that because each company is different, i.e. serving different publics, the best research techniques for him are likely to be different than for other companies.

As IMR practitioners we should never fear the innovative approach, so, take the sound basic techniques and refine and adapt them to suit the circumstances!

7.8 REFERENCES

1. Levitt, T. (1960). Marketing Myopia *Harvard Business Review*, July/August. 1960.
2. Kotler, P. (1972). *Marketing Management: Analysis, Planning and Control*, 2nd ed. Prentice Hall, Englewood Cliffs, N.J.
3. Kotler, P. (1975). *Marketing for non-profit Organisations*, Prentice Hall, Englewood Cliffs, N.J.
4. Kellogg, C.D. (1970). *IMRA Journal*, Vol VI No.2 pp.76–85.
5. Hudson, C.L. (1970) *IMRA Journal*, Vol VI No.2 pp.93–102.
6. Hird, M.W. (1973). *IMRA Majorca Conference, December 1973*. Unpublished Conference Papers.

7. Redwood, H. (1971) *IMRA Journal*, Vol VII No.1 pp.14–23.
8. Likert, R. (1967) The Method of Constructing an Attitude Scale *Readings in Attitude Theory and Measurement*, Wiley, New York.
9. Guttman, J. *et al* (1950) Studies in Social Psychology in World War II, *Measurement and Prediction*, Vol. 4, Princeton University Press, Princeton.
10. Thurston, L.L. (1928) Attitude can be Measured. *American Journal of Sociology* Vol. 33, pp.529–554.
11. Kelly, G.A. (1955) *Psychology of Personal Constructs*, Vols. I and II, Norton, New York.
12. Anderson, E.J., Tudor, R and Gorton, K. (1976) *Journal of the Market Research Society*, **18**, No. 4.
13. Bross. I. (1952) Sequential Medical Plans, *Biometrics*, **8**, 188–205.
14. de Bono, E. (1967). *The Uses of Lateral Thinking*, Pelican, Harmondsworth.
    de Bono, E. (1972). *Po: beyond yes and no*, Pelican, Harmondsworth.

Chapter 8

Intelligence aspects of IMR

Since IMR is largely the application of intelligence gathering this chapter may seem extraneous, but it specifically concerns itself with that ongoing data collection and analysis which is, to a large extent, the basis on which instant response to queries is based.

8.1 SOURCES OF MARKETING INTELLIGENCE

Much of the desk research side of IMR depends on the ready availability of data in structured form, and none more so than that concerned with competitors, economic and political trends, and acquisition analysis. There are, however, two major differences between regular IMR report preparation and writing and 'intelligence' reports. One is that much of the data for the latter are gathered over a long period of time, with no immediate use in view. The other is that intelligence reports rely much more heavily on making subjective decisions about the data and their interpolation.

A real fanatic for intelligence regularly culls a great number of sources from which individual items of information are collated, filed, and regularly reviewed. He or she does all this in the hope that the snippet of print from some obscure trade publication will yield a jackpot at some future time. We are aiming for the same goal, but without becoming an information officer rather than a marketing researcher.

The collection of intelligence is time consuming and, in many ways, drudgery. The information sources we use are many:

Trade reviews.

Marketing surveys.

Press reports.

Trade papers.

In-house sources such as salesmen.

Information services (see Sections 2.3 and 2.5).

Investment reviews from stockbrokers, etc.

Company reports and financial news services (Extel).

Companies House, where each Registered Limited Company has to file, annually, a Statutory Return of Directors and Shareholders together with a copy of its annual, audited accounts.

In these sources we are looking for information which will enable us to carry out several major functions. These include:

Providing details of our own company's position in its markets for forward planning.

Market monitoring to assess the relative strengths of competitors.

Maintaining a continuous watch on changes that could alter the competitive situation.

Preparing for acquisitions and mergers.

So, we should collect any item of news which throws light on markets; companies in the same fields as our own; technical information on products and technology. Other headings include quality of management, technical expertise, financial and shareholding information about our competitors.

For those lucky enough to have access to a properly run 'in-house' information department it is normally enough to ensure that the departmental head knows exactly what is required. This means delineating the areas of data that are likely to be needed for retrieval and storage, but, for the rest of us, it is just hard graft.

Because the information we collect is coming from such varied sources we have to evaluate it carefully. In order to ensure that the data, as far as possible, are comparable, a work plan should be produced. This overall work plan actually comprises two plans, one concerned with the data, the other with their use.

8.1.1 Data collection plan

To ensure that data are collected on a systematic basis we must apply the fundamental principles of IMR, for we need to:

(*a*) determine our information need;
(*b*) allocate our priorities (and try to anticipate needs);
(*c*) collect our information systematically and record it carefully;
(*d*) time-table evaluation reviews;
(*e*) evaluate on a regular basis;
(*f*) selectively monitor our data inputs.

This working method is essential to prevent us from getting bogged down in minutiae, for it is very easy to collect everything peripheral to our needs but, useful as this can be, it is time-consuming.

Hence the need to (*a*) determine our needs, and specify these in order to set a bound to our culling. Even at this point it is possible that more input is needed than we have time to handle—there is nothing more daunting than the pile of papers which have yet to be clipped! So we must (*b*) allocate priorities which will tie the degree of elaboration on a subject to its overall priority in our work.

Because data are flowing in from all directions (*c*) we must be completely systematic in our approach—an item of information buried in a pile of cuttings which need to be filed might not have been cut at all! In recording it (the transfer of salient points to a data base as an updating, etc.) we must ensure that the records include sufficient identification of source.

In time-tabling (*d*) we are taking into account the need to check data bases when particular flows of information are the norm—as in financial data collection when reviews of a particular firm would be tied to annual report publication and interim result announcements. Evaluation on a regular basis (*e*) enables a continuous picture to be built up—it also helps us in the preparation of a working time-table. If we know that we need a week each quarter for evaluating our data bases then this can be scheduled—otherwise we find ourselves forever grabbing a moment and getting nowhere.

The need (*f*) to selectively monitor our inputs is self-evident to anyone who uses, say, governmental statistics. As a result of long practice we learn to make the automatic adjustments needed to improve the quality of the data. The same need is even more essential in the case of the sources we are calling on in our intelligence work. One journalist may prove to be highly accurate, another gets 'scoops' but writes rubbish in the intervening period! We must learn, by checking and cross-referencing our checks, which sources can be trusted implicitly and so on, down the scale to those which just occasionally get something right! It also enables us to reappraise the situation when an editorial staff change is made on one of our source journals.

8.1.2 Data usage plan

In order to make the best use of the information we are collecting we must develop suitable data bases. These will vary from small market models to more elaborate financial analyses, so we should:

Monitor commercial activities on a standard basis.
Develop a market share matrix (possibly by using input/output analysis).
Standardize the financial information (see later in this chapter).
Continuously update the data bases, by reviewing all reports from every source.

8.2 PRACTICAL ASPECTS OF INTELLIGENCE GATHERING

Before moving on we must recap on the practice of intelligence, and it is worth doing this in some detail. The primary role of intelligence work is to keep us informed—and, preferably, enable us to anticipate change. It is, therefore, an extension of our daily work in IMR—so let us assume that the sources are to hand. Here we must take advantage of those others within the company who are also collecting information for their own disciplines. These include the engineering and design staff in manufacturing firms, the accounts (financial control) department, the sales office, etc. They will all have their own sources and we can pick their brains to ensure that we have access to these sources or, at least, know which we should best cull.

Filing requires that the data are cut from the source or written out (if a verbal input). Although the Xerox is a marvel of technology in this field, cutting and pasting to scrap sheets of paper is probably quicker—if messier—and handwritten notes are quite acceptable. Access to a copier becomes essential for cross-referencing (where two or more files should receive the same item), but here the relative merits of a further copy of an item, as opposed to notes referring to it, must depend on office circumstances. Before the data are filed salient points should be entered in the relevant data bases. Market information, estimates of market size or share, for instance, would be correlated with existing information and either used to update it if the source were dependable, or to provide further evidence of accuracy if not graded as to quality. Corporate information is treated in the same way, but here we have the base in the form of published information with a high level of reliability. Filing should then be done under three main headings—commercial, technical, and financial. So, with the basics behind us what are we aiming to do? The answer to that is probably to ask ourselves a series of questions on each of these filing areas.

8.2.1 Commercial

The information to be collected should encompass sales patterns, customers, pricing, delivery times, and so on—all the day to day data that are necessary to analyse a company's sales performance in the market place and compare it to other companies', including our own.

Among the commercial questions which we are attempting to answer are:

In which geographical areas do the companies under consideration sell?

Are these areas limited in size; are any companies expanding outside a traditional sales area? What will happen if they do so?

Are we all selling to the same customers or is the market stratified?

What are the factors for any division of the market and are these changing? (There may be two markets: one to distributors and the other to Original Equipment Manufacturers—OEMs.)

How do prices, discounts, special offers, relate between suppliers?

Is delivery a vital factor in capturing or holding customers and how well does the competition compare?

Each of us has a different list of questions to answer, therefore we must draw up our own list as our knowledge expands. When we have the questions the data we must collect become obvious.

8.2.2 Technical

Technical information falls into two broad areas—how competitive products compare with ours and how changes in technology or materials might affect the future of the product or the market.

For this reason we are concerned with catalogue information, which gives us product range, specification, price, technology, reliability, servicing, and, even, on occasions, size. From this we can work up a comparison chart listing all the relevant details, fully cross-referenced, from which we can keep abreast of changes which might have an impact on the market.

For technology and material changes one is reliant on journals outside the normal run. The best way to collate data in this area is to find a 'tame' engineer or designer and pick his brains twice a year! It is otherwise necessary to have a working knowledge of a suitable discipline or develop sufficient background to enable one to comprehend the impact of new materials, manufacturing methods, and technical changes.

8.2.3 Financial data

This is a much more complex sector since the data—though generally more easily accumulated—require more analysis. Ideally, a background in basic accounting is required, but the fundamentals are readily grasped and one can normally call upon the financial wizards of the company accounts department for help. From the financial information which one can collect (see Section 2.5) it is possible to build a profile of a company and watch its progress over the years. We can plot its changing fortunes, the development and decline of products, changes in market strategy, alterations in manufacturing efficiency, and the impact of changes in the company's markets and the economy in which it operates.

The three areas are taken individually, but it is important to understand their relevance. Commercial intelligence tells us about the products and their manufacturers in the market being researched; it also provides a preview of market changes.

Technical data let us compare products for quality, price, performance, etc.

Financial data give us an indication of the ability of a company to carry out investment, research, and also allows us to estimate the strength of their management through key accounting ratios (see Section 8.3).

8.3 INTERPRETATION OF COMPANY ACCOUNTS

The report and accounts published, in theory, by every company for each trading year is our most important source of data on companies. However, the information given in a set of accounts consists, in the main, of a large number of figures which can be confusing at first glance. One method of approach, which considers the general picture, results for the period, the financial position, and the 'small print', is to follow the same route through a financial report every time. (For an explanation of accounting terms used in this section see 8.3.5.)

8.3.1 The general picture

(i) We find out *what the Company does* from the Directors' Report.

The Chairman's Statement (if any) will amplify this considerably and also give a rundown of trading in the year (or other period) covered by the accounts.

(ii) We get an impression of *size* from:

The turnover figure (Profit and Loss Account)—a note will explain what turnover represents (e.g. value of goods sold, commission, income, etc.).

The total assets employed (i.e. fixed assets plus current assets plus investments or other assets).

The average number of employees (Directors' Report) and the total wage/salary bill.

(iii) We analyse the Company's *general trading pattern* from:

The breakdown of turnover and profits between different activities, where given (Directors' Report).

The value of export business (Directors' Report) in relation to total turnover.

In the case of quoted companies with overseas trading interests, geographical analysis of turnover (Directors' Report or Notes on Accounts).

(iv) It is imperative to look at the *accounting policies* of the company (to be found—if disclosed—in the Notes) in relation to its activities and if possible in relation to those of other companies in similar fields. From this we can see whether consistent and appropriate bases of accounting have been adopted, and if not we must make some adjustment to bring the accounts to a standardized base.

8.3.2 Results for the year (or other accounting period)

The Profit and Loss Account gives us trading data so we look at:

(i) Pre-tax profits

This is the central figure in the Accounts since it is this that measures the management ability of the Directors and ultimately controls what can be paid out as dividend or ploughed back to earn future profits.

The figures of pre-tax profits may be related to:

Turnover, as a net margin percentage

Capital employed, as a rate of return.

This year's profits may be related to last year's and the increase or decrease analysed between changes in volume of business and changes in profit margins.

(ii) Net trading profits

The profit earned before interest charged or received and certain other items. Adding back the figure for depreciation gives us:

(iii) Gross trading profit

This figure is a useful measure of overall 'efficiency' of manufacturing and marketing ability.

A time series of the ratio, Gross trading profit/Turnover, is a useful pointer to changes in a company's strength. An improving series is an indicator of some significance (especially in a competitor!) whilst fluctuation or decline is often adverse since it points to lower profitability or lack of management control.

(iv) Exceptional and extraordinary items

An *exceptional* item is a 'one-off' profit or loss arising from the normal trading of a business. An *extraordinary* item is a 'one-off' profit or loss arising outside normal trading activities. Exceptional items are included *but shown separately* in computing pre-tax profits; extraordinary items are shown separately *but after deducting taxation* and as an addition to profits after tax. They should both be disregarded in our computations.

(v) Earnings available for distribution to Ordinary Shareholders

This is the amount which the Directors can either *distribute* by way of dividend (giving the shareholders immediate income) or *retain* in the business to help finance future growth (thus effectively investing money in the business on behalf of shareholders).

(vi) Earnings per share (EPS) This is the result of dividing the net attributable profit (before extraordinary items but after minorities and preference dividends) by the number of shares in issue. Normally quoted in pence per share.
Price Earnings ratio (PE or PER)
This is the result of dividing the stock market price by the EPS.

(vii) Sources and Uses table.

For a quick overview of how the balance sheet has changed in the past accounting period we look at the 'Sources and Uses' analysis (or prepare our own). This table tells us where the money and assets of the company have gone, what changes there have been in borrowing, stocks, etc. It quickly summarizes the year—but it is no substitute for analysis. It can, however, give us an answer when the boss is breathing down our neck!

8.3.3 Financial position

Our interest in the 'balance sheet' has two major aspects: the *amount* of capital invested and the *deployment* of capital, or asset structure. The latter aspect also covers the company's liquidity situation.

If we are looking at a group of companies, the accounts will contain *two* balance sheets, one for the parent company itself and one for the group as a whole. The latter (the *Consolidated* Balance Sheet) is the more useful document.

(i) Capital employed

This is the sum of:

(*a*) share capital and loan capital where appropriate;

(*b*) reserves.

Reserves normally consist for the most part of retained profits of current and earlier years. They include the balance of the Profit and Loss Account itself. Profits will be retained either as a result of the deliberate re-investment of trading and other realized profits or because credit has been taken for unrealized profits e.g. a surplus arising on the revaluation of property used as trading premises. The item 'Share Premium Account' is also normally included with reserves, even if shown under a separate heading, and is included in the calculation of capital employed. (See Section 8.3.5 for a definition of these terms.)

For most purposes it is usual also to include *long-term borrowings* in the calculation of capital employed. The significance of the amount of capital employed is that it is a measure of the total economic resources devoted to the company. When the annual net pre-tax profit is related to it (i.e. pre-tax profit times 100, divided by capital employed), the resulting percentage rate of return on capital is a yardstick of the efficiency with which the resources have been used. It is, therefore, useful to develop a time-series of this ratio for use when we need to compare a company's performance either with previous years or with other firms.

(ii) Asset structure

The main points that we look for here are:

Liquidity position. What is the ratio of 'current assets' to 'current liabilities'? As a guide, a ratio of less than unity indicates weakness, and total dependence for solvency on trade credit and/or bank finance; a ratio of 2 or more indicates relative financial strength. The so-called 'quick asset' ratio relates debtors and cash (ignoring stock and work in progress) to total current liabilities. If this is less than unity, the business is presumably relying on a quick turnover of stock (and hence conversion into cash) to 'get by'.

Asset utilization. What are the ratios of stock and debtors respectively to turnover? The formula:

$$\frac{\text{Stock (or debtors)} \times 12}{\text{Annual turnover}}$$

gives the number of month's stock (or debtors) held. If these items are much less than 3 months, asset utilization may be considered good. We must, however, relate this to the type of trade or industry in which the Company is engaged.

Fixed Assets. These consist normally of property, plant, other equipment, and motor vehicles. The Note to the Accounts about fixed assets will indicate whether the property is freehold or leasehold, and whether included at cost or a professional valuation. If the current value of the property is thought by the Directors to be substantially at variance with the balance sheet value, the Directors' Report will contain a note to this effect. With regard to plant and machinery, if the net book value decreases in the year, this means that it is not being replaced as fast as it is wearing out or being scrapped. The relationship of the net book value of plant to its cost value will give an indication of the average age of the plant.

8.3.4 The 'small print'

Having examined the salient features, we must examine the Notes to the Accounts to see if there is anything which affects the impression so far gained from the accounts. For example, there might be a Note to the effect that the basis of stock valuation had changed. This would significantly affect the validity of the figure of profit or loss shown. We should remember, also, to look at the Auditor's Report. This should state that the accounts give a true and fair view of the financial position and result for the year. If the Auditor disagrees with the accounting treatment, valuation or disclosure of any items in the accounts, he will say so, giving his reasons and the £ amounts involved.

8.3.5 Dictionary of Accounting terms

Accounts

Accounts may be drawn up in various ways and cover different accounting periods. Annual accounts are usually audited (checked and certified by an independent qualified accountant) and follow the disclosure requirements of the Companies Acts (and the Stock Exchange). These are frequently called 'statutory' or 'published' accounts, usually cover a 12 month period, and will be sent to all shareholders and to the Registrar of Companies for public filing. 'Management' or 'interim' accounts are unaudited, and are for internal purposes only. They may be prepared on a monthly or other periodic basis, and contain details of every aspect of the company's operations. They will normally include a manufacturing, trading, and profit and loss account or detailed profit and loss account (as opposed to the short form 'statutory' profit and loss account), a balance sheet, and business statistics. The results of the management accounts are often compared with budget forecasts and are reconciled to the results shown by the 'published' accounts.

Accounting concepts

Accounting concepts are the broad basic assumption which underlie the periodic financial accounts of business concerns. The following are the most important:

(*a*) The 'going concern' concept which assumes that there is no intention to liquidate or reduce the scale of operations.

(*b*) The 'accruals' concept which assumes that costs are matched with relevant expenses wherever possible and dealt with in the financial period to which they relate.

(*c*) The 'prudence' concept which assumes that profits are not anticipated while provision is made for all known liabilities whether the amount is estimated or not.

(*d*) The 'consistency' concept which assumes that similar accounting treatment is given to like items from one accounting period to another.

Accounting policies

Companies are now required, under the U.K. accountancy bodies' statements of standard accounting practice, to disclose accounting policies followed for dealing with items which are judged material or critical in determining profit or loss for the year and in stating the financial position. These policies may, for example, cover such things as the accounting treatment given to depreciation, research and development, patents and trademarks, stocks and work in progress, long-term contracts, deferred taxation, hire purchase, leasing and rental transactions, conversion of foreign currencies, repairs and renewals, consolidation policies, property development, and warranties for products or services.

Associated company

This is a company in which the investing company holds 20% + of its equity on a long term basis *and* on which it exercises a significant influence *or* with which it has a joint venture or consortium interest. In every case the investing company will participate in commercial, financial, and profit distribution policies.

Appropriations

Distribution to various accounts, or earmarking, of net profits. Examples are transfers to reserves or distributions of dividends.

Capitalization

To carry forward into one or more future accounting periods any expenditure (e.g. R&D) the benefits or proceeds of which will be enjoyed in such future periods; to record capital expenditure.

Company

A company is a 'body corporate' with a legal personality which is distinct from the people who comprise it (normally incorporated under the Companies Act 1948).

Broadly speaking, companies are either quoted or unquoted, limited or unlimited, and private or public. A private company has a maximum legal membership of 50, restricts the right to transfer its shares, and may not offer its shares or debentures to the general public. Public companies are not subject to these restrictions. Quoted companies are also commonly referred to as public companies. Unincorporated concerns (e.g. partnerships) may include the word 'company' in their name but this is misleading since they are not companies in the strict sense of the word.

Debenture

A document evidencing a debt which may or may not be secured by a charge on the company's assets. Debentures are usually issued in series and debenture holders may be given the right to convert their debentures into shares of the company at a future date (convertible debenture).

Groups and group accounts

A group is a 'family' of companies, headed by a 'parent' or 'holding' company which owns one or more 'subsidiaries'. A subsidiary is defined in Section 154 of the Companies Act 1948 as being one where the parent company:

(*a*) holds shares and controls the composition of its board of directors, *or*

(*b*) holds more than 50% in nominal value of the equity share capital of the subsidiary.

The theory underlying group accounts is simple: since the various companies in the group are parts of one single undertaking, the group should produce comprehensive statements covering the financial condition and progress of that undertaking. This is normally done by 'consolidating' the accounts of all the companies in the group (in accordance with various rules contained in the

Companies Acts 1948 and 1967) from the viewpoint of the members of the parent company. The consolidated accounts comprise Notes, a consolidated Profit and Loss account, a consolidated Balance Sheet, and the Balance Sheet of the parent company.

Holding company

See 'Groups and group accounts'.

Parent company

See 'Groups and group accounts'.

Joint venture

A partnership whose object is confined to a particular project or series of transactions. No firm name is used and no liability attaches to the partners beyond the limits of the adventure.

Subsidiary

See 'Groups and group accounts'

Source and application of funds (Sources and uses of funds)

A statement covering a specific period which shows the sources of funds acquired and their distribution and general effect upon the various groups of assets, liabilities, and capital. The basis is a comparative balance sheet from which the changes in financial condition are derived.

PROFIT AND LOSS ACCOUNT TERMS

Turnover

Total sales; amounts received by an enterprise in respect of goods sold or services provided; may include or exclude sales within a group, or sales made as agent in addition to those made as principal; treatment of long-term contracts may vary between showing full sales value of contracts *completed* during the year and showing the estimated sales value of work *carried out* during the year.

Depreciation (Amortization)

Lost usefulness, or the diminution of service yield from a fixed asset or fixed asset group that cannot or will not be restored by repairs or by replacement of parts (caused by wear and tear from use, obsolescence through advances in technology, inadequacy, for example through unsuitability of asset to the business); normally based on cost (less grants and expected eventual scrap value) divided by the years of useful life of the asset.

Methods of depreciation:

(*a*) the straight line (or fixed instalment) basis, where a fixed percentage (calculated as above) is charged to the Profit and Loss Account each year.

(*b*) the reducing balance basis, where a fixed percentage is calculated on the diminishing value of the asset.

Deferred taxation

Inland Revenue rates of depreciation are often different from those used by companies, with a consequent effect on profits and tax payable. Deferred tax accounts are used to prevent undue fluctuations in tax charges which might otherwise occur. Transfers to these accounts will represent the amount of tax (at the current rate) on the difference between the net (or written down) value of assets as shown in the balance sheet and their net value so far as the Inland Revenue is concerned. The effect is to ensure that a charge for corporation tax is based on the profits actually shown in the Profit and Loss account, rather than on profit figures adjusted for tax purposes. This account may also be used to reflect future liabilities which could arise from the claim back of certain tax reliefs, e.g. stock relief.

Provision

A charge against profits for an estimated (or accrued) liability, or loss, or shrinkage in value, especially of stock or doubtful debts or fixed assets.

Extraordinary item

An item of financial importance which derives from events or transactions outside the ordinary activities of the business and which is not expected to recur frequently; the definition does *not* include items arising from ordinary activities of the business even if they are exceptional or abnormal on account of their size or incidence. Has to be shown separately in the Profit and Loss account.

Exceptional item

An item which is exceptional because of its amount or incidence but is otherwise part of a company's trading operations. Distinguished from 'extraordinary' items (see above). Usually shown with the pre-tax profit in the profit and loss account.

Profit

The excess of revenue, proceeds, or selling price over related cost.

Gross trading profit

Profit remaining after deducting all selling expenses but before depreciation charge.

Pre-tax profit

Profit remaining after deducting all expenses but prior to payment of tax.

Net profit

Profit remaining from revenue after deducting all related costs including tax (manufacturing, selling, administrative, financial, fiscal, and sundry).

BALANCE SHEET TERMS

Capital

The amount invested in an enterprise (partnership or company) by its owners; the amount so invested plus accumulated profits or reserves; total shareholders' funds.

Authorized capital

The maximum permitted share capital as stated in a company's Memorandum; may be divided into ordinary, preference, cumulative preference, or redeemable preference shares.

Issued capital

The total share capital, of all classes, issued to date; usually fully paid (i.e. shareholders have paid up the full nominal value of the shares they hold); may be equal to, or less than, the authorized capital.

Equity capital

A term used to describe all types of shares in a company which are not subject to a fixed rate of dividend *and* which would have unrestricted rights to share in the net funds remaining after all creditors had been paid off if the company were put into liquidation. Distinguished from 'loan' capital (see below).

Loan capital

The total debentures and other long term borrowings by the company; not a part of the shareholders' funds.

Reserve

A segregation, earmarking, or appropriation of profits; common headings of these accounts are: share premium accounts (these are known as 'statutory' reserves), capital reserve, general reserve accounts, general revenue reserve accounts, profit and loss accounts, retained profits. Reserves do not include 'provisions' (see '*Provisions*').

Capital employed

This is usually made up of issued share capital, retained profits, and long term borrowings and shows the total investment in a business.

Capital reserve

A reserve which is not regarded as available for distribution by way of dividend to shareholders.

Working capital

The excess of current assets (see '*Current asset*') over current liabilities (see '*Current liability*').

Asset

Any owned, physical object (tangible, e.g. plant) or right (intangible, e.g. patents) having a money value; an item or source of wealth expressed in terms of cost, depreciated cost, or valuation; any cost benefiting a future accounting period.

Current asset

An asset in which the enterprise deals and which it acquires for the purpose of sale; stages of conversion of such assets into cash (e.g. stock, debtors); prepaid expenses; shown at the lower of cost, replacement, or ultimate sale value.

Fixed asset

A tangible asset of a permanent nature used in the *production* of other goods and services; any item of plant; any capital asset or non-current asset; shown at cost or valuation less depreciation.

Other asset

An intangible asset not classified as current or fixed; this heading covers investments, goodwill, patents, etc.

Goodwill

The excess of the price paid for a business as a whole over its book value, or over the computed or agreed value of all tangible net assets purchased; profits in excess of the normal rate of return on capital. Normally, it is written down over a period of years.

Goodwill arising on consolidation

The premium paid by a parent company for the shares of its (consolidated) subsidiaries at the time of acquisition, reduced by the discount if any such shares were bought at a lower price.

Liabilities

Debts owed by the company for goods or services received; the title of the credit side of the balance sheet, often including total equity (or shareholders' funds) as well as obligations to outsiders.

Current liability

A debt owed by the company which is due to be paid within 12 months of the balance sheet date.

Contingent liability

An obligation, relating to a past event, which may arise in consequence of a future event which is considered possible but not probable—e.g. litigation or damages; costs arising from guarantees.

Deferred liability

An obligation which is not due to be paid within 12 months of the balance sheet date.

OTHER USEFUL TERMS

Brackets

Figures in brackets are minus, negative, or deductions of some kind. Figures may alternatively be shown in italics, although this convention is usually reserved for comparative figures.

Capital expenditure

If money spent is 'capitalized' and recorded as an asset in the balance sheet rather than being charged against profits in the profit and loss account, the profit for the period will obviously be that much higher (or the loss that much less). This will also affect calculations of return on capital. (See 'Capitalization'.)

Cash flow

Budgeting for cash flows (receipts and payments of cash) is a helpful management tool. The monthly (quarterly, etc.) net difference of cash in and cash out, when added to the existing bank balance, can show how much extra finance will be needed and when. Assumptions used (e.g. what the sales figures will be and how long it takes to turn a sale into cash) need to be clearly stated and both capital and revenue income and expenditure should be taken into account. The further into the future the forecast goes, the less dependable it will probably be.

Cost accounting

A method of trying to allocate costs and income to specific parts or cost centres: products, premises, people, etc., rather than giving an overall view as in the case of the published annual accounts. Used in pricing policies. 'Absorption' costing allocates *all* costs to a cost centre (thus producing a mini-profit and loss account) whereas 'marginal' or 'contribution' costing allocates directly related expenses, thus leaving a margin or contribution of profit to pay for fixed overhead costs. 'Standard' costing is based on budget targets (i.e. what a product ought to cost and generate in sales income) and this standard will be used to measure actual performance. Examination of the difference between standard and actual performance, and the reasons for it, is referred to as 'variance analysis'.

Exposure draft

An interim statement of standard accounting practice (SSAP—see later) which is published by the U.K. accountancy bodies for the comment by those interested or concerned. Has no binding effect until it is published as an SSAP. Rather like a Bill as opposed to an Act of Parliament. Many quoted companies tend to produce accounts which comply with exposure drafts before the relevant SSAP has been published.

Gearing

A term used to describe the relationship between the nominal amount of ordinary share capital on the one hand and loan and preference share capital on the other.

Inflation accounting

A method of restating profit and loss accounts and balance sheets in such a way as to demonstrate the effects of inflation on trading and assets.

Investments

May appear in the balance sheet as a heading which is regarded as being neither a fixed nor current asset. It usually includes quoted, unquoted, and trade investments as well as holdings in subsidiaries or associated companies. Current market values or directors' valuation are given as well as cost. Percentage held is given in the case of subsidiaries. For 'associated' investments see earlier.

Leasehold

A long leasehold is one with more than, and a short leasehold one with less than, 50 years to run.

Minority interest

The stake in a company held by a small group of outsiders. Appears as a deduction from funds available to shareholders in the profit and loss account and as a separate item in the capital employed section of the balance sheet.

Overtrading

Trading beyond the limits which can be supported by the existing financial resources of a business.

Prepayment

A payment to an outsider for services, etc., relating to the next financial year. To be distinguished from trade debtors (i.e. sales not yet paid for). These two are very often merged together when shown in the balance sheet.

Share premium account

If a company issues a share (e.g. an ordinary £1 share) and receives more for it than the nominal value (e.g. £1·50), the difference (50p) must be held in a special earmarked fund called the share premium account. This can only be used for the purposes set out in Section 56 of the 1948 Companies Act.

Standard accounting practices (SSAPs)

The U.K. accountancy bodies have promulgated a number of statements of standard accounting practice (SSAPs) in order to 'harmonize' the accounting treatment given to various items. Auditors are required by the accountancy bodies to comment on significant departures in their reports to shareholders if a company fails to observe one.

8.4 ACQUISITION ANALYSIS

8.4.1 Competitor analysis

Competitor analysis is a specialized area of IMR which has a bearing not only on both the management's investment decisions and marketing strategy, but also on acquisition studies. Primarily it is a tool by which we can keep a watching brief on our competitors in any market and through which we can compare our market and financial performance with theirs.

The analysis of this area has two main facets: the assiduous collection of commercial and technical data, and a close scrutiny of all sources of financial information. The inter-relationship of these provides an input through which the relative production efficiencies and overhead structures of competitors can be assessed and compared to one's own company and, further, if carried out on a regular basis, ensure that changes in the competitive situation can be quickly pinpointed. We have already discussed sources of such data (Chapter 2), which can be used with the proviso that these data particularize on competitors' market status as well as generalize on the market. Details of pricing and delivery patterns, raw material suppliers (and their pricing and delivery policies), geographical changes in markets, number of salesmen, etc., are all facts about one's competitors which are grist to the intelligence mill, especially when one can compare them with 'in-house' data.

Except for those working in true monopoly industries—and there are not many of those—the collection of competitor data is the most important task of IMR intelligence. Any work in studying a company's products revolves round the positions of those products relative to those made by competitors.

8.4.2 Marketing research in takeover and merger strategy

Acquisition study is a very specialized part of IMR—all of us might at some time find ourselves involved in a merger or takeover. It might be as a willing, or less than willing, participant, as an employee of a firm involved, or even as a shareholder in a company bidding or bid for.

What is the function of such a move? There are three main factors involved:

(*a*) as a defensive move—the usual reason for mergers;

(*b*) in order to extend the present bounds of business within the same industry;

(*c*) to diversify into new fields.

In reality all three of these factors are *defensive*, even if this is obscured by the bidder being a successful company. Any merger or takeover is aimed at securing a firm's sphere of influence whether immediately or in the longer term. It is in this that it becomes an important, if small, part of our work in IMR.

There is a need for an overall corporate growth strategy which includes a measure of growth by acquisition. It is at this level that IMR has so much to offer.

Let us look at the three reasons for merging or bidding and consider where we come in.

The *defensive* bid or merger is usually the result of IMR of some kind—even in informal and of the 'managing director is worried' style! By some means (usually an IMR study) the management has been made aware of the increased competition, or of new products which are cutting away at its established markets.

The '*extensive*' bid, rarely a merger in this case, comes from a definition of growth areas in current markets and the prospects of sales enhancement in the company's industry.

The '*diversification*' bid comes from a company, its markets well established and profitable, which desires to make the best use of its reputation or Stock Market worth to acquire companies which will provide it with new products to follow on from its present range—for nothing, it is said, goes on for ever.

What are our strategies in each of these cases?

In the case of a *defensive* move, we should already be aware of the situation from our market studies well before immediate action is needed. Once the required policy has been approved by the management, we should be able to pinpoint the future of the current product mix, those competitors particularly responsible for our declining market share, and the potential of a merger with one or more of these or some other company with suitable production capacity.

It may be that the answer to the question on the future of our current product range is negative—if so we must look at *diversification*. Should the answer be that the products have a useful life then our time can be allocated to the selection of suitable candidates for merger. This selection will include details of market shares, product capability, patent positions, innovativeness, management expertise, employee statistics, etc.—all of which should be in our intelligence files. With sufficient data available to narrow the choice the second marketing research phase starts—the preparation of the arguments for the bid or merger. These will cover the detailing of the present market position of the major firms within the market, the potential for each on an uncombined basis, and the change that would come from combination.

The steps we need to take in the *extensive* bid are similar to those already underlined, but there are additional factors which we need to look at in this case. In the first place it is unlikely that many companies are in every product area in the industry in which they operate and, second, it is even more unlikely that these product areas have similar growth rates or are as suitable for incorporation. Here, then, one needs to know which are growth areas, which provide best opportunities for sales enhancement (will the present sales team be able to handle these products or will additional specialists be required?), and whether products are compatible or competitive with any present lines.

With this information decisions can be made on the appropriate market areas to consider; at which point we once more come into our own in offering suitable candidates for consideration.

It is in acquisition study that the more specialized forms of research are needed, such as technological forecasting or long range planning (see Sections 5.2 and 9.3).

Diversification, to be successful, requires early selection of markets of greater long-term potential than our present mix. Mature markets may be useful for certain companies, but most will be looking for products to replace present mature or declining lines—or, perhaps, in the ultra-well managed firm, to replace lines which at the moment are only on the upward swing of their life cycles.

We should be continually using our intelligence data to report on the above markets and their suitability for integration into our company's present structure or a modified structure, and for the degree of compatibility with present product lines. For example, do they provide any areas of vertical or horizontal integration? The companies within the markets which could be acquisition candidates must also be screened regularly. This screening should cover in-firm capability, past operating record, future prospects, especially any reliance on personalities, position in the market, etc. A well integrated and efficient marketing research unit will be able to provide all these fundamental data, making the whole business of acquisition selection far more simple.

8.4.3 Financial implications

If ours is a *public* company one factor will loom large—the impact of an acquisition on earnings. We will be asked whether there will be a *dilution* of earnings per share. The relative value placed on the other company will reflect in the price we pay for it. This in turn, when related to the net attributable earnings, will either produce an increase or decrease in our price earnings ratio (PE). The PE is calculated by dividing the stock market price of our firm's shares by the earnings per share (EPS). As such the PE represents the number of years of earnings which investors are willing to discount when buying a share. A PE of 10 implies that the investors are willing to discount 10 years of earnings capacity at current levels and this, therefore, demonstrates a confidence level higher than that shown for a share which only rates a PE of 5. In fact the higher the PE the greater the expectation of growth—a PE of 10 indicates a belief that the earnings of a company will grow twice as fast as those of a company rated on a PE of 5.

If we make an issue of shares to shareholders in the company we are acquiring, or raise a loan from a finance house—perhaps, even, pay cash—the acquisition has a direct impact on that essential bottom line figure. In the case of a share issue we can calculate the impact of the new shares directly. We add the net attributable profit of the company to ours and divide by the new number of shares. If the bid is financed in some other form we must calculate the cost in interest charge terms and check to see whether the net after-tax cost of the interest is greater or less than the additional attributable profit.

If the earnings per share fall with a share issue bid or the net interest charge is greater than the extra income then we have *dilution*—a 'bad thing' in the eyes of the City. If, on the other hand, the earnings rise or there is a surplus of profit over interest cost then we have *earnings growth*—a much favoured position in the eyes of the investment community. Therefore, if we are working for a public company we should always check the ultimate cost or benefit in EPS and PE terms and give this impact in our reports.

For private companies the financial implications are less easy to determine, and we must rely on the management to indicate the constraints under which we will be working.

In the end the decision on whether or not to make a bid lies with the management, but it is as well to know that the borrowings level of the company has some bearing on the possibility of a favourable move following our report. A public company has its total borrowings set as a ratio of the issued share capital. To exceed this the board has to get the permission of the shareholders through the medium of an Extraordinary General Meeting (EGM). Because this takes time a sound proposal may fall since the finance director feels the need to maintain flexibility. In a private company the limits are often very tight and the room for manoeuvre more constrained. In either case a rough calculation could save us a great deal of fruitless work.

Chapter 9

IMR and its role in Marketing and Company Planning

9.1 THE MARKETING CONCEPT

In considering the role of marketing in the firm it has become common practice to start with an explanation of the 'marketing concept'. So let us stay with tradition and consider a classical statement of its meaning. Felton[1] offers the following basic definition:

> 'a corporate state of mind that insists on the integration and coordination of all marketing functions which in turn are melded with all other corporate functions for the basic objective of producing maximum long range profits.'

This statement immediately raises some problems if we look at the mixed economy of the United Kingdon in the middle of the 1970s: there is considerable argument today about whether or not the objective of an organization should be to produce maximum long range profits. This argument rages particularly strongly in connection with the nationalized industries, for governments often choose to use these industries as a means of promoting their natural economic objectives with the result that profitability may often not be the most important objective in the hierarchy of alternatives.

The marketing concept has also been interpreted to stress the focus on the customer. For example, in Kotler[2] there is an interpretation of the marketing concept defined in terms of customer orientation, integrated marketing, and customer satisfaction.

When we come to industrial marketing we have not just a customer, but a process by which a large number of individuals collectively behave in such a way that ultimately our products are purchased. This in turn means that although there may be some firms who are only concerned with the immediate customer (in the narrow sense) most firms find their business ultimately in the hand of a much wider group, either as final consumers or as individuals who influence the state of our economy and therefore the total demand for all raw materials, goods, and services.

9.2 THE MARKETING PLAN

Central to the operation of the company is the marketing plan: from it flows the estimates of demands on production, needs for raw materials, estimates of revenue and costs, and capital requirements. The marketing plan commonly consists of a detailed statement for the next year or two together with more sketchy figures stretching on to the next five years or perhaps to the next decade (depending on the nature of the business of the company concerned).

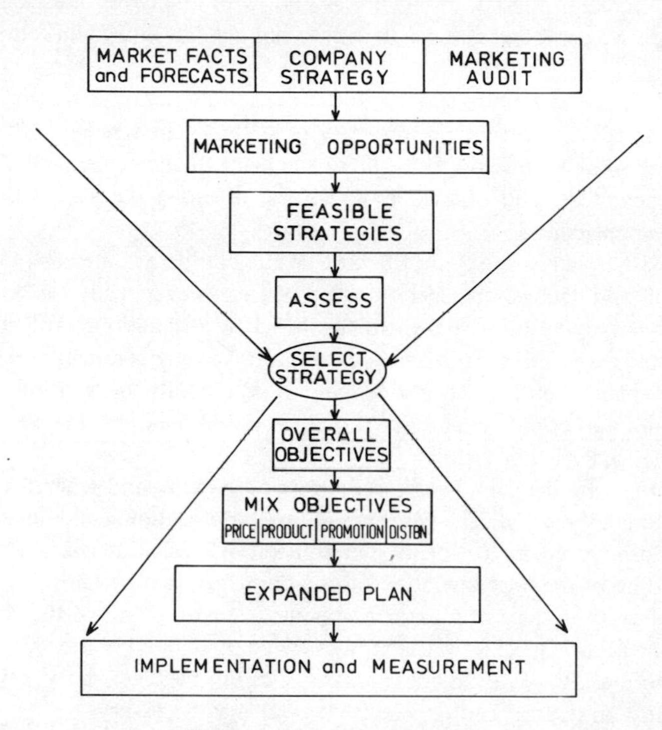

Figure 9.1 Route to a plan

The evolution of such a plan is shown in Figure 9.1.[3] This clearly defined pattern of events is, of course, an oversimplification. Making a plan is like driving in some unknown busy city where the signposting is slightly eccentric: sometimes you find hold-ups, delays, one-ways, detours, cul-de-sacs, and perhaps the need to retrace your tracks to some previous point in order to locate where you are and to check the suitability of your planned route.

The marketing plan starts with some understanding as to the general area of your business: the nature of your products, the generic needs you seek to meet in the markets you naturally serve, and the key technologies which you employ. How far these factors are likely to be open to variation is a function of circumstances: the longer you look ahead the more are you able to modify the set of assets and competences which characterize your organization. But in the one-year plan many factors are already pre-set.

So, your corporate (what-business-are-you-in) strategy is more or less given, and this input acts as an over-riding guideline to the planning process. There are two other inputs: external, the changing characteristics of the market, and perhaps an audit of the appropriateness of your existing marketing instruments.

Given, then, the inputs of facts, forecasts, and realistic assumptions, the planning process goes on to examine alternative feasible strategies. Sometimes alternatives are few and the strategy is clear; at other times the contrary is the case. There may be a number of segments at home and overseas and, with limited resources, a choice has to be made: what products, through what channels, to what markets, with what promotions?

In principle the procedure should be to identify alternative strategies and assess their economics: cost, revenue, probability of success. The strategy to be adopted is selected, and so on to develop the detail of the plan: budgets of capital, revenue and current expenditure, and of cash flow, setting of target dates and identifying of personal responsibilities.

Certainly the plan as the central feature of the company's forward look requires full, careful, and detailed consideration. Yet we can never really foretell the future and most plans have been shaken to the heart by the national and international lurches of the early 1970s. So we have to monitor the environment and be prepared to adapt the plan when changes in raw material availability, patterns of demand, and the discontinuities of politics and like problems reveal the need. The idea that a plan is set unchangedly is not valid.

When preparing the plan, keep careful note of the why and wherefores. This can help adjustment if need be. The value of the *process* of planning and linked budgeting has often been cited as a worthwhile spin-off: it really does leave us with an underatanding of the total operation of our company as a system.

Then follows the stage of measuring results at many points in the company and checking the accuracy: of forecasts of sales by company and industry, of the state of the world economy, of raw material prices, etc. But feedback is the key to keeping the company on course, and revising that course as necessary.

9.3 THE ROLE OF THE IMR IN COMPANY PLANNING

A firm undertaking company planning sets out to answer the questions:

'Where are we now?'

'Where are we likely to be in five years time?'

'Where should we be trying to get to in five years time?'

'How should we try to get there?'

Five years is a common planning horizon for firms serving industrial markets. Individual circumstances may require a shorter or longer period.

The role of IMR is to provide information on those matters external to the company that determine its present situation and condition its future prospects. This is crucial to the whole process. Unless judgments and projections are based on good information, the whole structure will be unsoundly based and policy decisions will be misguided; or, using the more succinct phrase:

Garbage in—Garbage out.

In practice, a company plan consists almost entirely of numbers. The criteria on which performance is judged are financial. The apex of the planning pyramid is a time series of financial accounts that describe the past and present performance of the company and project the performance that has been set as a target over the planning period. Detailed quantitative analyses, covering all relevant aspects of the company's activity, are carried out to 'explain' the past and present performance and are used as sources from which the target projections evolve.

IMR is primarily concerned with the analyses that 'explain' income from sales net of marketing costs and set the targets for this element of the forward plan.

The analysis of income from sales is best tackled by breaking down the total value into a set of product–market matrices. The number of Product rows and Market columns in a matrix is governed by individual circumstances. General guidelines are that a 'Product' should be defined as the single article or collection of articles offered by the company to satisfy a definable need. A 'Market' should be defined as a group of users and potential users who have a common need and who are likely to be subject to the same general set of external influences on their own businesses.

Having distributed net sales income over the product–market matrix we then are faced with explaining the value in each cell. This is done by constructing a profile of each cell. The profile covers the following information:

Total demand.

Our share of demand.

Main competitors with their shares.

Our relative standing on
product properties;
price—levels and structure;
delivery—quotation and reliability;
service—before and after sales.

Our marketing activities compared with competitors'
promotion—amount and quality;
selling—methods and intensity;
distribution—channels and mix;
technical service—amount and quality.

This process, when completed, answers the question, 'Where are we now?' as it relates to our standing and performance in the markets currently being served.

It also provides the basis of an answer, to, 'Where are we likely to find ourselves?' The first step in this is to estimate the forward movement in total demand, in quantity and value, in each product–market cell. Armed with the detailed analysis of our strengths and weaknesses provided by the cell profiles we can then form judgments of the likely movement in our share of demand and hence in net sales income. These judgments will take account, where relevant, of any increases or decreases in the strength of competition that can be anticipated from trends to date.

More positively, the information generated by the analytical processes is used, together with internal information on product profitability, in formulating business targets and in developing action programmes to achieve them. Preferred directions of change in the amount and type of marketing activity undertaken in various markets and for various products are worked out. The general objective is to maximize the advantage extracted from opportunites and minimize the effect of threats highlighted by the forward projections.

This process is common to all forms of planning. The aspect that distinguishes Company Planning is the extended time horizon involved and consequently the increased freedom to consider changes in things that are of necessity fixed in short-run plans. We can legitimately ask ourselves, 'What products supplied to what markets using what marketing resources offer the greatest expectation of profitable growth to the company?' This offers a substantial challenge to the marketing researcher. It involves the need to see the company clearly as an organic system within its industrial and commercial environment, to conceive sometimes radical ideas for change, and to demonstrate the validity of such propositions on the basis of solid information and sound reasoning.

The product–market matrix is a useful tool for generating ideas for development of the company's activities. The questions to ask are:

'What other markets, not currently served by us, have a demand for our products?'

'What other products, not currently supplied by us, are required by the customers making up the markets we serve?'

This leads to an extended matrix that can be examined for opportunities to exploit potential synergy. If any such opportunities are identified, the question of how best to pursue them calls for further research. The basic options are:

(i) Extending existing products into new markets

(*a*) Invest in new marketing resources.

(*b*) Acquire a company with suitable marketing expertise.

(*c*) Appoint suitable agents.

(*d*) Find suitable licencees for the products.

(ii) Additional products for markets in which the Company is established

(*a*) Invest in resources to develop new products.

(*b*) Acquire a company with suitable products.

(*c*) Take on marketing agencies for suitable products

(*d*) Obtain licences to manufacture suitable products.

Only thorough desk and field research will enable an appropriate choice to be made.

All planning is a team effort. It is difficult, and dangerous, to draw demarcation lines round the responsibilities of individual members of the team. The contribution of the marketing researcher is two-fold. As a specialist, he is responsible for ensuring that the planning team is provided with the best possible information based on the external market environment. As a member of the team his unique contribution should be a facility to place himself in the customer's shoes and interpret the reaction and response of the market to proposed strategies and actions as the company plan evolves.

9.4 REFERENCES

1. Felton, A.P. (1959). Making the Marketing Concept Work. *Harvard Business Review*, July/Aug., 55–65.
2. Kotler, P. (1976). *Marketing Management: Analysis, Planning & Control*, 3rd ed. Prentice Hall, Englewood Cliffs, N.J.
3. Fisher, L. (in the press) *Industrial Marketing*, 2nd ed. Business Books, London.

Chapter 10

Administration of an IMR Department

In the field of IMR the major proportion of the total effort takes place within integrated manufacturing and marketing organizations. The positioning, scope of activity, and public image of the marketing research function will, therefore, be conditioned by the quite complex relationships that arise. This chapter considers the administration of an industrial marketing research department within a typical integrated organization.

10.1 STAFF SELECTION

Some companies who manufacture industrial products will require to cope with large numbers of contacts, and hence with all the niceties of statistical approach and determination that this involves. In such a case the most suitable candidates may be science graduates, with a bent for mathematics, or alternatively graduate economists.

At the other end of the industrial scale, many companies in the basic industries may be able to list the entire group of European customers for a specific product on the fingers of two hands. In such cases they should all be contacted, but they will all have individual slants and vested interests which will colour their answers to our questions. This type of operation, therefore, needs a depth of industrial knowledge and a mature judgment of people to gain a sound interpretation. Such a background may well be found in a graduate of the science or technology relevant to the industry concerned (be it engineering, chemistry, medicine, physics, or biology, for example), but he will require some significant period of training on the job to acquire the necessary facility of judgment.

There is no intention, however, of suggesting that no non-graduate will succeed in this sort of job: there are plenty of examples to disprove such a proposition! The point that is implicit here is that in the selection of staff for IMR one has a different set of criteria from those established in consumer work. The level of scientific competence and maturity of judgment required in IMR will, in general, be markedly higher than those for interviewers consulting housewives about a preference between Brands X and Y.

It is appropriate at this point to mention that women play an effective part in IMR on equal terms with men. There is an occasional trauma amongst contacts at being entertained to lunch by a lady, but these are fast disappearing, and in many other respects a female marketing researcher may have the edge on a mere male in seeking information from male respondents. Chivalry is not yet dead!

Where to find these marketing researchers? An obvious route is to attract readymade specimens from other companies by advertisements in such media as *The Times*, *The Daily Telegraph*, *The Economist*, or the so-called 'Quality Sundays'. If you already have a well-established IMR unit then this is not usually the best source of new staff. The newcomer will have to be broken in to new concepts, new management policies, and the like, and one who arrives with considerable experience from other companies can find this hard to take.

Thus if we assume a preference for 'in-house' training then possibly the ideal arrangement is to take a young graduate with a year or so's experience in the marketing field. He can then broaden his experience and scope in marketing research for the usual 3–5 years and hopefully return (if that is his wish) to the marketing environment at a more senior level. A graduate fresh from college, on the other hand, would probably revel in the lack of constraints and the opportunities for creativity in the IMR field, and if he is then transferred to a totally commercial function will be distressed to find many more constraints being applied to his work.

A preference for a marketing background should not imply any specific type of person for the IMR job. The common impression that marketing or IMR is exclusively carried out by back-slapping hail-fellow-well-met extroverts is not true. Some of our best marketing researchers have come from a fairly rarefied R&D background. Such people may inject a meticulous approach into their work that can be very welcome. To perform the IMR job well, and to enjoy doing it, calls for a person who really finds it a pleasure to meet people. Such people may, however, have quiet, and far from florid, personalities.

10.2 LIBRARY AND OFFICE FACILITIES

This is a particular area where generalizations and a certain vagueness as to details is inevitable. There are lone-wolf marketing researchers whose total needs appear to be a desk at home, a telephone, a number of friends, and a long-suffering wife!

Turning again to the normal pattern we have assumed of an established department in an integrated company, the needs become rather more sophisticated.

The basics for a library will certainly include production and sales statistics so far as they are available from official government sources of both the home country and all overseas areas likely to be of commercial interest. To these will be added some, at least, of the relevant statistics produced by trade associations. Not all of these are readily obtained (at least at short notice) and recourse may be had to the official libraries to which reference may be made. (For further guidance see Chapter 2.)

Although there is no shortage of statistical background material for your library or information store it should be noted, however, that by one of those inscrutable natural laws:

(*a*) the information you want is rarely published in the required form;

(*b*) there is no correlation between the degree of official sponsorship of a publication and its reliability.

In addition to the statistics of immediate relevance there should, of course, be the appropriate books, periodicals, and journals relating to the industry or industries in which the integrated company operates. These will relate perhaps to the basic sciences and specific technologies of the industrial background. Also, no doubt you will add specialist subjects of concern and interests—treatises on statistical methods, for example, tomes on management, and current runs of periodicals belonging to relevant Associations.

Whilst it is not specifically a library matter, mention should be made of the desirability of having some form of systematic extraction of information items which can be recorded, indexed, and readily retrieved! There is a vast reservoir of literature and expertise on this subject, but, from a practical point of view, the most necessary capability of those handling the information store is knowing what to leave out. Much money, effort, and space can be wasted by preserving endless details of items which are of little or no residual interest.

The information store will comprise both published and private information. The latter aspect calls for some care in the dissemination of the contents of the store if confidences are not to be misplaced. This factor also draws attention to the fact that the manager of the information store should be on good terms with all the commercial people so that he or she (most commonly she in this case) can get a reasonable proportion of the vast store of marketing information that is constantly flowing into the company.

Turning now to office facilities, it should be emphasized that most IMR is an exercise in communication. It is, therefore, necessary to incorporate the most sophisticated communications facilities the company can afford. The telephone will be in constant use. A Telex will almost certainly be a valuable additional facility, and in the more grandiose units a computer terminal may be found.

Today's industrial marketing researchers feel almost naked without one of the small electronic calculators. From a management point of view this poses problems as we are now finding a tendency to assume that the calculator cannot lie. Certain basic attributes like adding, multiplying, and knowing where to put the decimal point may still be found to be of value!

One of the things one learns in practising marketing research is that old subjects never die. It is, therefore, useful after having written up a report to keep the working papers as well as the report (or pass them on to your successor). This will give you or the next man a head start when the subject inevitably rears its head again—possibly years later.

The business card is not quite as vital in meetings in this country perhaps as overseas. Nevertheless, all industrial marketing researchers should have them. Moreover, they should treasure the cards they receive and keep them in a card index system for future reference.

Copying facilities represent another item which can almost be taken for granted in a modern office of any size. The type of equipment should be adjusted in accordance with the needs expressed both in type and volume.

10.3 BUDGETING

In a typical company the marketing research function will have its overall size and costs determined by some sort of company establishment and revenue budget. The aim should, therefore, be:

(*a*) to find an agreed basis for the amount of this type of effort required by the company;

(*b*) to establish the extent to which the work should either be handled 'in-house' or be economically 'bought-in';

(*c*) to conduct the appropriate amount of work efficiently.

In general, managements are apt to regard marketing research as an expensive item, frequently because its costs are brought home to them as an 'overhead' or 'bought-in' item, whereas the costs of more mundane functions, such as accounts or general administration, are more acceptable.

Costs in money terms have become difficult items to quote as the passage of time may cause them to look ridiculous. Speaking, however, of conditions applying in the first half of 1977, the cost of a senior company-employed marketing researcher cannot be significantly under £350 per week to the company (if all costs are included) and may be higher if various administrative overheads are loaded on to the calculation.

It is not surprising, therefore, that the commissioning of work by outside consultants will be charged at a higher figure. The range of costs could be around £400–£600 per man week, or even more, according to the scope of the work and prestige of the consultant.

The cost advantage of conducting work in-house is, therefore, not terribly large, but there are additional advantages. These include certain aspects of confidentiality, the opportunities of more complete briefing, and therefore the final assurance that the work will really relate exactly to the information needed (which may not always be the same as the questions asked!).

Most companies in a substantial way of business have the need of a marketing research unit. Its size and prestige will derive from a multitude of internal pressures (of which more in the next section). It is important to remember that the company marketing research unit will cost much the same whether it is fully employed or not, hence the numbers employed should represent a constant minimum need.

Estimating the time for a job in man-weeks is an art to some extent. Most jobs will take longer than forecast since any unforeseen element (e.g. non-availability of respondents) can only slow the work down. Even a small study involving field work is apt to take 4–6 weeks, and larger jobs may run upwards of 20 man weeks. At or beyond this point some cold cost–benefit analysis may be desirable.

It is also necessary to allow a proportion of time for unplanned panic requests (management's panic, not yours, of course! No doubt this should not happen, but it always does, and some provision must be made for it.

The optimum working of the unit will depend upon an accurate assessment of the time taken for each job and a careful allocation of work in advance amongst the people available. Timing the job is perhaps the most exacting operation. In particular, care should be taken to avoid time being wasted during the drafting, editing, and reprographic stages of the report. The steam will have gone out of the effort by then and often the final stages can linger on far too long unless completion dates are strictly adhered to.

What ultimately emerges is that, within the integrated company marketing research unit, the budgeted costs in terms of manpower are set by overall company policies. To this extent the budget is measured more by work capable of being carried out within the pre-set manpower limits. This will, in turn, help to establish such additional items as the travel and entertainment budget for the unit (always an emotive subject!).

After manning levels have been set the capabilities of the company units can be examined to see if they will cover the whole range of company requirements. If not, work of some kind may be 'bought in'. This requires negotiation (see Chapter 11) and it should be possible to attach fairly firm cost figures to this work if the briefing has been thoroughly and soundly carried out.

An important aspect of this subject is the simple question of whether or not the calculated costs of this work are specifically or even notionally debited against the sponsoring unit. It is preferable that such calculations should not go beyond the notional stage, otherwise sterile arguments over money can interfere with the effective working of the unit—particularly when it is borne in mind that the saving achieved by not using a marketing research unit within the company is minimal.

10.4 RELATIONS WITH SENIOR MANAGEMENT

Unless you are employed by an exceptional company, you will have a Board of Directors probably without any direct experience at all of marketing research. They may well be wholly sympathetic, they may be deeply impressed by your pronouncements, but they will not have a full grasp of how you work, what your strengths and limitations are, or how to use you to the company's best advantage.

This is both a restriction and an opportunity. You may get asked to do some fairly ridiculous things, but you will have the possibility of implanting your own thoughts and methods on the work of the marketing research unit.

You should at all times be close to and friendly with the marketing function as a whole. It is likely that they will be the people who will use your results and recommendations in order to reach decisions.

Marketing researchers are surprisingly oblivious to the fact that the final report represents the sum total of outward evidence of the calibre of work performed. They will frequently have to be browbeaten into writing reasonably decent English, structuring their reports so that they can easily be followed towards a sensible conclusion, and making if possible specific recommendations arising from the work. It is one of the tasks of the man in charge to oversee this development and to direct the results to the appropriate people. (For guidance on the presentation of results see Chapter 6.)

In the last resort, it is not your own opinion of how useful you are that counts, but the opinion of you held by your management, bolstered by that of your colleagues.

10.5 THE POSITION OF THE MARKETING RESEARCH DEPARTMENT WITHIN THE ORGANIZATION

So far in this chapter the marketing research department has been referred to as the only one within the integrated organization, but it is by no means uncommon for more than one unit to operate in a single organization. In the extreme, it has been known for marketing research to be decentralized to the point where there is a 'development man' to be found in most of the commercial units. I regard this as decentralizing marketing research out of existence. The pressures on these 'development men' will tend to make them concentrate on short term commercial activities of immediate impact, so that the true function is clouded beyond recognition.

A divisional structure is more common in the typical organization, with each major integrated division having its own marketing research unit. These will probably need to be supplemented by a central marketing research unit covering such matters as the study of complete industries, the competitive impact of products handled in different marketing units, or matters pertaining to overall corporate planning.

Whether these market research units are divisionalized, centralized, or a combination of both, the principles involved in their location within the organization structure are likely to be broadly similar.

The first rule is to avoid being made too remote. In certain organizations the marketing research unit is located in a research and development area which may lead to the unit acquiring an 'ivory tower' reputation. This is death to effective marketing research.

In other organizations the MR function becomes wholly integrated with marketing as a whole. The danger here is analogous to that of the 'development man' mentioned above. Too many of the pressures are again likely to relate to immediate commercial problems and the true requirement of marketing research is likely to be thrust into the background.

Certain companies have a central presidential-type of decision-making group attached to the chief executive. This is perhaps the ideal point of responsibility for the marketing research function—after all, its most vital *raison d'etre* is to make easier the process of making reasoned decisions.

An often-overlooked aspect of the location of marketing research in the company structure is that of career development for the individual marketing researcher. The value of taking on a fledgling marketing man with perhaps one year's experience as the new marketing researcher was mentioned earlier. When after two to three years he moves on (as most of them do), the way will be open for him to return to marketing activities where he may use his broadened experience at a higher level. This is much easier if marketing and marketing research functions are close or integrated. If the IMR function is remote, there might well be difficulties in ensuring a reasonable channel of advancement for those who wish to move within the company.

Chapter 11

Consultants and their Role within IMR

In industrial marketing research, many projects are carred out by 'in house' researchers who are full-time employees of the sponsoring company; they carry out the desk and field research and write the reports themselves.

Over the last few years, however, one of the major changes in industrial research has been the growth in the use of the specialist industrial market research company (or consultancy), to carry out either the whole research project or just the fieldwork. This leads us to consider: when and what are the advantages of using a consultancy; and how to locate and select a research company.

11.1 DECIDING WHETHER OR NOT TO USE A MARKETING RESEARCH COMPANY/CONSULTANCY

In many highly technical fields where, frequently, a limited number of interviews are required, a company's research department conducts these interviews itself. This can lead to problems of security and ethics and in such cases a company researcher should always disclose to the respondent the company he works for. Further, if he promises confidentiality to the respondent, he must under all circumstances keep to his word, and, regardless of the demands of his company, he must never disclose the source of the information. Indeed, he should go further and ensure that it is not possible for the reader of the report to link a particular company with the information given. If this rule is not closely observed, the name of industrial marketing research will suffer, and obtaining information will become more difficult for everybody within the profession.

At the other extreme, where frequently hundreds of interviews are needed, it is usually far more practical to engage a marketing research company to carry out the interviews. Also, when anonymity is essential to the success of the project (for example, a new product or company image research), the work can only be carried out by 'outsiders'—in other words an IMR consultancy.

At this simple level, one can see the two ends of the spectrum—the end where the interviewing is usually done, and probably should be done, by the company's own researchers—and at the other extreme the situation where it is essential that a consultancy with a number of interviewers at its disposal should do the research. There is, of course, a very large 'grey area'. In this so called 'grey area' we could count examples such as:

Technical fields where a large number of interviews have to be carried out—so many that the company's own research department cannot handle it.

Where interviewing has to be carried out in a number of countries.

Where the interviewing has to be done in a very short period of time.

In these cases, whether or not to do a project 'in house' or to engage an outside research consultancy should be consciously debated before a final decision is made; indeed, in many cases the responsibility could be shared between the firm of consultants and an 'in-house' research department.

Whoever the interviewer is, bona fide research is done in the open, and as mentioned earlier, when a respondent is promised anonymity this promise *must* be honoured. Both the Marketing Research Society and Industrial Marketing Research Association have a very tight (joint) code of standards which clearly defines the responsibility of the marketing researcher towards the company that supplies the information (see Appendix for details).

11.2 HOW TO LOCATE AND SELECT A MARKETING RESEARCH CONSULTANCY

Locating suitable IMR Consultants has been made progressively easier over the years by the publication of several good Directories, one of which is the joint IMRA/EVAF publication, *European Guide to Industrial Marketing Consultancy*, which lists consultants alphabetically and also gives a cross-referenced list by types of industries in which the consultants specialize. For export marketing research the British Overseas Trade Board not only assist you with a grant towards part of the cost but will also supply a list of consultants to approach.

Selecting a particular IMR Consultancy to work with is perhaps an art rather than a skill. Many factors have to be taken into consideration, factors such as:

Reliability of the company.

Experience in your field.

Ability to work and 'get on' with them.

Competitors they are working for.

Their cost.

Let us look at these points one at a time.

(i) *Reliability*

If you have a particular consultancy in mind, talk to your colleagues about them. Ask them how this particular firm responds to crises—which unfortunately frequently happen in marketing research; whether they keep to the timing they have promised; whether their reports are accurate; whether their reports are understandable; whether the people that actually will work on the project are the people that you would meet when you discuss it, etc.

(ii) Experience in your field

It is sometimes useful to use a firm that has previous experience in your field. Experience has shown, however, that it is frequently far better to use a firm which is reliable, with whom you can work, and which shows a general competence, whether or not they have experience in your particular field. This is particularly true of relatively large scale industrial surveys where fieldwork techniques are probably far more important then specific knowledge of a particular product. When dealing with highly technical products, it might on the other hand be far more relevant to use people who have previous experience of the product.

(iii) Ability to work and 'get on'

Marketing research involves a great deal of personal contact. Contact between the actual user in the sponsoring company and his own marketing research department, contact between the marketing researcher and people in the marketing research consultancy, contact between executives at different levels in the marketing research consultancy and the sponsor. In a situation with this amount of personal contact, it is absolutely essential that people can 'get on'. It is impossible to define what is meant by 'get on' but nearly everybody can decide in one or two meetings whether he and the consultancy could, in general, work together satisfactorily. Although this might sound like a highly irrational comment, experience has shown that it is far better to sacrifice perhaps a little technical capability in exchange for being able to work closely together.

(iv) Competitors

It is always very useful to ascertain whether or not the research consultancy is at that particular time also working for competitors. That is not to say that a firm which has previously worked for a competitor should be ruled out. On the other hand, anybody who at exactly the same time is working for a competitor should be viewed very, very carefully. If you still decide to use this particular firm, make absolutely sure that totally different people within the consultancy would work on the two projects and that there is no possibility of a security leak.

(v) Cost

As mentioned earlier, research projects can be very expensive and very time consuming. It is, therefore, well worth setting a target budget before you go to a firm of consultants. In many cases, a research project can be as long as a piece of string. It could cost between £1000 and £10 000 depending on how detailed the information required is, and it is frequently better to set a limit and tie a project into a specific budget.

It is a waste of everybody's time and money to give a totally open brief which leads to a costing of many thousands of pounds when you already know you have only one or two thousands to spend. Again, experience has shown, it is often better to play fairly open cards with a consultancy and at least set a range that you would like the cost to be in.

Once all these points have been considered and discussed, it is time to draw up a brief to send to two or three consultants to ask them to prepare proposals on how they would handle this particular problem. In many cases you already know a particular firm of consultants or you have already worked with them, and it is far better to stay with somebody that you know and that you can work with than to go and ask everybody for quotes. There are, however, very good cases for asking two or three to quote—but do not ask six, seven, eight, or nine, a thing which frequently happens, because this again is a waste of time. Not only a waste of time for the consultants who prepare the briefs, but a waste of time for you who have to read the briefs in order to be able to select between them. When asking consultants to quote, do prepare a written brief so that each one can receive the identical specification. Then also be totally prepared—in fact request—to answer all questions the prospective consultants raise before they are required to submit their written proposal.

Once the written proposals are received, you and your colleagues, who will be involved in the research, can sit down, analyse them, and decide which one to use. Whom you use depends on so many circumstances that no general rules can be made—with the exception of one. Do not necessarily go for the cheapest. Look for the technical competence you require and accept the proposal that offers best technical competence—'technical' not necessarily in terms of knowledge of your product but in terms of research competence. Obviously price is of importance, but should never be the only criterion on which you select.

11.3 MULTI-CLIENT RESEARCH

Several marketing research consultants specialize in producing reports on particular market segments for general sale. They may initially approach a dozen or so companies who have a particular interest in the market to sponsor the work, or they may carry out the research first and then market the reports. In fact, proprietary lists of marketing research reports, which can be bought 'off the shelf', are now published.[1–5] The results of 'multi-client research' are, by nature, more general than a report produced to a single client's detailed brief. Multi-client research typically satisfies the basic questions of: market size broken down into individual products, market shares of the major manufacturers, together with an indication of future market structure and magnitude.

Points in favour of multi-client research are:

Speedier International Marketing Research.

Project costs reduced.

Increased market coverage of survey.

End-user tolerance to marketing research assisted.

Let us examine each of these points in more detail.

(i) Multi-client research as an aid to international marketing research

If you, as an 'in-house' marketing researcher, are asked to prepare a list of the top four European markets in which your company should launch its new product together with full market details of size, competitors, pricing structures, etc., within, say, two months, then you would be struggling! However, there is an excellent chance nowadays that somewhere there exists a multi-client survey which may, or may not, be up-to-date, but will give you at least the bare bones of your markets and, with more information gleaned from published sources and a few carefully chosen interviews, you should be able to put forward a reasonable report within the allotted time.

This is probably an extreme example, but multi-client research enables more resources to be expended at a given time as the cost is split between several clients; hence the cliché: multi-client for multi-country projects!

(ii) Multi-client research reduces project costs

It follows that if several clients are paying for the same research and that at the same time more man hours can be profitably spent on the project then the resulting reports will cost less per client and may be produced quicker.

As an example of this, the 1975 cost of producing 12 country reports on six electrical products was £20 000. Time spent on the project was 2 years and the cost of the set of 12 reports averages out at £100 per report for each participating company.

(iii) Multi-client research increases survey coverage

In many cases it may be desired to study a particular market in great depth, but the costs to a single sponsor cannot be justified. At this stage many projects are abandoned—they may never have got further than the marketing researcher's mind! In some instances, however, such as a Western European survey on Heat Exchangers and Pressure Vessels, several firms have sponsored a consultant to carry out the work to their mutual satisfaction. By-products to this kind of collaboration may be: marketing agreements between two participating firms; licensing agreements, and even full mergers, as on their own two or more clients may agree that in the longer term they cannot survive individually.

As the advantages of multi-client research become more apparent its use should increase and become a more accepted weapon in the market researcher's armoury.

(iv) Multi-client research aids end-users' tolerance to marketing research

Anybody who has tried to reseach an already over-researched market will understand this point. Many end users or equipment specifiers, e.g. Borough engineers, now refuse interviews automatically unless a very good case is put forward. If you can confidently claim that you are working for several would-be survey sponsors then the chances of success are correspondingly increased. Much multi-client research is often justified on these grounds as the IMR profession must be always on its guard against over-researching a particular market.

11.4 BECOMING A MARKETING RESEARCH CONSULTANT

After extolling the virtues of the marketing research company/consultant the more ambitious readers may be considering setting up as consultants on their own account.

Before any far-reaching decisions are made, make sure that you are prepared to commit yourself 150% and that you know your own market potential. Many intrepid entrepreneurs believe that marketing research projects can be sold 'off the shelf' like a can of oil, but this is not the case with IMR. The gestation period can often be in excess of a year. Let us consider some of the major pitfalls in greater detail—for those of you who are more determined!

(i) Client base

Few of us could afford to fund the multi-client type of research from the outset (unless you know a very generous bank manager!), so you would have to rely initially on the single client sponsorship mode of operation. This is fine provided you know a number of potential clients who could keep you in work for, say, the first twelve months in order that you can make a start on building up a reputation for producing good, reliable work on time. If you haven't got such a reliable client base (and beware of potential clients failing to fulfill their promises), then do not commit yourself until you have, as the recurring nightmare is not the project in hand, but the next one ....

(ii) Marketing and selling your research

It is much easier to carry out a research project, write the report, and then present the findings than to carry out a full marketing exercise on your clients.

It may seem paradoxical, but it is just as important for marketing research consultants to research *their* markets as it is for industrial companies to research theirs. Once you have done the necessary investigation you will then have to market your services and sell your capabilities in a way that not only brings in the immediate business but ensures the client will still require your services in the longer term. In other words you should help your prospective clients draw up the proposals so that they get the maximum benefit from the research. You should carry out the research to the best professional standards, and you should not only present the results but assist in the implementation of your recommendations wherever possible. By acting as a complete marketing consultant you are trying to ensure that when similar situations occur the Marketing Manager will not act before consulting you—which is the best possible way of ensuring continuity of business.

(iii) Cash flow

During the initial period you cannot expect to come out of a job with a vast profit. On the contrary, you will be struggling to break even. It is only when you start to sell a piece of similar research for the second or third time that you will begin to reap the benefits of setting up on your own.

Cash flow is a big headache, even for the most successful of businesses. It is not very prudent to accept a three-month assignment without making a percentage of the cost payable on signing the contract together with further progress payments at suitable intervals throughout the project.

This may be made feasible by producing interim reports so that your sponsor can satisfy himself that you are fulfilling the contract. Even when these provisions are made you may well be exposed to other risks, such as poor health and bad debts (as many bankrupts will testify!). It cannot be stressed too often that sound financial management is the key to any successful business. You should employ a respected accountant at the earliest opportunity to act as your advisor.

(iv) Practical problems

Until a nationwide force of interviewers has been built up (which is a very costly and time consuming operation), it would be foolhardy to accept an assignment that called for a full, nationwide series of interviews unless you are prepared to subcontract that part of the project to one of the fieldwork specialists set up for such a purpose. Frequently the new research company/consultant is asked to quote for carrying out mammoth surveys which have either been turned down by the experienced practitioners as being impracticable or prohibitive costwise. This is a problem which often confronts the new consultant. He may be too worried about the possibility of upsetting a prospective client to state that:

(*a*) A job cannot be done or is outside the consultant's scope.
(*b*) The consultant's time costs money! Large companies have a habit of 'trying it on' with small consultancies.
(*c*) The client is not always right and on this particular occasion he is wrong.

So, beware of overstretching yourself and being too timid at the beginning. It is wiser to limit your work at the start to what you know you can de well, and leave the more ambitious projects until you are well established.

11.5 REFERENCES

1. *Directory and Year Book of Industrial Marketing Research in Europe*, (1976), European Marketing Association and the Counseil Européen pour le Marketing Industrial. Details over 700 market research reports which are available for sale 'off the shelf'.
2. *European Directory of Market Research Surveys*, (1976), SEMA. Details of over 1500 studies which are available from the METRA Group.
3. *International Directory of Published Market Research*, (1977), 2nd ed. British Overseas Trade Board in conjunction with Research and Finance Management (International) Ltd. Coverage is more than 3000 reports on industrial and consumer products from East European, Middle and Far Eastern, African and South American markets as well as more familiar areas.
4. *U.S. and Canadian Marketing Surveys and Services*, C. H. Kline & Co., 330 Passaic Avenue, Fairfield, N.J., 07006 U.S.A. Nearly 1000 multi-client marketing reports and syndicated continuing services available from 85 consulting firms including both consumer and industrial reports.
5. *International New Product Centre Newsletter*. Editions in Europe, U.S.A., and Japan bring news of new products and their markets. 24 editions per annum. Available from: International New Product Centre, P.O. Box 37C, Esher, Surrey, England.

Appendix

Code of Conduct

Introduction

This abridged version of the Code of Conduct of the Industial Marketing Research Association and the Market Research Society applies to all forms of market and social research equally including, for instance, consumer surveys, psychological research, industrial surveys, observational studies, and panel research.

It is to be noted that the Industrial Marketing Research Association and the Market Research Society are bodies of individuals. Where the Code refers to organizations, such as client companies or research agencies, it is incumbent on individual members in these organizations to ensure, to the best of their ability, that the organization fulfils the Code in this respect. (Guidance on this point is given to members in Part VI of this Code.) In this Code the distinction has been drawn between 'Rules of conduct', which are mandatory, and 'Good practice', which is recommended to members. These latter are items which the professional body wishes its members to follow when relevant but, because they cannot be formulated precisely for all circumstances, or it is recognized that members may not be able to adhere to them strictly on every single occasion, or they may not always be completely appropriate, or it is, as yet, premature to make them mandatory, the professional body does not feel it right to insist on their universal application. This does not mean that good practice is necessarily less important than the rules of conduct in a particular case and attention is drawn to Clause 1.5.

Definitions

For the purposes of this Code:

An informant

Is an individual person who provides information, either directly or indirectly, on which the results of a research project could, in whole or in part, be based.

An interview

Is any form of contact intended to provide such information, with such an informant.

The identity of an informant

Includes, as well as his name and/or address, any other information which offers a reasonable chance that he can be identified by any of the recipients of the information.

Records

Shall be deemed to include anything containing data whether primary as, for example, completed questionnaires or intermediate as, for example, computer print out. Besides the above, examples of records are interviewer schedules, self-completion sheets, tick lists and observational sheets, documents designed to be optically scanned, interviewer notes on semi-structured and unstructured interviews, tape recordings, photographs or films, video tapes, transcription sheets, edge punched cards and other forms of computer input, together with any documents necessary for their interpretation, e.g., coding and editing instructions.

Client

Shall be deemed to include any individual, organization, department, or division—including any belonging to the same organization as the research agency—which is responsible for commissioning a research project.

Research agency

Shall be deemed to include any individual, organization, department, or division, including any belonging to the same organization as the client, which is responsible for conducting, or acting as a consultant on, a research project.

Where two or more individuals, organizations, departments, or divisions are together concerned in commissioning or conducting a research project, they shall be jointly and severally responsible for the observance of this Code of Conduct.

Overseas research

Where research is carried out overseas, Parts I, IV, V, and VI of the Code apply. As in the U.K. it shall be the duty of members in agencies specifically to point out to their clients any variation from the Standard Conditions in Part III. Where the codes of local market research societies or the equivalent are registered with the professional body, members must observe any responsibilities to informants that are set out in them; in any case, they must observe all the provisions in either Part II of this Code of Conduct or Section III A of the Code of the International Chamber of Commerce.

PART I: CONDITIONS OF MEMBERSHIP

1.1 The acceptance of market and social research depends upon the confidence of the business community and other users, and of the general public, in the integrity of practitioners. Members of the professional body undertake to refrain from any activity likely to impair such confidence and to comply with whatever general professional Code of Conduct, other regulations and interpretations may be laid down from time to time by the professional body.

It is important to this end that members should consider at all times that the purpose of market and social research is the collection and analysis of information, and not the direct creation of sales nor the influencing of the opinions of informants. It is in this spirit that this Code of Conduct has been devised.

1.2 Membership of the professional body is granted to individuals who are believed, on the basis of the information they have given, to have the required qualifications. Membership may be withdrawn if this information is found to be inaccurate.

1.3 Membership may be withdrawn, or other disciplinary action taken, if, on the investigation of a complaint by anyone properly having access to a study, it is found that, in the opinion of the professional body, any important part of the work falls short of reasonable professional standards.

1.4 Membership may be withdrawn, or other disciplinary action taken, if a member is deemed guilty of unprofessional conduct. This is defined as a member:

(a) Misrepresenting himself as having qualifications, or experience, or access to facilities which he does not, in fact, possess.

(b) Being guilty of any act or conduct which, in the opinion of the Council, might bring discredit on the professional body or its members.

(c) Disclosing to any other person, firm, or company any information acquired in confidence during the course of his work regarding the business of a client, without the permission of that client.

(d) Having a receiving order made against him or making any arrangement or composition with his creditors.

(e) Being sentenced to a term of imprisonment by a Court of Law.

(f) Publishing, or otherwise disseminating, unjustified and unreasonable criticism of another member's work.

(g) Being guilty of any breach of the Rules of Conduct set out in subsequent parts of this document.

(h) Knowingly being in breach of any other regulations laid down from time to time by the Council of the professional body.

1.5 Failure to follow the good practice recommendations contained in subsequent parts of this Code shall not in itself constitute unprofessional conduct, but it may be taken into account by the Council when investigating a complaint against a member or when considering disciplinary action under any of the foregoing articles of this Code.

1.6 The Council will consider complaints in the light of the available evidence. It is empowered to call for such evidence from its members as seems necessary to investigate a complaint fairly. Membership may be withdrawn, or other disciplinary action taken, if a member should fail, without good reason, to assist the Council with its enquiries concerning a complaint against another member. The Council may also request any evidence which seems necessary from non-members of the professional body. No member will have his membership withdrawn, or other disciplinary action taken under this Code, without an opportunity of a hearing before the Council, of which he shall have at least one month's notice.

PART II: RESPONSIBILITIES TO INFORMANTS

Preamble

The general principle on which the following Rules of Conduct are based is that informants are to be protected by members in the following ways:

(a) by having assurances honoured,
(b) by being allowed to remain anonymous,
(c) by avoiding any adverse effects from the contact,
(d) by being able to refuse or withdraw from an interview at any stage,
(e) by being able to check the credentials of the interviewer.

Rules of conduct

To ensure the protection set out above, the following rules will be honoured by members:

2.1 Any statement or assurance given to an informant in order to obtain cooperation shall be factually correct and honoured.

2.2 Subject to the provisions of this Clause, and those of Clause 2.7, the informant shall remain entirely anonymous.

No information obtained about individual informants which includes their identity shall be revealed, either directly or indirectly, other than to persons engaged in the administration, checking, or processing of research in accordance with this Code.

No information obtained about individual informants which includes their identity shall be used, either directly or indirectly, other than for the administration, checking, or processing of such research.

Information about individual informants which includes their identity shall only be further revealed to, or used by:

(a) Persons requiring it in order to conduct or process further interviews, after the first, with the same informants—subject to the conditions in Clause 2.6.
(b) Persons requiring it for other purposes, provided informants have consented to their identity being revealed, after being told the general purpose(s) of this revelation and the general nature of the recipient(s).

The member responsible for the research project must ensure that persons receiving such information are themselves bound by this Code of Conduct, or agree to abide by it for this purpose.

(See also Good Practice Clause 2.8.)

2.3 All reasonable precautions shall be taken to ensure that the informant, and others closely associated with him, are, as individuals, in no way embarrassed, or adversely affected, as a direct result of any interview or interviews, including product test participation, or of any other communication concerning the research project.

(See also Good Practice Clauses 2.10 and 2.14.)

2.4 The informant's right to withdraw, or to refuse to cooperate at any stage, shall be respected, unless the enquiry is being conducted under statutory powers. No procedure or technique which infringes this right shall be used, except that of observing or recording the actions or statements of individuals without their prior consent. In such a case the individual must be in a situation where he could reasonably expect his actions and/or statements to be observed and/or overheard (though not necessarily to be filmed or recorded). In addition at least one of the following conditions shall be observed:

(a) All reasonable precautions are taken to ensure that the individual's anonymity is preserved. (See also Good Practice Clause 2.10.)

(b) The individual is told immediately after the event that his actions and/or statements have been observed or recorded or filmed, is given the opportunity to see or hear the relevant section of the record and, if he wishes, to have it destroyed or deleted.

2.5 Members shall do their best to ensure that, on request at the time of the interview, the informant is provided with:

(a) an assurance that the interview is part of a research project (see also Clause 5.5).

(b) the information that the work is carried out under this Code (if necessary explaining the ways in which this protects informants).

(c) the name of the interviewer.

(d) the name of the responsible member of the professional body, and

(e) before the close of the interview, the name and address of the organization conducting the survey.

These statements may, if preferred, be shown in writing to the informant, e.g. on a card. Members should also do their best to provide the above information if the request is made after the close of the interview. (See also Good Practice Clause 2.11.)

Where the design of a postal survey necessitates the use of an accommodation address, arrangements shall be made for informants to discover, after its completion and if they should so wish, the name of the responsible member of the professional body, and the name and address of the organization conducting the survey.

Ownership of 'cover' organizations, when not separately registered with the Department of Trade and Industry, shall be registered with the professional body.

2.6 Further interviews, after the first, shall only be sought with the same informants under one or more of the following conditions:

(a) if informants' permission has been obtained at a previous interview, or

(b) if it is pointed out to informants that this interview is consequent upon one they have previously given and they then give their permission before the collection of further data, or

(c) if it is essential to the research technique involved that informants do not realize that this interview is consequent upon one they have previously given, but they do give their permission before the collection of further data—as though this were a new interview.

In all cases, the member responsible for the original interview must ensure, or receive assurances, that such further interviews are themselves conducted in accordance with this Code of Conduct.

(See also Good Practice Clause 2.12.)

2.7 Where informants represent an organization, or are speaking for a function (e.g. marketing manager, managing director, etc.), then their organization may be listed in the report. It shall not, however, be possible for any particular piece of information obtained directly from an informant or otherwise provided in confidence to be related to any particular organization, nor for any individual informant to be identified, either directly or indirectly, except with prior permission from the relevant informant. This permission shall be sought before the relevant information is collected and the informant shall be informed of the extent to which it will be communicated. (See also Good Practice Clause 2.13.)

Good practice

In conjunction with the above rules of conduct, it is considered good practice:

2.8 For interviewers, coders, field office staff, and other persons who may see completed questionnaires or schedules containing informants' identities, to be aware of the contents of this Code and to have signed a statement to abide by the relevant sections. (See Rule of conduct 2.2.)

2.9 To be as open with informants as is practicable, either before the event or as soon as possible after it, about aspects of the research procedures that might concern them, such as the use of tape recorders, the nature of outside observers, etc.

2.10 When considering whether a research procedure would be permissible under Clauses 2.3 or 2.4, to remember that informants can be embarrassed not only by what has actually happened to them but also by what they can reasonably think may have happened or might happen. Such factors as the following should be taken into account:

(i) the subject of the research.

(ii) the informant's likely assessment of the possibility of his being identified.

(iii) the relationship between the informant and those he is concerned might be able to identify him.

(iv) whether the likely identification of the informant is as an individual or merely as a member of a particular organization, and

(v) the type of record used for the study.

2.11 Where possible and appropriate, for

(i) statements and assurances given before the interview to cover

(a) the nature of the survey and

(b) the length of the interview (minimum and maximum likely duration).

(ii) at least items (c) and (e) in Clause 2.5 to be left with the informant in writing after the interview, and

(iii) the informant to be told, on request, the reasons for asking personal questions.

2.12 When seeking further interviews, after the first, with the same informants, to bear in mind that procedure (a) in Clause 2.6 is the one least likely to cause annoyance or give offence.

2.13 When interviewing representatives of companies or other organizations:

(a) To make appointments for interviews in advance.

(b) If discursive interviews are used, for an exchange of information to take place, and not to use personal interviews to obtain a basic understanding of the subject where such an understanding could have been obtained through desk research, etc.

(c) For the nature and/or the sponsor of the survey to be revealed where use of the information that will be contained in the survey report might have an adverse effect directly on the informant's company (e.g. when interviewing a competitor or a potential competitor). The provisions of Clause 3.2 shall, however, still be observed.

(See also Rule of conduct 2.7.)

2.14 For everything possible to be done by the member and the interviewer to ensure a continuing climate of goodwill, responsibility, and trust. A meticulous standard of good manners should be maintained and everything should be done to leave the informant disposed to receive a future contact on another research project. (See also Rule of Conduct 2.3 and Clause 6.5.)

PART III: MUTUAL RESPONSIBILITIES WITHIN THE PROFESSION

The Mutual Responsibilities of Members from Client Companies and Research Agencies (or other members who use and supply research information or facilities)

A The relationship between a client and a research agency, or other research practitioner, will frequently be subject to a form of contract between them. This Code does not aim to limit the freedom of the parties to make whatever agreement they wish between themselves, provided that neither party shall be required to act in breach of any of the mandatory sections of this Code.

B In the absence of any agreement to the contrary, the following Standard Conditions shall govern the behaviour of client and agency. Furthermore, it shall be the duty of members in agencies specifically to point out to their clients any variation from these Standard Conditions.

Standard Conditions

3.1 Research specifications provided by a client, and proposals provided by an agency at the request of a client when the agency receives neither the commission nor payment for the proposals, remain the property of the client or agency respectively and their contents may not be revealed to third parties without permission. Cost quotations may, however, be revealed, so long as an individual quotation cannot be associated with a given research agency. (See also Good Practice Clause 3.12.)

3.2 Unless authorised to do so by the client, or instructed by a Court of Law, the research agency shall not reveal to informants, nor to any other person not directly concerned with the work of the study, the identity of the client commissioning the study. (See also Clause 2.13(c).)

3.3 All confidential material relating to clients, including the fact that they have undertaken, or have considered undertaking, research in a particular area, shall remain confidential to persons wholly or substantially engaged in the service of the research agency. Whenever the client has reason to suppose that, due to any change of control or direction of the agency, or to other circumstances, any person not wholly or substantially engaged in the service of the agency may have access to confidential material relating to the client, the client may require possession of any such material held by the agency notwithstanding Clause 3.8. (See also Good Practice Clause 3.13.)

3.4 If fieldwork is to be subcontracted to another agency the client shall be so informed before being committed to the project.

3.5 (a) When two or more projects are combined in one interview, or the same project is carried out on behalf of more than one client, each client concerned shall be informed of this fact before being committed to the project. (See also Clauses 3.10 and 3.12.)

(b) Research agencies shall take all reasonable precautions to ensure that interviewers do not combine two or more projects in one interview without permission from themselves.

3.6 The research agency shall provide to the client, whether in the report, proposals or elsewhere:

(a) A copy of the questionnaire or other schedule used (or, in the case of a shared project, that portion relating to the matter reported upon) and any relevant extract from interviewers' instructions, etc.

(b) An adequate description of the following:

(i) For whom and by whom the study was conducted.

(ii) The objects of the study.

(iii) The universe covered (actual, not just intended).

(iv) The size and nature of the sample and details of any weighting methods used: where applicable, the planned sample as well as the number of interviews actually achieved.

(v) The method of recruitment used for informants in qualitative research or other techniques involving prior recruitment of informants.

(vi) Weighted or unweighted bases for all conventional tables, clearly distinguishing between the two.

(vii) Where appropriate, and especially in the case of postal surveys, a statement of response rates and a discussion of possible bias due to non-response.

(viii) The method by which the information was collected (e.g. by personal interview, postal questionnaire, mechanical recording device, or some other method).

(ix) If any incentive offers were made to informants such as members of group discussions the details of the incentives and the stage at which they were offered and provided should be made clear.

(x) The time at which any fieldwork was done.

(xi) The field force and any field quality control methods used.

(xii) The names of any subcontractors used for major parts of the research.

(xiii) In the case of desk research, the sources used.

(See also Clause 3.14.)

3.7 On request the client, or his mutually acceptable representative, may attend a limited number of interviews to observe the standard of the fieldwork (he then becomes subject to the provisions of Clause 2.2). In the case of multi-client surveys, the agency may require that the observer is independent of any of the clients. The agency is entitled to be recompensed if the client's desire to attend an interview interferes with, delays, or increases the cost of the field work.

3.8 Completed records shall be the property of the research agency (but see Clause 3.9). The agency shall be entitled to destroy such records without reference to the client two years, but no sooner, after the end of the fieldwork.

3.9 After the research agency has submitted its report upon the study to the agreed specification, the client shall be entitled to obtain from the research agency the original records, or duplicate copies of them, relating to his report, provided that the client shall bear the reasonable cost of preparing such records in a permissible form, and that the request is made within the time limit set by Clause 3.8. Such records shall not reveal the identity of informants, unless one of the conditions in Clause 2.2 or 2.6 has been fulfilled.

3.10 Unless the prior consent of the client has been obtained, any findings deriving from the study, other than published information, shall not be disclosed at any time by the research agency to any person other than to the client commissioning the study. This refers only to studies exclusively commissioned by a specific client, or clients, and it does not refer to the research techniques used in the study, nor to methodological analyses, so long as there is no disclosure of any such findings.

3.11 Reports, and other records or documents relevant to the project provided by a research agency, are normally for use within the client company or its associated companies (including the client's marketing, advertising and other relevant and duly authorised consultants or advisers), or other previously nominated recipients. If the client intends a wider circulation of the results of a study, either in whole or in part, the research agency's name may not be quoted in connection with the study until:

(a) it has approved the exact form and contents of the publication or circulation' and

(b) it has agreed with the client which items under Clauses 3.6 and 3.14 may be provided by the agency to recipients of this wider circulation, on request and at the enquirer's expense if necessary.

(See also Clauses 3.16, 5.3 and 5.6.)

Good practice

It is good practice for:

3.12 The terms and conditions under which research is undertaken to be defined as precisely and thoroughly as possible in a proposal, tender, or quotation submitted and approved before work is put in hand. This should include as many of the items listed under 3.6 and 3.14 as are relevant and also should state for example: if, and over what period, work on the same subject will not be carried out for a competitor without advance permission from the client (unless this is stated specifically, the client does not have the right to exclusive use of an agency); whether the client's identity may or may not be revealed to informants; if any subcontractors are to be used for major parts of the project and, if so, their identities; if the project is not to be exclusive to the client (unless this is stated specifically it is assumed to be exclusive—see Clauses 3.5 and 3.10); and the ownership of the copyright (see also Standard Condition 3.1).

3.13 The research agency to take reasonable steps to ensure the security of reports, questionnaires, and other material which is confidential to any client. (See also Standard Condition 3.3.)

3.14 The research agency to provide to the client, in the report, proposals, or elsewhere, in addition to the items listed under Clause 3.6:

(a) Weighted and unweighted bases for all conventional tables, clearly distinguishing between the two.
(b) A discussion of the effects of the sample design employed, and of any weighting methods used, on the effective size of the sample.
(c) A discussion of any aspects of the research which may bias the results obtained from it.
(d) In the case of desk research, an assessment of the reliability of the sources used.
(e) The name of the executive responsible for the research (where more than one has made a significant contribution the name of each and his responsibilities should be given).

A list of any sampling points used in the research project and an adequate description of all quality control methods used also to be made available on request.

3.15 Members, when presenting the results of a project (whether such presentation is as written or oral description, or in any other form), to make a clear distinction between the objective results and their own opinions and recommendations.

3.16 The research agency to be informed in advance if the client intends a wider circulation of the results of the study, either in whole or in part, and given an opportunity to express an opinion on:

(a) the exact form and contents of the publication or circulation and
(b) the items under Clauses 3.6 and 3.14 which should be provided to recipients of this wider circulation, on request and at the enquirer's expense if necessary.

(See also Clauses 3.11, 5.3 and 5.6.)

PART IV: RESPONSIBILITIES TO OUTSIDE CONTRACTORS

Responsibilities to Outside Contractors and Field Workers (whether or not members of the professional body)

Definitions

In this section the term 'outside contractor' is intended to cover such bodies as 'field force' companies, data processing houses, 'in house' interviewers, freelance (part-time) interviewers, etc. For the sake of convenience the term 'operator' is used.

Rules of conduct

4.1 The operator shall not be asked to undertake any type of interview or any method of respondent selection, or any other form of work, which is elsewhere disallowed by this Code.

4.2 The operator shall be provided with sufficient information and guidance to enable Clause 2.5 to be met. (See also Good Practice Clause 4.4.)

Good practice

It is considered good practice that:

4.3 The terms and conditions on which work is commissioned from the operator should be clearly set out in writing and agreed by both parties before the work starts.

4.4 Every effort should be made to enable the operator to observe the recommendations of Clauses 2.11 and 2.13. (See also Rule of conduct 4.2.)

PART V: RESPONSIBILITIES TO OTHER THIRD PARTIES

Responsibilities to the General Public, the Business Community and other Institutions

Rules of conduct

5.1 Public confidence in market research shall not be abused.

5.2 No activity shall be deliberately or inadvertently misrepresented as being market research. Specifically, the following activities shall in no way be associated, directly or by implication, with market or social research interviewing:

(a) sales approaches for profit or the compilation of lists for canvassing.
(b) attempts to influence opinions *per se*.
(c) industrial espionage.
(d) enquiries about private individuals *per se*.

(See also Good Practice Clause 5.5.)

5.3 A member shall not knowingly disseminate conclusions from a given research project or service which are inconsistent with, or not warranted by, the data. He shall also do his best to restrain any such dissemination by another party which arises from research with which he has been connected. This especially applies to public opinion polls and to the use of market research findings in advertising and sales promotion. (See Clauses 3.11 and 3.16.)

5.4 Letters after names tend to be understood as indicating that the user has an academic or professional qualification. The use of letters after an individual's name such as AMIMRA or FMIMRA can be misleading: members should refrain from using them except in such a form and manner as the professional body, from time to time, shall permit. This, does not, however, preclude members, where relevant, from pointing out that they are Full or Associate members of the professional body.

Good practice

5.5 Quite apart from actually misrepresenting other activities as being market research (see Clause 5.2), it is good practice to take every precaution to avoid leaving informants after a legitimate interview with the impression that they have been subjected to misrepresentation. (See also Clause 2.5(a).)

5.6 It is not good practice to make, or to be a party to the making of, claims based on research without offering to provide details of the research methods. (See Clauses 3.11 and 3.16.)

5.7 If members are approached for an interview which is ostensibly market research but which they suspect or find out to be something else, it is good practice for them to obtain the name of the 'interviewer' and the name and address of the organization involved. If their suspicions are confirmed they should complain directly to the 'interviewer' and to the organization for which he is working and also report the facts to the duly appointed committee of the professional body. Members should report to the same committee any other cases of which they become aware of activities being misrepresented as market research, in breach of Clause 5.2.

It is also good practice for members to report to the committee any cases of which they become aware of market research neglecting its proper responsibilities to informants, as set out in Part II, or of research conclusions being disseminated which are inconsistent with, or not warranted by, the data on which they are based. This clause applies whether or not a member of the professional body is concerned in the activity on which the report is made.

5.8 Although members are in general at liberty to conduct research into the products or services of the client's competitors, or of other organizations or individuals, without their permission, nevertheless it is not good practice to do it in such a way as to affect their reputation adversely.

PART VI: PROFESSIONAL RESPONSIBILITIES

Rules of conduct

6.1 Members in client companies, if they commission market research work from persons or organizations not known to be bound by this Code of Conduct, shall ensure that they are familiar with its contents and agree in writing to abide by it as if they were in fact members. (See above for the special requirements regarding Part II when commissioning overseas research.)

6.2 A member shall not knowingly place a fellow member in a position in which he may unwittingly breach any mandatory part of this Code of Conduct.

6.3 The most senior member within the hierarchy of an organization (or members if two or more are of equal status) who is a member of the professional body shall take all reasonable steps (e.g. by the display or circulation of suitable notices) to ensure that all relevant individuals in that organization are familiar with this Code of Conduct, and that the working arrangements of the organization are such that the Code is unlikely to be breached through ignorance of its provisions. This, of course, does not absolve members of the professional body in the organization of their own individual responsibilities.

Good practice

6.4 It is good practice for senior members in research agencies (see Clause 6.3) which conduct product tests or do other forms of research which involve the possibility of risk to informants, however slight, to ensure that the agency indemnifies itself against claims for compensation by carrying appropriate insurance.

6.5 It is good practice when considering interviews with members of small populations likely to be of interest to researchers to be especially careful to avoid unnecessary interviews, since there is a particular danger that such populations may become 'over-researched'. For the same reason it would be good practice for members interested in such populations to combine to undertake syndicated research rather than each separately commissioning their own projects. (See also Clause 2.14.)

6.6 It is not good practice for a member to take advantage, without permission, of the unpublished work of a fellow member in another organization. Specifically, it is not good practice for a member to carry out or commission a research project based on a proposal prepared by a member in another organization, unless permission has been obtained from that organization.

6.7 When writing to the press, or making any similar communication, members are at liberty to claim membership of the professional body if they so wish. It is not good practice, however, to do this in any way which would imply that they are writing or speaking on behalf of the professional body, unless they have the authority of Council, or some duly delegated individual or committee, to do so.

6.8 Guidance to members aware of an actual or potential breach in the mandatory parts of this Code of Conduct:

Four circumstances can be distinguished:

(a) Where the member is instructed to breach a mandatory part of the Code by his superior in the organization.

In these circumstances the member must not, of course, obey the instruction. He should explain this to his superior, by reference to this Code if necessary, and may ask the duly appointed committee of the professional body to confirm to the superior that the required action would be a breach of the Code. In cases where it is not completely clear whether or not the proposed action would be a breach of the Code, it would be good practice to consult the duly appointed committee, which is prepared to advise members before a decision is taken.

(b) Where the breach is about to occur on a survey with which the member is connected.

If the member is aware of a breach before it has taken place, he should do his best to prevent it, lest he be considered to be a party to the breach. Where the member is not the individual responsible for the survey he should point out, in writing, to the person responsible for the project that the proposed action would be a breach of the Code. (Copies of any written communications should, of course, be retained.) If necessary he should also seek the support of other members of the professional body working for the organization, especially the senior member (see Clause 6.3), and may request advice from the duly appointed committee of the professional body.

(c) If a member only becomes aware of a breach on a project with which he is connected after it has taken place, he should:

(i) Ensure that those responsible for the survey are aware that it is, in fact, a breach, and thus attempt to prevent a recurrence.

(ii) Ensure that all concerned in the organization do their utmost to minimize any damage caused by the breach. If difficulties arise in this respect because the member is not the person responsible for the research, then he should proceed as in the appropriate part of Clause 6.8(b) above. If required, the duly appointed committee of the professional body is prepared to give advice in these circumstances and, in extreme cases, a written report should be sent to the committee.

(d) Where a member has no connection with the project but becomes aware of a breach, he should remind the person responsible for the project, if he is a member, of his responsibilities. If the person responsible for the project is not a member, he should inform the senior member of the professional body (see Clause 6.3) in the organization. Such communications should preferably be in writing. (Copies of any written communications should, of course, be retained.) If the breach continues, the member should proceed as in Clause 6.8(b) or (c)—in particular seeking the support of other members of the professional body in the organization and, if needs be, informing the duly appointed committee of the professional body.

Index